MEET ME UNDER THE CLOCK
At Grand Central

A Family History and Memoir:
Fullers & Vestners, Merceins, Dwights & Webbs,
New England, Brooklyn & New York

Eliot N.Vestner, Jr.

ISBN: 1439270449
ISBN-13: 9781439270448

CONTENTS

Dedication v

Introduction ix

  1. Eliot's Story 1

  2. Priscilla Alden Fuller: Flatbush Girl 45

  3. Fullers, Merceins, and New York in the Nineteenth
     Century 81

  4. Dwights, Webbs, & the California Gold Rush 105

  5. Charles Humphrey Fuller: Church and Politics 125

  6. Eliot and Priscilla: Courtship, Marriage and the Great
     Depression 147

  7. The Second World War, Bronxville, New York 185

  8. Postwar Germany, 1947-52 211

  9. Getting Educated in the Fifties 249

10. Korea and the Home Front, 1953-55 261

This is a story of family; but it is primarily the story of my parents, Eliot and Priscilla, from their first date under the clock at Grand Central Terminal in Manhattan, through courtship and marriage, the Great Depression, the Second World War and the postwar occupation of Germany, to their final safe harbor in Freedom, New Hampshire. It's not the whole story; it's my version of their story, and it only scratches the surface of their lives. It surely isn't the story they would tell. They lived their lives; I didn't. One thing is sure: Priscilla wanted a child, and on August 4, 1935 she got one. She may have wanted more, but that was it. From then until my father's death in 1983, the story is about the three of us.

I never called Eliot and Priscilla by their first names: they were always "Mom" and "Dad," and that's how I usually refer to them in the memoir portion of the book. For the period before I was born, it seems appropriate to call them by their proper names. But I haven't been entirely consistent (in my defense, I will simply quote Emerson: "a foolish consistency is the hobgoblin of small minds").

Several themes run through the story. Religion is one: from Puritans, Separatists and Congregationalists, to Methodists and Episcopalians, generations of Fullers took their religion seriously. Public service is another. Eliot served more than twenty years in the Army. Most of the other characters served in the military, in a public position, or sought elective office. The preeminent example is William Bradford, who for many years served as Governor of Plymouth.

Money and finance have also played a big role in the history of the family. Eliot and Priscilla lived through the Great Depression. But before that, there were recurring financial crises, from early Plymouth through the financial panics and depressions of the nineteenth and twentieth centuries. Eliot and Priscilla's ancestors experienced their own versions of the Great Depression. Each financial panic seemed, to those caught in it, to be the worst ever, only to be followed by one that proved even worse.

The people in this story are a restless lot; few of them stay put for long. They cross the ocean, brave the wilderness in search of land, cross the continent in search of riches, leave the farm for the big city, move every few years within the city, and move from city to suburb.

* * *

I begin with Eliot's story and his first experience away from home, one that set the future course of his life: his service on the Mexican border, March 1916.

"People are interested in themselves, so it is not surprising people want to tell their own story...But the big question is, why should readers who don't know us be interested in our story?" Ben Yagoda, author of *Memoir: A History*

INTRODUCTION

Boston, March 26, 1995, 7:30 A.M. The commute was easy: a ten minute walk along Devonshire to the Bank of Boston at 100 Federal Street. But this morning was different. One block, and I was breathing hard, feeling like I'd just run a mile. I stopped and leaned against a building. The street was crowded with people fast-walking to work in the financial district. I turned and made my way against the tide back to the apartment. Louisa, my bride of seven months, called the doctor and drove me to the emergency room at the Massachusetts General Hospital. That afternoon I was on an operating table. Two surgeons probed my heart found a blocked vessel and inserted a stent. Lying there watching what they were doing on the screen, awed by their skill, I thought how much better to be a doctor than a lawyer or a banker.

Three weeks later I was back at work, the oldest senior executive at the bank, out of touch and irrelevant: blindingly obvious to everybody, but not to me. Facts are facts: college, law school, twenty-five years in Manhattan, ten years in Boston, marriage, children, divorce, remarriage, heart attack—my life had flashed by, like an express train barreling through the station. I was no longer a young man with a future. I had become what I never wanted to be and never thought I would be—an old man like my father.

Eliot Noble Vestner died on March 2, 1983 at home in Freedom, New Hampshire. In the weeks after he died I went through his stuff. His desk was crammed full of carefully bundled items: old pens that you had to dip in ink; pencils, long, medium and short, separately bundled; string, tinfoil, and rubber bands; paperclips sorted by size and stored in old match boxes; stamps, carefully removed from letters and stored in envelopes marked "stamps," intended for a collection; a dozen old wallets, long since emptied; drawers with old road maps going back to the early fifties, ancient artifacts predating the interstate highway system; about a dozen old cigar boxes, one stuffed with silver dollars; a giant vase filled with hundreds of matchbooks from hotels and restaurants all over the world; and old newspapers, the oldest yellowed at the edges and falling apart, road signs of his life:

The Dallas Evening Journal, June 30, 1916, with a lead article announcing "Vanderbilt's New York regiment passes through Dallas today on way to the Mexican border"

The New York Times, July 23, 1916, with a full page photo showing a group of dusty and tired national guardsmen, gathered at the close of a hard day of searching for Pancho Villa and his army

The New York Times, November 11, 1918: "Armistice signed, End of the War! Berlin seized by Revolutionists"

The New York Times, May 22, 1927: "Lindbergh does it! To Paris in 33 ½ Hours; Cheering French carry him off field"

The Sun, October 29, 1929: "Stocks Off In 16 Million Day; Prices Slump from Ten to Thirty Points"

The New York Times, November 9, 1932: "Roosevelt Winner in Landslide; Democrats Control Wet Congress"

The New York Times, December 11, 1936: "Edward Vll Renounces British Crown"

The New York Times, September 3, 1939: "Britain and France in War at 6AM; Hitler Won't Halt Attack on Poles; Chamberlain Calls Empire to Fight"

The Sun, May 7, 1945: "Germany Surrenders"

He saved *Newsweek*, April 23, 1945, with FDR on the cover and *Life,* the same April 23, 1945, with new President Harry Truman on the cover. He saved old *Holiday* magazines: the October 1959 issue was devoted to New York, his old home town; and he saved *The Saturday Evening Post*, March 21, 1964, head-lined "The Secret of the Beatles... Their Incredible Power to Evoke Frenzied Emotions Among the Young."

Priscilla Fuller Vestner, my mother, had died fourteen years earlier in November 1969, yet her things were still all there in the house, just as she had left them: clothes hanging neatly in the closet, shoes carefully lined up on the closet floor, pen and paper on her desk, books and files in order—as if she would re-appear any minute.

The house where they lived and died was filled with lots of stuff. I kept the old newspapers and magazines, but what to do with a hundred perfectly useable pencils or Priscilla's clothes? I cleaned out most of it. When Penny and I divorced in 1991, she got the house. She wanted it, I didn't: too many memories. Now, there is hardly a trace of our family in that house. It's as if we had never lived there.

* * *

Back in the fall of 1955, on the verge of retirement and looking for their first permanent home, Eliot and Priscilla fell in love with the old Rogers farm in Freedom, a village of about 315 people at the southern edge of the White Mountains, two-and-a-half hours northwest of Boston. They closed the deal in November of 1955.

For me, that house was a magical place. Vacation didn't start until the moment I got out of the car under the tall pines, and my mother came running out of the house, a big smile on her face, and put her arms around me. It was usually dark when I arrived; the sky was always full of stars, and the stars seemed so close it was hard to believe they were so far away.

In my mind's eye I can still see her sitting on the sofa in the sun-filled library, working at a big table, glasses perched on her nose, surrounded by genealogy charts. Her charts were handmade, straight lines fanning out across the page filled with names and dates. Her sources: letters and notes written long ago by aged relatives alive during the second half of the nineteenth century. No matter how big the sheet of paper, she couldn't get more than four generations on a page. Some charts started with her and worked back; others started with her ancestors and worked forward. The names extended outward like a flight of Canada geese. At the outer edges of the formation, the information got fuzzy; she was clearly frustrated.

Her handwritten pages traced her family back to Elizabethan England. Bradfords and Fullers sailed on the *Mayflower* and settled Plymouth in 1620. Generations later her grandfather, Humphrey Fuller, born and raised in Hebron, Connecticut, left the Fuller farm in about 1850, went to work for a bank on Wall Street, met and married her grandmother, Isabelle Mercein of New York City. At about the same time Eliot's grandfather, Johann Vestner, left Altdorf, Bavaria, traveled by land to the port city of Bremen, and from there sailed to New York City. In 1861 Johann married Eliot's grandmother, Margaretha Ramming, also a Bavarian immigrant. The Fuller and Vestner families merged on May 28, 1931, when Priscilla Alden Fuller married Eliot Noble Vestner at St. Paul's Church, Brooklyn, New York.

Eliot's family left a sparse record. Johann Vestner worked hard but never made it out of the tenements of Lower West Side Manhattan. Johann's son and Eliot's father, George Vestner, became a lawyer and moved uptown. I've tried to tell their stories. If they were around to see the results, they'd probably say I got it all wrong. Why didn't they leave more of a record so I could get it right? They'd say they were too busy trying to earn a living. For Johann, it was a struggle to survive; for George, it was a struggle to get ahead. They both worked right up to their final sickness and retired to the grave. They were serious, hard-working men.

My father was also serious, but as a young man he apparently had a light side. In 1985, a woman saw my name in an Irving Trust Company annual report and wrote, asking if I was the son of Eliot Vestner. I said I was, but that he had died in 1983. She sent me photos taken at Ocean Beach, New Jersey in 1919, showing a young skinny guy in a bathing suit holding a dark-eyed girl on his shoulders. The girl wore a black bathing dress down to her knees with black stockings. The woman said she had known my father and that "he was a lovely person and a lot of fun" (maybe she was the dark-eyed girl in the picture). I never thought of him as "a lot of fun." But I didn't know him back then, when he was twenty-two, single, and just home from the war.

Priscilla's family left a rich paper trail, particularly the men. Starting with Governor Bradford of Plymouth Colony, they were actively engaged in the issues of their times: war, politics, religion, and business. We know less about the women. For most, there's only a birth, marriage, and death record—sometimes not even that, not even a name. The absence of a record reflects the circumscribed role and status of women that prevailed even into the later years of the twentieth century. Those "invisible" women bore the children—as many as a dozen—raised and educated them, suffered through miscarriages, high infant mortality, and early childhood disease that often led to death. They also made and repaired the clothes, tended the vegetable gardens, fed the family, nursed the sick, mothered their husbands, cared for their aging parents, and developed their own web of connections in the community. They are the unsung heroines of the family.

Because there is so much more material on the Fuller family, the Fullers take up more space than the Vestners. But that's simply a matter of the available material, due in part to their earlier arrival and their greater fecundity. I attach no importance to the arrival date. Bradfords, Fullers and Vestners were all immigrants and they all came to this country to start a new life, as have millions of others.

I. Eliot's Story

Mexican Border, March 15, 1916: In the early morning, Brigadier General John Pershing, U.S.Army, led 4,800 men and 4,175 horses across the border at Columbus, New Mexico in hot pursuit of Francisco ("Pancho") Villa, a Mexican bandit with a large popular following in Northern Mexico. The week before, Villa had raided Columbus, leaving twenty dead Americans. The American troopers stationed at Columbus had killed close to 100 of Villa's men.

The cross-border raid was the last straw. President Woodrow Wilson, under pressure to do something, mobilized the army and ordered Pershing to capture Villa.[1] By April Pershing's troops, deep inside Mexico, had run into trouble. His advance units were routed near the city of Parral by a large Mexican force, with ten dead, twelve wounded, and twenty-four captured. Wilson faced a dilemma: reinforce Pershing and go to war with Mexico, or retreat to a defensible position closer to the U.S. border and leave the pursuit of Villa to the Mexican government. Wilson chose retreat.

That spring and summer, an army assembled on the Texas side of the border. In June the New York Seventh Regiment—all young men from the city— arrived in McAllen, Texas. They were a small part of the 110,000-man force assigned to duty on the border. Eliot Vestner, age eighteen, was one of the approximately 200 men in Company E.

Eliot was a New York City boy. Born December 19, 1897, he grew up in an apartment at 282 West 114th Street, a middle-class neighborhood one block south of Morningside Park and a short walk to the new Morningside Heights campus of Columbia University. The name on his birth certificate was "Noble

---

1   Herbert Molloy Mason Jr., *The Great Pursuit* (New York; Smithmark, 1970), 1-26; 64-73; Henry Bamford Parkes, *A History of Mexico* (Boston; Houghton Mifflin Co., 1960), 356. One of several contenders for the Mexican presidency during the long and chaotic Mexican revolution, Villa thought that U.S. President Woodrow Wilson had betrayed him by supporting a rival. In his anger, he had executed Americans in Mexico.

Ellis Vestner." At his confirmation, he was "Noble Elliott Vestner." [2] When he graduated from PS (Public School) 186 in 1913, he was "Noble Eliot Vestner." By the time he joined the Army, he had become "Eliot Noble Vestner." "Eliot" was a better first name than "Noble." With "Noble" as a first name, he had probably taken a lot of kidding in school. It took eighteen years, but he finally got the name he wanted.

Eliot's father, George Vestner, commuted to his downtown law office at 35 Nassau Street on one of the elevated railways lines running the length of Manhattan. Noisy and packed tight with commuters, some of whom hung on for dear life, the trains careened around corners on seemingly rickety supports up to sixty feet above the street, where people got around mostly on horse-drawn coaches and trolleys.[3] In 1905 George probably switched to the new West Side subway line, which opened that year and ran along Central Park, stopping a few blocks from the Vestner apartment.

The El curve at 110th Street (Zeisloft, The New Metropolis, 1899)

---

2   "Noble," Ruth's family name, was an odd choice for a first name; odder still that George, a sensible man, would let that pass. Eliot's confirmation certificate is in my personal files, which can be accessed through email to <evestner@comcast.net.> Every document referenced in this book that does not include a specific citation, including diaries and letters, is from my personal files and can be similarly accessed.
3   Edwin G. Burrows and Mike Wallace, *Gotham, A History of New York City to 1898* (New York; Oxford University Press, 1999), 1053-58.

Eliot got his early education in the New York City public school system, graduating in 1913 from PS (Public School) 186 at 145th Street, and in 1916 from Hamilton Institute for Boys, a private school at West 89th Street. At Hamilton he took regular pre-college classes in history, classics, English, and math. Hamilton also gave the boys military training under Captain W. B. Porter of the New York National Guard.

Eliot in uniform, Hamilton Institute for Boys

The school newspaper—*The Hamilton Echo*—proudly noted that "Graduates have successfully entered Harvard, Yale, Cornell, Princeton, Dartmouth, MIT, Union, Trinity and RPI." Eliot did not go on to college.[4] Immediately after graduating from Hamilton, he joined the New York Seventh Regiment.

---

4   Hamilton was described as "a day school making a specialty of college preparation" in Porter E. Sargent, *Handbook of the Best Private Schools in North America* (Boston; Press of George M. Ellis Co. 1915), 47. From school data it appears that roughly 75 percent of graduates went on to college. But in the overall population, the percentage of college graduates was tiny, less than five percent of Americans were college graduates; less than fifteen percent even graduated from high school. Eliot was always embarrassed that he had not gone to college, and usually added a year of college to his resume. On his "Army Personnel Placement Questionnaire," April 14, 1944, he stated that he graduated from high school and then attended City College of New York for one year—1916. According to his official army record, he attended "Harvard University in Massachusetts" in 1916.

3

He joined the army to get away from home, earn a paycheck, and put some excitement into his life. In June 1916, his parents were separated; his older sister was living in Manhattan with their father; Eliot was living in Brooklyn with his mother, Ruth Noble Vestner. The bond between mother and son was unusually strong and she depended on Eliot for emotional and financial support. She did not want him to leave home. But at eighteen, he could and did join the Army without her permission. While there must have been considerable tension between mother and son, Eliot was not exactly breaking away from his mother; his army paycheck took care of rent and groceries for the Brooklyn apartment they shared.

After basic training, Eliot and the rest of the Seventh Regiment boarded the train headed for McAllen. Until the arrival of the troops, McAllen, with a railroad depot, a hotel, bars, stores, and a population of 1,200, had been a sleepy Texas border town. In the summer of 1916, the local population was dwarfed by the arrival of 12,000 soldiers, most of them young and single. The soldiers constructed a sprawling tent city outside of town. They were kept busy with drills, long hot marches, target practice, parades, maintenance of the horses and vehicles, housekeeping, construction, and daily inspection. Heat, boredom, and rattlesnakes were the enemy. Under the hot Texas sun the soldiers sweated through their woolen pants and shirts.

Eliot on the Mexican border spring 1916

Downtown McAllen 1916: Eliot on left

The boys at dinner: Eliot fourth on right

A shower was a bucket of water once a week or a plunge in the canal that ran through camp. Some of the boys who had joined the regiment wished they hadn't. On July 15, 1916 *The McAllen Evening Sun* reported that two privates got drunk, broke into a store, stole a bottle of whiskey, and were promptly arrested. One of them had a postcard in his pocket: "Dear Mother—Please get me out of here. It is hell."[5]

Eliot liked his army service on the border. Promoted first to corporal and then to sergeant and platoon leader, he thrived. Pictures show a tall skinny guy with a grin on his face, obviously having a good time. But his service came to an end in the winter of 1917.

That winter, President Wilson faced the prospect of U.S. entry into the European war and prudently agreed to withdraw Pershing's troops from Mexico in exchange for assurances of security along the border. Most of the troops were withdrawn in February 1917. Despite the mobilization and cost of the border campaign, the Army never came close to finding Villa.[6]

---

5   *The McAllen Evening Sun*, July 15, 1916, unattributed column headed "Privates Raid Border Stores."
6   In 1919 Villa agreed to lay down his arms in return for a grant of 25,000 acres and a hacienda in Canutillo, thirty-five miles south of Parral in the Chihuahua district, and about 600 miles south of El Paso, Texas. On July 20, 1923 Villa was assassinated in his Dodge touring car as he drove through the center of Parral, possibly on his way to meet a girlfriend. See Mason, *The Great Pursuit*, 137-139.

Eliot left the Army and went to work on a construction crew. But he was out of the army for only a couple of months. In April 1917 Congress declared war on Germany and that month he re-joined the Seventh Regiment.[7]

As the U.S. entered the war, Eliot and millions of other Americans were only one or two generations removed from Germany. Before the war, German-Americans had been a large and respected immigrant group. But in April 1917, being German suddenly became a liability. The Captain of Eliot's Company, Leo Knust, was a career officer in the Army, but he had been born in Germany and was abruptly removed from command on the eve of his company's departure for France. The war unleashed a torrent of anti-German sentiments; sauerkraut became "liberty cabbage;" a St. Louis mob lynched a German-born American for no other reason than his German origin; schools banned the teaching of German and required loyalty oaths of teachers; and the government created study courses that drew a clear bright line between the "autocratic" and "barbaric" Germans and the "democratic" and "humane" French and English, ignoring any details that might complicate the picture.[8]

Eliot's generation was eager to serve, and the enlistment centers were overwhelmed with young men trying to enlist. Behind that eagerness was a sophisticated government propaganda campaign that created enormous social pressure on the men to join up.[9]

In the summer of 1917, Eliot was transferred to the 165th Regiment of the newly formed 42nd (Rainbow) Division. The Division's chief-of-staff was Colonel Douglas MacArthur, later its commanding officer. Most of the men transferring were drawn by lot; Eliot was a volunteer. His new regiment had a long and distinguished history as the old 69th New York. Known with good reason as the "Irish Brigade," the 69th had fought with distinction throughout the Civil War. Father Francis Duffy, Chaplain to the 69th, described the Irish reception for

---

7   Wilson had won re-election in 1916 on a peace platform. But by 1917, German submarines were attacking U.S. ships. On March 1, 1917, newspapers published an intercepted telegram from the German Foreign Minister, Zimmerman, to the German ambassador in Mexico, inviting Mexico to join the war on Germany's side against the United States. In return, Germany would see that Mexico recovered some of its lost territory, including New Mexico, Texas, and Arizona. The "Zimmerman telegram" inflamed public opinion and triggered U.S. entry into the war. War was declared April 6, 1917. See David Kennedy, *Over Here, the First World War and American Society* (New York; Oxford Press, 1980), 10. See also *History of Company "E," 107th Infantry, 54th Brigade, 27th Division 1917-1919* (New York City, War Veterans' Association, 1920), 31.

8   See Kennedy, *Over Here*, 54-57.

9   Henry Berry, *Make the Kaiser Dance* (Garden City, New York; Doubleday, 1978), 369. Kennedy, *Over Here*, 144-151. The draft was a curious mixture of romance and compulsion, with President Wilson describing the draft as mass volunteerism, while simultaneously calling for people to be vigilant that all eligible young men register as required.

Eliot and his fellows on August 18, 1917 as they passed into the 69th Regiment Armory in mid-Manhattan:

> Our 2,000 lined the walls and many perched themselves on the iron beams overhead. They cheered and cheered and cheered till the blare of the bands was unheard in the joyous din—till hearts beat so full and fast that they seemed too big for the ribs that confined them, till tears of emotion came, and something mystical was born in every breath—the soul of a Regiment. Heaven be good to the enemy when these cheering lads go forward together into battle.[10]

Stirring words; but Father Duffy was skeptical of the newcomers who had to prove themselves to the Irish boys. Eliot was joining a tight-knit group. Did he realize what he was getting into when he volunteered to leave his old regiment, made up largely of Protestants like himself, to join an Irish Catholic regiment where he'd be an outsider and have to prove himself all over again? He may have seen that some good friends were being transferred and made a snap decision to join them without giving the matter much thought.

On October 31, 1917 Eliot shipped off to France with his new unit on *The America*. He got his first taste of war when the convoy entered the zone of acute submarine peril four days off the French coast. Those last four days, zig-zagging through the cold, dark Atlantic to avoid the German U-boats lying in wait, must have been the longest four days of his life.

They arrived at Brest on the French coast and were immediately transported by train to the North, where they were "billeted" in haylofts on French farms, described by one soldier in a letter home: "There are three classes of inhabitants in the houses—first, residents; second, cattle; third, soldiers."[11] On Christmas Day 1917, General Pershing reviewed the regiment. A year earlier, Pershing had been a one-star general in charge of 4,000 U.S troops on a fruitless search for Pancho Villa; now he was a four-star general commanding an army in France that would grow to two million within the year.

On March 1, 1918 Eliot's regiment was sent to the front in the Luneville-Baccarat sector in the Vosges Mountains, the final training area for U.S. troops. There, they could get a taste of combat under the watchful eye of the more

---

10   Francis P. Duffy, *Father Duffy's Story, a Tale of Humor and Heroism, of Life and Death with the Fighting Sixty-Ninth* (New York; George H. Doran Co., 1919), 18.
11   Duffy, *Father Duffy's Story*, 41.

experienced French 7th Corps, which had been fighting the Germans for over three years.

Somewhere in France, winter, 1918

Luneville-Baccarat had been relatively quiet, with French and Germans observing a tacit live and let live approach to the war. But the Americans, spoiling for a fight, stirred things up. The Germans retaliated. The regiment had its first experience with German artillery when a trench collapsed under a direct hit, burying thirty-eight men alive.[12] Most of the bodies were never recovered. The regimental history described the artillery fire directed daily at the men that March:

> Probably no one who had not experienced it can realize the suddenness and violence with which modern artillery can execute

---

12   See Henry J. Reilly, *Americans All: the Rainbow at War* (Columbus, Ohio; The F.J.Heer Printing Co., 1936), 138-145; Duffy, *Father Duffy's Story*: 76-77.

9

a surprise attack. Until seen it seems impossible to convey to another the way in which a quiet peaceful section of country...can suddenly be torn to pieces.... Sections of trenches and dugouts go up in the air, machine guns are blown to pieces, trees are rooted up their fragments scattered in every direction. Human beings who a few seconds before were sound physically...apparently safe and enjoying the scenery, suddenly are wounded or dead, mangled by fragments of shell!

The batteries from which the shells come cannot be seen. The enemy's trenches... are apparently vacant...Then without warning and in many cases before the discharge of the guns... can be heard, the screeching shells arrive bursting with tremendous force. They sometimes stun and always shock the nerves of the men not hit.[13]

That same March, another company of the 165th was virtually wiped out in a mustard gas attack:

The men were prompt in putting on their masks as soon as the presence of gas was recognized, but it was found impossible to keep them on indefinitely and at the same time keep up the defense of the sector. Immediately after the bombardment, the entire company area reeked with the odor of mustard gas...

By about midnight some of the men were sick as a result of the gas, and as the night wore on one after another they began to feel its effects on their eyes, to cry, and gradually go blind, so that by dawn a considerable number from the front line had been led all the way back and were sitting by the Luneville road, completely blinded, and waiting their turn at an ambulance...

By ten o'clock in the morning, fully two-thirds of the company had been blinded...[14]

13   Reilly, *Americans All*, 167-68.
14   Reilly, *Americans All* 162.

The Germans had first used chlorine gas against the Allies in 1915. By the time Eliot arrived, both sides were deep into gas warfare. All soldiers were issued gas masks and trained in defending against gas attack. The gas used against Eliot's regiment in March 1918 was mustard, not usually fatal but bad enough: it disabled by burning skin and lungs and causing blindness. Phosgene was worse. Virtually odorless and hard to detect, it killed by suffocation. By the end of the war, gases had been developed that penetrated gas masks.[15]

With nerve-shattering artillery bombardment, poison gas, rapid-fire machine guns and other killing weapons, Eliot was in the middle of what was then the most destructive war in human history.

By the end of March, Eliot's division had finished its training. That was also the point of greatest peril for the Allies. With the signing of the Russian peace treaty, the Germans were able to send sixty divisions to the Western front and mount a major offensive, breaking through the British-French lines, threatening Paris and the channel ports. It was a looming disaster. The Germans were trying to end the war in one quick strike before U.S. forces achieved critical mass in Europe. They almost succeeded.

The French 7th Corps was sent in to the big battle, leaving Eliot's Rainbow Division in charge of Luneville-Baccarat, the first American division considered ready to take over a sector. By June 1918 the extraordinarily rapid buildup of American forces had offset the German advantage, enabling the French and British to concentrate all their experienced divisions at the front and blunt the German offensive.

That June, Eliot was transferred to the 59th Regiment of the 4th Division, presumably part of an effort to strengthen this newly-arrived division with some experienced men.[16] During July, his new regiment saw action in the Aisne-Marne offensive, part of the successful effort to drive the Germans back from their furthest point of penetration. By early August the 59th had relieved Eliot's old unit at the Ourcq River. In his memoirs, General Pershing recalled that "some of the bitterest fighting of the war occurred on this line." Eliot's unit went on as part of the American First Army to fight at the St. Mihiel salient in September, a battle that engaged 400,000 Americans, and later in the final battle on the Meuse-Argonne

---

15   When it entered the war, the U.S. had no experience in gas warfare; by the end of the war, the U.S. was the largest producer of poison gas in the world. If the war had extended into 1919, a large percentage of artillery shells on both sides would have contained poison gas. See Shipley Thomas, *The History of the AEF* (New York; George H. Doran, Co., 1920), 401-410. The major nations agreed to ban chemical warfare in 1925, a treaty that was finally ratified by the US Senate in 1975.
16   According to Eliot's Certificate of Discharge, he was transferred on June 3, 1918. Pershing apparently viewed the Rainbow Division as a source of replacements for other divisions. During the war, the 4th Division received 19,588 replacements. See Shipley Thomas, *The History of the AEF*, 455.

front during October and into November that engaged 1.2 million Americans, more than any other military action in U.S. history.[17]

The Armistice, November 11, 1918, officially ended the fighting with more than two million American soldiers on the battlefield and two million more in the U.S. ready to go. In just two months of fighting, Eliot's 4th Division, with a full complement of 32,000 men, had lost 2,611 men killed and 9,895 wounded—a 39 percent attrition rate.[18] Eliot was among the fortunate 61 percent who survived without injury.

The First World War, A Photographic Essay, ed. Laurence Stallings

One month after the Armistice, Eliot was on duty with the military police in the Paris Headquarters District.[19] That December the Allied armies, including Eliot's unit, moved into occupying positions on the West bank of the Rhine.[20] He was stationed on the Rhine from December to April, when he rejoined his old unit, Company F 165th Regiment, and sent a card to his anxious mother in Brooklyn:

17   John J. Pershing, *My Experiences in the World War* (New York, 1931): 210, 294-295.
18   See Christian A. Bach and Henry Noble Hall, *the Fourth Division, its Services and Achievements in the World War* (published by the Division, 1920).
19   A Card dated December 1918 with the stamp of the Paris Provost Marshal, permitted Eliot to be absent from quarters until midnight when not on duty. If he was out on the town and stopped by an MP, all he had to do was flash that card and he would be okay.
20   The Armistice provided for a fifteen-year occupation of the Rhineland by Allied troops, creating a buffer between Germany and France. This "foreign" occupation on German soil caused resentment in Germany. Hitler was able to capitalize on that resentment. His first foreign policy triumph occurred when he reoccupied the Rhineland with German troops in 1936 without firing a shot.

My Dear Mother: Just a greeting to you, for Easter, on the eve of my departure for home. If all goes well, I am sailing for America about April 9th and will arrive in a week's time. Received your letter addressed to Co. F. 165th, in which I was more than surprised to hear of Fathers illness. If this card gets home ahead of me, I would advise you not to get in the rush and jam that is bound to occur when the division arrives. But let me surprise you at the house. Sincerely, Eliot.

He arrived in New York April 20, 1919. On April 26, the Mayor's Committee of Welcome gave a dinner dance for the men at the 69th Regiment Armory, with music by the New York City Police Band.[21] The officers of the regiment dined at Sherry's, then one of the fancier New York City restaurants.

The next day the 2,700 men of Eliot's regiment led by their colonel, William Donovan, marched the four miles from Washington Square to 115th Street. Donovan insisted that all his officers march the entire route, an order that endeared him to the men but not to the officers, accustomed to parading on horseback. The old veterans of the Civil War, Eliot's grandfather John Noble among them, were assembled in the reviewing stand at 105th Street. There was one accident along the parade route: a waiter slipped and fell out of an upper window at Delmonico's, corner of Fifth Avenue and 44th Street, landing on Mrs. E. P. Whitehead, a visiting Chicago socialite. She died of shock; the waiter survived.[22]

Eliot was honorably discharged, May 7, 1919, with the rank of sergeant. He was twenty-one and he had to get a job.

He saw his opportunity on Wall Street. Largely as a result of the war New York City, not London, was now at the center of world finance. Investors were bullish on American business prospects (between February and May General motors shares went from 130 to 191; International Mercantile Marine shares, from 23 to 47), and the market was experiencing unprecedented trading volumes (the exchange had to close on May 31 to catch up with all the paperwork). Eliot signed up for a course at the Henry L. Doherty School for Securities Salesmen. The advertisement for the school announced that the course would start in September 1919, it would be free and it wouldn't be overly demanding: a "few lectures and comparatively little textbook work."

---

21   *The New York Times* April 27, 1919, 12 (unattributed column). For dinner, the men were served vegetable soup, roast chicken, peas, roast potatoes, Neapolitan ice cream, cake, coffee, mineral water, cigars and cigarettes—no mention of beer or wine. In 1919, the temperance movement was in full bloom and Prohibition was about to become the law of the land.

22   *The New York Times*, April 29, 1919.

In the fall of 1919, as Eliot was learning how to sell securities, the optimism of a rising market suddenly turned sour. That November the market crashed.[23] Eliot received his certificate of graduation on March 13, 1920. Despite the swooning stock market, he used his army contacts and managed to line up a job at the securities firm of Kissel, Kinnicutt & Co., with offices at 14 Wall Street.

Eliot was working at the Kissel firm at noon on September 16, 1920. As he later recalled, the normal hum of office activity was interrupted by a tremendous explosion: the building shook, windows shattered, and crowds poured into the street. A powerful bomb had exploded only a block and half away instantly killing thirty and injuring many more. The building at the corner of Wall and Broad, long the home of the Morgan bank, still bears the marks of the great explosion, the cause of which, despite a well-publicized investigation led by Attorney General A. Mitchell Palmer, has never been determined. Since 1920 was the year of the red scare, most people, Eliot included, assumed it was the work of anarchist terrorists. In 1919, booby-trap bombs had been mailed to prominent persons across the country; more powerful bombs exploded in major cities. Those explosions, accompanied by anarchist leaflets declaring war on capitalism, killed and injured people.[24]

As the 1920 fall election campaign swung into high gear, it must have seemed to Eliot that the country was in bad shape. The Wall Street explosion and other terrorist bombings were only part of the big picture that fall. It was the fourth straight year of double-digit inflation; unemployment was on the rise; there were major strikes in the meatpacking and steel industries as the new labor movement flexed its muscles. The Ku Klux Klan was growing and spreading, its membership now five million, and race riots had erupted in Chicago, Knoxville, Omaha and Washington D.C. President Wilson had suffered a serious stroke the previous fall and there was a leadership vacuum at the highest level of government. To Eliot, it must have seemed that the euphoria of victory had all too quickly evaporated.

After about a year at the Kissel firm, Eliot moved to the National City Company, the securities affiliate of National City Bank. He was assigned to the

---

23   The Dow Jones average went from 119.62 on November 3, 1919 to 63.9 on August 24, 1921, a drop of 46.6 percent, one of the worst declines on record.

24   See John Brooks, *Once in Golconda, A True Drama of Wall Street 1920-1938* (New York; Harper & Row, 1969), 1-21. U.S. Attorney General A. Mitchell Palmer, relying on wartime legislation (the Sedition Act of 1918, and the Anarchist Act of the same year), raided homes, arrested suspected terrorists and deported hundreds. One of his key lieutenants was 24-year old J. Edgar Hoover. Many people believed Palmer used the bombings to go after radicals, union leaders and others. But the anarchists and their bombs were real.

New England region as an institutional bond salesman. In 1923 he was based in Hartford, living at the YMCA in New London, and taking the train to New York City on weekends to be with his mother in Brooklyn.

He started out at National City making $1,500 a year; by 1923 he was making $2,400.[25] He tried to build up some savings with a United States Government Thrift Card, which promised to pay five dollars on 1 January 1923 provided he pasted sixteen 25-cent thrift stamps, one in each of the boxes. Like a Chinese fortune cookie, each box contained words of encouragement: "Waste not; want not," "If you want to succeed, save," "A penny saved is a penny gained," etc. He never got beyond the first stamp; the space for his next stamp—"Your second stamp here," is still blank.

* * *

In the spring of 1923 Eliot left National City for a job at Dow Jones as a financial news reporter for *The Wall Street Journal*. It was his third job in three years. His paycheck was the same ($2,400) but since the Dow Jones offices were in Manhattan, he could live at home. As a financial news reporter he would be a cut above a bond salesman, and it was an open secret that financial news reporters at the *Journal* were privy to all kinds of interesting financial information that could prove useful in buying and selling stocks, which in 1923 were moving up again.

His social life was conducted under the watchful eye of his mother. He had accepted an invitation to a house party in Stamford, Connecticut for the weekend of February 16-17, 1924. The invitation had come with the suggestion that he escort a girl from Brooklyn, Priscilla Fuller, who had also been invited. The small group was to meet at 9:30 in the morning under the clock at the main information booth, Grand Central Terminal. He didn't know anything about Priscilla. He kept a little book filled with the addresses of girls. One of them, Justine Sackett, lived near Stamford and worked for an advertising agency in New York. She was going to be at the house party. At least there'd be someone he knew and liked. An entry in Eliot's day book for the previous June described a weekend at the beach with Justine, dining, dancing and swimming. His day book contained names and phone numbers. He had intended to start a diary but gave it up after a few days.

---

25   Eliot's salary of $2,400, in purchasing power, was the equivalent of about $29,000 in 2007 dollars. See <www.measuringworth.com> All translations of old dollars into current dollars that appear hereinafter are based on this website, which was accessed March 18, 2010.

In 1924, Eliot was an attractive man. Over six feet tall, he smiled and laughed easily; he was athletic and full of energy and vitality. According to at least one girl he knew at the time, he was fun to be with.

Early 1920s, Eliot on left

He was also ambitious. But if asked, would he have been able to explain exactly what he was ambitious for? He might have said he wanted to "make something of myself," "be somebody," "get ahead." In 1924, Wall Street seemed to offer plenty of opportunity to get ahead.

It's hard to tell how, if at all, the war had affected him. He had survived combat without visible wounds, and his lifelong love of the Army suggests that for him the war had been a largely positive experience. The Army had promoted him, given him authority, offered him camaraderie, order, security, prestige, and the sense that he was part of something big and important. Shortly after his discharge in 1919 he had joined the New York National Guard. By the winter of 1924, he had devoted four years to the Guard with every reason to believe he would soon receive his officer's commission.

Although seemingly self-assured, there was something about him that suggested he wasn't quite comfortable in his own skin, something that suggested uncertainty about where he stood, a slight self-consciousness, even awkwardness, with other people. Who was he and where had he come from?

* * *

Let's go back seventy-five years to October 29, 1849, when Eliot's immigrant grandfather, Johann Vestner, arrived in New York harbor on the *Hudson*, a relatively small and crowded ship that had left the German port of Bremen sometime in September.[26] The officer making up the ship's manifest listed him as "J. Vestner???" age 28 from Germany.[27]

A ship similar to the Hudson, ca. 1849

26   A relatively small ship, approximately 117 feet long and weighing 386 tons, the *Hudson* might have carried a few dozen passengers in comfort, but when J. Vestner sailed it was a very crowded ship with 300 names on the manifest. Built in New York in 1840, the ship on which Johann arrived was purchased in 1849 by the Bremen firm of Konitzky & Thiermann and renamed the *Hudson*, replacing a ship of the same name lost on a voyage from Puerto Rico to Bremen in January 1849. See Palmer, List of Merchant Vessels, at < www.geocities.com/mppraetorius/com-ma.htm>. Last accessed June 2008.
27   Entry "J. Vestner???;" *Hudson* Passenger Manifest, October 29, 1849, in Family Tree Maker's Family Archives, *Passenger and Immigration Lists: 1820-1850* (CD # 273) from National Archives Microfilm Series M237, Roll # 84: 1459.

What do we know about Johann Vestner's life before coming to America? Not much. He was born December 16, 1816 in the town of Altdorf, about fifteen miles southeast of Nürnberg, one of the principal cities in the Kingdom of Bavaria.[28] He was the bastard son of Margaretha Vestner and Heinrich Roth. The birth record is short and to the point:

> Unmarried Margaretha Vestner's, oldest daughter of dayworker Johann Vestner from here, premarital son is born Monday the 16th of September in the evening at 6 o'clock and baptized Wednesday the 18th by me, Godfather was Johann Vestner, the given father of the child is Heinrich Roth, citizen's son from here, midwife was Muller.[29]

Johann's unmarried mother, Margaretha Vestner, was Eliot Vestner's great grandmother. She was the daughter of Johann Vestner and Anna Barbara (Friedel) of Altdorf. Johann's father (Eliot's great grandfather) was Heinrich Roth, also of Altdorf. Johann took his mother's name and presumably she raised him in Altdorf as her only child. Eight years after Johann's birth, in 1824, his father, Roth, married Anna Haas of Altdorf. Margaretha Vestner never married, lived her life in Altdorf, and died in 1860.[30]

---

28   Johann was a Bavarian. Bavaria was an independent kingdom, one of the dozens of small Germanic states; it would not become part of a unified Germany until 1871. Johann may have thought of himself as a "Frank," since Franconia had only recently been incorporated into the new Kingdom of Bavaria under Napoleon around 1806.

29   "Baptism Book, 1816," Parish of Altdorf, Fi. 7-13, No. 3: 217/No. 174 (Evangelical Central Archives, Regensburg, Germany).

30   Johann's family had lived in Altdorf at least since 1680, the year his ancestor Georg Vestner was born. By the 1840s "Vestner" was a fairly common name in Altdorf, as well as in and around the city of Nürnberg

Teacher's college in Altdorf around 1830, when Johann Vestner was a boy

Vestnertor ('Vestner Tower') old Nürnberg

Altdorf had once been a famous university town. By 1816 the university had closed, but there was a teachers college. With professors and students the town probably retained some of its old sophistication. Johann's early life included compulsory schooling, probably not beyond his sixteenth year. At about sixteen or earlier, he probably apprenticed to a master cabinetmaker. After years of apprenticeship, he may have attained the status of master cabinetmaker in Altdorf with his own apprentices, but I doubt it. If he had been a master cabinetmaker, I doubt he would have left. But that's speculation. All we know is that when he arrived in New York, age thirty-three, he considered himself a cabinetmaker.

19

What were Johann's reasons for leaving the familiar surroundings of Alt-dorf and undertaking the long, uncomfortable and dangerous journey across the ocean? What were his first impressions of New York? What did he do when he arrived? He left no diary, but other Germans coming at the same time did, notably Friederich Nohl and Michael Radke, and their diaries probably speak for Johann as well.[31]

Nohl was well-to-do and had served in the Prussian parliament. He sailed from Bremerhaven with his wife and six children and arrived in New York City on October 22, 1849, just nine days after J. Vestner's arrival. Nohl was on his way to the farm he had purchased in Ripon, Wisconsin. Michael Radke, with a wife and three children, sailed from Bremerhaven to Baltimore in March-April 1848, also en route west.

Nohl sailed on the *Emigrant*, at 900 tons a much larger ship than the *Hudson*. The *Emigrant* accommodated 196 "B Deck" passengers and 19 in upper-deck first-class cabins. Nohl was able to provide cabin accommodations for his family, which he described as "small" but "well furnished." As to the two bunks in each cabin: "the mattresses... are damned hard and I didn't want to stay longer in them than absolutely necessary." He was happy with the food: "simple, but hearty and good," noting that even the people on B Deck, who paid less than half of what he had paid, were provided with "simple but good food." Nohl looked at his fellow German passengers, especially those from Bavaria, with a jaundiced eye:

> It turns out that the greater half of the passengers comes from Bavaria...there were a lot of trashy passengers.... Many passengers travel only with a rucksack. It would be interesting to write the life histories of all the passengers, although the backgrounds of many of them don't seem impressive. If you look at these people, you shouldn't be surprised that the Germans in America don't have a good reputation.

---

31   "The Trip Diary of Friedrich Nohl, 16 September 1849 to 20 December 1849" is included in James Nohl Churchyard, *Our Family Museum* (1996). Contact James Nohl Churchyard, 1894 Santa Margarita Drive, Fallbrook, CA 92028 for information. Eva Krautein translated the diary, originally in German. Nohl, born in Prussia in 1807, was a pastor and owner of an agricultural school. He sold his school and had ample funds available for emigration to the United States. He died in Ripon, Wisconsin, August 1882. Before coming to this country he had been a member of the Prussian Parliament. Michael Radke was a distiller from Prussia with a wife and three children. See Sabine Jordan, trans. *Immigration Diary of Michael FriedricRadke, 1848* (privately published in 1982). <http://www.ingenweb.org/infranklin/pages/tier2/radke1848.html.> Last accessed February 2010.

When Nohl's ship arrived at New York Harbor, a pilot came on board to steer them into the harbor, followed by a medical examiner and customs officials. Nohl's description of their arrival conveys a sense of what Johnann Vestner would have seen on his arrival:

> In the early morning everybody is on deck. The B Deck passengers are cleaning themselves up. Straw and old clothes are being thrown into the ocean. It is almost impossible to recognize them, because everybody has dressed up so much. The doctor came on board to check the health situation. This is satisfactory, and so, after an hour, we are towed by steamer into New York. Unfortunately it is raining terribly and we can't enjoy the beautiful sights of New York.
>
> About 10 o'clock we are in New York harbor. Suddenly, one hundred seedy fellows (sharks) climbed on the ship and tried to meet the passengers. Many are welcomed by relatives and friends, and there were several touching scenes. In the afternoon I debarked from the ship and was happy to have firm soil under my feet.... I ran around in the immense but terribly dirty New York till evening and found the houses for which I had addresses. New York is much livelier than Hamburg and Brussels, Berlin, etc. In the main streets there is so much dirt that the passing vehicles sink in to the axles. In New York you find many beautiful buildings and squares and vitality as only London and Paris have. The harbor is a forest of masts and you have to remember exactly the place where your ship from the homeland is if you want to find it again.[32]

The Nohl family baggage was transferred to a steamer that would take them to Albany on the way to Wisconsin.

Johann Vestner's ship was smaller, it was overcrowded, his accommodations were undoubtedly below deck, and his crossing would not have been as comfortable as Nohl's. A contemporary description of the sleeping arrangements in steerage, deep in the bowels of the ship, suggests what it might have been like for Vestner:

---

32 *Nohl Diary*: 5. "Sharks" were probably runners, paid by the lodging houses to bring customers; they were notorious for stealing baggage and money from newly-arrived immigrants. See Edwin Guillett: *The Great Migration* (New York; Thomas Nelson & Sons, 1937), 185-186.

besides two tiers of berths on the sides, the vessel was filled with a row of berths down the centre, between which and the side berths there was only a passage of about three feet. The passengers were thus obliged to eat in their berths. In one were a man, his wife, his sister, and five children; in another were six full-grown young women, whilst that above them contained five men, and the next one eight more."[33]

Bad enough on a fine day and a calm sea; in bad weather the passengers in steerage, many of them sick, would have been crowded below with the hatches closed and no bathrooms.

Michael Radke, a distiller, had a longer and more arduous crossing than Nohl. His ship, the *Johanis*, left Bremerhaven on March 5, 1848 and didn't arrive in Baltimore until April 29, a voyage of fifty-five days that included at least two life-threatening storms, as Radke noted on April 11, "Violent storm... it seems as if all of us will perish," and on April 20, "During the day the storm grew stronger and stronger, so that we saw around us high mountainous waves and deep abysses.... We give up hope of surviving the furious, foaming, wildly raging sea."

Crossing the ocean was dangerous business; but there were powerful forces propelling Nohl, Radke and Johann Vestner towards America. For Nohl, the reasons were largely political. In his diary entry for October 13, he said, "Today is my wedding anniversary. Three years ago, I was very sick on this day. If I hadn't been sick and if the political situation hadn't become so miserable, I wouldn't be here." As a member of the Prussian Parliament, Nohl was involved in the political turmoil of 1848, which led to revolution and violent repression. Radke was fed up with the poverty and social structure back home:

It was my desire to bring my children...to a place where they could find work and bread, as long as they would work hard and be frugal, where each of them could prepare for a happy and calm future. In Germany the poor man compared to the rich man is like a despised creature, or like a scarcely noticed creeping worm, who must slither and creep along in the dust in order not to be stepped on to death....Once the poor man

---

33   Guillet: *The Great Migration*: 67-68, quoting a contemporary description of accommodations aboard the *Thomas Gelston* from Londonderry, Ireland.

completed his day's work, what did he earn for his sour sweat? Only 7½ to 10 silver groschen—which is 20 cents in American money—and on that the poor man is supposed to live with his family, pay his rent and pay his royal taxes.

Was Johann Vestner, like Nohl, disillusioned with the political situation? Was he, like Radke, fleeing poverty and a rigid social structure that left him without hope for his future? What were the conditions in Bavaria at the time that caused so many to come to America?

When Johann Vestner was growing up, Bavaria was virtually a feudal society, dominated by a landed aristocracy. Most Bavarians worked on farms or at trades. Life was short; children died at birth or at a young age, usually from infectious diseases. During the 1840s repeated crop failures, particularly potato rot, led to famine conditions. Because the potato was a relatively cheap and nutritious staple in Bavaria as it was in Ireland, a shortfall in the potato supply had grave consequences. With diminished supply, the cost of potatoes and other basic food products skyrocketed. At the same time the industrial situation was changing fast: factories and machinery were replacing individual craftsmen. Famine and unemployment created fertile conditions for radical political change. In the 1840s, Karl Marx and Friedrich Engels were writing and expounding their ideas about revolution and communism, ideas that were taking root in the German states. And then there was the army. Military service was compulsory and Johann, thirty-three in 1849, was at risk of being called up.

Johann's timing could not have been worse. Traditionally, a young man seeking to become a cabinetmaker would start as an apprentice in the shop of a master and proceed by stages to the point where he could expect to become a master with his own shop and clientele. But with the end of the Napoleonic wars in 1815, things began to change. European markets were flooded with cheap furniture manufactured on the machines that made Britain the early leader in the new industrial age. Machine-made furniture was driving down prices and wages in local German markets. Declining farm income in the 1830s and 1840s made matters worse: local farmers no longer had the money to buy fine furniture, and displaced agricultural workers left the farms to become apprentice craftsmen. There were too many cabinetmakers and not enough business.

During those same years, glowing letters from Germans in America published in local newspapers, and numerous travel and advice books, painted a rosy picture of life in America, and in particular of New York, as a place where Germans would feel entirely at home.

German immigrants landing in New York in the 1840s and 50s were joined by Irish, unemployed English factory hands, frustrated political radicals, Italian veterans of the 1849 War for Independence, and many others. At mid-century, the port of New York was the main U.S. entry point for European immigration.[34] Between 1840 and 1859 more than 3 million immigrants, roughly 40 percent Irish, 32 percent German, and 16 percent English, entered New York Harbor to live and work in the city or to continue their journey west. During that tumultuous period, the population of New York City swelled from 313,000 to 814,000.[35] The Germans, like the Irish, were driven to America largely by politics, poverty, and potato rot.

When Johann Vestner's ship docked, he may have been accompanied by friends or cousins from Altdorf, but he was not accompanied by any other Vestners. As he walked down the gangplank and out into the crowded streets, he knew he had to find a place to sleep. He had probably been advised to find a respectable German boarding house.

Another piece of advice he had probably received was, "Don't trust anyone with your money, and watch out for smooth-talking swindlers looking for naive German immigrants," advice that would have made Johann suspicious and guarded in dealing with strangers. Early on his first morning in New York, he was probably directed to the German Society, formed in 1784 to provide advice and counsel, employment assistance, and financial aid to German immigrants. They probably referred Johann to a German cabinetmaking establishment; the Germans dominated the woodworking trades.

From his arrival in 1849, Johann Vestner lived and worked in anonymity. There is no record of him in New York until 1861. Officially, he did not exist. But we can make an educated guess about his life. He probably lived in a boarding house with other single men from Bavaria, and socialized mainly with his fellow Bavarians (each of the German states had its own particular dialect, food and customs). He may have tried to learn English, and perhaps made some progress; but he could get by perfectly well in German, which was the primary language of his friends and co-workers, and he could get all his news from one of the many local German-language newspapers. Culturally and socially he was more Bavarian than American. He wasn't any different from other immigrants,

---

34   Burrows and Wallace, *Gotham*, 735-747.
35   Burrows and Wallace, *Gotham*, 736.

who tended to settle into their own ethnic enclaves, hearing the comforting sounds of their native language, smelling familiar smells, eating familiar foods, observing familiar customs, and socializing with family and friends from their home regions or towns in Germany, Ireland, or England.

New York was a tough place for cabinetmakers. In Germany, it took a long time for an apprentice to become a master cabinetmaker, and the work was done to a high standard. Johann's local cabinetmaker's guild in Altdorf would have had strict rules that governed exactly how the cabinets were to be made and sold. In America it was very different. There were no guilds, no rules, and the market was a free-for-all. That may have come as a rude surprise to Johann.

In New York, a few highly skilled and well-paid cabinetmakers worked in high-end custom furniture shops like Duncan Phyfe's. But most shops had to meet the demand for cheap furniture. By and large, cabinetmakers worked in small sweatshops that competed by driving down wages. If some poor cabinet-maker didn't want to take a pay cut, his boss had ten eager prospects just off the boat willing to work for less.

New York cabinetmakers had earned on average $12-15 per week in 1836. That information, relayed to Germany and perhaps read by Johann Vestner, would have attracted a lot of interest among cabinetmakers. That was good pay. But by 1850, New York cabinetmakers were earning less than $5 a week.[36] Some cabinetmakers were successful; most were not. Ernest Hagen, a German cabinetmaker who had come to New York from Germany in 1844, described the business as it was in the 1850s:

> The work was all done by hand, but the scroll sawing, of course, was done at the nearest sawmill..... The journeymen cabinet makers had to supply their own tools and work benches. They had only wood stoves in the shops and no steam heating what-ever...Amongst the most prominent cabinet makers of the East side was Henry Weil, who had a large shop on Essex near Riv-ington Street, and sent most of his goods to New Orleans. He died rich leaving a fortune of about 4 Millions...Weil made those ugly heavy veneered 8 cornered high post bedsteads of which you find so many down South....Attorney Street, which is 12 blocks east of the Bowery... was quite a center for the

---

36   Ernst, *Immigrant Life in New York City*: 80-81, 102-103.

small cabinet makers then. Wenzels saw mill was located there
and the cabinet makers seemed to cluster around it...[37]

Most of the work was done in small shops, which tended to specialize
in a single piece of furniture (veneered box sofas, French bedsteads, bureaus,
high bookcases, etc.). From Henry Weil's experience, it was possible for a
cabinetmaker to make a fortune by organizing the production and sale of
cabinetry crafted by men like Johann Vestner. Hagan himself worked in the
200-man shop of the leading New York cabinetmaker of the 1850s, Charles
Baudouine, who operated his factory at the corner of Broadway and Anthony
Street and also became a multi-millionaire in the business. Weil and Baudouine were the exceptions. The great majority of cabinetmakers struggled to
make a living.

Responding to cut-throat competition and low wages, the German craftsmen, led by refugee intellectuals who had fled in the aftermath of the 1848
revolution, formed the earliest American labor organizations. In 1850, 800 of
the city's 2,000 cabinetmakers formed an association that posted handbills in
immigrant boardinghouses, directing new immigrants to shops offering adequate wages. During the 1850s, German-led associations of cabinetmakers, car-
penters, and upholsterers all went on strike for higher wages and achieved some
success. But it was only temporary. With the financial panic of 1857, followed
by rising unemployment, wages fell, and by 1860 cabinetmakers were again
struggling to make a living.[38]

Despite the conditions, Johann was apparently doing well enough to
get married. On October 28, 1861 "Johann Vestler," age forty-five, married
Margaretha Ramming in a ceremony performed by the Reverend August H.
M. Held, the first pastor of St. John's Evangelical Lutheran Church at 79
Christopher Street.[39] The bride was twenty-seven and single, from Unter-
dornlach, another small Bavarian village, and she had arrived in November

---

37   Ernest Hagen, "Personal Experiences of an Old New York Cabinet Maker" (Brooklyn, NY, 1908), 3-4
(Courtesy, The Winterthur Library, Joseph Downs Collection of Manuscripts and Printed Ephemera, No.
88x207.1, Col. 32).
38   Ernst, *Immigrant Life in New York City*: 108-111, 120.
39   "Marriage Register," St. John's Evangelical Lutheran Church, 79 Christopher Street, October 28,
1861. Although "Vestler" is not quite "Vestner," immigrant names were frequently misspelled in official
registers, directories, and census documents.

1859 on the *Republik* from Bremen, Germany.[40] She was Eliot Vestner's grandmother.

On or about August 2, 1863, Margaretha gave birth to a son, George John Vestner.[41] There is no birth certificate, but a substantial number of births weren't registered in those days, and Margaretha almost certainly used the services of a German midwife. George was born during the New York City draft riots, when city officials were more concerned with avoiding the mobs than registering births.

When George was born, the Civil War was still raging and German immigrants swelled the ranks of the Union army. At thirty-eight with wife and child, he would have escaped the net cast by the 1863 Draft Act, which focused on unmarried young men between the ages of eighteen and thirty five. Through the war years, he pursued his cabinetmaker's trade. The Vestner family lived on the Lower West Side, within a small area defined by Chambers Street to the south, West Houston to the north, Hudson Street to the West and West Broadway to the East.

Johann and Margaretha's neighborhood was a mix of German, Irish, and English. They were only a few blocks west of the most concentrated German-speaking section of the city known as "Klein Deutschland" (Little Germany). It was an area extending north from Bayard Street to East 14th Street, and west from the East River to the Bowery, with saloons, wine gardens, beer halls, concert halls, club rooms and theaters.[42] The Irish, in particular Mr. Dooley, had their own take on the Germans in Little Germany:

That's as far as I care to go, havin' lived f'r manny years among th' Germans. I'm not prejudiced again' thim, mind ye. They make good beer an' good citizens an mod-rate polismen, an' they are fond iv their fam'lies an' cheese. But wanst a German, always Dutch.

---

40   Margaretha Ramming was born January 26, 1835 to Adam Ramming and Margaretha Gade of Unterdornlach. She arrived in New York on November 7, 1859. *Germans to America*, Vol. 13, August 1859-December 1860: 62. While Margaretha headed for New York, other members of the Ramming family had left Germany in 1854 and settled in Baltimore, Maryland. Her brothers may have advised her to go to New York, perhaps thinking she'd be better off striking out on her own. Or, equally likely, perhaps Margaretha had an independent streak and wanted to distance herself from her brothers. See *Passenger Lists of Vessels Arriving at Baltimore, Maryland, 1820-1891*. Microfilm Roll M255_10. Five Rammings: Christian, thirty-two; Adam, thirty; Friedrich (or Frederica?), twenty-eight; Adam, five; and Johann, nine months, arrived in Baltimore on the *Ceres*, December 1854.

41   In the 1900 census, George reported his birth date as August 2, 1863, consistent with what he reported in his marriage certificate in 1891. See Federal Census 1900, New York Roll 704. ED 587, VDL 154, Sheet 23, Line 43. But his death certificate lists his birthdate as August 13, 1864. See Certificate of Death, No. 7203, March 18, 1934 (New York City Municipal Archives).

42   Burrows and Wallace, *Gotham*, 745. See also Ernst, *Immigrant Life in New York City*: 43 (showing geographical distribution of Germans and Irish, district by district, in New York City 1855); and Stanley Nadel, *Little Germany* (Champaign, Illinois; University of Illinois Press, 1990). If Little Germany had been a city, it would have ranked just behind Berlin and Vienna in the size of its German population.

Ye cudden't make Amereicans iv thim if ye called thim all Perkins an' brought thim up in Worcester. A German niver ra-aly leaves Germany. He takes it with him wheriver he goes. Whin an Irishman is four miles out at sea he is as much an American as Presarved Fish. But a German is niver an American excipt whin he goes back to Germany to see his rilitives. He keeps his own language, he plays pinochle, he despises th' dhrink iv th' counthry, his food is sthrange an' he on'y votes f'r Germans f'r office, or if he can't get a German, f'r somewan who's again' th' Irish. I bet ye, if ye was to suddenly ask Schwarzmeister where he is, he'd say 'At Hockheimer in Schwabia.' He don't ra-aly know he iver come to this counthry. I've heerd him talkin' to himsilf. He always counts in German.[43]

Schwartzmeister, with a giant stein of his favorite beer, sitting with friends in an outdoor beer garden in little Germany, perhaps with the Vestners at the same table, buckling under the weight of a platter of steaming sausages, pork, bacon and sauerkraut, undoubtedly could have given a hilarious description of the Irish in New York.

By 1863 Johann Vestner was visible, with name and address listed in the city directory. He was now "John Vestner, cabinetmaker," presumably earning enough to pay the rent and put food on the table.[44] He probably belonged to at least one "Verein" (club), consisting of men in his trade and from his part of Bavaria. For most immigrants from the German states social life revolved around the clubs. Some clubs were mutual benefit societies, which collected dues and insured members against the expense of sickness and death. Most of the clubs were for recreation. They organized song festivals, parades and summer outings to Long Island, New Jersey and up the Hudson. A summer outing might involve hundreds and include gymnastic exhibitions, sharp shooting, plays, group singing and dancing.[45]

John and Margaret (she had anglicized her name too) undoubtedly had a favorite local beer hall—there were hundreds of them in Little Germany—where they could gather with their friends and neighbors, gossiping, drinking, eating, and singing German songs.[46] In the summer the beer halls became beer gardens. From their picture, John and Margaret were loyal customers of their favorite beer hall.

43   Finley Peter Dunne, *Observations by Mr. Dooley* (New York; Harper & Brothers, 1902), 83-84. "Preserved Fish" was a prominent New York City shipping merchant in the early 1800s.
44   *Trow's New York City Directory*, entries for "John Vestner," 1863-67.
45   Stanley Nadel, *Little Germany*, 107-112.
46   Ernst, *Immigrant Life in New York City*, 130. Germans dominated the beer business.

Johann and Margaretha Vestner 1864-66

By 1870 John, along with all the other New York cabinetmakers, was probably struggling to earn money (after being listed in the New York City Directory every year from 1963 through 1967, his name once again disappears from
the official record). Ernest Hagan described the "great change" that struck the
New York cabinetmakers in the late sixties:

> The western factorys drove every thing else out of the market.
> All the smaller cabinet makers were simply wiped out, there
> are very few left now which make a scant living…and even the
> larger establishments have a hard time in competing with the
> western concerns of Grand Rapids in Michigan and other out
> of town houses.[47]

On August 6, 1872 John Vestner died from an attack of diarrhea, possibly
cholera, rampant in the crowded and dirty downtown tenements. His death was
quick; no more than a couple of days from beginning to end. His last residence

---

47   Ernest Hagan, *Personal Experiences,* 14.

was a three-family house at 82 Thompson Street, near Spring Street, 90 Sixth Avenue, and Laurens, all places John had lived during the past ten years. Having once crossed the ocean, John lived the rest of his life within a very small area on the Lower West Side of Manhattan. The doctor who signed his death certificate wrote John's name as "Fesner," later crossing it out and inserting "Vestner." The certificate listed John's occupation as "cabinetmaker," noted his age, that he had been in New York for twenty-three years, and recorded his birthplace simply as "Germany." [48]

John left few possessions, but one that survived the years is a tiny locket with a picture of his mother, an early daguerreotype, probably taken just before he sailed for America in 1849.

John Vestner's mother, Margaretha Vestner, ca. 1849

John rests alone in a one-hundred-square-foot plot at Cypress Hills Cemetery, Brooklyn. Founded in 1848, Cypress Hills was non-sectarian and

48   Death Certificate, John Vestner, New York City, August 6, 1872, No.125974 (New York City Municipal Archives).

relatively inexpensive. New York City prohibited burials in the downtown area, and an uptown burial would have been expensive.[49] Margaretha took title to the burial plot and paid $55 cash (about $1,000 in current dollars), suggesting that John's business may have enabled him to put some money aside or purchase life insurance to provide for his widow. An ornate granite gravestone inscribed in German, with a small sculpture of a hand holding a tool, marks his burial place

> Here rests in God
> Our husband and father
> John Vestner
> Born 16 Dec 1816
> Died 6 Aug 1872
> Peace for his ashes
> He is not dead, but
> Remains forever in our hearts[50]

Margaret Vestner moved with her son across the river to Brooklyn and rented an apartment at 8 Throop Street.[51] In 1878 she married Carl Heinrich Hautan (known as "Henry"), a fifty-two-year-old widower and butcher living at 655 Washington Street, Lower West Side of Manhattan.[52] They were married in the same Evangelical Lutheran Church where she and John Vestner had married in 1861, and the Reverend Held similarly blessed her new marriage. Like Margaret, Henry Hautan had been born in Germany.[53]

George Vestner, nine when his father died in 1872, was fifteen when his mother remarried. He was an only child. His mother saw to it that he received an education: in the public school system and later at a German-American private school in Brooklyn. She was determined that he would not follow in his father's footsteps as a struggling cabinetmaker. At about the age of sixteen,

49   Burrows and Wallace, *Gotham*: 582.
50   I am indebted to Christa Bleyleben for translating the inscription into English.
51   The Brooklyn Directory, 1875 to 1877, lists "Vestner, Margaret, wid. John" at 8 Throop Avenue. It would have been relatively easy for Margaret to visit John's grave in Cypress Hills from Throop Avenue.
52   Marriage Certificate, Margaretha Barbara Vestner and Carl Heinrich Hautan, New York City, November 17, 1878, No. 6570 (New York City Municipal Archives)
53   Margaret lived at 655 Washington Street for the next thirty-seven years. Widowed in the 1890s for the second time, she died at home on August 13, 1915. Death Certificate, Margaretha Hautan, August 13, 1915, No. 24215 (New York City Municipal Archives). The certificate lists "senility" as a contributing factor in her death, but the main cause was "arrhythmia," or irregular heartbeat. She was buried in the Lutheran Cemetery at 355 Bleeker Street.

George went into the law. On July 31, 1879, George Wager, a lawyer at 12 Chambers Street in Manhattan, filed an affidavit with the Court of Appeals:

I George W. Wager, an attorney of the Supreme Court practicing in the City of NY do hereby certify that George Vestner commenced a service as clerk and student at law in my office on the first day of April 1879.

In 1879 most aspiring lawyers arranged to clerk for a practicing lawyer. Clerks weren't paid; they usually had to pay for the privilege. The period of clerkship varied, but when the lawyer in charge was satisfied, he made a recommendation to the court and his clerk was admitted to the bar. After a year of clerking, George became a lawyer. The 1880 city directory lists "George J. Vestner, Lawyer," with his office at 320 Broadway, living with his mother and stepfather at 655 Washington Street. In fact, George was little more than a messenger and office boy in the law office of John Joseph Adams, a prominent New York lawyer and political figure.[54]

In 1880 there was a move to upgrade the legal profession, led by well-known New York City lawyers such as former Mayor George Templeton Strong. Strong, senior partner in what was then the largest law firm in the city with six lawyers, believed there were too many unqualified lawyers. Strong was a Columbia graduate, and he focused his energies on strengthening and expanding Columbia Law School. With some of his like-minded colleagues, he established the Association of the Bar of the City of New York with screening and grievance committees. In its first year the new bar association, dominated by a small group of elite Manhattan lawyers, admitted only about 450 out of more than 4,000 lawyers in the city.[55] George Vestner was not a member.

In 1883 George got his first big break. John J. Adams, newly elected to Congress, took his promising nineteen-year-old clerk to Washington. Serving as Adams's private secretary, he also attended classes and graduated from the Columbian University Law School, now known as the George Washington University Law School, and served as chief clerk to the Hydrographic section of the

54   John Joseph Adams, born New Brunswick Canada, 1848, died New York City February 16, 1919. Adams emigrated from Canada in 1864, graduated from Columbia Law School in 1876, and was elected to Congress from Queens, 1883-1887.
55   Burrows & Wallace, *Gotham*: 967-968.

U.S. Coast and Geodetic Survey.[56] After two terms, Adams returned to New York and resumed his law practice with George as his partner.

Energetic, popular and a good organizer, George also looked out for himself. In 1888 he was president of the Arlington League. *The New York World* described the members of the League as "several hundred prosperous and intelligent young men whose object was to secure mental recreation and social engagement."[57] The article went on to describe one of George's outings on June 18, 1888: a party barge and boat trip on Long Island Sound, five hundred gentlemen and ladies, a band, dancing, food, drink and cigars. Unfortunately the party ran into a thick fog on the way home in the evening and had to put in at Flushing Bay, Queens. The paper reported "There were several young ladies whose parents did not know they were out and they dreaded the consequences of being found out." The fog didn't lift until 3:30 A.M. Until then the party was stranded, nothing to do but dance, drink and eat. They landed back at the West 10th Street pier at 5:30 A.M., met by an excited and worried crowd, doubtless including the parents of the girls who "dreaded the consequences of being found out." George, of course, had planned ahead, the reporter noting that "President Vestner found a cab he had ordered before starting, and which had been waiting since 10 o'clock" the previous night.

Soon after he returned to New York in 1887, George began seeing Ruth Noble. In 1889 he inscribed a two-volume set of Victor Hugo's *Hunchback of Notre Dame* "R.N. from G.J.V. 1889." The pristine condition of the two volumes suggests she never opened them; Ruth was no intellectual. Courtship led to engagement; but on the eve of their marriage, George received a curious letter of advice from a friend who wrote at the end of the letter "please destroy this":

> In this, the most important act of your life, you can never expect, or hope for happiness unless you enter the state with the firm resolve to cut loose from the association of those who have held you in vice-like [sic] grasp for years. I do not refer to men, or women, alone, I combine the forces. Do! I implore you (as I would my own brother) shun their society... She is a brave girl surely, to trust her happiness to the keeping of a Club man... I have a perfect horror of such.... Now you ought to make up your mind to gather in all the reins that other people have been pulling and placing them in this noble young ladies' [sic] hand...

---

56 *Report of the Superintendent of the U.S.Coast and Geodetic Survey* for the fiscal year ending June, 1886 (Government printing office, Washington, D.C. 1887), 145.

57 "OUT ALL THE NIGHT IN A FOG" *The New York World*, June 19, 1888, (unattributed article).

The trouble with you is that you have exercised little caution,
and less judgment in the selection of your male associates....[58]

George's friend, who signed his letter "K.L.W.,"obviously thought George
ran with a fast crowd. Odd that "K.L.W." would take it on himself to chastise
George on the eve of his marriage. The worst he could say was that George
was a "Club man." George probably belonged to a men's club. He undoubtedly spent time with other men, some good, some not so good, and enjoyed a
night of poker. He probably liked an occasional afternoon at the racetrack; and
he probably had an eye for the ladies, not all of them "proper." Unfortunately,
"K.L.W." doesn't go into specifics. The letter suggests George may have been an
interesting guy with some rough edges, perhaps a convivial drinking companion. Curious, that of all the letters George must have written and received, only
the letter from "K.L.W." survived the years. Perhaps he took the advice to heart,
at least initially and with good intentions.

George Vestner, ca. 1889

---

58   Letter, undated, from K.L.W. to George Vestner.

Ruth Vestner, ca. 1889

George and Ruth were married on August 19, 1891, in the Calvary Baptist Church at 57ᵗʰ Street near Sixth Avenue.[59] George was twenty-eight, Ruth twenty-five. The marriage was announced in most of the New York City newspapers—in 1891 New York had about a dozen daily papers—and from the reports it was quite an event, with two hundred guests, described as "the greater portion of the smart set in town." The "knot was tied" by the Rev. Dr. MacArthur, pastor of the church; the bride was attended by a page (her nephew), two bridesmaids (cousins from Albany) and a maid of honor (her sister Sally); the groom had his best man and three ushers, one of whom was the bride's brother. The bride's gown was described as "of the richest white silk, slightly rounded at the throat and with long pulled sleeves," with a "tulle veil, fastened with diamonds." The bride's step-mother wore black silk—not a good omen. William Noble, the bride's uncle, made his apartment at 246 Central Park West available for a reception and supper, described as "sumptuous," furnished by "the well known caterers, Pinard and Co." One reporter, obviously enjoying himself, called the supper "a monument to their gastronomical skill...nothing

---

59   Marriage Certificate, Ruth Noble and George Vestner, New York City, August 19, 1891, No. 9804 (New York City Municipal Archives).

was neglected that refined taste, liberal expenditure and the most unwearied exertions of a genial host could do toward insuring the pleasure and enjoyment of the guests." Among the guests seated in the "spacious and beautiful rooms" of the Noble residence were ex-Mayor William H. Wickham, ex-Congressman Adams, department store magnate John Wanamaker, Mr. and Mrs. John W. Noble, parents of the bride (he was described as owner of "one of the largest racing stock farms in the country at Metuchen, N.J."), and "Mr. and Mrs. Henry Hautaun," parents of the groom.[60] After the wedding, the new Mr. and Mrs. Vestner left for a trip south to Old Point Comfort, Virginia, a popular seaside resort.

The fashionable uptown wedding, following his law partnership with former Congressman Adams, put the finishing touch on George's move up from the tenements of lower Manhattan. In sharp contrast to his father, George was prosperous, prominent, had made what appeared to be a good marriage, and clearly had a future. He was at the top of his game.

George Vestner's bride was the daughter of John W. Noble and Eliza Woodhall.[61] Eliza, born in England, arrived in New York in 1858 and married John sometime before 1866. John Noble was fifteen at the outbreak of the Civil War, but by the end of the war he was in the Union army serving in one of the New York regiments.[62] After the war, John was an Inspector with the New York City Police Department. Ruth's mother, Eliza, died in 1872 and John remarried.[63] By 1880, he had retired from the police force, and gone into the real estate business with his brother William. He was successful enough to acquire and operate a large horse breeding farm in New Jersey. For the rest of his life he was actively involved in real estate, horse breeding, politics, and veterans' affairs. He died in 1933, age eighty-five. *The New York Times* printed his obituary:[64]

---

60   Selected quotes from various undated newspaper clippings contained in a scrapbook.
61   Birth Certificate, July 13, 1866, New York City, No. 2020 (New York City Municipal Archives).
62   John Noble's tombstone at Kensico Cemetery in Westchester County is inscribed "Veteran of the Civil War," and his active leadership in Civil War veterans' affairs supports the claim of war service. But of the John Nobles who served from New York, none is listed as John W., and none of the ages are even approximately consistent with John W. Noble's birth date of 1846. Of course his record may be buried somewhere, or he may have lied about his age.
63   U.S. Census 1870, Series M593, Roll 996, 606. John is recorded as married to Eliza with two children: Ruth, four and Charles, two. John and Eliza were twenty-three and John was then an "Inspector" with the police. Eliza died December 18, 1872 of "Bright's Disease," a general term then used to describe a variety of kidney diseases. Death Certificate, Eliza Noble, New York City, December 19, 1872, No. 136364 (New York City Municipal Archives).
64   John Noble died March 14, 1933. See *The New York Times*, March 15, 1933 (Obituaries), 20.

John W. Noble, Civil War veteran, Commander of the John A Dix Post of the G.A.R., who formerly was president of the Fifth Assembly District Republican Club, died yesterday in the Lutheran Hospital of pneumonia at the age of 87. Before his retirement from business he had been associated with his brother, William Noble, as part owner of the Grenoble and Empire Hotels in this city and the Hotel Fort William Henry at Lake George. He had long resided at the Hotel Endicott, Eighty-First Street and Columbus Avenue. Surviving are a son, John W. Jr., and two daughters, Mrs. Ruth Vestner and Mrs. Sadie N. Bean.

After the marriage, George and Ruth Vestner moved into their own place at 282 West 114th Street on the Upper West Side of Manhattan, a block to the east of Morningside Park.

As a bright young lawyer with Washington experience, George was ambitious to get ahead in New York City politics. He started as a low-level volunteer in the Tammany organization, which in 1887 controlled all the levers of power in the city. Richard Croker, the Tammany boss, could make or break the career of an ambitious young man like George Vestner. The potential rewards for party loyalty must have been tempting, but George probably saw that as a German there wasn't a bright future for him in a political organization dominated by the Irish. And George must have seen that Tammany was a thoroughly corrupt organization, engaged in ballot fraud, and payoffs at every level of government (it cost $300 to be a cop, and up to $25,000 to be a police captain).[65] He would have to pay a substantial sum to achieve public office; and if he did that, he would become part of the corruption himself. George made a critical decision: he transformed himself from a Tammany man to an anti-Tammany man. In doing so he joined his law partner, Adams, and many of the leading citizens of the city in the reform movement. George gained a respectable reputation, but he risked losing any chance for a future in politics if the Tammany Democrats survived the challenge. Boss Croker had a long memory.

---

65   See Gustavus Myers, *The History of Tammany* Hall (New York; Published by author, 1901). Myers provides a detailed summary of Tammany corruption during the period 1888-1900 uncovered by various State investigating committees, notably the Lexow Committee of 1894.

In 1894, the reformers, led by William Strong, an independent Republican, beat Tammany. Strong, accompanied by his lawyers, Adams and Vestner, was sworn in as Mayor on December 13, 1894:[66]

> Col.William L. Strong, who will succeed Thomas F. Gilroy as Mayor on Jan. 1, was sworn in by Justice Barrett just before 11 o'clock this morning....With plenty of ostentatious flourish, they [court attendants] cleared a pathway for a party of five men.... Chairs were knocked over and a few corns were trodden on, but...up to the bar walked Mayor-elect Strong in tow of ex-Congressman John J. Adams, and followed by...George J. Vestner, Col. Strong's secretary.

The reformers included both Democrats and Republicans. What united them was the cause of clean government; they wanted to reclaim the city from Richard Croker and Tammany Hall. But the reform movement also had a class and religious element. The city's social elite, mainly old-line Protestants, disdained the newly arrived Irish and their Catholicism. The Irish dominated Tammany; Tammany, through its control of the Democratic Party, ruled the City; to the reformers that was an intolerable state of affairs.

George Vestner was an ardent supporter of Grover Cleveland, who in 1884 had been elected president of the United States, the only Democrat to be elected president since before the Civil War. Cleveland had risen from mayor of Buffalo to governor of New York on a platform of clean government, a sound dollar backed by gold, and tariff reform.[67] George and his fellow Cleveland Democrats were also called "Gold Democrats." *The New York Herald* printed an 1892 letter from George on tariff reduction, a hot topic:[68]

> I have read with considerable satisfaction to myself your editorials on the tariff in the past few days. They are admirable, and enough praise cannot be given by your readers for the plain,

---

66   *The New York Times*, December 13, 1894 (clipping, without page number or attribution).
67   Cleveland lost in 1888 but was re-elected in 1892—the only U.S. president re-elected after having been defeated.
68   Tariff reform was the central issue that separated Democrats and Republicans in the 1890s. Republican Congressman McKinley, in 1892, led a successful effort to raise tariffs. In theory, this would make imported goods more expensive and less competitive with American-made goods, thus protecting American jobs. In reality, higher tariffs simply led to higher prices and higher corporate profits for U.S. manufacturers. The Democrats were for lowering tariffs, arguing that lower tariffs would force lower prices, which would more directly benefit American workers.

straight forward manner in which you show the fallacy of 'protection to the American workingman.'

I credit myself with some amount of reasoning power, but I must admit that even as good a democrat as I believe myself to be, I often have been befuddled by the buncombe put up by the 'high priests of protection' to prove their theories.

I have heard the question put in the form you have presented it, but have never seen it in print. It seems to me to be the most thorough and comprehensive article on the tariff which has ever been put in type, and I think the National Democratic Committee could do nothing better than send hundreds of thousands of copies broadcast through the country. G.J.V.

In 1893 George was thirty and probably earning a good living as a lawyer. That year, he was appointed receiver for Harry Ely, a real estate dealer. The *Times* reported that Ely's income was $20,000 (about $456,000 in 2007 dollars), his expenses $22,000 or $23,000, and that "he spent just what he wanted to and placed no restriction on his wife's expenses..." But 1893 was no ordinary year. Ely had fallen victim to a full blown financial crisis. Stock prices plummeted, banks failed, and many people lost their life savings and their jobs as unemployment rose to twenty percent of the workforce. The resulting depression spread across the country and had a major impact on national politics. George, trying to make his way in the world and accumulate some savings, probably owned some stocks; if so, he would have lost money, perhaps a lot of money. Most likely, he kept some money on deposit with a bank. If so, he would have moved fast to get his money out when the bank runs started in June 1893. The banks continued under siege through July and into early August when all the New York banks temporarily suspended payments. It was a harrowing time. The "Depression of 1893" had the same effect on George's generation as the Great Depression of the 1930s did on a later generation.

The Depression had a major impact on the presidential election of 1896. That was George's biggest year in politics; the year he almost made it; the year of the most dramatic presidential election since 1860. The Democrats were the party in power, led by Grover Cleveland, and they were blamed for the Depression. At their nominating convention in 1896 the Democrats broke free of Cleveland and the Eastern wing of the party, nominating a Westerner, William

Jennings Bryan. With his stirring oratory, Bryan gave voice to all the anger felt by Western farmers and Southerners, who had been hit hard by the Depression; their targets were Wall Street and big business. Bryan ran on a platform that included currency devaluation (expanding the volume of silver coins and paper money), a graduated income tax, and support of labor unions—all "hot button" issues. Bryan's nomination and the radical Democratic platform caused many Democrats to walk out and form their own party.

Bryan scared the daylights out of the New York legal and financial establishment. Cleveland Democrats deserted the party in droves and formed a third party: the "National Democratic Party." The National Democrats nominated a seventy-nine year old Civil War general, John Palmer. They didn't expect Palmer to win; he merely provided a spot on the ballot for Democrats who couldn't stomach voting for Bryan or the Republican, William McKinley.

In the election of 1896 George ran as the National Democratic Party candidate for New York State Assembly from the 21st District, embracing a wide swath of the Upper West Side, from 81st Street to 120th Street. George believed in sound money backed by gold and clean government; he was against the tariff.

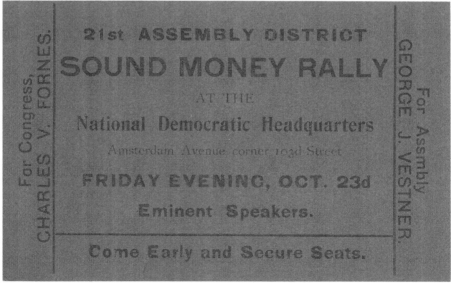

A sound money rally, 23 October 1896

The New York papers ran flattering profiles of George and his career, reported his attacks on Tammany and printed letters of support: ("George J. Vestner...is a very bright young lawyer. If elected, he will represent the people faithfully and honestly...A vote for Vestner is a vote for an honest man.") John Noble, George's father-in-law, helped George finance his campaign.[69]

Tammany filed a protest with the police department and tried to disqualify George. They vilified him as a self-righteous reformer who would surely close the bars on Sundays. One news article described Tammany "Myrmidons... flocking to the assistance of the local heelers, entering the saloons and tearing from the walls the handsome features of Mr. Vestner, which his friends, with great liberality, have posted throughout the district."[70] George had two opponents: a Republican, George C. Austin, and the Tammany Democrat, Thomas J. Murray.

The Democrats took a licking in 1896. Austin won, Murray finished second, and George came in a distant third. George was bucking the tide, which clearly favored the Republican candidate in his district.[71] At thirty-two George had no future in the regular Democratic Party. He had opposed Tammany, and the Tammany boss, Richard Croker slammed the door on his once promising political career.

He continued to be active behind the scenes, serving as an officer of his district Democratic Committee, and on a committee of distinguished citizens formed in 1901 to elect a reform mayor. When his mentor and law partner, John Adams, retired in 1904, George moved his office downtown to 29 Broadway. Like most lawyers, he was a solo practitioner and a generalist. But George also specialized in bankruptcy; business was good for him when it was bad for everyone else, and during his lifetime the boom and bust cycles of the American economy guaranteed that bankruptcy law would be a bread and butter business for him.[72] But George was also an investor, and those same cycles made it dif-

---

69   Undated and unattributed news article; ("Not the least of the influences brought to bear in Mr. Vestner's behalf is that of his father-in-law, Mr. John W. Noble, the well-known builder. He is making the candidacy his own personal affair...").
70   Undated and unattributed news article; a "myrmidon" is a loyal retainer or hireling. A "heeler" or "ward heeler" is a local worker, a soldier in the army of the big political bosses.
71   A local issue probably sealed his fate. Post-election analysis suggested that many New Yorkers were outraged at the strict enforcement of the law against drinking on Sunday, initiated by Theodore Roosevelt, who in 1896 was New York City Police Commissioner. Roosevelt was a reformer; he enforced the saloon law uniformly without regard to the political influence of the saloon owner. The problem was that a lot of people who might otherwise have voted for George thought that closing down the saloons on Sunday went too far, and they were prepared to vote for the Tammany candidate on that basis, Tammany making it clear that they favored simply ignoring the law as unfair to working people (rich men being able to drink in the privacy of their clubs). George was certainly not a prig—he had, after all, been chastised for his loose habits—and he almost certainly wouldn't have been against drinking in a bar any day of the week; but as an upstanding lawyer, he probably decided that he couldn't publicly support violating the law. That cost him votes.
72   U.S.Census 1910, Manhattan Ward 12, New York, New York, Roll T624_1027, 18A, Enumeration District 1431, Image 118. George's entry describes him as a lawyer in general practice working out of his own office. A *New York Times* report of April 27, 1904 notes that he was then handling the bankruptcy of Baxter & Co, a sizeable trading company specializing in stocks and cotton. See also *Gould's Lawyer's Diary*, 1881; *Bender's Lawyer's Directory* 1898; *New York State Lawyer's Diary and Directory,* 1903, cited in email from Dawn Tybur, researcher, New York State Library, 29 December 2003.

ficult for him to accumulate capital for his retirement. Just at the peak of the cycle, his stock portfolio telling George that he had finally achieved a measure of wealth, another Wall Street panic with plunging stock prices would bring him back to reality. That happened at least four times during George's adult life: 1893, 1907, 1920 and finally 1929.

In 1895, George and Ruth started their family. Marguerite ("Marge") was born in 1895, Eliot in 1897. By 1900, George had a full house, with wife, daughter, son, and Ruth's twenty-eight-year-old nephew.[73]

In 1902 the Vestners started to move around a bit. That year they lived at 51 West 106th Street; in 1905, 113 Manhattan Avenue; in 1907, 71 West 103rd Street—all within blocks on the Upper West Side. In 1908 they moved to 74 West 103rd Street. Since that was following the stock market crash of 1907, they probably moved to take advantage of cheaper rents. From 1909 to 1911 they lived farther up the West Side, at 625 West 140th Street. By 1912 George and Ruth, with their children, had moved to 601 West 137th Street; in 1914 they were living right around the corner at 52 Hamilton Place. From 1900 to 1914 Eliot and his family lived in eight different apartments, moving at least every two years. Like most people then, the Vestners were renters. Home ownership was for those with enough capital to buy or construct a splendid town house. Landlords often gave a month's free rent to new tenants, creating an incentive to move from one apartment to another when the lease term expired, usually in two years. For George there was another consideration. Most of the moves landed the Vestners conveniently close to George's yacht club, first located at 108th Street on the Hudson River and later at 138th Street.

George was a passionate boater. He loved the feeling of power behind the wheel of a fast boat, on the Hudson or up in the Thousand Islands on the St. Lawrence River. He was a founding member and director of the Motor Boat Club of America (later the Colonial Yacht Club) an event important enough to warrant coverage by the *Times* in the fall of 1905.[74] In September 1908, George was commodore when the club hosted a national racing carnival with speed boats from around the country. Next year, the *Times* reported on the club's annual meeting, at which "a committee was appointed to make arrangements for some suitable recognition of the untiring services of the retiring Commodore, George J. Vestner."[75]

---

73   U.S. Census 1900, Manhattan, New York, New York; Roll: T623_1006, 23A Ancestry.com. *1900 United States Federal Census* [database on-line], Provo, UT, USA.
74   *The New York Times*, October 25, 1905, 11.
75   *The New York Times*, December 5, 1909, Part 3, C7.

Commodore Vestner.

George and his boat, ca. 1905

43

George behind the wheel, ca. 1912

In 1915, George and Ruth separated.[76] What happened? Did she say, "George, this is it? If you want to move, move. But we're staying put?" Or possibly she said, "George, it's the boat or me!" Or, perhaps George had never really abandoned the life of a "club man" that his friend had warned him about back in 1891; possibly George was spending too much time at work and at pleasure with his friends; possibly he was keeping a mistress.

Ruth took her son, Eliot—he was seventeen at the time—and moved to Brooklyn.

In 1924 Eliot was twenty-six; still sharing an apartment with his mother, who undoubtedly dreaded the prospect that he might meet the "right girl" and leave her to fend for herself. She would do everything in her power to make sure that didn't happen. Ruth Vestner was a serious woman and not to be trifled with. Any young woman coming into Eliot's life would have to deal with her.

Early Saturday, February 16, 1924, Eliot took the subway from Brooklyn to Grand Central, hoping to get to the main information booth by 9:30 A.M., the time he and the other house party guests, including his blind date Priscilla Fuller, were to meet. A fly on the wall would have seen a girl standing under the clock, bundled up in winter hat and coat, holding a suitcase, looking at her watch and obviously waiting for someone. Priscilla always arrived early.

---

76   In 1915, there was a stigma attached to divorce, and getting a divorce was difficult. New York State required proof of adultery. The other option was to establish residence in Idaho or Nevada and file for divorce out there.

2. Priscilla Alden Fuller: Flatbush Girl

At age eleven, Priscilla Alden Fuller started a diary and kept at it the rest of her life.[77] Her first entries, for August 1911, record a summer trip from Flatbush to Winthrop, Maine with her older sister, Dorothy:[78]

> 4 August: Dorothy & I started for Winthrop in aft. Took the stemer [*sic*] "Priscilla" to Fall River. Got there at 5 A.M."

> 5 August: Took train to Boston, and Boston to Winthrop. Great! Cottage right by the lake. Very tired.

Winthrop is a small town eight miles west of Augusta, wedged between two large lakes, Marancook and Cobbosseecontee. Priscilla's mother, Mary Fuller, had been raised in Winthrop back in the time of the Civil War. Most summers, the Fullers rented a lake cottage in Winthrop. While Mary and the children enjoyed the cool Maine summers, Charles Fuller stayed home and worked. In an early August 1906 letter to Priscilla, he complained about the heat:

---

77   The diary of Priscilla Fuller Vestner covers the years 1911-14, 1917-24, 1932-36, 1949-50, and 1957-69. All diary quotes and references are to those volumes, hereafter referred to as "Priscilla's Diary." The diary can be accessed by email to <evestner@comcast.net.>
78   Priscilla Alden Fuller was born October 7, 1899, to Charles and Mary Fuller at the Fuller home, No. 2 Tennis Court in Flatbush. She was preceded by Dorothy (1889), Everett Webb (1892), Randolph Mercein (1893), and Ruth Dwight (1896).

My dear Priscithouski.

Your nice letter enclosed in Mamma's was very welcome and you are the first one of the four kids to write...I hope it is not so hot on the hill today as it is here. I am glad you are all out of it. I went to a big picnic last Thursday—750 men—and we all sat down to dinner in our shirt sleeves....Last night I went to the club. Very few there and I came home early. Mrs. Covell & kids came home yesterday & I guess they are sorry they did. It is so hot here....I hope to leave here the 29th at night & be in Norway Thursday morning.[79]

For Priscilla, spending a month in Winthrop meant hiking, swimming, and fishing with her older brothers, Ran and Everett. In the summer of 1911 the boys had just graduated from Erasmus Hall in Flatbush and were set to go to Amherst College, their father's alma mater. Summer in Winthrop was relaxed and unscheduled:

6 August: Sunday. Nothing much. Doesn't seem like Sunday. No church, no best dresses, no nothing.

9 August: Walked to the village in morn. With Ran, there & back 5 miles. Fishing with boys in aft. Caught 3 Suns.

10 August: Hunted bait with Ran in morn. Swimming in aft. Can almost swim. Fishing with the boys. Nothing!

16 August: Nothing in morn. Ran & I walked around lower lake in aft. 12 miles. Saw 13 new birds. Quite tired in eve.

20 August: Nothing in morn. Walked around by Cousin Al's farm in aft.

The rest of August passed much the same way. Some days she caught something; some days she didn't. Some days the boys took her along; some days they didn't. Usually when they went out in the canoe, they left her behind—at eleven, the boys didn't think her swimming was up to the challenge of capsizing

---

79   Letter, dated August 2, 1906, from Charles H. Fuller to Priscilla.

in the middle of the lake. Her mother was a Webb, and there were a lot of Webbs to visit—the 1910 census shows more than twenty Webbs living in or near Winthrop.

Priscilla, 11, on Mt. Pisgah near Winthrop; Brother Everett
keeping an eye on his youngest sister

Albert ("Cousin Al") and Frank Webb were Mary Fuller's cousins; both lived on farms with large families.[80]

On September 3, summer was over and it was time to go home to Flatbush:

2 September: Started for Portland in morn. Lunch there. Cape Elizabeth in aft. Took Old Colony at 6:00 in eve.

3 September: Sick till 10:00. On deck all morn. Ate a big dinner, slept on deck all aft. Flatbush at 6:30 P.M.[81]

---

80   U.S.Census, 1910, Albert Webb family at Series T624, Roll 542, 228; Frank Webb family at Series T624, Roll 542, 232
81   There were automobiles on the roads in 1911, but the roads were limited and generally unpaved; there were also trains running up and down the coast. But it was relatively pleasant and efficient to travel most of the distance from Winthrop to Flatbush by boat.

No. 2 Tennis Court ca. 1911

Entry to Tennis Court ca. 1911

The home she returned to at 2 Tennis Court was a three-story brown-shingled Victorian, with lots of rooms, a big front porch, and a second floor balcony. Steps from the front porch led to a broad lawn. Tennis Court in its entirety ran about 275 yards from Ocean Avenue at one end to 18th Street at the other, accommodating ten or so similar homes, separated by grass, gardens, hedges, and trees. An architect, writing about the area in 1908, described Flatbush as a "realm of light and air," and Tennis Court as "one of the handsomest and most exclusive sections in Flatbush."[82]

Tennis Court had been farmland only a few years before. The farmland was developed in the 1880s when Flatbush was connected by rail to Brooklyn. When the Fullers bought the house in 1892, Flatbush had become a "bedroom community;" the women managed children and home while the men commuted to their offices in downtown Brooklyn and Manhattan, by ferry across the East River or by crowded trolley across the still relatively new Brooklyn Bridge, completed in 1883 and one of the engineering marvels of the age.[83] Flatbush, with its excellent schools, numerous churches, and efficient public services, was a good place to raise a family.

Priscilla's good friend, Helen Roberts, was a neighbor; her uncle Will Redfield, her aunt Ellie and their children lived next door. There was at least one actual tennis court positioned between two of the houses, used by all the families on the block. The Knickerbocker Club graced the 18th Street end of Tennis Court. In the summer of 1911, tennis at the Knickerbocker Club with its four clay courts was a formal and leisurely affair: the men wore dress shirts and long pants, the ladies wore long dresses and blouses buttoned up to the neck.

Tennis at the Knickerbocker Club, 1893

82   Herbert Foster Gunnison, *Flatbush of Today* (Brooklyn, N.Y; All Souls Church, 1908), 84.
83   Flatbush was annexed by the City of Brooklyn in 1894.

Tennis Court in 1911 was an intimate, upper-middle-class suburban neighborhood, largely insulated from the rough, crowded Irish, Jewish, Italian, and Caribbean neighborhoods that were increasingly shaping twentieth century Brooklyn. But time has not been kind to Tennis Court. One hundred years later, all the old houses have been replaced by ugly six-story red-brick apartment buildings constructed in the 1920s and showing their age. It takes an act of imagination to recapture Tennis Court as it must have been in 1911.

Tennis Court, 2006

Sunday was family day, and the Fullers were a big family: Priscilla, her brothers and sisters; Charles Fuller's brother-in-law, Will Redfield, and his family; Mary Fuller's mother (Fanny); Mary's sister, Annie Holt, husband Will, and their son Kenneth; a variety of Merceins (Charles Fuller's mother was a Mercein), and many others.

Sunday started with the service at St. Paul's Episcopal Church, a short walk from Tennis Court. Charles Fuller was head of the vestry. His particular interest was the Sunday school; he believed teaching Sunday school was a calling that required training and constant Bible study. It was not something to be taken lightly. Dr. Jackson, the minister, was a close family friend. Pris was either attending or, as she got older, teaching Sunday school. For the Fullers, church was a serious matter.

After church, Charles Fuller presided over Sunday dinner at a table set for as many as twenty, prepared and served by a cook and maid. Sunday dinners depended on help in the kitchen, and managing the help wasn't easy. On February 22, 1914 Pris noted, "The Heisers came to supper. 11 eating and Ella out!!" She helped serve dinner that night. The Fullers replaced Ella with Lavinia, but one day Pris noted, "Lavinia left after supper for good. Bang!" Ella and Lavinia were probably overworked and underpaid.

After dinner, depending on the weather, there might be a walk through nearby Prospect Park, or music, games, and talk in the big living room followed by a light supper, homework for Pris and her sister Ruth, and bed.[84] During the week, meals were less formal.

Priscilla was expected to help around the house. That meant clean her room; plant, weed and water the garden; pull dandelions out of the lawn; do office work for her father, who paid her; cook and clean for her father when her mother was away; polish the silver tea pots, and occasionally help serve dinner when the Fullers entertained. Sometimes she was able to eavesdrop on her parents and their friends. Her diary for January 14, 1914 notes: "Papa had a dinner party, Covells, Taylors & others...R {Ruth} & I sat in hall closet & listened. Fun!" Unfortunately, she doesn't say what they talked about.

Pris, Ruth, and Pris' close friend Helen Roberts, wrote a weekly newspaper (subscription two safety pins) and produced plays (admission ditto). Sometimes they did John Alden and Priscilla Mullins of Plymouth, with Pris, the taller of the two, as John; other times they did the prince and the princess: Pris was always the handsome prince; Helen the beautiful princess, doubling as the dragon that the prince had to slay before the princess could be freed from the tower. Ruth was production manager and in charge of the box office.

---

84   Prospect Park, about five hundred acres, was designed by Frederick Law Olmsted, and is considered one of his finest creations, rivaling if not surpassing Central Park.

Priscilla and Helen Roberts playing dolls, ca. 1912

Priscilla, No. 2 Tennis Court ca. 1913

Priscilla also wrote poetry. In 1908, *The Brooklyn Daily Eagle*[85] published one of her poems:

> The Crocus to the Lily said,
> 'Oh, Lily, do pop out your head!'
> And all the little bird lets cried,
> 'Yes, Lily dear,' tis Eastertide.'

> And so the Lily raised its head,
> And to the little Crocus said,
> 'I thank you for your kindly warning,
> I quite forgot 'twas Easter morning.'

Next year, they published another:

> The city's noisy avenues,
> The country's shady lanes,
> The city's big department stores,
> The stage-coach or the trains?

> A crowded trolley up Broadway,
> A row upon a lake,
> An auto down to Brighton Beach,
> A pretty drive to take?

> And as for me, I think I'll have
> The country's balmy air,
> A little farm house, way in back,
> And out of everywhere.
> PRISCILLA FULLER (age 10).[86]

When she wasn't writing poetry, acting, or doing her chores, she climbed the big trees on Tennis Court and played long-forgotten games: German bat ball, wave, Sherlock Holmes, hide-and-go-seek, hospital, mumblety-peg, skip

---

85 *The Brooklyn Daily Eagle* was Brooklyn's main newspaper from its founding in 1841 to its demise in 1955. Walt Whitman was the editor from 1846 to 1848.
86 Undated clippings from *The Brooklyn Daily Eagle* for 1909 and 1910, respectively.

rope, marbles, and shipwreck. Her brothers played checkers with her when they came home, and she gleefully noted whenever she won.

She attended Mrs. Perkins' School in Flatbush until she was eleven, at which point her teacher, Mary Kirk, wrote that she was ready for sixth grade in the public school.[87] She outlined what Priscilla had presumably learned:

> *English*: Study of the parts of speech, structure of the simple sentence, dictation, reproduction, composition, memorizing of poetry, oral and written spelling, letter writing, Arnold & Kittridge's Mother Tongue Vol 1 completed.
>
> *Reading*: Cyr's Fourth Reader, Carpenter's Readers.
>
> *Arithmetic*: Fractions and decimals completed, denominate numbers, Smith's Intermediate Arithmetic, Milne's Arithmetic.
>
> *Geography*: South America and Europe studied in detail, map modeling, geography scrap books kept, Dodge's Elements of Continental Geography.
>
> *History*: Colonial history of the U.S. read, discussed and main points memorized; Gerber's Story of the Thirteen Colonies.
>
> *Art*: Freehand drawing and coloring, principles of design, applied design.
>
> *Nature Study*: Recognition and study of common trees, wild flowers and birds according to season.

The next year she entered PS 139 in Flatbush, completing grades six, seven, and eight. In the winter of 1912, school was a source of some anxiety, judging by the exclamation marks in her diary:

> 26 Jan. Friday. School. Math test! Oh my I hope I passed!!!!!!
>
> 30 Jan. Tues. Not much work in school.... Hope I get promoted!
>
> 31 Jan. Wed. School. Promoted!!!!

---

87   Letter, dated June 1, 1909, from Mary F. Kirk to "To whom it may concern."

She graduated in January 1913 in the Erasmus Hall High School auditorium. The highlight, as reported in the *Eagle*, was a debate: "Resolved: that the Assassination of Julius Caesar was for the Good of Rome." Priscilla's father was chairman of the judges' panel, which ruled for the negative.[88]

That summer, she joined the Campfire Girls, the girls' answer to the then recently-formed Boy Scouts.[89] She also started going to summer camp, something she would do every summer as she moved from camper to junior and then senior counselor at Miss Hart's Camp for Girls at Silver Lake, New York, one of the early Adirondack camps, located about thirty miles north of Lake Placid. Miss Nina Hart taught English at Packer Collegiate Institute in Brooklyn, and became a lifelong friend and mentor, but she was always "Miss Hart." As a counselor, Pris—her friends called her "PAF" or "Yippy"—got $75 for the summer plus room and board. By 1922 she was getting $100, and she was in charge of athletics, taking the girls on long hikes and canoe trips, and teaching them to play tennis and ride.

Priscilla at camp, Silver Lake, New York, ca. 1917

---

88   *The Brooklyn Daily Eagle*, January 28, 1913.
89   The Campfire Girls was founded in 1910, about the same time as the Boy Scouts and by the same men and women active in formation of the Scouts. It was intended to be the girls' equivalent of the scouts. Today, the organization is called "Campfire Girls and Boys," and boys make up 46% of the active membership of 750,000. The Girl Scouts was founded in 1913, and there was an early effort to merge the Girl Scouts and Campfire Girls, but they remained separate. See Alice Marie Beard, "Historical Origins of Camp Fire" http://alicemariebeard.com/campfire/history.htm. Last accessed March 18, 2010.

Priscilla on her horse, Silver Lake, ca. 1919

Campers and counselors all wore white middies with a colorful scarf and headband, bloomers, and stockings up to their knees. In their spare time, the counselors swam, rode, played tennis, flirted with the few men around who had a full set of teeth, and posed for the camera. There wasn't much to do or places to visit outside the camp; the nearby village of Hawkeye didn't have much going for it, just a general store and an old hotel. The big event of the season was a three-day expedition up Whiteface Mountain, at 4,600 feet one of the highest in the Adirondacks and visually striking with its open rock face. The counselors making the trip hiked, camped, toasted marshmallows, sang, and froze around the fire at night, returning to camp exhausted but triumphant in their conquest.

Getting back to Flatbush from Silver Lake was an adventure:

29 August: Fri. Up at 5 A.M. Billy Lewis, Rosemary, Nannette & Choodie Nichols & I left at 5:30. Auto to Port Kent. Train to Westport. Boat to Montcalm. Train to head of Lake George. Boat to end of L.G. Wonderful sail. Train to Albany.... Night boat to N.Y. Wonderful dinner. Danced in dining room. On deck after.

30 August: Sat. Landed at 8:30. Taxi to breakfast at Schrafft's. Said good-bye to Billy etc., at Grand Central. Home at 11. Great to see everyone. Slept with Ruth all P.M. Sick all night.

In the fall of 1913 she started at Packer Collegiate Institute in Brooklyn, which would take her through two years of college.[90] When not in school she and her friends went to the movies, or to more serious things like concerts, lectures and theater at the Brooklyn Academy of Music, which occasionally featured Sarah Bernhardt and Maude Adams, two of the most famous actresses of the time. On May 2, 1917, Pris and her sister Ruth went to see Maude Adams in *A Kiss for Cinderella*. Pris, who had a crush on the beautiful Maude Adams, and Ruth waited in vain at the stage entrance to catch a glimpse of Maude.[91]

There were convenient movie theaters in Flatbush—the Linden, Strand, and Parkside among others. The movies, a new form of entertainment, cost a nickel and were silent. There was usually a pianist sitting at the front of the theater to supply mood music. As films became more sophisticated, orchestras were employed to provide the musical effects, including the sound of galloping horses, gunfire and other effects. The actors pantomimed and occasionally held up cue cards to help the audience. Priscilla, Ruth and their friends saw all the great names of silent film: Charlie Chaplin and Mary Pickford in *Poor Little Rich Girl*, Douglas Fairbanks in *Mark of Zorro*, George M. Cohan in *The Meanest Man in the World*, Norma Talmadge in *Poppy*, and Wallace Reid in *Believe Me Xantippe*. After the movies, it was tea or perhaps dinner at a Flatbush restaurant, like Huyler's, Schrafft's, Schmidt & Horchette, or Joe's & Beckman's. In the summer, she and her friends took the trolley to Brighton Beach on Coney Island, with its great amusement park, or Long Beach, farther out in Nassau County. If they wanted the excitement of Manhattan, all they had to do was walk over the Brooklyn Bridge or take the subway. One day she and Ruth went into Manhattan for lunch but had trouble making up their minds:

> Ruth & I went over to New York. Got lunch at Mary Elizabeth. Too dainty & expensive, so we went to a cafeteria. Too

---

90   Packer, founded in 1845 as the "Brooklyn Female Academy," was renamed when Harriet Packer donated $65,000 after the school building burned down. The new building was completed in 1854, and the school reopened under its new name. Packer combined elementary school, high school, and junior college, and was one of the top academic schools in the city.

91   Priscilla's Diary, May 2, 1917: "Ruth & I went to see Maude Adams in *A Kiss for Cinderella*.... Great play. Waited at stage entrance & saw the hero & some others come out but not her." Maude Adams (1872-1953) was probably the most popular stage actress of her day, famous for her leading roles in *Peter Pan* and other James Barrie Plays. *A Kiss for Cinderella* by Barrie was her last performance before she retired in 1918. The play opened at the Empire Theater in New York, December 25, 1916 to rave reviews and ran for 152 performances. One reviewer described Maude as "utterly winsome." See "History of Maude Adams," from *Utah History Encyclopedia*. < www.media.Utah.edu/UHE/a/Adams_Maude.html> Accessed March 18, 2010. See also Phyllis Robbins, *Maude Adams: An Intimate Portrait* (New York; G.P.Putnam's Sons, 1956).

greasy and cheap. Went to the Metropolitan Museum and then walked to 42nd St. Got a meal at Mirror's.[92]

"Mirror's," apparently, was okay. Two weeks later, Pris and Ruth were in Manhattan again, this time shopping for a suit. They found one, after trying eight stores. Sometimes it was easier to stay in Flatbush and shop on Flatbush Avenue, the great shopping street that ran through the heart of Brooklyn and an easy walk from 2 Tennis Court.

When Priscilla was in grade school, automobiles were rarely seen. By 1917, they were more common, but driving was still an adventure on the mostly unpaved roads; with few service stations, every driver had to be his own mechanic. That year, Ruth was dating Sid—actually she was dating Sid's car; Sid, probably a very nice guy, was incidental. On May 11, 1917, returning from a drive out on Long Island with Ruth and Sid, Pris noted in her diary: "Three punctures & home at one...Great time nevertheless." They had to leave the car and take the train home, a mortifying experience for Sid, who generally didn't seem to have much luck with the Fuller family. On another ride out along the Long Island shore with Sid and Ruth, Priscilla got sick, "most in Sid's lap" as she described it.

Until she was eighteen, a "date" would mean going to the movies with one of her brothers, or a young man might visit the family in the evening for music and games. All the local clubs—the Midwood, Montauk, or Heights Casino—held regular dances and friends had informal dances at their homes. The girls were all friends from Packer; the boys all local and known to the families. The dances weren't all lemonade and cookies. On July 18, 1917 she noted: "Squin's dance...good time....Boys got hold of applejack."[93]

In 1917 Pris was dating a variety of boys, including Conrad Shumway, whose brother Lowell had started courting Ruth. It didn't take Lowell long: it was barely ten days from the first mention of Lowell Shumway in her diary of August 18 ("Lowell Shumway came to see Ruth in evening") to her entry for August 27 ("He and Ruth got engaged in eve!"). The Shumways lived in Brooklyn, so the Fullers were probably well-acquainted with Lowell and his family. Lowell would have known Pris' brothers at Amherst, where they all graduated about the same time.

Her main beau that year and next was Alan Colcord, another Brooklyn boy. At first he called on her at home, spending evenings with the family, playing

---

92   Priscilla's Diary, April 9, 1917.
93   Hard cider.

checkers and making fudge in the kitchen. On April 4, 1918, they stepped out: "Alan Colcord took me to 'Seventeen' in N.Y. Dandy play. Mirrors after. Good time." On November 2 they had another big date in Manhattan: "Alan C & I saw 'Daddies' at Belasco Theatre in eve. Very funny & good. Crowd coming home. Taxi from Pacific St. B.R.T wreck at 7 P.M." There was a little more excitement that night than they had expected. The B.R.T. (Brooklyn Rapid Transit) was what they would have taken to get home, and the "wreck" occurred near the Prospect Park station in Flatbush, where they would have gotten off. The rush hour train was moving much too fast as it entered a corkscrew tunnel and smashed head on into a concrete partition, splintering the crowded wooden cars. It was the biggest subway disaster in New York history, and the second worst railroad wreck in U.S. history, with 102 dead and 100 injured.[94]

That Pris, at nineteen, was able to go into the city with her date for an evening illustrates the dramatic social changes taking place during and after the First World War. When her mother and father were courting in the early 1880s, an evening date in the city, just the two of them, would have been out of the question. Priscilla and her friends moved in a world unimaginable to their parents, who undoubtedly worried about this new generation and where it was headed. But with sons in the army, the Fullers had more serious things to worry about. From the declaration of war against Germany in April 1917 until the Armistice in November 1918, daily life in the Fuller family took place against the backdrop of the Great War.

Long before the United States got into it, people with friends in Europe were keenly aware of the personal cost of the war; by 1917, battlefield casualties were well over one million.[95] The last major war fought by the U.S., the Civil War, was ancient history; the veterans of that bloody war were fast disappearing. The most

---

94   In November 1918, the motormen of the BRT were on strike. The company, trying to freeze out the strikers, began using inexperienced employees as motormen. One of those, Edward Luciano (known as "Billy Lewis"), was put in charge of a train on the Coney Island line. Luciano had received two hours of training compared with the usually required sixty hours. Falling behind schedule with a crowded rush hour train, Luciano tried to make up time and lost control. His train blew through stations without stopping and entered the "S" curve in the tunnel under Malbone Street/Prospect Park at an estimated speed of somewhere between thirty and seventy mph. The speed limit in the tunnel was six mph. The wooden cars at the front of the train derailed, and the cars behind crashed into the front cars jamming them into the concrete walls of the tunnel. Most of the people in the front cars died. The operator, and top management of the BRT, were arrested, tried for manslaughter, and acquitted. The BRT, deluged with lawsuits, filed for bankruptcy.
95   Pris received a letter from a friend in the winter of 1914: "Isn't this war awful? I have a friend in France and a good many of her friends have been killed or wounded." She also had a treasured first edition of the poetry of Rupert Brooke, a handsome English officer and poet who died in 1915. Brooke's poem, "1914," epitomized the enthusiasm of young men going off to war: "Now, God be thanked Who has matched us with His hour, And caught our youth, and wakened us from sleeping…"

recent U.S. military experience had been on the Mexican border; Ran Fuller, Pris' brother, served there as a lieutenant after graduating from Amherst.

Lt. Randolph Fuller, Mexican border, summer 1916

A new generation of Americans, raised in peaceful times, seemed to welcome U.S. entry into the European war. Priscilla's Diary for June 5, 1917 says it all: "Conscription day!" Ten million men registered for the draft as they were required to do under the new conscription law. Conscription Day was a success, due in no small measure to the Administration's carefully orchestrated campaign to whip a willing nation into a patriotic frenzy. That same day, Pris started work as a volunteer with the Red Cross. [96]

Later in the summer, her brother Ran left for army camp at nearby Bay Ridge. As Pris noted "mother, Ruth & I went down to 1st Cavalry Camp at Bay Ridge, foot of 67th St. in aft. Looked over camp & watched Retreat."[97] On November 26, 1917 Ran sailed for France as a lieutenant in Company "B," 106th Machine Gun Battalion, 27th Division. Her brother Ev, a chemist and a lieutenant serving in the army's chemical warfare section, was stationed in Washington and left for France the following August 1918, where he was assigned to the army's special chemical warfare laboratory located outside Paris.

There were daily reminders that the United States was fully committed to a big war. The girls at Packer couldn't take showers because of a coal shortage; with Daylight Saving Time initiated as a war measure in 1918, clocks had to be reset; male friends were going off to war, writing letters home from the front, or coming home with injuries and stories to tell; Sunday sermons incorporated patriotic themes; men in uniform came to dances; there were parades and military drills to watch (on February 3, 1918, Lowell Shumway, now a lieutenant in the army, took Pris and Ruth, to the Hippodrome in Manhattan to see the 308th Infantry engage in bayonet drill, march and sing); there were patriotic movies (*Johnny Get Your Gun*), patriotic songs (*Over There*), and soldiers's songs (*Its a Long Long way to Tipperary*); there were huge public rallies with popular entertainers, like Douglas Pickford, to sell war bonds.

On May 20, 1918 Pris was anxiously preparing a talk she was to give at St. Paul's:

> 20 May. Mon. School. At Montague library all aft, looking up references for talk in chapel on 'France in the war.' Up till 11:30 writing up notes. Recited it to Ruth. Took 45 minutes!

> 21 May. Tues. School. Learnt speech all aft in library. Tried out parts of it to D. Hoffman in chapel at 5.... Recited to Ruth while she made fudge.

> 22 May. Wed. School. At 8:15 gave talk in chapel on 'France in the war.' Lots of fun.

---

96   David M. Kennedy, *Over Here, the First World War and American Society* (New York; Oxford University Press, 1980), 147-153. President Wilson described the draft as a "selection from a nation which has volunteered in mass."
97   Priscilla's Diary, August 28, 1917.

Families with sons and brothers at the front were keenly aware that bad news could arrive any day. Margie Catlin was the family's main source of information on Ran, who apparently addressed most of his letters from the front to his fiancée. What she probably did not read in those letters were the details of Ran's life under enemy fire. The company historian, recalling action on the Hindenburg line toward the end of the war, filled in some of the details of Ran's life at the front:

> At one point several gas shells landed on the road directly in front of us and the gas alarm was given. That meant everything had to be dropped on the spot and gas masks adjusted. Then we groped and stumbled and choked for breath, but managed to push on until Lieutenant Fuller tested the air and found it clear.
>
> We had to make two trips along that road carrying equipment entirely by hand. Each way it was a good mile and a half, and to use an inelegant but vivid phrase we "sweated blood." The road was being irregularly shelled and on the second trip "Clint" Swan, Frank Lynch and several others were hit with shrapnel and had to be carried to the rear.
>
> When we had completed the second trip and before the gun positions had been selected, we were all crowded into a small... trench for rest and safety. We got neither. For we were hardly settled before two "whizz-bangs" landed on the parapet of the trench, killing Goldie Hardgrove and George Staudenmayer, wounding several others, and jangling our nerves like broken fiddle strings. That was probably the worst moment any of us ever experienced. We were for the moment pretty nearly demoralized,..But thanks to Lieutenant Selby's presence of mind we didn't have time to think about it. He hustled us out of the trench and we started moving our equipment further forward...
>
> We had been working for about half an hour when Lieutenant Fuller returned from Company Headquarters with a clear conception of what was to be done and with definite ideas about

the way to do it. With him came one of the best of soldiers and staunchest of men—Sergeant Miller of the Australian Division...I should like to state here unqualifiedly that Lieutenants Fuller and Selby and Sergeant Miller were the three men to whom the credit is due for B Company's wonderfully efficient work under all kinds of difficulties during the Hindenburg Stunt. Of the men in B Company who deserve medals for gallantry and resource under fire Fuller and Selby head the list. I have mentioned these men because I personally saw what they did and because they stand out more prominently in my memory for that reason.[98]

Americans at home, secure from gas and "whizz bangs," felt the need to participate in the war effort. Miss Hart ran the Silver Lake Camp with an iron hand, and she was determined to do her duty. The summer of 1918 the girls at camp were required to take military drill twice a week, and Pris got a kick out of her role as drill sergeant. On 17 July she noted, "Military drill at 7:30. Learned right flank march." On 31 July she noted, "Drilled Co. B all evening. Much fun." The girls in Co. B probably didn't think it was all that much fun.

When the war ended, Pris wrote, "Peace! Whistles began at 5 A.M. School let out after chapel...went to N.Y. 5th Ave. & 42nd & got in crowd.... Great excitement. Armistice signed!" Sunday November 17, there was a special peace service at St.Paul's Church. The war was over but not the dying. Preoccupied by the war, Pris doesn't mention the Spanish flu pandemic, which was far deadlier. By the time the disease had run its course in 1920, somewhere between 50 and 100 million had died from it, including some 675,000 in the U.S. alone. The crowds celebrating the end of the war ensured that the disease would spread rapidly from November through the winter of 1919.[99]

Ev and Ran Fuller survived the war without injury. On December 16, 1918 Pris wrote, "Everett home from France! Some shock! Came on the *Leviathan*. He went to see Gertrude in eve." Everett didn't waste any time. On 22 December: "Ev at Gertrude Gladdings. He & she engaged in eve! Ye gods!!"

98   Leslie S. Baker, *the Story of Company B, 106th Machine Gun Battalion, 27th Division, U.S.A.* (New York; Company B, 1920), 46-47.
99   See <http://virus.stanford.edu/uda/> Last accessed March 18, 2010.

Lt. Everett Fuller and new bride, Gertrude Gladding, 1919

Lowell Shumway, home on leave, didn't waste any time either. He married Ruth on March 4, 1919. In her diary, Pris reported: "Ruth's wedding at 8 in the chancel of St. Paul's. I was maid-of-honor. Small reception after. Danced, ate, caught bouquet. _Much_ fun!"

Lowell, an Amherst graduate, was an athlete and a fierce competitor. Ruth, with her deep brown eyes, dark complexion and perfect figure, was the beauty of the Fuller family. In Ruth, Lowell would have a warm, gentle and gracious wife, qualities that perfectly complemented his fierce competitive drive. Their life together would be one of love, devotion and tragedy.

Ruth Fuller and Lt. Lowell Shumway, just married, 1919

65

On March 18, 1919 Brother Ran arrived from France on the *Missouri*; the next day he was home on leave.

Armed with her camera, Pris joined the estimated one million people who filled the streets of New York City on March 25, 1919, as the 27th Division, over 20,000 men, staged its victory parade along the traditional route up Fifth Avenue from Washington Square to 110th Street. *The New York Times* captured the seriousness of the soldiers just back from the front:

> Between the two banks of color, as brilliant as colored silk and bunting, gay dresses, pretty girls and myriads of be-ribboned children could make it, stern-faced men, clad in sober olive-drab and bearing their battle equipment, looked more formidable than ever.[100]

In her diary for that day she noted: "No school because of parade. Father, Margaret & I saw 27th parade from balcony, 5th Ave & 21st St. Great! Ran marched. Some crowd! Ran, home to dinner."[101]

In the winter of 1919, the war and its aftermath weren't the only important things in her life. She had to get a date for the senior prom. On February 19, 1919 she noted, "Clinton can't go to the Prom with me." Clinton Swan, a young lawyer in Brooklyn, had served in France with Ran. On February 24: "Alan C. called up in eve. He can't go to the Prom! Wrote Pitman Buckley & asked him!" On February 25: "Pit Buckley called up & can go to the Prom! Joy!" February 28 was the big night:

> Excitement! Home early. Bought hat at Mrs. Jones.' Orchids (4) came in P.M.! Senior Prom in eve. Took Pitman Buckley. Wonderful time. Wore orchid dress. Gym all fixed up with ceiling, & library with little lateral alcoves with tables, rugs and cushions inside. Only punch & frappe to eat. Stopped at one. Went & came in taxi.

The girls all carried dance cards, with the names of the boys they were to dance with written in.[102]

---

100   *The New York Times,* March 25 1919, 5.
101   Lt. Randolph Fuller was discharged April 21 1919.
102   The names in parentheses were those of the girls with whose dates Priscilla was dancing.

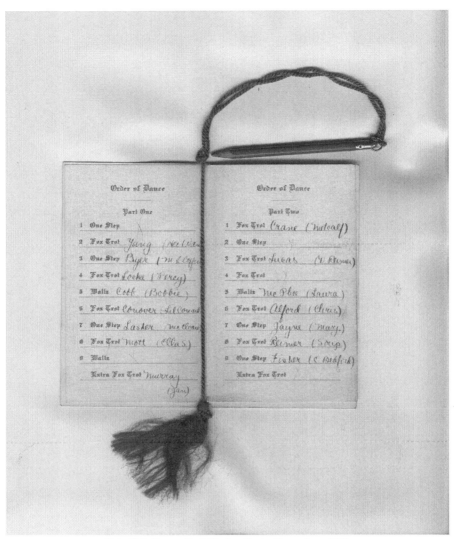

Priscilla's Dance Card, Packer Senior Prom, June 1919

Priscilla's card shows twenty dances: waltzes, fox trots, and one steps, and the music they danced to, long forgotten numbers like: "When You Come Back," "Land Where the Wild Flowers Grow," "Missouri Waltz," "My Sweetie," "Do It for Me," and "Chu Chin Chou" The "punch" served at the dance almost certainly contained no alcohol—by February 1919, the sale of alcohol had been

67

permanently banned by Constitutional amendment and the entire country was now "dry."[103]

In June 1919 she graduated from Packer. The essence of the graduation sermon was captured in a *Daily Eagle* article:[104]

WAR FREED WOMEN SAYS RECTOR MELISH

"They Think Independently Now," He Tells Packer graduates

Pris described her graduation as "sad but wonderful." She was an achiever: straight As and winner of the Athletic Association award. In *Love Scenes from Shakespeare*, presented by the class, she was Celia in *As You Like It*. In the 1919 Packer yearbook, Priscilla was voted "most talented." In "Class Knocks," the "knock" on Priscilla was that she needed "to lose her rep." In the class prophecy, the lines on Priscilla were

> Priscilla still is our talented one,
> She can play any instrument under the sun,
> And can play her way in and out of love,
> And is never caught by a turtle-dove.[105]

Under her picture her classmates wrote: "Seeing only what is fair, sipping only what is sweet." Today, one might say "sounds like a Pollyanna." But in 1919 the description would not have carried that implication. Eleanor Porter's novel, *Pollyanna*, had been published in 1913 and was still popular. Pollyanna was admired for her cheerful optimism.

Pris managed to get in trouble occasionally, but trouble wasn't her thing. Diary references to trouble are few and far between. In 1917, the French teachers bawled her out for goose-stepping up and down the hall.[106] On March 12,

---

103   The Eighteenth Amendment to the Constitution, establishing a uniform nationwide prohibition against the manufacture or sale of all alcoholic beverages, was ratified on January 16, 1919, only nine weeks after the armistice. Prohibition reflected the belief that alcohol was at the root of a number of social ills: crime, gambling, adultery, divorce, homelessness, poverty, etc. Adoption of the Constitutional Amendment followed a long and persistent campaign by churches (Baptists and Methodists) and organizations like the Prohibition Party, Woman's Christian Temperance Union and the Anti-Saloon League.

104   *The Brooklyn Daily Eagle*, June 9 1919 (unattributed article).

105   *Year Book of the Class of 1919, Packer Collegiate Institute* (Brooklyn, N.Y. 1919), 31, 81, 83, 100.

106   The "goosestep" was the traditional marching style of the German army. Any Frenchwoman in 1917 would have been outraged at girls mimicking the German goosestep.

1919 she wrote in her diary: "Scolded in Chapel & by Miss Dunlap for neglecting home-work." In May on a senior house party to Tom's River, New Jersey, she and a couple of other girls skinny-dipped in the ocean, and there's a picture of her and her friends with cigarettes hanging out of their mouths. Not much to show for nineteen years. But then, maybe she didn't report everything in her diary.

When she graduated from Packer, Pris had two years of college under her belt. She had to get a job and get serious about finding a man. With her usual diligence, she had written a profile, marked "PRIVATE" with the title "My Ideal Man-Nov. 15, 1917:"

Taller than I
Brown hair with reddish tinge
Dark gray eyes
Hair not parted in the middle
Rather large mouth
Smooth face (good complexion)
Strong, lean and a little homely

Musts:

Clean-physically & morally
Sense of humor and vivid imagination
Love animals
Love out-doors, camping, etc.
Ambitious & have ideals & ideas
Wholly unselfish, appreciative
Love me better than anything (except honor)

Preferably

Rather wealthy (crossed out)
Comfortably rich
No mother
Smokes only a pipe.[107]

---

107 Note by Priscilla, November 15, 1917.

She stood only five feet four inches, so finding a man "taller than I" wouldn't be a problem, and it would have been easy finding somebody "a little homely." But "vivid imagination," "wholly unselfish," "appreciative," "comfortably rich" and "no mother"—that was setting the bar pretty high. She would clearly have to make some compromises.

In the fall of 1919, back from Miss Hart's camp and with no school, she was at loose ends. She played a lot of tennis, mostly with Ruth, and went to Forest Hills on Labor Day to watch Bill Tilden beat Norris Williams in the semi-finals of the U.S. Open; she was a ribbon girl in her brother Ev's wedding; she and Ruth took long walks in the sand on Brighton Beach, quiet and deserted in the fall.

Pris and Ruth dressed for tennis, 1919

She also took a secretarial course at Heffley Business School in Brooklyn, which she described as "rather fun, but busy people." Late in the fall, she started her first full-time job as supervisor of play for the girls in the lower school at Packer and secretary to Miss Nelson on the faculty. Her salary was $60 a month. She did research on playground management at the library, taking notes on books such as *Playground Technique and Playcraft* by Arthur Leland (1909), and

Organized Games for the Playground, by Robert Wood (1911), and writing up detailed descriptions with diagrams of "Squirrels in Trees," "Dodge Ball," "Fox and Geese," and "Last Couple Out." Five years later, in September 1925, she resigned from Packer to go to work for the telephone company. An article in the *Eagle* noted that:

> It will be a matter of regret to many children that Miss Priscilla Fuller, supervisor of afternoon play, will no longer be with them in the garden and playground.[108]

She was equally serious about her teaching in the Sunday school at St. Paul's, although there were Sunday mornings when she would have preferred not facing the class. After a late night out on September 20, 1919, she noted: "S.S. & church, 10 kids there. Hope they were gladder to see me than I was to see them." In 1921 she completed a year-long course in religious education given by the Episcopal Diocese. When she finally resigned her teaching position in the fall of 1925 she received a letter from one of her students:

> Will you please come back and teach our class on Sundays! We study by ourselves so that Mr. Webber will not give us another teacher.[109]

Eighteen months after graduating from Packer, shortly after her twenty-first birthday, she played a small part in a very big event—the first presidential election in which women could vote.[110]

That year the Democrats put up Governor James Cox of Ohio for president and a young up-and-coming politician, Franklin Delano Roosevelt, for vice president. Warren Harding, a handsome senator from Ohio who looked presidential, and Calvin Coolidge, who had risen to national prominence as governor of Massachusetts by breaking the Boston police strike, were the Republican candidates for president and vice-president. On August 29, 1920, Charles Fuller, as head of

---

108   *The Brooklyn Daily Eagle,* September 5, 1925: 8 (unattributed article).

109   Letter, dated October 21, 1925, from Marion Griffith to Miss Priscilla Fuller.

110   A Constitutional amendment giving women the right to vote was ratified August 18, 1920. It had taken seventy years, from the first meeting of the women's suffrage movement in Seneca, New York in 1848, through civil disobedience, jailings, organizational work in every state, close defeats in the U.S. Senate, stubborn Southern opposition, and final passage of the amendment by the Congress in 1919 to the final cliff-hanger conclusion: ratification by a one-vote margin in the Tennessee House of Representatives on August 18, 1920, Tennessee being the thirty-sixth state to ratify.

the St. Paul's vestry, hosted a church visit by Cox. Pris noted: "Sun. Church at 11. Introduced to Gov. Cox, Dem. Pres Candidate there with father."

Priscilla's father was an active supporter of the Democratic ticket, Cox and Roosevelt. From her diary, Priscilla's political preferences are clear:

> Democratic meeting at Erasmus in eve. Big crowd. Father opened it & mother & I sat on the platform. Heard Franklin D. Roosevelt (Vice Pres Candidate); awfully nice & attractive.

But the Democrats were on the defensive, blamed for everything that was going on in the country in 1920, from inflation and unemployment to strikes and terrorist bombings.

On November 2 Pris reported: "Voted in A.M. after waiting 1¼ hours on line. Voted for Cox...." When the results came in, she was mad: "Harding & Coolidge elected; also Miller (Rep) for Gov. All wrong!" Harding and Coolidge won by twenty-six percentage points, a stunning repudiation of Wilson and the Democrats, and the widest popular vote margin in our history.

Although women had gained the vote, that hard-won right wasn't the breakthrough its proponents had hoped for and expected. In 1920, women were still far short of equality in educational opportunity and the workplace. College and business were still largely for men only. Women had entered the workforce in large numbers during the war, but later the men moved back into their old jobs and the women by and large moved back into the home.[111]

After graduating from Packer, Pris had wanted to finish her last two years of college at Swarthmore, perhaps become a teacher or a lawyer like her father. But she was not quite the independent new woman that the Reverend Melish had described in his graduation sermon at Packer commencement. The war really hadn't made that much of a difference, at least in Priscilla's life. She was an obedient and loyal daughter and Charles Fuller, having put her two older brothers through Amherst, decided that Pris had had enough education at Packer. So she entered the workforce: as teacher, and secretary.

By the early 1920s, all her brothers and sisters were married. Priscilla was single and living at home. Priscilla's diary was sparse, factual and short on introspection; it nevertheless suggests what her life was like in those years immediately after the war. Nineteen twenty-one was a typical year:

---

111 See Kennedy, *Over Here*, 284-288. Despite high hopes that the war would revolutionize American society, women actually made up a smaller percentage of the labor force in 1920 than they had in 1910. There was intense pressure on women to give up their wartime jobs to returning veterans.

January: Priscilla spent half the month making daily visits to Ruth, hospitalized with rheumatic fever. The fever would leave Ruth with a permanently crippled heart. Mary Fuller was away visiting family, so Priscilla was left to take care of her father: fix his meals and keep him company in the evening. She put on a "Salmagundi party" (pirate theme) for her Sunday school class. She had a couple of dates at home (checkers and cards); a movie date—*Last of the Mohicans* ("gooey"); and a date to hear the famous Burton Holmes give a travelogue on the Middle East.[112]

February: Ski outing to Buck Hill Falls, Pennsylvania,[113] with Chauncey W. Baxter (otherwise known as "Chan") and eight others—five boys and four girls—plus "Mr. and Mrs. Thayer chaperones." She and Chan took the train from Hoboken, arriving at 9:30 in below-zero weather with plenty of snow on the ground and had a late dinner "a deux." The next day, the group skied and rode toboggans.[114] In the evening they bowled, played checkers, twenty questions, ping-pong, charades, and other games, and took long walks through the snow-covered Pennsylvania woods. The following Monday, after getting home late the previous night from the weekend, she was on stage in a Packer play, *A Thousand Years Ago* (for which she had rehearsed during the month) and danced into the early morning hours. Her diary comment: "Tired." Later that month, she hosted a Packer class luncheon at the Pennsylvania Hotel in Manhattan for twenty-five classmates.

February-April: Chan Baxter, a Columbia graduate, took her to six Columbia basketball games, mostly won by Columbia's opponents. Her diary entry for March 12: "Columbia 21 Dartmouth 26. Dinner first at Enrico's & dance after. Peachy time." Columbia beat CCNY 15-14. Pris' comment, "Most exciting thing ever, nasty jews, etc," reflected the passion of that rivalry: Columbia, the establishment university, vs. CCNY, heavily immigrant and Jewish. It also reflected the views of the old-line Protestants on the changes taking place in Brooklyn.

---

112   Burton Holmes (1870-1958). At a time when traveling around the world to faraway places was uncommon, Burton Holmes' travelogues were famous. Formally dressed, he performed for large and enthusiastic audiences, and was a pioneer in combining lecture with motion pictures.
113   Buck Hill Falls, in the Pocono Mountains of northwestern Pennsylvania, is a 2-hour drive from New York City. It was a planned community, owned by Philadelphia families and developed early in the twentieth century, consisting of cottages, an inn, a golf course, tennis courts, hiking and riding trails, and winter ski facilities.
114   In order to ski, she and her friends had to hike up the hill, carrying heavy wooden skis on their shoulders. The first ski lift wasn't installed until 1934 in Woodstock, Vermont (a rope tow powered by an old Ford Model T engine).

March: She attended the Ellsworth School for Secretaries, receiving a proficiency certificate for "speed and accuracy," typing forty-seven words per minute on her borrowed Underwood.[115] Later in March she went with Chan Baxter to the "Little Men and Women" dance at the Heights Casino—an indoor tennis club in Brooklyn Heights. On March 31 she went with her family to a Packer block party that raised $2,600 for the school.

April: "Alan C." took her for a ride to Coney Island in his new car and taught her how to drive. She finished *Main Street* (Sinclair Lewis's popular new novel) and graduated from Teachers's Normal School at St. Anne's in Brooklyn, run by the Episcopal Diocese of Long Island. She went to a dance at the Heights Casino and to a Democratic Party affair with her father and mother. One evening Chan and his family all came to the Fuller house for supper. Channing Baxter knew how to impress the ladies: as Pris noted in her diary, "Chan brought roses for all the females."

June: She took up golf. In 1921 golf was popular, as Bobby Jones, handsome and talented, was just beginning to win golf tournaments. Her first time out she shot one hundred—for nine holes. She practiced in the Fuller backyard, played with Chan Baxter, and by the end of the season got her score down to seventy-three for nine. That June her brothers (class of 1915), their wives, and her father (class of 1878) all went to Amherst for commencement, reunions, and a dance at the Chi Psi house, which kept her up until 2:30. Her comment: "loads of boys there; met about 30 people."

July-August: She was a senior counselor at Silver Lake Camp.

September: Chan and Pris drove out to Amagansett on the Long Island shore to visit his family for a week of golf, tennis, swimming and parties. The only other September diary entry is for Sunday the twenty-fifth: "Early church. Tennis all A.M. & P.M. 10 sets."

October-November: She devoted six weekends to football games with her boyfriend Chan: Columbia-NYU (19-0); Columbia-Williams (0-20); Columbia-Ohio University (21-23); Columbia-Colgate (14-21); Princeton-Harvard (10-3); and Army-Navy (0-7). After the games, it was usually dinner and dancing. When they weren't going to football games, they played golf or Chan came over to the house for an evening of cards.

In 1921 Pris was twenty-two and old enough to live her own life. But she was still living in her father's house. Her diary for 1921 suggests she had a

---

115   "Underwood" was the brand name of the most popular typewriter and the original "word processor;" the keys were stiff and hard to press down, and you had to change the ribbon periodically, getting ink all over your hands in the process. Corrections were made by special pencil, rubbing out the mistake and typing over it.

pretty good social life, but she also spent many long evenings by herself, curled up with a book in her father's library.

Six days a week she went to her job supervising afternoon play at Packer. As a faculty member she was involved in a variety of Packer activities, including substitute teaching and organizing a filing system for Dr. Denbigh, the head of the school. Sunday was church and Sunday school. Sunday evenings she worked with Helping Hands, a charitable organization run by St. Anne's in Brooklyn, provided she could get her brother-in-law or someone else to escort her home in the evening.

She was seeing other men besides Chan Baxter, but he was clearly her favorite, and their relationship seemed to be going strong right up to the end of 1921. Her diary is blank for the first four months of 1922, and by April Mr. Baxter is no more—gone, vanished into thin air. No explanation.

* * *

In the early 1920s, American culture was changing fast. Skirts were up and would continue to rise during the decade, tracking the stock market.[116] Frederick Lewis Allen, writing in 1931, recalled some of the other changes taking place:

> Supposedly "nice" girls were smoking cigarettes—openly and defiantly, if often rather awkwardly and self-consciously. They were drinking—somewhat less openly but often all too efficaciously. There were stories of daughters of the most exemplary parents getting drunk—"blotto," as their companions cheerfully put it—on the contents of the hip-flasks of the new prohibition regime, and going out joyriding with men at four in the morning. And worst of all, even at well-regulated dances they were said to retire where the eye of the most sharp-sighted chaperon could not follow, and in darkened rooms or in parked cars to engage in the unspeakable practice of petting and necking.[117]

Pris had been brought up to respect her parents' values. But she was also a "modern" woman, part of the postwar generation. Though she may not have

---

116   See Frederick Lewis Allen, *Only Yesterday* (New York; Harper & Brothers, 1931), 103-104. Allen describes Professor Hystrom's graph of skirt-length during the twenties, showing that in 1919 the average distance of the hem above the ground was about 10 percent of the woman's height, reaching 25 percent of her height by 1927 where it remained through 1929.
117   Allen, *Only Yesterday*: 90.

done everything Allen describes, she probably gave her parents some sleepless nights.

During 1923 and the first part of 1924 she lived pretty much as she had in 1921. There were some new things. On February 6, 1923, she mentions listening to a new toy—radio. It was "lots of fun."[118] Nicholas Robert Gilbert Jr., ("Bob G"), Alan Colcart, and Remsen Albert replaced Channing Baxter. In January 1923 she was out seventeen nights with one of those three. Then Don Love, a polo-playing Yale grad, moved in and monopolized her time, taking her to hockey games, horse shows, polo matches at his riding club in West-bury, dances at the Biltmore, concerts (Fritz Kreisler at the Academy), movies (Marion Davies in *Little Old New York*), and dinners at the Crescent Club or the Bossert. The Bossert Hotel, constructed in 1913, was one of the grandest hotels in Brooklyn, and the Marine Roof at the Bossert was a hot spot for dinner and dancing in 1924. Priscilla and Don Love were spending a lot of time together.

That was Priscilla's life as of February 1924. Young and single, she may have dressed in the latest fashion and perhaps looked like a Roaring Twenties girl, though it's hard to imagine her getting "blotto" or going too far in the back seat of a car. But I didn't know her then.

To get a better understanding of Priscilla, let's briefly (or perhaps not so briefly) interrupt the chronology and go back in time to look at her family history.

Priscilla's roots go back to old England, to the sixteenth century, to the Bradfords of Austerfield, Yorkshire, and the Fullers of Redenhall, Norfolk.[119] Priscilla's sixteenth-century ancestors were self-described "yeomen," a cut below "gentlemen" in the English pecking order. They were merchants and landown-ers, the hardworking and prosperous backbone of England.

Edward Fuller was born in 1575; Samuel Fuller, in 1580; William Bradford in 1590: all during the reign of Queen Elizabeth. Instead of living out their lives as prosperous merchants and landowners, Bradford and the Fuller brothers turned their backs on ordinary life and joined a religious sect, known as the Separatists,

---

118   Westinghouse had created the first broadcasting station on November 9, 1920 to broadcast the Harding-Cox election returns to people in the area with radio sets. By 1923, people were discovering that they could listen to music and other things on the new radio sets, and radio was rapidly gaining traction as a new form of entertainment. The Fullers, however, had yet to acquire a radio.

119   A lengthier version of the Plymouth story, including a discussion of Puritanism, Separatism, and the beliefs that inspired Bradford and the Fullers, is contained in Appendix 1. In addition to Bradfords and Fullers, Priscilla's other ancestors, born about the same time in sixteenth-century England and who also settled Plymouth Colony, included John Alden, Myles Standish and George Soule. Their respective lineages to Priscilla are set forth in Appendix 2. For simplicity's sake, the narrative focuses mainly on the Edward Fuller line. In the eighteenth century, Bradfords and Fullers merged when Emma Dyar Johnson, descendant of William Bradford, married Humphrey Taylor Fuller, descendant of Edward Fuller.

an extreme version of Puritanism. Their families tried to talk them out of their religious enthusiasm but to no avail. Because the Separatists insisted on their own forms of worship outside the established church and in defiance of the Queen, they were regarded as outlaws and harried by the authorities. Around 1610 many of the Separatists, including Bradford and the Fullers, fled England, lived for twelve years as exiles in Leiden, Holland, and left in the fall of 1620 to found a religious community on the Atlantic coast. They left Holland not to seek freedom of worship— they already had that in Holland. They left because they were uncomfortable with the very tolerance that allowed them to live and worship in Holland. They wanted to establish their own exclusive community with only a single church—theirs.

Priscilla's ancestors—Bradford and the Fullers, but also Myles Standish, John Alden, Priscilla Mullins and George Soule—sailed on the *Mayflower,* leaving Southampton, England in early September and reaching Cape Cod in November 1620.[120] A month later, they discovered a good harbor and land ideal for settlement at "Plimoth," so described on their map.[121] Indians, who outnumbered the newcomers (later called "Pilgrims"), were watching.

---

120   Most of what we know about Priscilla's ancestors is from Bradford's history: Samuel Eliot Morison, ed., *Of Plymouth Plantation 1620-1647* (New York; Alfred A. Knopf, 2001) (hereinafter, "Bradford Journal"). Other books about Plymouth include G. Mourt, *A Relation or Journall of the beginning and proceedings of the English Plantation settled at Plimoth in New England* etc. (London 1622, reprint, ed. by George B. Cheever, New York, 1848) (hereinafter, "Mourt's Relation"); Eugene Aubrey Stratton, *Plymouth Colony* (Salt Lake City, UT; Ancestry Publishing, 1986); and Nathaniel Philbrick, *Mayflower* (New York; Viking 2006). The story Priscilla grew up with was a relatively straightforward story of pious and heroic pilgrims, persecuted in England and finding religious freedom in the virgin forests of New England with the help of friendly natives.   Recent histories present a more complex version, more critical of the Pilgrims, their sometimes ruthless treatment of the "savages;" their endless problems with the investors who financed their voyage, and their human shortcomings.

121   The Pilgrims were familiar with Captain John Smith and his book, *A Description of New England,* published in 1614 which included detailed information on the coast, including a map showing "Plimoth" harbor just north of Cape Cod. The Pilgrims interviewed Smith for the position of military leader, but according to Smith, they felt they could get what they needed "more cheaply"out of his book.   In landing at "Plimoth," the Pilgrims had stumbled upon an abandoned Indian settlement, the inhabitants apparently the victims of a plague that had wiped out up to ninety percent of many settlements along the coast. In the spring, the Pilgrims were visited by a native who spoke some English; he described the fate of the earlier settlement: "he told us the place where we now live is called Pautuxet, and that about foure yeares agoe, all the Inhabitants dyed of an extraordinary plague, and there is neither man, woman nor childe remaining..." *Mourt's Relation,* 50-51, 58. In 1617, a plague had quickly spread up the New England coast, virtually wiping out Indian villages with death rates approaching 100%. Instead of finding thickly settled villages and thousands of warriors prepared to fight, the Pilgrims found abandoned villages, cleared fields, and very few Indians. They were the beneficiaries of one of the deadliest epidemics in human history; they saw the hand of God at work. For a discussion of the plague that ravaged the coastal Indian communities, see Dean R. Snow and Kim M. Lanphear, "European Contact and Indian Depopulation in the Northeast: the Timing of the First Epidemics," *Ethnohistory,* Vol. 35 (winter 1988): 1-32.

"Okay, I'll be nice, but they'd better not stay long."

Accustomed to relatively mild winters, the first New England winter caught the Pilgrims by surprise.[122] The first settlers at Jamestown in 1607 had suffered

---

122   Karen Kupperman, "The Puzzle of the American Climate in the Early Colonial Period," *American Historical Review*, 87 (1982): 1260-1289. European misconceptions about the North American climate persisted for many years until actual experience forced an acknowledgement that North American weather patterns were quite different and unrelated to longitude and latitude.

a high first year death rate; the settlers at Plymouth similarly suffered. In the winter of 1620-21 Plymouth lost 50 of 101.[123] Neither Edward Fuller nor his wife survived the first winter.[124] Their son Samuel, age twelve when the group landed, was brought up in the care of Edward's younger brother, Dr. Samuel Fuller, Plymouth colony physician and deacon of the church.

Priscilla's ancestors who did survive led the colony through the dangerous challenges of its early years: William Bradford, governor for most of the years from 1621 to 1657 and whose history of Plymouth colony is one of the classics of American literature; Myles Standish, their military leader, a man with a short fuse who inspired fear among the Indians; John Alden, whose marriage to Priscilla Mullins in the winter of 1620-21 was transformed into legend by Longfellow; and Dr. Samuel Fuller, whose diplomatic missions north to the much larger Massachusetts Bay Colony in 1630 allayed suspicions of Plymouth church practices and contributed to the development of the New England Congregational Church.[125]

The sons and daughters of Bradford, Standish, Alden, and Fuller gradually moved out from the original settlement and Plymouth, though surviving in history, eventually disappeared as a political entity.[126]

* * *

After the passing of the first Plymouth settlers, Priscilla Fuller's ancestors lived in Barnstable, Dedham and Braintree, Massachusetts; East Haddam and Hebron, Connecticut. They were farmers, soldiers, public officials, innkeepers, and slave-owners: Samuel Fuller of Barnstable in his will bequeathed "the Indian Joel" to his son; Col. John Dyar of Canterbury bequeathed three slaves: "negro

---

123   The difficulty of establishing a permanent settlement on the Atlantic coast was a matter of record. In the first attempt, at Roanoke off the North Carolina coast, the settlement had vanished, the settlers, victims of either starvation or hostile Indians. Jamestown had barely survived—during the first year 66 of 104 settlers died, mainly from disease. In 1607, the Popham settlement at the mouth of the Kennebec River in Maine, lasted just one year through a very cold New England winter

124   *Bradford Journal*: 446.

125   Dr. Fuller's diplomatic mission is described in his three letters to Bradford from Boston, Salem and Charlestown, contained in Governor Bradford's *Letter Book*, reprinted in *The Mayflower Descendants* (Boston; Massachusetts Society of Mayflower Descendants, 1905), 7: 79-82.

126   The colonies of Maine and Plymouth were combined with Massachusetts Bay on October 7, 1691. The last meeting of the Plymouth General Court was held June 8, 1692. On April 5, 1693 the Plymouth Church set apart a day of thanksgiving "that the government over us is yet in the hands of saints." Though disappearing as a political entity, Plymouth's historical importance survived as the origin of certain American institutions, such as self-governance and civil marriage; as starting point for the Congregational Church (Fuller's mission persuaded the Salem Puritans to follow the Plymouth model); and as an inspirational story of faith, courage and resourcefulness in the face of life-threatening conditions. See Samuel Eliot Morrison, *By Land and By Sea* (New York; Alfred A. Knopf, 1953), in particular, Chapter X: "The Pilgrim Fathers: Their Significance in History."

woman Gene;" "negro man Sham," and "negro child Rose." Jedediah Johnson of Canterbury was recorded in the 1820 census as owning one male slave.

Farming and raising large families were their main occupations. Their families ranged from seven to as many as fourteen children. But the sons of large families needed to inherit part of the family farm to start their own, which were invariably much smaller than those on which they had been raised.

When John Fuller, son of Samuel Fuller, moved from Barnstable to East Haddam in 1696 he acquired a farm of hundreds of acres. But he and his wife Mehitable Rowley had seven sons and each son got one-seventh of the Fuller farm (their five daughters got mainly pots and pans). John's sons had sons, and the land was again divided. But there was only so much good farm land in East Haddam, or in all of New England for that matter, and finally the land gave out.

About 1850 Priscilla's grandfather Humphrey Roger Fuller, one of ten children of Humphrey Taylor and Emma Johnson Fuller, left the family farm in Hebron (most of his brothers and sisters had already left), moved to New York City, married the daughter of a prominent New Yorker and went to work as a clerk in a bank on Wall Street.

3. Fullers, Merceins, & New York in the Nineteenth Century

In the early evening of May 20, 1893, Humphrey Roger Fuller was riding the trolley from Brooklyn to Flatbush for a family dinner at his son's new home, 2 Tennis Court, a short walk from the Prospect Park station. Humphrey's wife had died six weeks earlier and he was under considerable pressure as chief financial officer of a bank fighting for survival in the midst of the latest Wall Street financial crisis. The next day the *Times* carried the following news item:[127]

Humphrey R. Fuller Drops Dead
Humphrey Rodger [sic] Fuller of 107 Macon Street, Brooklyn, dropped dead last night on Flatbush Avenue, opposite the Willink entrance to Prospect Park, just as he was stepping off a street car.

Mr. Fuller was born at Hebron, Conn., and was sixty-seven years of age. When a young man he came to New York, where he secured a position as cashier in the Bank of America on Wall Street. He has been in the banking business ever since. His son, Charles H. Fuller, is a lawyer in the Potter Building.

Humphrey arrived in New York City in about 1850, age 24. For a farm boy from Hebron, Connecticut, the city would have been a rude shock. New York: crowded and noisy; Hebron; mainly farmland. New York was exciting,

---

127 *The New York Times,* May 21, 1893, (unattributed article). Isabelle Fuller died April 6, 1893 at the Fuller home in Brooklyn. Humphrey and Isabelle are buried side by side in the cemetery at Ballston Spa, near Saratoga, New York, next to the graves of Humphrey's father and mother. The Fuller graves are located in the Village of Ballston Cemetery at the corner of Ballston Avenue and West High Street.

growing, money-making; the most exciting place in Hebron was the old Hebron Hotel, long owned and managed by Humphrey Fuller's uncle Erastus. The people in Hebron were mainly Congregationalists and Episcopalians descended from old New England; New York City was a mix of virtually every religion on earth, and the number of immigrants from foreign countries landing in New York harbor on any given day far exceeded the entire population of Hebron.

Humphrey secured a position as clerk at Bank of America, one of the many banks on Wall Street. [128] On July 17, 1853 he married Isabelle Mercein in the Mercein's Fourth Street town house. The Reverend Thomas Fitz Randolph Mercein, an eminent Methodist minister and the bride's younger brother, performed the ceremony in the presence of various Merceins.[129]

Two men were notable by their absence: the bride's father (Priscilla's great-grandfather) Thomas Royce Mercein, who had died in 1843, and the bride's grandfather, Andrew Mercein, who had died in 1835. Each had been a significant figure in the early days of the city.

Andrew Mercein: In 1779, Andrew Mercein was sixteen and living with his mother in New York City. His father, a watchmaker, had disappeared on a trip to New Orleans, where he had intended to establish a home for the family. The Merceins were recent immigrants from Geneva, Switzerland. The Revolution was in its third year and the city was occupied by British soldiers. One day, Andrew caught the attention of a British press gang on the lookout for able-bodied young men to serve in the navy. They snatched him off the street and delivered him to a British warship lying in the Hudson River. In an unguarded moment and under cover of darkness, Andrew dived into the water fully clothed and made his escape as British sentries fired at him.

During the rest of the war, he apprenticed to a baker who supplied bread to the British army. Apparently, there were times when bread was scarce even for

---

128   Bank of America, a New York State bank founded in 1812, was acquired in 1928 by A.P. Giannini's Bank of Italy, which then assumed the name of the much smaller New York bank.

129   Among the Merceins most likely present were Mary Stanbury Mercein, Isabelle's mother and widow of Thomas R. Mercein; Mary's mother, Elizabeth Stanbury, eighty-eight, born on the Isle of Wight; Eliza Anne Mercein Barry, long separated from her husband, John Barry, after a bitter and highly-public legal conflict; Rosalie Mercein with her husband Henry Heiser, a New York merchant, and their seven children; and Imogene Mercein: thirty-seven, unmarried. Of Isabelle's brothers, Andrew, a sailor, had drowned at sea in 1822; Daniel was a merchant with a growing family in Mississippi, and Thomas Fitz Randolph, the youngest, was a minister in the Methodist Church at Sheffield, Connecticut. See U.S.Census 1850, Roll M432_ 555, 41.

the British, and Andrew made money by selling it at a hefty markup (selling six penny loaves as fast as he could for "a hard half dollar a-piece").[130]

In 1780, he married Elizabeth Royce. He was seventeen, she was eighteen. Two years later, he witnessed the events that marked the end of the war: the British evacuation from New York as the royal band beat a farewell march; the evacuation of the loyalists with their wives and children, boarding ships to take them to "the bleak and barren soil of Nova Scotia"; the triumphant entry of Washington's "weather-beaten" troops.[131]

After the war Andrew operated a successful bakery business at 93 Gold Street in lower Manhattan. In 1786, at the age of twenty-three, while listening to the Presbyterian preacher in the Dutch Reformed Church in Manhattan, he experienced a religious "awakening" that changed his life. He was persuaded to join the Methodists at the John Street Preaching House and thereafter Methodism became the driving force in his life.

Andrew's conversion experience wasn't unique; it was typical of what was going on in the rest of the country. He was part of the greatest religious revival in American history—the "Second Great Awakening"—during which emotionally-driven, evangelical faith spread like fire.[132] It was a time of explosive religious growth for Baptists, Methodists, and other evangelical groups, but particularly for Methodists, described by one historian as "the most powerful religious movement in American history."[133] In Andrew Mercein's time, Methodism grew faster than any other denomination, its growth propelled by ardent converts like Mercein, and by a cadre of itinerant preachers. Part of Methodism's appeal was its optimism, teaching that one could earn salvation by doing good, in sharp contrast to the gloomier vision of the New England Puritans, who held that salvation was restricted to the predestined few.

Andrew's fellow members at the John Street church were men like himself: tradesmen and artisans. Andrew served as trustee and class leader, contributed

---

130   John Fanning Watson, *Annals and Occurrences of New York City and State in the Olden Times* (Philadelphia; Henry F. Anners, Chesnut Street, 1846), 327.

131   Watson, *Annals and Occurrences*, 326-328.

132   The first great awakening had taken place in the early eighteenth century, led by Jonathan Edwards preaching in Northampton, Massachusetts, and other notable New England preachers. The second great awakening took place starting in the late eighteenth century continuing into the next century. The formal beginning of the Methodist church in America dates from the Christmas Conference in Baltimore, held in 1784, when the church organization and leadership were established. With the Anglicans discredited by the Revolution and New England Puritans split between Congregationalists and Presbyterians, the Methodists and the Baptists found fertile soil for their missionary zeal.

133   Dee Andrews, *The Methodists and Revolutionary America, 1760-1800* (Princeton, N.J; Princeton University Press, 2002), 4. See Gordon S. Wood, *Empire of Liberty* (New York; Oxford University Press, 2009), 581-608.

money for the construction of additional Methodist churches, and worked among the poor during the smallpox epidemics that struck the city in the late eighteenth century. In 1805, having made his fortune, he turned the bakery business over to his son and moved across the river to Brooklyn, then a small country village with more cows than people.

Andrew absorbed the Methodist teaching that one should evidence desire for salvation by doing good.[134] Among other things, he was a teacher at the Sands Street Church, which he helped establish in 1816; a founder of the "Assistant Society," formed in 1813 for "relieving and advising the sick and poor during the winter season;" president of "A Society to Prevent and Suppress Vice in the Town of Brooklyn;" chairman of the Board of Trustees of Brooklyn and a leader in obtaining a village charter from the State in 1816; organizer of Brooklyn's first public school in 1816; founder of the Apprentice's Library in 1823; organizer of the Brooklyn Savings Bank, chartered in 1827 as "a secure place of deposits for the savings of tradesmen, mechanics, laborers, minors, servants and others who wish to lay up a fund for sickness, for the wants of a family or for old age." Mercein's stern morality was evident in the statement: "In no case whatsoever will loans of money be made to individuals." [135]

Andrew's wife, Elizabeth, died in 1830, the fiftieth year of their marriage. During their life together, Elizabeth bore twelve children, of whom only two, Thomas Royce and William, survived infancy.[136] Known in his old age as "Father Mercein," Andrew died in 1835 after leading his last Bible class. In the words of one Methodist historian, Andrew "died in peace, and in full assurance of a glorious immortality."[137]

Thomas Royce Mercein. Born to Andrew and Elizabeth Mercein in 1783, Thomas Mercein was raised as an apprentice in his father's bakery business and went on from there to be a master baker, lawyer, legislator, public official, army officer, businessman, civic leader and man of letters.

---

134 Andrews, *The Methodists and Revolutionary America,* 445
135 Henry Reed Stiles, A *History of the City of Brooklyn* (Albany, N.Y; John Munsell, 1870), Vol. 2: 13-14, 25-26. See also *The Brooklyn Daily Eagle,* April 17, 1882, 4; June 21, 1884, 4 (unattributed articles).
136 Following Elizabeth's death, Andrew married Charlotte Gault, an Episcopalian who converted to Methodism and taught at the Sands Street Church.
137 Andrew died June 29, 1835. Much of the discussion of Andrew Mercein's life and his part in the church is based on Joseph B. Wakeley, *Lost chapters recovered from the early history of American Methodism* (New York; Carlton & Porter, 1858), 559-562, and Edwin Warriner, *Old Sands Street Methodist Episcopal Church of Brooklyn, New York* (New York; Phillips & Hunt, 1885), 462-466

Mercein married Mary Stanbury of New York City in 1802.[138] Between 1803 and 1825, Mary gave birth to twelve children, of whom eight survived to adulthood. At the time of his marriage, Mercein was managing his bakery business and practicing law.[139]

In the spring of 1806 Mercein was asked by the city to organize one of the first four companies of the New York Seventh Regiment.[140] War fever was running high in New York. British warships stationed off Sandy Hook just outside the harbor were boarding and searching U.S. vessels. The British ship *Leander* had fired on a U.S. sloop from Delaware, killing a well-known New Yorker. After a public funeral the crowd, probably including Mercein, adjourned to the Tontine Coffee House at the corner of Wall and Water streets to hear angry speeches and adopt resolutions against the British.

Tension with Britain continued to build during the next six years, as the Royal Navy, seeking to enforce a blockade of the continent during the Napoleonic wars, boarded and searched U.S. vessels. Mercein, in addition to his bakery business, law practice and increasingly serious military obligations, was elected to serve in the New York legislature from 1810-1812.[141]

War broke out in June 1812. Mercein's Seventh Regiment was called to active duty. With New York vulnerable to British invasion, the city established a "Committee of Defence," chaired by Mayor De Witt Clinton. Mercein, then a major in the army, served as treasurer to the committee, which met daily to assess the British threat and prepare the city's defenses. As treasurer, Mercein arranged for $1 million in bank loans to cover defense expenditures. Since New York was in far better financial shape than Washington, he also lent city funds to the national government to defray its expense in defending the city, riding his horse to Washington to negotiate the terms of the loan with the War Department.[142]

---

138   They married April 17, 1802. Mary was the daughter of Daniel and Elizabeth Stanbury of New York. See "Mercein Family Records" in *The New York Genealogical and Biographical Record,* Vol. 44: 339-340 (New York; NYG&BS, 1913).

139   In 1806, there was no law school or bar exam requirement. A man could practice law by reading law books and spending time with other lawyers. Mercein was recognized as a distinguished lawyer. See Fitz-Greene Halleck, Joseph Rodman Drake and James Grant Wilson, *The Poetical Writings of Fitz-Greene Halleck* (New York; D. Appleton & Company, 1869), n26, 27, which describes Mercein as a "lawyer of distinction."

140   Hopper Striker Mott, *The New York of Yesterday* (New York; Putnam's, 1908), 61. Colonel Emmons Clark, *History of the Seventh Regiment 1806-1889* (New York; Seventh Regiment, 1890), 45.

141   *Laws of the State of New York in Relation to the Erie and Champlain Canals* (Albany, N.Y.; E & E Hosford, 1825), 592-593, listing the members of the legislature for 1810-1812.

142   Letter by James Monroe, Secretary of War, to Thomas R. Mercein, January 30, 1815, *American State Papers*, 18th Congress, 1st sess., Finance, Vol. 5, 37.

In 1814, with the British occupying Washington, the White House and Capitol in flames, and rumors that the British were outfitting an immense fleet to invade New York City, the Committee of Defence launched an all- out effort to complete construction of defensive works at the city's most vulnerable points.[143] Major Mercein was given command of the North Battery with sixteen big guns overlooking the Hudson. The rumored British fleet never appeared in New York Harbor, and the war ended in the winter of 1815.[144] The Committee of Defence adopted a resolution recognizing Mercein's wartime service:

> Resolved unanimously that the thanks of this Committee be presented to Thomas R. Mercein, Esq., for his assiduity and faithful discharge of the important duties of Treasurer, for the regularity of his accounts and vouchers, for encountering the fatigue and expense of going to Washington at an inclement season, and particularly for his correct, prompt and satisfactory settlement of accounts with the General Government.

> Resolved that Five hundred dollars be appropriated to the pur- chase of Plate which he be requested to accept for his services above expressed.[145]

---

143   The most vulnerable points were regarded as Sandy Hook, Harlem Heights, and the boundary between Brooklyn and Long Island, where it was feared the British might land troops, cross into Brooklyn and use that as a launching point for an attack on the city.
144   The fleet sailed for New Orleans, where, on January 8, 1815, Andrew Jackson won a decisive victory over the British. A treaty ending the war had been signed December 24, 1814, but news of the treaty didn't reach New Orleans until after the battle. See Gordon Wood, *Empire of Liberty*, 695.
145   Mott, *New York of Yesterday*, 59-64. The resolutions were adopted March 4, 1815. Apparently an engrossed copy of the tribute and the plate with inscription: "Presented to Col. Thomas R. Mercein by the Committee of Defence of the City of New York, 4 March 1815" were, as of 1908, in the possession of the Heiser family.

Portrait of Thomas R. Mercein, ca. 1815

Later that year, in the largest demonstration of military strength seen in New York, 25,000 troops paraded down Broadway. The *Evening Post* observed that "the troops made a splendid appearance and the regiment commanded by Colonel Mercein attracted particular attention." Mercein continued to serve as colonel and regimental commander until his retirement in 1818. The regimental historian described Mercein as "one of the ablest and most distinguished military officers of the period."[146]

---

146   Clark, *Seventh Regiment*, 80, 90.

During the war, Mayor Clinton appointed Mercein New York City Comptroller. He was an innovative comptroller. To improve the city's reputation in the market and its ability to sell bonds, he created the first sinking fund, dedicating specific city revenues to debt repayment: standard financial practice today but cutting edge then.[147] In 1815 he bailed the city out of a precarious financial situation. The federal government owned several parcels of land in downtown Manhattan, originally intended as the site of office buildings but no longer needed with the nation's capital in Washington. [148] Negotiating with federal authorities, Mercein assembled a block of prime property, now known as "Bowling Green," and auctioned off seventeen parcels. The auction raised $164,783, which he then applied to the retirement of city debt.[149] Mercein purchased lot 9 for himself.

Retiring as comptroller in 1816, Mercein resumed his bakery business. He also joined the St. Nicholas Society (with Washington Irving, Hamilton Fish and other prominent New Yorkers), served as a founding member of the Literary and Philosophical Society (with De Witt Clinton, James Kent and others) and the New York Historical Society, and was among the initial contributors to New York University.

As president of the Society of Mechanics and Tradesmen, Mercein gave the keynote speech on November 25, 1820, commemorating the opening of a new library for apprentices. The large audience included the mayor as well as members of the city council and state legislature. His address reflected the liberal reform spirit of the time (and perhaps Mercein's own personal experience): that study, hard work and clean living will lead to success. "Who can tell" he asked his audience, "how many Franklins may be among you?...Who can tell how many Fultons may yet spring from the Institution this day opened?" He warned

---

147   At the time, the city borrowed on the assumption that the debt would be repaid by revenues available when the debt became due. All municipalities, and even the federal government, operated that way.
148   Alexander Hamilton, Secretary of the Treasury and the leading New Yorker of his time, needed congressional support for his controversial plan to assume all state debts incurred during the Revolution, a step that established the credit of the new government and set the country on the course of prosperity. To obtain that support, Hamilton agreed to give up New York's claim to be the nation's capital and support a location between Virginia and Maryland. The bargain was struck at a private dinner, giving Jefferson and Madison what they wanted—a southern capital situated next to Virginia—and Hamilton what he and President Washington wanted but couldn't get because of Jefferson and Madison's determined opposition.
149   "Fifth Avenue Around 58th and Central Park in 1858," <www.oldandsold.com/article> (the web site is no longer operational). Mercein paid $8,250 for his lot. While the present purchasing power of $164,783 would be about $2.5 million, a better measure of the relative magnitude would be share of Gross Domestic Product, which would translate into about $2.6 Billion in current money. See <www.measuringworth.com.>

the young apprentices "to avoid the alluring but fatal paths of vice and dissipation." Later, the apprentices checked out some three hundred books.[150]

The most important event of Mercein's lifetime was the completion of the Erie Canal in 1825. The canal, connecting Lake Erie to the Hudson at Albany, was by far the biggest and most successful public works project of its time. Following the financial crisis of 1817, the canal project put large numbers of otherwise unemployed men to work, pumping money into a depressed economy. De Witt Clinton, Mercein's friend and mentor, was the driving force behind it. [151]

The canal produced dramatic and lasting changes in American life. Before the canal, there was nothing linking the nation's interior to the East Coast. For all practical purposes, East and West were separate countries. After the opening of the canal, the produce of the West flowed into New York City and on to Europe; the goods of the world flowed through New York City to the West. [152] The impact on food prices was huge. Take one example: the canal cut the cost of transporting a ton of flour from Buffalo to New York City from $120 to $6; it cut the time from three weeks to six days.[153] The results for New York City were equally dramatic. Before, New York vied with Boston, Philadelphia, Baltimore and New Orleans for commercial preeminence. After, New York was without a rival as the nation's preeminent port, commercial and financial center.

With its completion, there was an outpouring of New York pride; the state, denied federal support, had financed the entire project on its own. [154] There had to be an appropriate celebration. At a meeting of the chamber of commerce, Mercein was selected to be an organizer of the statewide celebration.[155]

---

150   T.R .Mercein: *Address to Mechanics Society, 25 November 1820* (New York; W.A.Mercein, 1820); Tom Glynn, *Books for a Reformed Republic: The Apprentices' Library of New York City*, 1820-1865 (Austin, Texas; University of Texas Press, 1999), 347-353. The first item of expense in the library budget was for candles, so that it could be open in the evening for the apprentices and mechanics who worked all day. See Marci Reaven, Steven J. Zeitlin, Martha Cooper, *Hidden New York* (New Brunswick, N.J.; Rutgers University Press, 2006), 63.
151   This discussion of the Erie Canal draws heavily on Peter Bernstein's excellent book, *Wedding of the Waters, the Erie Canal and the Making of a Great Nation* (New York; W.W.Norton & Company 2005).
152   Uniting East and West put the South at a severe disadvantage in the Civil War.
153   John Steele Gordon, *The Great Game* (New York; Scribner, 1999), 56-57
154   President Madison vetoed the bill that would have provided funding for the canal. New York State then funded the entire project, which at $7 million was about twenty times the cost of other contemporary canal projects. To give some idea of the size of the project relative to the size of the economy, cost relative to GDP would be about $129 Billion in current dollars. The state financed the project through bonds backed by its credit and certain tax revenues. As construction proceeded and the success of the canal appeared less doubtful, the bonds found an increasingly enthusiastic market in Europe and Britain. The entire cost was recouped within nine years from canal tolls. See Bernstein, *Wedding of the* Waters, 190-191, 230-236.
155   Resolutions adopted at a meeting held September 12, 1825, Chamber of Commerce room, Tontine Coffee-house, New York City. See < http://www.history.rochester.edu/canal/bib/colden/App02.html.> Last accessed March 18, 2010.

Mercein's organizing committee planned an elaborate celebration that lasted for the better part of two weeks. Early on October 26, 1825, a fleet of boats, led by the *Seneca Chief* with Governor Clinton on board, entered the canal from Lake Erie. During the next eight days the fleet slowly made its way down the canal, cheered on by crowds, the cheers accompanied by the boom of strategically-positioned, large-caliber cannon. The traveling dignitaries ate and drank their way down the canal, stopping for celebratory breakfasts, dinners, and suppers at virtually every town along the route, enjoying at one stop "fat ox roasted whole" and the "ruby bright wines of the best vineyards of Europe." After entering New York Harbor, Governor Clinton's fleet gathered in a circle off Sandy Hook. Before a distinguished audience, the governor lifted two kegs filled with water from Lake Erie and emptied them into the Atlantic Ocean.[156]

In the evening there was a grand parade up Broadway to City Hall, "the largest of the kind ever witnessed in America." City Hall, lit up like a Christmas tree, was the scene of a spectacular display of fireworks with rockets "uncommonly large." City Hall Park was "filled to overflowing" with "not less than eight or ten thousand admiring spectators." [157]

The next evening, Mercein and his fellow organizers put on "The Grand Canal Ball" and midnight supper for three thousand invited guests. A few days later, the *Seneca Chief* and the rest of the fleet headed back to Buffalo with kegs of Atlantic water.

The canal was an immediate success. Incomes and property values all along the canal route and in New York City soared and the city, now handling an increasing share of the nation's trade, enjoyed a long period of prosperity.[158] As president of the Equitable Fire Insurance Company and investor in prime city real estate, Mercein became a wealthy man.[159] Under Mercein's leadership, the

---

156   One of the kegs is on display at the New York Historical Society.

157   The description of the celebration, from the launching of the *Seneca Chief* at Buffalo to the final ball is based on William L. Stone's "Narrative of the Festivities, etc." prepared for the organizing committee, the text of which may be found at < http://www.history.rochester.edu/canal/bib/colden/App18.html. > Mercein was apparently known as a good event organizer. Seven years later on 30 May 1832, he organized a special dinner in honor of Washington Irving, the nation's preeminent man of letters, at the City Hotel, New York's finest, attended by three hundred prominent citizens. The dinner committee was a who's who of the New York elite, including Cornelius Low, Peter Schermerhorn, George Strong, and others. Chancellor Kent presided. See Walter Barrett Clerk, *The Old Merchants of New York Cit y* (New York; Carleton Publisher, 1863), 322.

158   From 1825 to 1836 the value of real and personal property in New York City increased from $101 million to $310 million. Bernstein, *Wedding of the Waters*, 349.

159   In 1823 a group of investors formed the Equitable Fire Insurance Company at 46 Wall Street, with an initial capital of $300,000. Trow's: *New York City Directory*, 1823 (Business section). Mercein was elected president and served in that position for the next twenty years. In 1826 Mercein developed a row of nine Federal houses on property he owned between MacDougal Street and Sixth Avenue, an area known as "Waverly Place."

Equitable managed to survive the great fire of 1835, which destroyed much of downtown Manhattan and bankrupted twenty-three of the twenty-six New York fire insurance companies.[160]

In the spring of 1837, prosperity came to a sudden end and the nation experienced the most devastating financial crisis in its history up to that point. Thomas Mercein left no diary that might tell the story of the crisis and how it affected him and his family, but a contemporary, Philip Hone, did. Hone, like Mercein a wealthy and distinguished New Yorker, described the failure of his son's business and his own heavy losses:

> Saturday March 4....This is a dark and melancholy day in the annals of my family. Brown & Hone stopped payment today, and called a meeting of their creditors. My eldest son has lost the capital I gave him, and I am implicated as endorser for them to a fearful amount... This is a heavy blow for me, and added to the difficulty I experience in raising money on my property to meet my own engagements, almost breaks me down..." [161]

On March 17, Hone noted "The great crisis is near at hand, if it has not already arrived. The banking house of I. and L. Joseph...stopped payment today..." The failure of the seemingly solid House of Joseph, triggered by defaulting Southerners short of cash from falling cotton prices, set off a panic that led to a string of failures.[162] On May 8, Hone sounded a desperate note: "Where will it all end? In ruin, revolution, perhaps civil war." Two days later the stock market collapsed and bank depositors panicked. Hone, trustee of the Savings Bank, described the run on his and the other New York banks:

> Wednesday, May 10...The volcano has burst and over-whelmed New York...a day of unexampled excitement, and a ruthless run upon all the banks...

---

160   Moses King, *King's Handbook of New York* (New York; M. King, 1893), 640. The Equitable was liquidated in 1889. During its life, the company never failed to pay a dividend; dividends ranged from a low of 8 percent up to 40 percent. *The New York Times*, May 8, 1889, 8 (unattributed article).
161   Allan Nevins, ed., *The Diary of Philip Hone, 1828-1851* (New York; Dodd, Mead and Company, 1927, Kraus Reprint Co. 1949), 245. Another New York diarist estimated Hone's losses at about $200,000, which in current dollars, measured as share of GDP, would be about $5,000,000. The Nevins edition of Hone's diary is abridged; the complete diary running to well over one million words is at the New York Historical Society on microfilm.
162   *Gotham*: 611-612.

The press was awful. The hour for closing the bank is six o'clock, but they did not get through the paying of those who were in at that time till nine. I was there with the other trustees and witnessed the madness of the people. Women were nearly pressed to death, and the stoutest men could scarcely sustain themselves...but they had strength to cry "Pay! Pay!"[163]

The governor deployed the National Guard to restrain the crowds on Wall Street.[164] The Wall Street panic was accompanied by hundreds of business failures and bankruptcies of formerly well-to-do New Yorkers. Fortunes made during the boom in property values melted away; elegant homes and rich furnishings were put on the market and sold for whatever the owners could get. After a brief but illusory recovery, the Bank of England, which had precipitated the 1837 crisis by raising its interest rate, did the same thing in 1838, and with the same results. British investors withdrew from the American market, businesses fell on hard times, and depression followed. The nation didn't fully recover until after the Mexican War and the California gold strike of 1848.[165] Appeals to the federal government fell on deaf ears. President Martin Van Buren, responding to calls for assistance by the New York merchants, took the position that people should not look to the government for help:

---

163   *Diary of Philip Hone*: 257. In 1837, money was largely in the form of gold and silver. Bank depositors were entitled by law to receive payment in gold or silver, commonly referred to as "specie." Financial panics inevitably led to runs on the banks, as deposits were not insured and the banks held only a limited amount of gold and silver in their vaults.

164   Allan Nevins and Milton Halsey Thomas, ed., *The Diary of George Templeton Strong* (New York; The Macmillan Company, 1952), 1: 65. The crisis in New York quickly became a national crisis, but President Martin Van Buren declined to use the powers of the federal government to stem the tide. The complete Strong diary is located at the Columbia University Library.

165   Like most financial crises, there were multiple events that led to the 1837 crisis. The Bank of England, seeking to reverse the flow of capital out of England, raised its interest rate and achieved its objective. British investors drew funds out of the U.S. market, which in turn led to collapsing prices, especially in speculative western railroad securities. There were also domestic triggers. The Jackson Administration, seeking to curb western land speculation, had issued a treasury circular requiring that Federal lands be paid for in hard money (gold and silver). At the same time, the administration also distributed the national surplus among the banks in the various states according to population. Those two measures drained the reserves of the New York City banks by forcing them to ship their hard money to banks in the south and west. As a result, the New York banks began to call in loans to compensate for the loss of reserves, which led to some well-publicized bankruptcies. Lacking strong reserves, the banks were ill-equipped to meet the demands of increasingly panicked depositors. Jackson's earlier destruction of the Second Bank of the United States removed an institution that might have helped in the crisis. See Peter L. Rousseau, "Jacksonian Monetary Policy, Specie Flows and the Panic of 1837," *The Journal of Economic History*, 62 (June 2002): 457-488.

Those who look to the action of this government for specific aid to the citizen to relieve embarrassments arising from losses by revulsions in commerce and credit, lose sight of the ends for which it was created, and the powers with which it is clothed... The less government interferes with private pursuits, the better for the general prosperity.[166]

Mercein, like Hone, had furnished the capital for his son's business venture and lost heavily when the business failed. Men like Mercein and Hone, wealthy in 1836, were no longer wealthy at the end of 1837.

The financial collapse also ruined Mercein's son-in-law, destroyed the marriage of his daughter, and precipitated a dramatic and bitter lawsuit by his son-in-law against Mercein. In addition to providing a glimpse into Mercein family affairs, the suit and resulting decisions up to the United States Supreme Court formed the basis for modern custody law and the role of the courts in deciding custody cases.[167]

John Barry, a prominent businessman from Nova Scotia, married Mercein's daughter, Eliza Ann, in 1835. As a condition to the marriage, Mercein had extracted from Barry an agreement that Barry would move to New York so that Eliza could be close to her family. Barry did so. Assisted by a loan from Mercein, he set up a business on lower Broadway selling lamps and fine china. The business lasted just ten months. In August 1837, three months into the financial crisis, Barry was forced to call in his creditors and declare bankruptcy. Mercein arranged a quick sale of Barry's business inventory and applied the proceeds to what Barry owed him, leaving Barry with nothing. Barry was furious. Expecting to be accommodated as family, Barry was shocked, describing Mercein as "gruff," "surly," "cold-hearted," and "narrow-minded." Mercein, hit hard by the crisis, was in no mood to be generous.

Disillusioned by his New York experience, Barry was more than anxious to return with wife and children (son and daughter) to Nova Scotia. But Eliza Ann refused to leave her father's comfortable house. In a fit of anger, Barry packed his bags, snatched his son, and moved out of the Mercein house. She asked him to return. He refused. She wrote him, reminding him of their prenuptial

---

166   See Bernstein, *Wedding of the Waters*: 306-307. Van Buren, blamed for the crisis and for doing nothing, lost badly in the 1840 election.
167   The facts of the case are set forth in the report of *People Ex. Rel. John A. Barry vs. Thomas R. Mercein*, which consumes virtually the entire issue of the *New York Commercial Advertiser*, 28 August 1839 (New York Historical Society). The case was not concluded until 1847.

agreement and reaffirming that she would not return to Nova Scotia. He responded with an ill-considered angry letter, renouncing the marriage and "declaring his unalterable determination never to be reunited to her on this side of the boundless ocean of eternity."

After he cooled down, Barry was anxious to reconcile with his wife, but Mercein would have nothing to do with Barry, declaring him *persona non grata*. Mercein made it clear that he would keep Eliza Ann and her daughter in his house for as long as she wished to stay and that the only communication he would accept from Barry would be a proposal for "separation unto death."

Barry brought suit in the New York Chancery Court to force the return of his wife and daughter. Barry contended that his tyrannical father-in-law was keeping his wife and daughter from him (that Barry was keeping his son was apparently not an issue in the case). Chancellor Wallworth heard the case in Saratoga. The judgment and opinion of the Chancellor, which went against Barry, were printed in the *New York Commercial Advertiser* for all to see. The Chancellor found Eliza Ann's attachment to her father's house most peculiar and clearly disapproved of separation, but he refused to compel Eliza Ann to return to her husband:

> Neither this court nor any other court in this state has any jurisdiction or authority to compel a wife to return to the bed and board of her husband and to the performance of her conjugal duties, where she voluntarily absents herself from him, either with or without justifiable cause....

> But, I will therefore only say here... that a Christian wife and mother should suffer long and much before she can be justified in resorting to the doubtful and dangerous expedient of separating herself permanently from him whom she has once chosen for the partner of her bed and bosom, thereby placing both herself and him in the undefined and dangerous situation of a husband without a wife, and a wife without a husband.

As to custody, the Chancellor ignored the traditional legal view that the husband as head of the house was legally entitled to secure the return of his child. Instead, he determined that in this case the mother was the best person to entrust with the care of the infant child. Barry appealed all the way up to the

U.S. Supreme Court, but to no avail.[168] The decision marked a dramatic change in the law. At the time Barry brought his suit, he could have been reasonably confident of securing the return of wife and child; after the decision, a father could no longer be so confident, and a wife might well gain both independence and custody.

By 1843, Thomas Mercein could look back on his life with some pride. He was a successful man by any measure: distinguished military and business career, public and philanthropic service, highly-regarded by his peers, loving father surrounded by a large family. But he had lost heavily in the financial crisis and depression that followed; he was no longer the wealthy New York merchant he had been before 1837. And Barry was obsessively pursuing the lawsuit and tarnishing Mercein's reputation. In 1843, the suit was already five years old and would go on for four more years. On October 24, 1843 Mercein died suddenly, possibly of a heart attack. He was sixty years old. [169]

* * *

Had he lived to 1853, Thomas Mercein might have doubted Humphrey Fuller's ability to provide for Isabelle in the style to which she was accustomed. But Isabelle was thirty-one and staring spinsterhood in the face. That she had a proposal in hand from a respectable young man was undoubtedly a great relief to her mother.

With their marriage, Humphrey and Isabelle lived at the Mercein home in downtown Manhattan, Humphrey walking the short distance to Wall Street where he was employed at Bank of America.

---

168   See *People v. Mercein*, 8 Paige 47 (New York Court of Chancery, 1839); 3 N.Y.Sup.Ct. 399 (1843); 25 Wendell 66 (Court for the Correction of Errors, New York, 1843); 46 U.S. 103 (U.S. Sup. Ct, 1847). For a good discussion of the case and its significance, see Hendrik Hartog, *Man and Wife in America* (Cambridge, MA; Harvard University Press 2000), 193-218.
169 Death Register, Thomas R. Mercein, New York City, October 24, 1843, citing the cause of death as "spining" (New York City Municipal Archives). Mary Mercein, Isabelle's mother, continued to live at 4th Street in downtown Manhattan. Two of her children inherited their grandfather Andrew Mercein's passionate attachment to the Methodist Church. Thomas Fitz Randolph Mercein became a prominent Methodist minister and writer; Imogene Mercein was an active member of the Methodist Ladies Home Missionary Society, which brought social reform and the Methodist religion into the heart of the notorious five points section of the city. Her eldest son, Daniel, moved to Mississippi and raised a family there, including a son, Thomas, who later married into the Schley family of Milwaukee. A descendant, Thomas R. Mercein, today lives with his family in Darien, Ct.

Isabelle Mercein Fuller, about the time of her marriage to Humphrey Fuller in 1853

Two years later Humphrey and Isabelle moved across the Hudson River to Newark.[170] A rail link connected Newark to the Hudson River Terminal at Jersey City where Humphrey could catch the ferry to downtown Manhattan.

When Humphrey boarded the train at Newark, took a seat and opened his newspaper, there was one big issue that dominated the news: slavery, and the escalating conflict between North and South. Every day Humphrey would have read about some aspect of that overriding issue: southerners, using the Fugitive Slave Law to hunt down escaped slaves in hostile northern cities; the conflict over extending slavery to the new western territories; civil war in Kansas between pro-slavery marauders from Missouri and armed abolitionists; the *Dred Scott* decision, which put the Supreme Court squarely on the side of slavery;[171] the formation of the new Republican Party by opponents of slavery; John Brown's attempt to capture the arsenal at Harper's Ferry and instigate a slave rebellion.

With his orderly banker's outlook and his bank's southern business relationships, Humphrey may have been rather conservative, looking askance at the

---

170   *Pierson's Directory for the City of Newark*, 1856 to 1857. Humphrey and Isabelle were listed as residing at 31 Camp Street, corner of Orchard.

171   *Dred Scott v. Sandford*, 60 U.S. 393 (U.S. Sup. Ct.1857). The Supreme Court, Chief Justice Roger Taney writing the opinion, decided that slaves or their descendants could never be citizens of the United States, that slaves were property, and that Congress lacked authority to prohibit slave-owners from taking their property into federal territories. In effect, the court gave its blessing to the extension of slavery throughout the West.

northern abolitionists stirring up trouble and the new Republican Party with its anti-slavery stance. The implications of the slavery issue for Western expansion and railroad profits were beginning to cause concern for investors and lenders. That would have caught Humphrey's attention. He knew that if borrowers defaulted and stock prices plunged, there would be another financial crisis, and his bank would be in the middle of it.

By 1857, the stock market had grown in size and importance; it had captured the popular imagination, as men and women from all walks of life—merchants, doctors, lawyers, clerks, and their wives—bought stocks from brokers. A generation had forgotten about the panic of 1837.

In September 1857, the market, reacting to banking and brokerage failures of late August, turned volatile. Bank depositors, fearing the worst, began withdrawing gold and silver from the New York City banks.[172] On September 12 the *Central America*, carrying more than fifteen tons of gold from California to New York, went down in a hurricane off the South Carolina coast.[173] News of the disaster heightened public concern, and the banks were forced to pay out more gold and silver to their anxious depositors. Running short of reserves, the banks began calling in their loans to brokerage firms which then had to sell off their securities to repay the bank loans, further depressing securities prices.[174] In the process, several prominent brokerage firms went bankrupt, and Wall Street panicked.

On Friday and Saturday, October 9 and 10, thousands of bank depositors lined up to retrieve their deposits, knowing that those at the head of the line would probably get their money and those farther back might well leave empty-handed. The banks barely survived the weekend. Withdrawals continued unabated on Monday. On Tuesday all hell broke loose, as an estimated 25,000 people crowded the Wall Street area, choking off the entrances to all the banking

---

172   On August 24, 1857, the New York office of the Ohio Life Insurance and Trust Company suffered a large embezzlement and was unable to collect on loans to western railroads. Short of cash, it stopped honoring depositors' claims. That was immediately followed by the failure of a well-known New York City brokerage firm. For a discussion of the causes of the panic, see Charles W. Calomaris and Larry Schweikart, "The Panic of 1857: Origins, Transmission, and Containment," *The Journal of Economic History*, 52 (Dec. 1991): 807-834.

173   The *Central America* was a three-masted wooden side-wheel steamship. The fifteen tons of U.S government gold was valued at $20 per ounce. The total value was $10 million, with a 2007 purchasing power of about $245 million. As a share of GDP, the current value would be about $35 Billion. That was in addition to the personal wealth of 581 passengers, of whom 425 were lost at sea as the vessel sank two-hundred miles off Charleston harbor.

174   Because banks were legally required to honor a depositor's demand for gold or silver in satisfaction of the deposit liability, maintaining adequate gold and silver reserves was critical. But bank reserves were never enough to stem a full-fledged panic.

offices.[175] George Templeton Strong, in his diary entry for those days, described the scene:

> Oct. 13 (Tues.): "Here is the 'crisis' at last....learned there was a run on the American Exchange Bank. Went into the street [Wall] and found it pretty densely crowded. Over a dozen banks... had stopped. A steady stream was setting in toward the counter...of every other bank in the street....depositors were calling for gold....At a little after two the Bank of New York, our oldest bank, had stopped..."

> Oct. 14 (Wed.): "We have **burst**. All the banks declined paying specie this morning."[176]

Another observer recalled the scene at Humphrey's Bank of America:

> Men were lined up in rows...swearing and fighting for the first chance to draw their funds. Some of the banks had guns from the Seventh Regiment to have ready for an emergency. I remember at the Bank of America there was a particularly long line of depositors...The Cashier informed the President that their funds were getting low. The President said "Get up the kegs of silver; it is nearly three o'clock and you can keep on paying until closing time." The Cashier pointed to a keg on the floor and said "That is our last keg!" The President, who was an old gentleman, was so shocked that he fainted there in the presence of the depositors.[177]

Bank of America, along with all the other New York banks, suspended payments to depositors.[178] Since the New York banks were at the center of the nation's banking system, banks around the country quickly followed suit.

175 James L. Huston, *The Panic of 1857 and the Coming of the Civil War* (Baton Rouge, LA; Louisiana State University Press, 1987), 22-23.
176 *Diary of George Templeton Strong*, 2: 360-61.
177 Henry Dexter, "Reminiscences of the Panic of 1857," *American Historical Magazine* (November 1906), 459. See also Burrows and Wallace, *Gotham*, 842-847.
178 Because they were legally obligated to pay depositors in gold or silver, the banks had to obtain a special dispensation from the Legislature to suspend payment.

With people hoarding gold and silver and banks lacking the reserves to support their normal lending activities, credit dried up; businesses, starved of credit, failed; the ranks of the unemployed grew, and investors, rich in August, were broke in October. A diary entry by Strong described the city in late October:

> Oct. 22 (Thurs.): "Depression continues...We are a very sick people just now. Walking down Broadway you pass...buildings begun last spring...that have gone up two stories, and stopped...Almost every shop has its placards...announcing... vast reduction of prices, sales at less than cost...This is far the worst period of public calamity and distress I have ever seen, and I fear it is but the beginning."

This was a crisis with international dimensions; that winter, panic spread from the United States to England and France. Even the Bank of England appeared uncertain in its moves.[179]

The sheer panic eventually subsided, but effects lingered on until well into the Civil War years. Just as the panic of 1837 was a searing personal experience for Thomas Mercein, the panic of 1857 was probably a similar experience for Humphrey Fuller. It was Humphrey's first brush with financial panic, but not his last.

At the end of the day, Humphrey returned to a scene of domestic tragedy, all-too-common in nineteenth century America—infant mortality. Isabelle bore Humphrey five children between 1856 and 1862: Henry; Elise Mercein; Charles Humphrey; Randolph Mercein; and Rosalie. Of the five, Henry, Randolph and Rosalie died within the first year; only Elise and Charles survived. Charles Fuller was Priscilla's father.

---

179 *Diary of George Templeton Strong*, 2: 367; "Like us, France and England have swelled up; like us they seem about to *burst*. There is pressure on the Bank of England and panic on the Bourse...The 'Old Lady of Threadneedle Street' is flustered." The financial crisis of 1857 was directly caused by panic, but behind the panic were real events. As in 1837, the Bank of England raised its interest rates and British investors shifted capital from the U.S. to Britain; the end of the Crimean War saw European grain production increase, leading to falling prices for U.S. producers; a number of western railroads, deprived of British capital, were forced to declare bankruptcy; western settlement slowed down, western land speculation collapsed, and land prices fell, causing speculators to default on their bank loans, etc. As in 1837, the Federal government played virtually no role in the crisis. And as in 1837, financial panic was followed by a lengthy depression with high unemployment.

Charles Humphrey Fuller, age 3, 1862

Humphrey and Isabelle lived through hard times: financial crisis, family tragedy, and then the Civil War.[180] Humphrey kept his head down, worked at his job, took care of his family, and didn't go off to war.[181] In 1864, the Fullers moved across the river to Brooklyn, where Humphrey and Isabelle both had family. With a population of around 250,000 Brooklyn, smaller than New York City but larger than Newark, was graced with attractive single-family homes, lawns, parks, and churches, lots of churches.[182]

---

180   The U.S Census 1860, Series M653, Roll 810, 395 shows Humphrey, thirty-five, working as a book-keeper in a bank. Isabell, thirty-eight, was home with their children and Irish servant, Mary Matthews, eighteen.
181   When the Conscription Act was passed in March 1863, Humphrey was thirty-eight and within the age range of men subject to the draft. But even in the highly unlikely event that his name was drawn (the category of men 20-35 was to be exhausted first before older men were called), he could have purchased a substitute. His chances of being called in the draft were slim. See Thomas H. O'Connor, *Civil War Boston, Home Front & Battlefield* (Boston; Northeastern University Press, 1997), 138-141. Of those eligible for the draft in Massachusetts, less than one-half of one percent actually ended up serving.
182   In Brooklyn, the Fullers lived first at 232 Bergen Street, about five blocks from the waterfront in what is now Cobble Hill, a fashionable part of town, later moving to 445 Franklin Avenue, further from the waterfront and the hustle of the expanding city.

Humphrey prospered in the postwar years.[183] It seemed, though, that boom always led to bust. Postwar prosperity was fueled, in large part, by the continued development of the railroads, the biggest transportation revolution of the century. Railroad securities dominated the stock and bond markets; railroad bonds were sold in Europe and the U.S. and the railroads used the money to build lines from one end of the country to the other. The railroads depended on the European market to sell their bonds, but in 1873 the Europeans had their own problems and stopped buying. The railroads, over-extended and unable to raise money, began defaulting on their obligations and the price of railroad securities plunged. Brokerage houses holding railroad securities were unable to repay their short-term bank loans, and pretty soon it was just like the autumn of 1857.

On September 18, 1873 several major Wall Street firms failed, notably Jay Cooke & Company, a major banking firm and a big investor in the railroads. That set off another panic in the stock market and a run on the banks.

Humphrey, now chief financial officer at Bank of America, nervously watched his dwindling supply of reserves disappear as angry and panicked depositors crowded into the bank, desperate to get their money. As in 1837 and 1857, the New York City banks were finally forced to suspend payment and close their doors until things quieted down.

With bank credit unavailable, about five thousand businesses went into bankruptcy. Unemployment reached very high levels, and a long depression followed, lasting through much of the 1870s.[184] Humphrey's bank survived and he kept his job.

Nine months after the 1873 panic Humphrey and Isabelle Fuller, with their daughter Elise, sat in the Adelphi Academy school chapel at Lafayette Avenue and St. John's Place, Brooklyn, waiting for the graduation ceremonies to begin.[185] It was June 20, 1874, and their son Charles, age fifteen, was about to graduate.

---

183   U.S. Census 1870, Series M593, Roll 949: 473. The 1870 census got three of the four Fuller names wrong: "Fuller Ham," "Isabella," "Ellen," and "Charles." Humphrey reported stocks and bonds valued at $2,000, a big improvement over the $300 he had claimed in 1860. Humphrey's personal property would have a current value of about $35,000 in terms of the consumer price index. But the relative importance of $2,000 was much greater than that. In terms of per capita gross domestic product (a rough measure of the average wage), $2,000 in 1870 would be comparable to $481,000 today. In other words, $2,000 was nothing to sneeze at in 1870.
184   See Frederic S. Mishkin, "Asymmetric Information and Financial Crises," *Financial Markets and Financial Crises*, ed. R. Glenn Hubbard (Cambridge, MA; National Bureau of Economic Research, 1991), 69-108. One factor in the 1873 crisis was that the railroads had issued a large volume of complex securities that plummeted in value when investors realized there was no tangible value behind them.
185   Founded in 1863, Adelphi was located in the Bay Ridge section of Brooklyn. It was the first high school in New York City to admit women, and by Charles Fuller's time girls were enrolled in all departments. Over 140 years later, it is still a top-rated preparatory school. Humphrey Taylor Fuller, a widower then living with his son, died in Brooklyn, May 18, 1977.

18 Sept. 1873: Investors running to sell after news of the failure of Jay Cooke & Company
(Photo of a painting by Howard Pyle, published in Elisha Benjamin Andrews,
The United States in Our Own Time, New York, Charles Scribner's Sons, 1903)

Humphrey Fuller was undoubtedly dressed in his three-piece black banker's suit. The ladies, more colorful in long dresses and big floral hats with all manner of exotic bird feathers, discreetly flicked their fans back and forth to keep cool. The Fuller group may have included old Humphrey Taylor Fuller, now 88, his joints stiff from a lifetime of farming, his mind verging on, if not deep into, senility. Headmaster Sprague opened the ceremonies and called on young Fuller to deliver the salutatorian address. As reported in *The Brooklyn Daily Eagle*:

> Mr. Charles H. Fuller delivered an oration in Latin, whereat the audience was greatly edified and looked as though they understood every word! The address was delivered with fluency, and in a manner which showed that the orator understood what he

was saying, which is more than can be said of many orators in classic tongues at this day in schools and colleges.[186]

It was a long afternoon with poetry readings and six orations, including "The Higher Education of Girls," a controversial topic in those days when higher education was considered bad for a young girl's health.

That fall, Charles Fuller began his freshman year at Amherst College in Massachusetts. There were prominent Amherst graduates in Brooklyn, notably the Reverend Henry Ward Beecher, class of 1834 and minister of the Plymouth Church in Brooklyn. Beecher was the most famous minister in America and a star on the lecture circuit (the year Fuller graduated from Adelphi, Beecher was charged with seducing the wife of his best friend, but acquitted after a sensational trial that was front page news). The Reverend Dr. Richard Storrs, class of 1839, was minister of the Church of the Pilgrims and another national figure. Professor W. C. Peckham, Amherst class of 1867, was on the faculty at Adelphi.

At Amherst, Fuller was a diligent scholar. He graduated in 1878, age nineteen, with a Phi Beta Kappa key and the prize for political economy. After attending Columbia Law School, he was admitted to the New York Bar and started his law practice in 1880. In the early 1880s, Fuller and his father probably commuted together by ferry across the East River to their offices in the Wall Street area (even after the opening of the Brooklyn Bridge in 1883, the ferry would have been a more comfortable commute than the jam-packed trolley that crossed the bridge). Fuller also got around to other business. He met, courted and married Mary Everett Webb from Winchester, Massachusetts, Priscilla's mother.[187] Charles and Mary shared common New England roots. Having examined the Fuller roots, let's at least take a look at Mary's parents, who like the Fullers were descended from English Puritans.

---

186   *The Brooklyn Daily Eagle*, June 20 1874, 2 (unattributed article).
187   In those days, courtship could be a rather complicated minuet, requiring time and patience for the man to win over both the girl and her family. See Edmund Morris, *The Rise of Theodore Roosevelt* (New York; Coward, McCann & Geoghegan; 1979), 119-125; describes young Roosevelt's courtship of Alice Lee in 1879 and his strategy for winning over Alice's family as well as Alice.

4. Dwights, Webbs, & the California Gold Rush

Mary Everett Webb, Charles Fuller's young bride, was the daughter of Francis Everett Webb and Mary Frances ("Fanny") Dwight, each of whom participated in large events of the nineteenth century.

Fanny Dwight. Born in 1828 to Mary Moore Farrell and Joseph Dwight, cashier of the local bank, Fanny grew up with her two sisters in Hallowell, a town of about 2,500 people.[188] Hallowell lies on the western side of the Kennebec River two miles south of Augusta, the state capital, and five miles east of Winthrop. The streets of Hallowell, with old Federal-style homes, lead down to the small commercial center and harbor on the river. When Fanny was a young girl, Hallowell was thriving, with shipyards, daily steamer service to Boston, an ample supply of lawyers and doctors, excellent schools, a granite quarry, and a winter ice business. Great blocks of ice were cut from the river by strong men and shipped to ports as far south as Cuba.

---

188   Fanny was a descendant of John Dwight, who left Dedham, England in 1635 and settled in Dedham, Massachusetts. Dwight was part of the great Puritan migration, a movement of some 20,000 Puritans from England to the Massachusetts Bay Colony between 1630 and 1642. Dwight was a prominent landowner in Dedham, and one of twelve at the first Dedham town meeting. He served as Selectman from 1639 to 1655, and was a trustee of the first publicly supported school in New England. Dwight's son Timothy was also a Dedham selectman. He negotiated land acquisitions from the Indians, including some difficult negotiations with Metacom, Chief of the Wampanoag, who, as "King Philip," led the Indians to war against the English in 1676. Timothy Dwight served as captain in the militia during King Philip's War. He lived to be eighty-eight, married six times, survived five wives, and produced fourteen children. Mary Fuller's Dwight ancestors migrated from Dedham to Western Massachusetts, where they were "thrifty farmers," innkeepers, military officers, and judges, and from there to Hallowell, Maine.

At some point Fanny met Cyrus Clark Richmond, youngest son of a widow living in nearby Winthrop.[189] Cyrus and Fanny may have had an "understanding" before Cyrus left for San Francisco in the spring of 1849 to make his fortune.

In setting out for California in the spring of 1849, Cyrus was part of a national craze. California had become a U.S. possession only in February 1848 with the formal end of the Mexican War.[190] Gold deposits had been discovered in January at John Sutter's sawmill, south fork of the American River, Sacramento Valley. Sutter tried to keep it secret but couldn't.[191] Men began heading for the valley, surreptitiously at first. Then the trickle turned into a stream. From all over California men abandoned their farms and businesses; workmen walked off the job; sailors deserted their ships; soldiers deserted their regiments: all heading to the valley. In the fall of 1848, Eastern newspapers began publicizing the gold strike and the news reached Europe, South America and Asia. By spring, a torrent of men was heading for the valley from all over the world.

To the residents of Winthrop, California was as exotic and far away as Timbuktu. A lot of people in Winthrop thought the California gold craze was a hoax; they assumed Cyrus would be back, tail between his legs, nothing to show for it.[192] But he was determined to prove himself, and the California gold rush was his big opportunity.

Arriving in San Francisco the first week of June 1849, Cyrus was among the early arrivals from the East Coast. He found a small town with a generous harbor that a year earlier had boasted a population of 800. By the time Cyrus arrived, the population had grown to about 2,000 with new arrivals every day. It was a man's town: from April 1849 to April 1850, 60,244 men and 1,979 women arrived in San Francisco.[193]

189   Cyrus Richmond was born July 14, 1825. His father, Capt. Leonard Richmond of Winthrop, Maine, was born January 25, 1789, and died June 28, 1832. He was a veteran of the War of 1812. His mother was Nancy Sweet, also of Winthrop. Cyrus's grandfather, Capt. Nathan Richmond, was a native of Winthrop and a Revolutionary War veteran. Cyrus had an older brother, Arnold Sweet and an older sister, Nancy, both of whom lived in and around Winthrop. Joshua Bailey Richmond, *The Richmond Family 1594-1896* (Boston; J.B.Richmond, 1897), 213.

190   On February 2, 1848, the U.S. and Mexico signed the Treaty of Guadalupe-Hidalgo in which Mexico ceded California, Nevada, Arizona, New Mexico, Colorado and Texas to the United States.

191   Immediately after the discovery, Sutter tried to establish his ownership of the land through written confirmation by Colonel Richard Mason, then the U.S. military governor of occupied California. Mason turned him down on the basis that, in January 1848, California was Mexican territory. See Rand Richards, *Mud Blood and Gold, San Francisco in 1849* (San Francisco; Heritage House Publishers, 2009), 8-9.

192   Letter, dated June 27, 1850, from Cyrus to his mother: "How do all the people in Winthrop. Do they still think that California is a hoax? Time will prove all things." *C.C. Richmond Letters*, SMC 11, Box 13, Folders 3 and 4, California State Library, Sacramento, CA.

193   *Hallowell Gazette*, November 30, 1850, 1, col. 7, reporting the arrival of a steamer in New York carrying a large number of persons returning from California "sick of Chagres fever, worn out from their hardships in California, absolutely penniless..." As for the proportion of male to female arrivals, see entry for April 15, 1850 in <http://www.sfmuseum.org/hist/chron2.html.> (last accessed March 18, 2010). Most of the men passed through San Francisco on their way to the Sacramento Valley.

Cyrus described San Francisco in a letter to his brother: the harbor was clogged with abandoned ships because "the crews have left and gone to the diggins [gold mines]"; gambling was the town's biggest business, and as for the city's main hotel, the Parker House, "the whole house is full of gamblers;" shovels, needed for gold prospecting, were selling for twice the price back east, but clothing was "cheap as dirt." Because women were scarce, it cost Cyrus as much to get a shirt washed as it did to buy a new one.[194] The medium of exchange was "gold dust." There was no paper money and coins were scarce. It wasn't actually "dust," but tiny flakes and kernels of gold carried around in bags, generally valued at about $16 per ounce, and weighed in the shops on scales.[195]

Shortly after he arrived, Cyrus acquired a lot at the corner of Montgomery and Stockton, built a store, and set up his wholesale pharmacy business: "C.C.RICHMOND & CO." Within a year the business was thriving. He had a profitable side line lending money at 10 percent monthly interest.[196]

A family friend from Maine, checking in on Cyrus for his older brother Arnold, advised Arnold not to worry:

> I find your Brother in good health and spirits and up to his eyes in business. I should think according to appearance that he was in as good business as anyone...and makes loans at 10 per cent per month...they all say as near as I can find out he is worth about 75,000....

Arnold Richmond must have been impressed; $75,000 was a fortune back in Winthrop.[197] Arnold, obviously skeptical about how long the gold craze would last, tried to persuade Cyrus to invest some of his San Francisco income in good, solid, Winthrop property. Cyrus preferred the investment returns in San Francisco: "I have been thinking about sending some money home to invest, but while it yields me the income it does I cannot make up my mind to."

194   Letter, dated June 30, 1849, from Cyrus to his uncle, *C.C.Richmond Letters*.
195   As to the use of gold as the currency of San Francisco, see *Mud, Blood and Gold*, 63.
196   His interest income of about $12,775 yearly would be about $350,000 in current dollars. Cyrus had to share that with his business partner, Dr. Maginnis, back in Winthrop. See letter dated June 27, 1850, from Cyrus to his mother: "Business is first rate now, better than it ever was before....I have four clerks... then another store on Clarks Point where I have two clerks," *C.C. Richmond Letters*. Money lending at ten percent a month was not unusual in San Francisco. See Le Roy Armstrong and J.O.Denny, *Financial California* (San Francisco; Coast Banker Pub. Co., 1916), 54-58. Early San Francisco banking houses included Palmer, Cook & Co, Baldwin & Co, Wells & Company and Dunbar & Co. All had failed by the end of 1851.
197   Letter, dated May 21, 1850, James W. Sayward to Arnold Richmond, *C.C. Richmond Letters*. In current dollars, Cyrus' share in the business, assuming he was in a 50/50 partnership, would be worth about $1 million.

Cyrus returned home on a visit in the fall of 1850. In a letter to his mother, he was concerned about what might happen to his business, given the epidemic of fires in San Francisco; he also took steps to ensure that he had money available when he got home, informing his mother that

> I have sent by this steamer a draft to the Northern Bank Hallowell to be collected and held in their hands subject to my own order. I have requested them to send you a duplicate certificate of "deposit...[198]

The cashier at the Northern Bank was Joseph Dwight, Fanny's father and Cyrus's banker. Before leaving San Francisco, Cyrus encouraged his mother to go over to Hallowell and show the gold samples he had sent home to his "particular friends....You know very well who I mean." Once home in Winthrop, it didn't take long for Cyrus to propose. They married in Hallowell, December 30, 1850. In March, they set out for San Francisco.

Fanny and Cyrus weren't the only young people making the trip—thousands were leaving small towns and farms in New England and heading to San Francisco.[199] In October 1850, the *Hallowell Gazette*'s California correspondent reported the arrival of a ship in San Francisco with thirty to forty girls from Boston and "a larger sprinkling of Maine girls, and we doubt not their friends will be glad to learn that their prospects are good..." [200]

It was not just about getting rich or finding a husband. It was also about escaping the confinement of the small town for the freedom of living three thousand miles away from the watchful eyes of parents, grandparents and neighbors.[201]

In the spring of 1851, there were basically three ways to get from Hallowell to San Francisco: the overland route by wagon and mule across the West; the long

---

198   Letter, dated June 27, 1850, from Cyrus Richmond to his mother, *C.C. Richmond Letters*. It would take a while for that draft, sailing around Cape Horn, to get to Hallowell. The bank would then "collect" the draft by communicating with the company where Cyrus had his account, perhaps a Boston bank or one of his suppliers. Having made those arrangements, Cyrus could call on the Northern Bank for cash (in the form of gold and silver coins) to use during his visit and return trip.

199   See William Strauss and Neil Howe, *Generations: The History of America's Future, 1584 to 2069* (New York; HarperCollins, 1991), 206-216, describing the "gilded generation" born around 1825. Other girls were going from New England to San Francisco in the mid-nineteenth century. See Diantha Lamb Barstow, *The Colemans of California* (Baltimore; Gateway Press, 2003), 75-81.

200   *Hallowell Gazette*, October 19, 1850, 2, col. 6.

201   New York was another city drawing the young and adventurous from all over the world. Just as Cyrus and Fanny were striking out for San Francisco, so Humphrey Fuller was leaving the family farm in Connecticut for New York City. And the same thing was happening in Europe—Johann Vestner left his small Bavarian town and sailed to New York in 1849, joining the millions of Irish and Germans leaving their small towns for New York and points west.

voyage around Cape Horn; or the shorter route across the Isthmus of Panama. Cyrus chose to take his bride by way of Panama. They sailed by steam ship from New York to Aspinwall on the Atlantic coast of Panama. From Aspinwall it was sixty miles to Panama City on the Pacific.[202] Crossing Panama, they covered the first half by flat-bottomed boat up the Chagres River to Gorgona. At Gorgona, they hired mules and a guide to take them through thirty miles of jungle to Panama City.

Though it was quicker than going around Cape Horn, Panama exposed them to the risks of cholera, typhoid fever, yellow fever and malaria. There were other risks. In November 1850, five travelers en route to San Francisco drowned on the Chagres; in March 1851, about the time Fanny and Cyrus were sailing from New York to Panama, eleven travelers—six men, three women, and two children— were murdered on the Chagres by a gang of locals "who hated the whites."[203]

Cyrus and Fanny arrived in San Francisco the afternoon of May 3, 1851 after six to eight weeks of travel. They checked into the new Union Hotel, which impressed Fanny with its elegant furnishings: she was "astonished" to find such a magnificently furnished hotel in San Francisco. But that night San Francisco experienced its fifth and worst great fire in the space of two years. This one burnt down their hotel, destroyed much of the city and virtually the entire business district. In just ten hours the fire consumed eighteen blocks and two thousand buildings.

In a letter to her mother-in-law, Fanny described the trip and the events surrounding their arrival in San Francisco:

My Dear Mother,

I presume you will have seen in the paper before receiving our account of the terrible fire that has again visited this city... It was the first large fire I ever was in the midst of for so we seemed to be and as we were most fortunate to escape not only with our lives, but with all our baggage.

We arrived about 4 o'clock on Saturday afternoon May 3rd after a most delightful voyage of seventeen days from Panama.... How I wished every day that all at home could see us, and know how comfortably, and with how little fatigue we got along. Going up the Chagres River and the ride from Gorgona

202   In 1851 construction of a railroad across Panama had just begun and would not be completed until 1855
203   *Hallowell Gazette*, November 30, 1850, 2, col. 5; March 29, 1851, 2, col. 5.

to Panama which is such a "bug-bear" to almost every one in the States was a charming excursion, the scenery magnificent, the foliage on the trees, the vines and flowers, the natives' "ranches" scattered all along the banks of the river, and on the sides of the mountains, every thing one saw and heard, was beautiful and romantic and strange.

Panama, I must confess, I was disgusted with. It's true there are some things to interest one there, some pleasant walks... and some old Cathedrals to visit; but I think one day there would fully satisfy my curiosity, for with every natural advantage, except perhaps the heat of the climate, it is one of the most filthy, disagreeable places I was ever in. Acapulco, where we stopped nearly two days on our way up, is a much smaller but decidedly much more pleasant Spanish town. It is a famous place for fruit, and you may be sure, Cyrus obtained a good supply of Pine Apples, Bananas, Limes, and Oranges, on which we have almost lived ever since.

When Cyrus and Fanny arrived in May 1851, San Francisco had exploded from the small boomtown of 1849 into a city of about 25,000, bursting with energy. Municipal government was not up to the challenge, and the result was a breakdown of law and order. Every day thousands arrived in search of riches. Gambling, prostitution, crime, arson, public drunkenness, cholera and small-pox were all thriving. [204]

California had become a State the year before Fanny arrived, but she talked about it as if it were a foreign country. She was optimistic, though shocked by the prices:

I like San Francisco very much. Tis true, I think I could be well contented any where with my husband, but aside from that I think I shall like the place. Cyrus has many acquaintances here and we made several very pleasant ones on our way. Within a very short walk are four ladies whom I like much besides those

---

[204] See San Francisco History Index at < http://www.zpub.com/sf50/sf/hgpop.html.> (last accessed March 18, 2010). The population estimates for the years 1849 to 1852 lack precision, and there are different estimates, but in 1849, the population appears to have grown from 850 to 25,000; by 1852, it had reached about 36,000.

in the house Tis quite amusing to go out shopping here, and
mark the great difference in the prices of goods, in California
and the States. ...Bonnets which could have been bought in the
States last Autumn for fifty cents here, with a little trimming
on them, are sold for twenty dollars. But of course everything
has increased ten-fold in value, since the fire.[205]

In 1851 San Francisco was not without culture: the city had daily newspapers, theater, opera, elegant hotels, dances and balls, and churches. For Fanny,
there would have been a much wider range of cultural and social opportunities
than she had experienced in Hallowell. But the challenges of living in San Francisco under the constant threat of earthquakes and fires were daunting. From
the day of her arrival in 1851 she would have experienced three significant
earthquakes and two major fires during the course of the year.[206]

San Francisco undoubtedly tested Fanny's New England values. There were
people there who shared those values, but in 1851 it was a den of iniquity
compared with Hallowell or Winthrop. Sarah Royce, a young woman brought
up in the East and living in San Francisco in 1850-51 with her husband, found
men and women who shared her moral and religious values. But she was also
disgusted by much of what she saw: loose women, adultery, divorce, drunkenness, rampant speculation, reckless spending, cheating, and street crime.[207]
Sarah was particularly upset by the women who appeared to be refined and morally upright, but who succumbed to money and flattery and abandoned their
husbands.

In one of his letters back home, Cyrus described San Francisco as a whirl-
pool that could easily drown a young man from New England:

But I would not advise young men to come if they are making
a good living at home, for here they are away from home surrounded by every vice. No sin which you could think of but
what is here to entice and destroy. No laws no formal society.
No parents to give advice and look after the young and I know
of many who before they came here never knew what it was to
drink, never gambled in their life....Now, they are drunkards

---

205   Letter, dated May 12, 1851, from Mary Frances to her mother-in-law, *C.C. Richmond Letters*.
206   The fires were May 4 and June 22, 1851; the earthquakes were May 13 to 17, November 12 to 15 and
December 26, 1851. <http://www.sfmuseum.org/hist/chron2.html.>
207   Sarah Royce, *A Frontier Lady's Recollections* (New Haven, Yale University Press, 1932), 107-119.

and gamblers and have lost all respect for themselves or the parents who have watched over them from childhood...They have found every thing so perfectly different from what they expected that now they care not what becomes of them ...and the old song as regards California is true:

Them now drinks who never drank before
And them who always drank now drinks the more[208]

Cyrus and Fanny lived on Jackson Street. Cyrus's first pharmacy, at Jackson and Stockton, had been destroyed in the great fire that swept the city the night of 4 May.[209] By December 1851 Cyrus had acquired a much larger and grander store on Jackson Street, a brick building between Montgomery and Sansome. He and Fanny had probably converted the top floor into a comfortable apartment. Describing it to his worried mother, he emphasized that it was "perfectly Fire Proof." In the same letter he assured his mother that he and Fanny were "well and happy and she never enjoyed so good health in her life as she does now."[210]

Arnold Richmond was still asking his friends in San Francisco to check on his younger brother. B.W. Sawyer wrote back to Arnold:

I presume you would like to hear from your Brother C.C.... he is well and says he is doing a first rate Business, and I should so Judge by appearances, he has moved from his store in Jackson street to a fire proof building on Montgomery street, a much more desirable location for his trade, his store is fitted up in splendid style and makes quite a show.[211]

Cyrus had recovered from the fire of May 1851; but he and others, fed up with the arsonists and criminals who seemed to do as they pleased, formed the

---

208   Letter dated June 30 1849, from Cyrus Richmond to his uncle, *C.C. Richmond Letters*.
209   The *San Francisco Directory* (San Francisco; Charles P. Kimball, 1850), lists the Richmonds as living at Jackson Street. The *Hallowell Gazette,* August 9, 1851, 3, col. 2, reported that "in a list of the sufferers by the fire, Mr. C.C. Richmond's loss is put down at $6, 500,"about $182,000 today in terms of the consumer price index. But that understates the real difference. Relative to per capita gross domestic product (a proxy for the average wage), the value of $6,500 today would be about $2.6 million.
210   Letter dated December 4, 1851, from Cyrus Richmond to his mother, *C.C.Richmond Letters*.
211   Letter, dated December 28, 1851, from B.W. Sawyer to Arnold Richmond, *C.C.Richmond Letters*.

San Francisco Committee of Vigilance.[212] Organized in June, the constitution described the conditions that led to its formation:

> Whereas it has become apparent to the Citizens of San Francisco that there is no security for life and property, either under the regulations of Society as at present exists or under the laws as now administered, therefore the Citizens whose names are hereunto attached do unite themselves into an association for the maintenance of the peace and good order of Society and the preservation of the lives and property of the Citizens of San Francisco and do bind themselves each unto the other to do and perform every lawful act for the maintenance of law and order and to sustain the laws when faithfully and properly administered but we are determined that no thief, burglar, incendiary or assassin shall escape punishment, either by the quibbles of the law, the insecurity of prisons the carelessness or corruption of the Police or a laxity of those who pretend to administer justice. [213]

Within a week, the committee had organized itself and acquired a headquarters on the west side of Battery Street between California and Pine Streets. When summoned by bell, members were expected to drop what they were doing and immediately go to headquarters. When a prisoner was to be tried, the members would be called to act as a jury, hear evidence, convict, or acquit by majority vote, and carry out the sentence. The members, who as a matter of course would carry pistols, were bound "to defend and sustain each other in carrying out the determined action of the Committee at the hazard of their lives and fortunes."

During the committee's first week several members caught a "John Jenkins" in the act of stealing a safe. The membership was summoned; Jenkins was tried, convicted, and hanged—all in the course of a day. On July 11, an Englishman,

---

212   Porter Garnett ed., *Publications of the Academy of Pacific Coast History*, Vol. 1, No. 7, Papers of the San Francisco Committee of Vigilance of 1851, (Berkeley, CA; University of California, Berkeley, July 1910). The papers include the signature pages, showing Richmond's signature as # 311. The membership eventually grew to 711.
213   Mary Floyd Williams, *History of the San Francisco Committee of Vigilance of 1851* (Berkeley, CA; University of California Press, 1921), 205. See also Selected Correspondence of Robert Effinger, California History, Vol. 82, No. 1, *The Magazine of the California Historical Society* (2004), 65.

James Stuart, was tried, convicted and hanged. Stuart had confessed to multiple crimes, including murder.

On August 21, the committee caught, tried, and convicted two men, Whitaker and McKenzie, of robbery and arson. But the sheriff, coming in the middle of the night with an armed force, removed the prisoners to the city jail. The next day thirty-six armed members of the committee forcibly retrieved the two men, and within twenty-four hours they were hanging from wooden rafters outside Committee headquarters, cheered on by a large crowd.[214] Whitaker and McKenzie were the last to be hanged. As the local authorities stepped up the pace of law enforcement, the committee faded into the background.

During its brief one-hundred-day life, the committee arrested ninety-one, hanged four, whipped one, deported fourteen to Australia, and handed fifteen over to the authorities. The rest were presumably discharged.[215] There is no record of how many criminals fled the city on their own to escape vigilante justice.

Warmly supported by the local newspapers and probably by a majority of the people, the committee was not universally popular. The governor, mayor and some judges were, not surprisingly, hostile. After the executions of August 24, a San Francisco judge described the committee as "nothing else but murderers. [216] But it appears to have largely accomplished its purpose: inspiring fear in the hearts of would-be criminals and ridding San Francisco of some bad characters.

In May of 1852, Cyrus was anxiously awaiting his partner, Dr. Magginis of Winthrop. He was hoping to buy out Magginis's interest and resolve their disagreement over the value of the business.[217] But Cyrus was struck down by smallpox or typhoid fever and died on June 1, 1852.[218]

---

214   George R. Stewart, *Committee of Vigilance, Revolution in San Francisco, 1851* (New York; Ballantine Books, 1964), describes the executions and events surrounding them.

215   See Stewart, *Committee of Vigilance*, 288.

216   *Hallowell Gazette*, August 16, 1851, 2, col. 6. Judge Harvey Brown was a notable and vocal opponent of the committee.

217   Letter, dated December 4, 1851, from Cyrus to his mother, *C.C. Richmond Letters*.

218   The *Sacramento Daily Union*, on June 4, 1852, reported the death of "C.C. Richmond, druggist, of San Francisco." The Richmond obelisk in the Winthrop cemetery cites smallpox as cause of death. The Dwight family history cites typhoid. See Benjamin W. Dwight, *The History of the Descendants of John Dwight of Dedham, Massachusetts* (New York; John F. Trow & Son, 1874), 2:930. Both diseases were common in San Francisco, 1852. "Richmond, C.C., born Maine d. 1852 age 25" was buried in Yerba Buena Cemetery, Grove No. 1801. In his will, dated March 28, 1852, Richmond left Fanny a life interest in one half of his estate, with the rest going to his brother Arnold, sister Nancy and their heirs.

Cyrus and Mary Frances Richmond, Priscilla's grandmother, ca. 1852

Fanny may have enjoyed her time in San Francisco, and as a widow her prospects for remarriage in a city with about fifty men for every woman were excellent. But she apparently had no stomach for life as a young widow in San Francisco. Her gold rush adventure was over. She returned immediately to her family and settled down to life as a widow in Winthrop and Hallowell. Six years later she married Francis Webb, a rising young lawyer in Winthrop.

Francis Everett Webb. Francis Webb was the youngest of seven children of Samuel Webb and Oliver Lambert of Winthrop, Maine.[219] His father, Samuel Webb, served as president of a local literary society, the Anderson Institute, a forum for discussion of scientific and philosophical subjects. Webb also served as a Justice of the Peace and for several years operated a general store in town. He died 17 April 1840, apparently insolvent.[220]

Francis Webb was eleven when his father died. Forced to find work, he started out as a farmhand and day laborer. Studying at night, he eventually managed to obtain a teaching position at a school in Augusta. The head of the school was impressed with Webb and loaned him the funds to attend Bowdoin College in Brunswick, Maine.

Webb graduated from Bowdoin in 1853, Phi Beta Kappa and at the top of his class. At his graduation, he delivered the valedictory address. Offered a teaching position in Greek and Latin, he chose instead to pursue a career in the law. He clerked for a judge, was admitted to the Kennebec County Bar in 1856 and set up his law practice in Winthrop.

At some point during the 1850s, Webb began courting the young widow, Fanny Dwight Richmond, a frequent visitor to her late husband's family in Winthrop. Webb was handsome, Fanny was attractive, and they were both about the same age. They married on December 30, 1858.[221] In 1862 Fanny gave birth to their first daughter, Mary Everett; in 1865, she produced another daughter, Annie Dwight.

Webb was elected to the Maine Legislature in 1860. On April 24, 1861, with the onset of the Civil War, Governor Israel Washburn called Webb and his fellow legislators to an emergency session. In his opening address Washburn referred to "combinations" against the laws of the United States by the "slave-holding states," which "have, for their real object and ultimate purpose, the destruction of the government." He urged the legislators to support

---

219   Francis Webb was descended from Christopher Webb, who left England in 1642 and settled in Braintree, Massachusetts, part of the Puritan migration to the Massachusetts Bay Colony. Webb's son, Christopher 2nd, was born in England. He was a lawyer, surveyor and selectman of Braintree. He represented the town of Braintree during the crisis of 1688, when the English revolted, deposed their king, and installed William and Mary on the throne. In Boston, the colonists put the colonial governor, Edmund Andros, in jail and then met to determine what should be their course of action given the chaotic situation in England. That was the high water mark of Webb political activity. The Webbs migrated from Braintree to Maine; first to Skowhegan and eventually to Winthrop, by virtue of marrying into the Lambert family, among the early Winthrop settlers.

220   His widow died 11 August 1866. Samuel and Olive Webb are buried in the Maple Cemetery in downtown Winthrop. Their seven children have produced numerous descendants many of whom live in and around Winthrop. A descendant of Francis Webb's brother, Samuel Webb Jr.,Lee Davis, lives in nearby Monmouth. Lee is a veteran of the Second World War. Recently widowed, Lee has five children and at least two grandchildren.

221   *Vital Records of Hallowell, Maine,* "Marriages, 1797-1860."

President Lincoln's call for troops to aid in "suppressing" those combinations.[222] Webb and his fellow legislators voted to raise five Maine regiments, including the famous Twentieth that repelled the Confederate assault on Little Roundtop at Gettysburg, the turning point of the Civil War.[223]

At thirty-two Webb suffered from a heart condition, and was not physically qualified for military service. But the war affected everybody, including the Webbs. His sister-in-law, Ella Louisa Dwight, had married a young naval officer, Walter Titcomb (son of a famous Hallowell sea captain).[224] Before the battle of Mobile Bay, Titcomb had written to his father:

> Farragut is about to attack Mobile: he has not men enough now; and there will be hot work before he gets in.... I have offered my services for the impending fight, and asked to be transferred temporarily to some vessel that will take an active part in the engagement. I came out here to fight for the cause; and I wish now to do all in my power to advance it; and I will never go home and have it said that I lay idle at the Navy Yard while gallant men were struggling to take Mobile. Have I done right, father?[225]

Titcomb was an officer on the Monitor *Tecumseh,* which struck a torpedo and sank. He went down with his ship leaving a twenty-three-year-old widow with one child.

During the war years, Webb practiced law, served in the Legislature, and as town treasurer and director of the Winthrop School. In 1864, he was re-elected to the Legislature. After the war, Governor Joshua Chamberlain, Webb's old colleague on the Bowdoin faculty, appointed him state banking commissioner.[226] In 1869, the citizens of Winthrop again chose Webb to represent Winthrop in the Legislature.

---

222   Address by Governor Israel Washburn to the Legislature, April 24, 1861, *Maine Public Documents,* 1861 (Bowdoin College Library). The resolution of the Legislature responding to the governor is attached to the printed copy of the Address.

223   See Edward Longacre, *Joshua Chamberlain, The Soldier and the Man* (Conshohocken, Pa.; Combined Publishing, 1999). The Twentieth was led by Colonel Joshua Chamberlain, who had been a colleague of Webb's on the Bowdoin faculty. Chamberlain was awarded the Medal of Honor, promoted to general, and after the war served as governor of Maine.

224   The first ironclad ship, designed for the U.S. Navy in 1862, it rode low in the water, had a revolving turret with guns and thick armor.

225   *Dwight Family,* 2: 930-31.

226   See *Annual Report of the Bank Commissioners of the State of Maine,* 1867 (Maine Public Documents).

Francis Webb, rising young lawyer, 1866

The evening of November 19, 1869 Webb relaxed over dinner and wine with a neighbor "in his usual good humor and sociability." He awoke in the early morning with a painful attack of angina and died within the hour.[227]

Articles about Webb by those who knew him, published after his death, tell us something about how he appeared to his contemporaries. His pastor, the Reverend Edward P. Baker, described Webb as

---

227   *Lewiston Weekly Journal,* November 25, 1869: December 2, 1869 (Obituaries).

The idol of his own and the stay and support of other house-
holds, a much-beloved Sunday school teacher, a steady and
hearty supporter of gospel institutions, a school director and
the town treasurer, a brother of high mark in the Masonic fraternity, a lawyer surrounded by a numerous clientage...and at
the time of his decease, county attorney and a member of the
legislature elect. He occupied a large place among us...

And he was all this amid much bodily infirmity. With the
relentless hand of disease fastened upon him...he has supposed
for years that an early and probably sudden death awaited him.

Baker went on to describe Webb's "hidden life:"

He lived, to a certain extent, a hidden life. He appeared to the
casual observer to be only a moral man; but there was really
much of spirituality in him. He had a deep reverence for God,
and a hearty love for divine truth. He was a constant student
of the Bible. He loved to teach in the Sabbath school. Though
he never said he was a Christian, yet his intimate friends have
felt, that in this regard, his deeds spoke louder than his words,
and that he had the power, though not the form, the substance,
though not the sign....[228]

Following Webb's death, the Legislature devoted the session of January 12,
1870 to his memory.[229] Representative May of Winthrop offered his perspective
on Webb as lawyer and friend:

As a legal counselor, he was eminent in his profession; as an
advocate he was reserved and diffident. He possessed a keen
intellect and a well balanced mind, and when aroused, seldom
failed in convincing his auditors of the justness of his cause.
Although he earned his bread by his profession, he strove to
discourage litigation; ever counseling his clients to reconcile
their differences if possible....

228   *Lewiston Weekly Journal,* December 2, 1869.
229   *Daily Kennebec Journal,* January 13, 1870.

He was a congenial companion, a profound scholar, and within the circle of his acquaintance universally beloved. His sparkling wit and repartee, his social bearing and keen perception, made him the favorite of his townsmen.

Although successful in law and politics, Webb was not driven by ambition for higher office. That puzzled some of his contemporaries, who regretted that his "excessive modesty," "distrust of his own powers," and seeming lack of ambition prevented him from achieving the higher office warranted by his abilities. Webb's response to those urging him on to greater things: "My ambition for this world is only to do good and prepare for the life to come."

Webb may have had his eye on the "life to come," but he also left his widow with a comfortable estate.[230] After Webb's death, Fanny and her two daughters continued to live in Winthrop until 1874, when she moved with her daughters to Winchester, Massachusetts. There, she oversaw the wedding in 1884 of her eldest daughter, Mary Everett, to Charles Fuller, a young lawyer from Brooklyn.[231]

* * *

Mary Fuller, age 4, in 1866

---

230   In the 1870 U.S. Census, Kennebec County at 685, Fanny Dwight Webb reported real estate of $5,000 and personal property of $28,000, about $550,000 in current purchasing power but a much larger sum in terms of the economy as it was in 1870 (closer to $5 million).

231   Fanny's other daughter, Annie Dwight, married John Page, an older Haverhill lawyer, in 1886. Page, who was seventeen years older, died in 1893.and Annie Page later married William W. Holt. See U.S. Census 1900, Roll T623_668, 13A. Their son, Kenneth Holt, was born July 7, 1901. He was Priscilla's favorite cousin.

Mary Fuller, 1888, 26 years old

Mary Fuller, fifth from left, back row; Charles Fuller, right end back row,
June 18, 1887, Iona Island on the Hudson

In the group photo, Mary Fuller stands out in the middle, slim and straight, in a high-necked dress, with a great white plume in her hat.[232] She and her friends are all young, trying to look casual in their suits and long dresses. In the same photo, her husband, short (he was 5'6") and slightly stocky with a cap and small mustache, seems to be saying something amusing that makes the girl next to him laugh.[233] In that photo they're frozen in time, forever young and starting out.

About the time of the photo, Mary Fuller's mother, Fanny, married Judge Henry Carter of the Haverhill municipal court. It was her third marriage. Fanny and the judge lived in Bradford, a suburb of Haverhill, and Mary was a frequent visitor with her children. In an 1897 letter to her mother, Mary Fuller discussed sleeping arrangements for a pending visit:

> About sleeping when we get to your house, I think you would better not make any change about your sleeping. You will need your good night's rest after the days with your grandchildren. Let Dorothy sleep on the lounge in my room, Everett in his crib & Randolph & Ruth in bed with me.... If Charlie is there for a night or two, let him sleep on the sofa down stairs. I don't mind piling up any way 3 or 4 deep if necessary, for the sake of being in Bradford with you again.[234]

Mary clearly looked forward to visits with her mother; "Charlie" and the judge, perhaps less so.

Mary Fuller was primarily devoted to home and family. But she had outside interests. On January 28, 1897 *The Brooklyn Eagle* reported that

---

232   In 1887 hats with all manner of bird feathers and even birds themselves were in fashion. But the feathers were gathered by hunters at a terrible cost to the bird population, especially the heron and egret population in south Florida. In 1896 Mrs. Augustus Hemenway of Boston read a bloody description of a Florida plume hunt and, with her cousin Minna Hall, organized the Massachusetts Audubon Society. Other Audubon societies were organized state by state with the express purpose of ending the trade in birds and their feathers. Within a few years, the societies secured laws in most states prohibiting the hunting of birds for their feathers, as well as Federal legislation banning the interstate shipment of birds or feathers. That effectively put an end to the use of bird plumes in ladies' hats. It was also the beginning of the conservation movement. In Florida, however, policing the new prohibitions was dangerous business; at least one warden, Guy Bradley, was murdered in the line of duty.

233   In his 1892 passport application, Fuller described himself as 5'6" tall, blue eyes, light brown hair, with a small brown mustache, *U.S. Passport applications 1795-1905* (National Archives Microfilm Publication M1372).

234   Letter, dated July 29, 1897, from Mary Fuller to her mother.

Notwithstanding the inclement weather of last evening the third meeting of the Midwood Club Literary Circle of Flatbush held in the women's parlor of the club house was well-attended. The principal topic of the evening was "Mark Twain and his writing." A paper on that author's literary career was read.... A review of "Personal Recollections of Joan of Arc... came next, followed by a paper on Joan of Arc as a historical character, read by Mrs. Charles H. Fuller....[235]

She also traveled. In the summer of 1901, having had her last child, Mary sailed to Europe with her husband. Fanny moved into the house at 2 Tennis Court to oversee the five Fuller children, including Priscilla, age eighteen months. On their return, the Fullers made the *Eagle*'s list of noteworthy passengers arriving on the *Deutschland*, then the fastest ship on the Atlantic.[236] In 1906 Mary and Charles took an extended trip by boat down the coast to Jacksonville, Florida. Fanny again looked after the children. During the trip their boat docked in Brunswick, Georgia and Mary wrote her mother how excited she was to see that "the dock was full of real Southern darkies." [237] Mary Fuller, unlike her mother, had led a sheltered life.[238]

Fanny Dwight Webb died at eighty-five on April 12, 1912 in Brooklyn. By then Fanny had outlived three husbands. Though she often visited Winthrop and Hallowell, there is no evidence that she ever returned to San Francisco.

---

235 *The Brooklyn Daily Eagle*, January 28, 1897, 4 (unattributed article).
236 *The Brooklyn Daily Eagle*, August 1, 1901, 2 (unattributed article).
237 Letters, dated May 1906, from Mary Fuller to her mother.
238 .*The New York Times*, April 20, 1912, 15 (Obituaries). Fanny's third husband, Judge Henry Carter, died January 24, 1898, age eighty-three. See "Deaths," *Commonwealth of Massachusetts Department of Public Health Registry of Vital Records and Statistics*, 1898, Vol. 481: 443.

5. Charles Humphrey Fuller: Church and Politics

Charles Fuller was an Episcopalian, a scholar (he was an omnivorous reader and student of history), a lawyer and a politician, roughly in that order. He specialized in commercial law from his office at 346 Broadway in the Wall Street area.

In 1889 Fuller's father was an active member of the Central Congregational Church on Hancock Street, Brooklyn, and Charles was president of the Young People's Association. In November 1889, Fuller and his brother-in-law, William Redfield, presided as auctioneers at a doll sale to raise money for the church's annual Christmas distribution of coal, groceries, and clothing to the poor. [239] The following November, Fuller, "with Brooklyn's most prominent Congregational ministers and laymen," attended an evening dinner meeting at the Congregational Club to hear President Merrill Gates of Amherst speak.

Gates' subject was education for citizenship. He emphasized the critical role of the mother in educating her children for citizenship, suggesting the wisdom of keeping an open copy of the Constitution on a table in the parlor. Gates moved on to the role of the college, noting the increasing demand for courses in "political economy," so that college men—the "leading minds" of their generation—would be well-equipped to serve as leaders in the political affairs of the nation. Fuller, winner of the prize in "political economy" at his Amherst graduation, probably agreed with all that.

---

239   *The Brooklyn Daily Eagle*, November 15, 1889, 1 (unattributed article). Redfield had married Charles Fuller's sister, Elise Mercein, in 1885. He was then an accountant with the J.H.Williams Company in Brooklyn, a tool manufacturer.

When Gates finished, Dr. Richard Storrs, eminent pastor of the Church of the Pilgrims,[240] rose from the audience and proposed a motion of thanks for such a stimulating talk. But Storrs, Amherst class of 1839, also felt the need to say a few words about "political economy":[241]

> The department of the college that bothered me most was not Greek or mathematics, but political economy. It is likely that it is taught more luminously now. Indeed, when I left college my thoughts were tangled about nothing so much as political economy and they have not straightened out yet.

Storrs next launched an attack on the "mugwumps": the idealistic young men who had deserted the Republican Party and become Democrats over the issues of clean government and sound money:

> I was brought up as an old fashioned Republican, a Whig, and have kept to my original judgment, looking with wonder upon those who wander into the new paths. The element of mug-wumpism has been bred among the learned men, wherefore I say that if education is to have this effect what is the use of it? I believe in the common sense of the American people and think that when great problems come they are to be faced not by experts but by the robust, vigorous common sense of the people. It was that which carried us through the civil war. It is that, and not political economy, which has built the nation. [242]

Storrs suggested that far more important than the study of "political economy" was the role of the father in the home. He deplored the way children were

---

240   Burrows and Wallace, *Gotham*, 1233. Richard Salter Storrs, born in Braintree Massachusetts and educated at Amherst College, served as Pastor of the Church of the Pilgrims from its inception in 1846 until shortly before his death in 1900. He was one of the most famous and influential clergymen in the country, but was overshadowed by Henry Ward Beecher of the nearby Plymouth Church, a more emotional and charismatic preacher.
241   *The Brooklyn Daily Eagle*, November 25, 1890, 1 (unattributed article).
242   In the 1884 election the Republicans nominated James G. Blaine as their presidential candidate. Disgruntled Republicans viewed Blaine as a crook, deserted the party, and supported Grover Cleveland, the Democratic candidate. At the time party loyalty was regarded as very important; Republican loyalists scorned those deserting Republicans as "Mugwumps." Cleveland attracted a large following of reform-minded Republicans ("Mugwumps") with his program of civil service reform, lean government, tariff reduction, and honesty in government and politics. See Charles and Mary Beard, *A Basic History of the United States* (New York; Doubleday, 1944), 325.

being brought up without a strong paternal influence: "The father comes home late at night, goes away early in the morning, and his children, therefore, in early life hardly form an acquaintance with him. Here I am reminded of the story of the little boy who was crying. His mother asked him what was the matter, and he replied, "The man who lives here Sundays just hit me."

Fuller, twenty-six, represented everything that Storrs, seventy, detested. Fuller was one of the "learned" young men; he had won the prize for "political economy" at Amherst; he was an ardent reformer; he may have started out as a Republican, but he was now a Democrat. To Storrs, the Democrats were the party of the South, the party of disloyalty and rebellion. Fuller commuted into the city and worked long hours, leaving Mary Fuller at home to raise the children; just the sort of parenting that Storrs deplored.

Storrs' anger and disappointment were directed at the younger generation that had come of age after the Civil War. It was the old story of generational conflict: an older generation, saw change and didn't like it. And yet, Storrs had a point in valuing common sense over book learning and criticizing the absence of fathers from the home.

But Fuller was more than just a hard-working lawyer commuting into Manhattan. He was an engaged Christian. At St. Paul's Episcopal Church he taught school, served as superintendent of the Sunday school, and on the vestry. Charles and Mary Fuller had both been brought up in the Congregational Church of their ancestors, and the decision to join St. Paul's could not have been taken lightly. During the 1880s, Brooklyn had two of the most prominent Congregational churches in the country: the Church of the Pilgrims, led by Richard Storrs, and Plymouth Church, led by Henry Ward Beecher. One of those would have seemed a logical choice for Fuller. But St Paul's, an easy walk from Tennis Court, had the advantage of convenience. Also, he may have been drawn to the warmth and formality of the Episcopal service, and he liked the Rector, the Reverend Dr. Townsend G. Jackson. As a student of history, Fuller may have thought about his Plymouth ancestors when he joined St. Paul's. They might have looked askance at Fuller's new church affiliation; but they would have conceded that he was indeed a serious and devout Christian.

In 1898 Fuller was appointed secretary of the Sunday School Commission of the Episcopal Diocese of Long Island. After a two-year study, the Commission found the teaching of religion in the churches unsatisfactory, and recommended a required course of study for the teachers, who "must be taught how to teach and what to teach." Fuller presented and defended the recommendations before a Sunday schools convention. Several ministers suggested the recommendations for teacher training were "a little too hard on the teachers, who were most generous in giving their time and services." There was a "lively and vigorous" discussion, after which a motion was made and carried to soften the recommendations.[243]

As a member of the St. Paul's vestry and for many years its head, Fuller was deeply involved in raising the money for a new building. The original church, built in 1836, was replaced in 1874, but the larger building could no longer handle the growing congregation. The new building was completed for Easter Sunday 1900. Fuller was still raising funds to pay for it in January 1901, when he and his organizing committee arranged for a concert at the Knickerbocker Club.[244]

The church was his first love, but politics was a close second. From 1892-1894 he was president of the Flatbush Democratic Club and a member of the Executive Committee of the King's County Democratic organization (Brooklyn was in King's County). At that time he began to play a leading role in the reform movement.[245] Fuller, Redfield, and other young men (including George Vestner in New York) felt a burning desire to change local politics. Educated, successful, idealistic, and largely Protestant, they saw the Democratic Party as a "machine" run by corrupt Irish bosses: Richard Croker in New York, Hugh McLaughlin in Brooklyn. The bosses controlled the spoils of office and doled out plum government positions and contracts to their friends and loyal supporters, who were in turn expected to kick back a portion of their salaries or fees. The bosses viewed politics as a business and reformers like Fuller and Redfield as meddlesome amateurs. Fuller and Redfield preferred to see the issue as clean versus corrupt government, and were willing to put their principles ahead of party loyalty. But the argument was also about class, religion, ethnicity, and length of time in America.[246]

Fuller and Redfield worked together on the great local issue of 1895— whether Brooklyn should consolidate with Manhattan to form a Greater New York City. The proponents of consolidation presented the voters with visions

243 *The Brooklyn Daily Eagle*, November 21, 1900, 3 (unattributed article).
244 *The Brooklyn Daily Eagle*, December 30, 1900, 23; February 13, 1901, 3 (unattributed articles).
245 Fuller was chosen as a member of the "Committee of One Hundred" to reorganize the Kings County Democratic Party: *The New York Times*, December 23, 1893, 9 (unattributed article).
246 The regular Democrats sometimes hired hoodlums to break up reform meetings, as on November 3, 1894. The first speaker was Fuller's good friend and fellow St. Paul's vestryman, Henry Sherrill. As Sherrill attempted to explain the benefits of electing the reform ticket, hecklers drowned him out with "vile epithets." The next speaker was given the same treatment. The police finally arrived and dispersed the hoodlums. That was Brooklyn politics.

of municipal grandeur (consolidation would cement New York's position as the nation's premier city) as well as more practical arguments, such as the real prospect that Brooklyn would soon run out of water while Manhattan had plenty.

The previous year the citizens of Brooklyn had voted narrowly in favor of consolidation by a margin of 277 votes out of 129,211 cast. But Redfield, Fuller and others organized a League of Loyal Citizens and campaigned to kill the whole idea of consolidation. They argued that Manhattan was a social and political failure and that Brooklyn enjoyed superior municipal government. Some, like Storrs, argued that Brooklyn would be swamped by "the political sewage of Europe," losing its distinctive New England and American character. That argument may have had relevance in a few white Protestant enclaves like Brooklyn Heights or Tennis Court, but it ignored the observable fact that in 1895 Brooklyn had already become a large polyglot city, with Irish, Italians, Eastern European Jews, Germans, and blacks—not too different from Manhattan.

The League of Loyal Citizens, with more than 70,000 supporters, mounted a vigorous political campaign to set aside the referendum results. But Senator Thomas C. Platt and the Republican machine in Albany outgunned them. Platt saw consolidation as a means of gaining Republican control of a larger New York City by diluting the power of the Tammany machine that controlled Manhattan. Legislation setting a date and a process for consolidation was rammed through the legislature. After the mayors of both New York and Brooklyn vetoed it, Platt rammed it through again. Governor Levi Morton was under intense pressure to veto the bill, but he needed Platt's support for his own presidential aspirations. Visions of the presidency dancing in his head, he signed the bill, and Brooklyn officially became part of New York City on January 1, 1898.[247]

Fuller and Redfield were also deeply involved in the 1896 presidential campaign. They were both Democrats, but when their party nominated William Jennings Bryan they, like George Vestner in Manhattan, were horrified. They were Democrats who believed in limited government and sound, gold-backed, money. They saw Bryan and his followers as hell-bent on cheapening the value of the

---

247   If Platt saw this as a victory over Tammany, he would be in for a surprise when a Tammany candidate won the first mayoral election for the new Greater New York, expanding Tammany's power over a much larger city.

dollar.[248] But they were not prepared to become Republicans. So they did as George Vestner; they joined a new political party of disaffected Democrats—the National Democratic Party—and ran for office on the National Democratic ticket. They did not expect the National Democrats to win. They would be content with a McKinley victory, because McKinley was for "sound" money and Bryan was not.

On October 2, 1896 an item in *The Daily Eagle* noted that:

> A most promising sound money Democratic Club has been organized in the 29th Ward of Brooklyn. The headquarters are located at 2 Tennis Court…. A most vigorous intelligent and aggressive campaign will be prosecuted. An effort will be made to get all sound money democrats of the Ward, whatever their past affiliation into the club…

The Fuller home at 2 Tennis Court was to be the headquarters of the sound money Democratic Club.[249] Fuller was a "sound money" Democrat; he believed in a dollar freely convertible into gold and backed by ample gold reserves in the U.S. Treasury. That was why Fuller, Redfield and like-minded Democrats were called "Gold Democrats." They believed inflation was bad for the country; they were tight money men. But below the surface of the money issue, the Gold Democrats believed in the status quo. Fuller, Redfield and their friends were mainly upper-middle-class bankers, lawyers and corporate executives, many of them products of Eastern colleges and universities. Bryan, on the other hand, represented the "masses." He was the pied piper of the have-nots: the poor, the unemployed, the struggling farmers from the West and the South, the factory workers, the legions of people who owed money to the banks.

Fuller campaigned tirelessly, speaking before different audiences several times a week. On October 24, the *Eagle* reported a speech by Fuller. headlined: "Sound Money Mass Meeting in Flatbush Last Night, Candidate Fuller's Address":

> Mr. Fuller also spoke of the claims of the silver men that this campaign is a contest on behalf of the poor against capitalists.

248 That, of course, is what made Bryan so popular among the western silver mine owners and the farmers. Bryan advocated making dollars convertible into either silver or gold at a ratio of 16:1—sixteen ounces of silver would be priced the same as one ounce of gold. Since the supply of silver was large and growing, the government could print more dollars and more money would be in circulation, an increasing portion of it backed by silver. The expected effect would be to inflate prices, to the advantage of farmers and workers and the disadvantage of bankers. Farmers and small businessmen, many of whom owed money to the banks, would be able to repay their loans in cheaper dollars.
249 *The Brooklyn Daily Eagle*, October 2, 1896, 11 (unattributed article).

He referred to one kind of capitalist of the 'Hannah' type, whom the demagogues were so fond of denouncing, but called attention to the fact that there were hundreds of thousands of capitalists consisting of poor widows and others of small means which had their savings invested in securities, and that a free coinage policy aimed at the so-called capitalists would injure these numerous small capitalists much more than the few wealthy ones. The latter could stand it, but the former would be ruined.[250]

The reporter noted that Fuller was "generously applauded." The reformers put up a full slate of candidates for public office: Redfield ran for Congress, Fuller for State Assembly. McKinley won in a landslide, and Republicans easily beat most of the young reformers—Fuller and Redfield included. But the purpose—to beat Bryan—had been achieved.

In 1897, Fuller and Redfield again bolted the party and joined the fight to elect Seth Low the first mayor of the new Greater New York. Low, president of Columbia University and a former mayor of Brooklyn, was running on a Citizens Union "good government" ticket; his high-minded campaign energized the reform crowd in Brooklyn, and his appearances generated large and enthusiastic crowds. Fuller helped form a Seth Low Club in Flatbush and spoke out during the campaign.

Low ran a strong race, beating the Republican candidate and finishing a respectable second. But the election was a solid victory for the Democrats and Tammany Hall. Asked his opinion of the election and the reform movement behind Low, the crusty old Hugh McLaughlin, heaped scorn on the reformers, said they would always be ineffective, and compared them to the anti-immigrant "Know-Nothing" movement of the 1850s:[251]

It is the most wonderful thing in the history of politics—Low's vote is. It cannot be analyzed by any living being except those who were interested in bringing about that result. Look back to 1854, 1855, 1856.... Do you get the idea? The same spirit which prevailed in those past times prevailed in the Low party yester-

---

250   *The Brooklyn Daily Eagle*, October 24, 1896, 5 (unattributed article).
251   The "Know-Nothing" movement was essentially a middle-class Protestant reaction to Catholic immigration and Irish Catholic political activity in the cities. The movement was made up of disaffected Democrats and Whigs, and operated under the name of the "American Party," winning political elections at the local and state level in the early 1850s. When a member of the party was asked about its activities, he was supposed to answer "I know nothing." The American Party platform included restrictions on immigration, and requirements that political offices be filled by native-born Americans. The movement had a brief life, but in the North it formed the backbone of the new Republican Party that triumphed with Lincoln in 1860.

day. Sure! It was the Know Nothing system in those years. It was the American Protective Association yesterday, supplemented by the support of so-called high toned Roman Catholics... There is a passage of scripture which says: 'Lord, forgive them; they know not what they do.' You get the idea, don't you?[252]

Fuller and Redfield saw Hugh McLaughlin as representing everything that was wrong with politics.

* * *

President McKinley led the nation out of the depression precipitated by the panic of 1893, but was assassinated following his re-election in 1900. His successor, Theodore Roosevelt, presided over a period of prosperity. By 1904 things were humming: the Treasury had accumulated large gold reserves; prices were rising gently; the deficit had shrunk; the U.S. was becoming the world's biggest exporter with a favorable trade balance of almost $500 million (about $12 billion in current dollars); and there was a bull market in stocks on Wall Street.[253]

Automobile parade down Fifth Avenue, New York City, 1904 (Old N.Y.World Staff Photo)

252   *The Brooklyn Daily Eagle*, November 3, 1897, 1 (unattributed article).
253   Mary Jane Capozzoli Ingui, *American History 1877 to the Present* (New York; Barron's, 2003), 42-46. For translating 1904 dollars into current dollars, see www.measuringworth.com

Fuller ran again for the state assembly in 1904. That year, Roosevelt, running at the head of the Republican ticket, swept New York in a landslide. In Brooklyn the Republicans made significant gains, picking up three seats. But Fuller managed to buck the Republican tide and win a tight race, unseating the incumbent Jacob Remsen in his largely Republican district by 9,145 votes to 9,000 for Remsen.[254] *The New York Times* ran a profile of the new assemblyman:

> Assemblyman Charles H. Fuller of the Flatbush District of Kings County came to the Legislature with the prestige of having defeated Jacob D. Remsen of gas legislation fame. Remsen had been in the Legislature for years and was something of a figure. Representing a strong Republican district, his defeat came as a great surprise, and there was a natural curiosity about the personality of the man who had successfully opposed him. Those who asked to have the man who had beaten Remsen pointed out to them saw a stockily built man of medium height with a countenance that suggests pugnacity.
>
> The impression of force and determination which one gets from Mr. Fuller on first meeting he fully sustains upon further acquaintance. While his legal training restrains him from rushing into the fray of debate heedlessly, he is always ready to take part in a discussion upon any measure of importance, and generally his views are so well digested as to give him the best of the argument...
>
> Mr. Fuller...did not seek the nomination. He was importuned by the leaders of his own party and prominent Republicans in the district as well to make the race.... Mr. Fuller is what as known as a Cleveland Democrat. He does not always vote for party measures, believing that the sentiment of his district is broad and liberal enough to permit him to exercise independent judgment.[255]

---

254   *The New York Times*, November 10, 1904, 2 (unattributed article).
255   *The New York Times*, May 14, 1905, 6 (unattributed article).

Fuller served a single term. In the fall of 1905 he was the Democratic candidate for judge of the municipal court of New York but lost to Republican Lucien Bayliss. Charles Fuller did not want to be an Assemblyman; he wanted to be a judge.

In 1906, he was the Democratic candidate for the New York State Senate in the Eighth District and won by 767 votes. Charles Evans Hughes, Republican candidate for governor, carried Fuller's district by 7,000 votes. Once again Fuller managed to win against a strong Republican tide.[256]*The New York Times* reported:

> One of the surprises of the election relative to Senators was the defeat of Senator Charles Cooper in the Eighth District by Charles H. Fuller, who appears to have won out by a comfortable margin.... It was a great victory, as the district was Republican by thousands.... This year he was drafted to make the fight against Cooper in an overwhelmingly Republican district. Fuller is the highest type Senator elected by the Brooklyn Democracy in years.[257]

The same paper later looked back on Fuller's senate record, describing him as "straight as a string":

> Mr. Fuller had an enviable record in the State Senate, where he put in a great deal of painstaking work as a member of the Finance and other important standing committees. His work there gave him ample opportunity to demonstrate his ability. All his confreres in the Legislature agree that he is as straight as a string and a fearless and uncompromising exponent of all that is best in public life... He was Chairman of the State commission that worked out the comprehensive plan for the husbanding of the State's water resources, which now is in a good way of being applied as the State/s policy.[258]

Senator Fuller also cast a vote on at least one issue that would come back to haunt him. A bill to restrict racetrack gambling came up for a vote. Fuller

256   Edgar L. Murlin, *The New York State Red Book* 1908 (Albany, N.Y; J.B.Lyon, 1908), 76-77.
257   *The New York Times*, November 8, 1906, 4 (unattributed article)
258   *The New York Times*, September 26, 1909, 10 (unattributed article).

was not in favor of gambling, and there was strong opposition to gambling in his district. But the district also included two racetracks: Brighton Beach and Sheepshead Bay, and the racetrack interests pressed him hard, threatening his political future if he voted for the bill, which of course he did.[259] The bill passed by a single vote, and he undoubtedly made some powerful enemies with that vote.

Fuller's two years in Albany cost him time away from his Wall Street law practice. As an investor he must have been alarmed as he watched the nation come close to a complete financial meltdown.

It started in April 1906. Wall Street was roiled by the worst natural disaster in the nation's history: the virtually complete destruction of San Francisco by earthquake and fire, an event that caused financial repercussions around the world, followed in 1907 by yet another Wall Street panic.[260] Fuller may have been shaken, but he probably did a brisk business in bankruptcies. He also pursued his dream to become a judge. Giving up his Senate seat in 1908 after a single term, he received the Democratic Party nomination for judge of the municipal court of New York. He lost in a close race.

Fuller remained a figure in the political life of the city. His name came up as a candidate on an anti-Tammany reform ticket for Brooklyn borough president in 1909.[261] In 1910, he was called before a legislative committee investigating charges that racing interests had sought to defeat the racetrack bill by bribing legislators:[262]

> The appearance of former State Senator Charles H. Fuller of Brooklyn...in the committee room at City Hall caused the rumor that more evidence of legislative bribery or attempted bribery was about to be heard. But any such hope was short lived. Mr. Fuller, who is a lawyer, and in 1908 represented the Eighth Senatorial District of Kings County in the State Senate, said he had read the testimony of Senator Travis printed in yesterday's newspapers and that he could not recall the luncheon referred to by Travis....

259   *Report of the Joint Committee of the Senate and Assembly of the State of New York to Investigate Corrupt Practices...* (Albany; J.B.Lyon, 1911), 1143-1148.
260   The "lesser" shocks included, among other things: congressional legislation providing for the regulation of railroad rates; a $29 million fine levied against Standard Oil for antitrust violations; the collapse of the copper market, and a failed bond offering by New York City.
261   *The New York Times*, September 26, 1909, 10.
262   *The New York Times*, November 20, 1910, 12.

'I cannot recall it at all' said Mr. Fuller. 'And of one thing I am certain. I did not say to Senator Travis that I had been approached with any pecuniary offer to influence my vote on the Hart-Agnew bill.'

'Were you ever approached with any intimation that a very juicy melon was about to be cut by the turf interests?' asked Mr. Bruce [M. Linn Bruce, counsel for the committee].

'No,' replied Mr. Fuller, 'and the only intimation I had that money was being offered to influence votes was through the newspapers at the time.'

Mr. Fuller added that he had voted for the anti-race track gambling measure.

The *Times* article summarized a longer exchange between Fuller and Judge Bruce, committee counsel, who pressed him hard on the issue.

In 1912 Fuller served as president of the Brooklyn League, a civic organization of prominent Brooklyn men.[263] As president, he organized a fiftieth-anniversary celebration for the New York veterans of the Battle of Antietam, the bloodiest one-day battle in American history, fought on September 17, 1862. A long article in the *Times* described the gathering:

Wearing as of old their blue cadet caps with crimson braid and gold letters, the handful of survivors of the Eighty-third and Eighty-fourth Regiments together with several hundred old soldiers from other commands organized in New York for the defense of the Union, mingled joyously under the trees around the pavilion in Music Grove, grasped hands and recalled incidents of the war. When their deeds of heroism were lauded by the speakers, those who fought fifty years ago were deeply moved and there was scarcely one but drew his handkerchief to dry tears from his eyes.

---

263   The Brooklyn League, through its committees, was actively engaged in a wide range of civic improvement activities: the subway system, railways, sewage disposal, dock and water front, education, environment, and real estate taxation. Members sought to influence the shape of legislation in Albany and Washington insofar as it affected Brooklyn.

The event drew an audience of over 5,000 to Prospect Park. There was a military concert by Shannon's Twenty-third Regiment Band, speeches, canon salutes, a parade and review, and a seated dinner at the Armory. The veterans were growing old, another war was on the horizon, and there wouldn't be many more events for the Civil War men. They were the surviving members of the nineteenth century's "Greatest Generation." Charles Fuller sat at the head table and was introduced as one of the distinguished men of Brooklyn.[264]

Charles and Mary Fuller with daughters, ca. 1915

* * *

As Fuller presided over the Antietam celebration, a bitterly-fought presidential campaign was underway with three major contenders: President William Howard Taft, Republican; former President Theodore Roosevelt, Progressive; and New Jersey Governor Woodrow Wilson, Democrat. Fuller's brother-in-law, William Redfield, campaigned hard for Wilson, who won.[265]

---

264 *The New York Times,* September 22, 1912, 11.
265 See John Milton Cooper, Jr., *The Warrior and the Priest, Woodrow Wilson and Theodore Roosevelt* (Cambridge, Mass; Harvard University Press, 1983), 143-229. Professor Cooper provides a stirring account of the campaign of 1912

The president appointed Redfield the first secretary of commerce.[266] As a member of the Cabinet, Redfield served at the highest level of government from 1913-1919, a tumultuous time in American history during which much of the foundation was laid for modern America.[267]

Redfield was a driven and brilliant man. Starting out as a clerk at the J.H.Williams Manufacturing Company in Brooklyn, he worked his way up to president. At the time of his appointment, he was a leading national expert on business efficiency, having written an influential book, *The New Industrial Age* (published in 1909).

The appointment did not sit well with Wilson's campaign manager, William McCombs:

> I was astounded when informed that the President had chosen Redfield...Redfield was without any following at all...He was in disfavor with Democrats of his home county of Kings...[268]

Redfield was not a Democratic Party loyalist; he and Fuller had often bolted the party on matters of principle. He was appointed because Wilson respected his intellect, his business experience and his deep knowledge of one of the central issues of the campaign, the tariff.[269] William Gibbs McAdoo, Wilson's Secretary of the Treasury and fellow member of the cabinet, had his own perspective on Redfield and his appointment:

> With Brandeis [Wilson's first choice] out of consideration, and the inauguration at hand, it looked as if we might go to Washington minus a Secretary of Commerce. While House [Col. Edward M. House, Wilson's confidant] and I were talking over the situation, the name of William C. Redfield of Brooklyn

---

266   The Department of Commerce and Labor had been created in 1903. Labor and Commerce were separated into two departments in 1913.

267   The graduated income tax, the Federal Reserve System, the Federal Trade Commission, mobilization of the entire economy for war, and the United Nations all had their origins in the years of the Wilson administration.

268   William F. McCombs, *Making Woodrow Wilson President* (New York; Fairview Publishing Co. 1921), 217-218. McCombs' remark about Redfield being in "disfavor" with the party in Kings County reflected McCombs' close Tammany ties and Redfield's tendency to operate independently of the party.

269   Asked for an estimate of his new cabinet, Wilson said that "Redfield possessed much the best analytical mind..." From the Diary of Colonel House, April 1, 1913, Arthur S. Link, ed., *Papers of Woodrow Wilson* (Princeton, N.J; Princeton University Press, 1978), 27: 253.

came up as a possible choice... Redfield was an executive in a large manufacturing concern, and was considered by all who knew him as a business man of experience and capacity. He had served as a member of Congress, where he had a reputation as a tariff specialist. He not only knew a great deal about that complicated subject, but he had a faculty of presenting very dry and dreary tariff information in digestible form. I was favorably impressed by him. Governor Wilson agreed with House and myself as to Redfield's qualifications, and he was appointed. [270]

Redfield was an ardent internationalist, intimately familiar with government and business in Europe, Latin America and Asia. He had traveled the world, and was an outspoken advocate of free trade, tariff reform, and U.S. business expansion abroad. His views and experience fit nicely with Wilson's own thinking.

Wilson's cabinet meetings were apparently friendly and informal, with the tone set by the unfailingly gracious and courteous president, who regarded his cabinet as family. Redfield described his first cabinet meeting:

A group of ten men, some of them old acquaintances, gathered around a table in a quiet room of small dimensions, talked freely with the President and with one another about current affairs. The most noticeable thing was the lack of formality...It was much more like the meeting of friends having a mutual interest and a common chief than like anything more formal.[271]

---

270 William Gibbs McAdoo, *Crowded Years* (Boston, Mass; Houghton Mifflin Company, 1931), 183.
271 The description of the first cabinet meeting is from Redfield's article in *The Saturday Evening Post* May 10, 1924.

Wilson's first cabinet meeting, March 1913; Redfield is sixth to the left of the president
(Harris & Ewing)

Redfield, as a congressman, had impressed Wilson with his mastery of the arcane details of the tariff, an issue that had long divided Democrats and Republicans. [272] Following his election, Wilson made tariff reform his first major legislative initiative, taking on the Republicans and the powerful interests that supported high tariffs (the sugar and wool lobbies, among others). Wilson cast the fight as one for the working man and small business against big business and the "monopolists." He and Redfield also saw the tariff as the main impediment to expanding export markets. In August, the Congress was embroiled in a hot debate over the tariff. The president asked Redfield to go to Maine and do his bit for the "cause":

My dear Mr. Secretary: I hate to burden you with extra tasks, but we have a most important and interesting Congressional

---

272   Tariffs are duties paid on imported goods. For example, when the U.S. imposes a tariff on imported sugar, the result is to increase the price of imported sugar in line with domestic prices. The intent is to protect the domestic producer against lower-priced competition. Of course that leads to retaliation by the country affected, which then levies its own tariff on some other U.S. products. Republicans favored high tariffs to protect American manufacturers, the Republicans' main source of campaign contributions; Democrats viewed high tariffs as a cause of price inflation and an economic benefit to a small group of wealthy businessmen. Redfield believed that tariff protection made business less efficient and competitive than it might otherwise be if tariffs were removed and American companies had to compete on even ground with the Europeans.

Uncle Will as secretary of commerce

election pending in Maine and nobody could be more service able in the speaking campaign which is about to begin
up there than you, yourself. The issue is to be the tariff. We
are to be challenged to justify the pending action of Congress

about the import duties. Nobody can expound that matter better than you can....I wonder if you would be willing to do this for the cause.[273]

Redfield played his part in the great battle for tariff reform, which resulted in a legislative triumph for the president.

In August 1914, the European war broke out. This was viewed as both crisis and opportunity. It was a crisis, because U.S. foreign trade, heavily dependent on the British merchant marine, came to a virtual standstill. But it was also an opportunity, for the United States to acquire its own shipping fleet and capture markets hitherto dominated by the Europeans. Redfield, never one to mince words, spoke out for taking advantage of the opportunity:

> It would seem plain that our resources are undiminished, our capital secure, our labor safe, that we are saving when others are losing, that we are living when others are dying, that with us the path is upward and with them it is in large measure downward. It seems certain that one result is to be our own greater industrial independence.

He transformed the commerce department into a much more effective instrument of U.S business expansion overseas.[274] As a principal adviser to the president on matters of foreign trade and commerce, he drafted and fought for legislation to strengthen U.S. trade.[275] With his aggressive leadership on

---

273   Letter, dated August 12, 1913, from Woodrow Wilson to William Redfield, William Cox Redfield Family Papers, 1821-1959, Library of Congress. See Ray Stannard Baker, *Woodrow Wilson, Life and Letters, 1913-1914* (New York; Doubleday, Doran & Company, Inc., 1931), 4: 93-130, for a history of the struggle in the congress leading to passage of tariff reform in September 1913.

274   Redfield greatly expanded the foreign trade activities of the Commerce Department. He increased the appropriation for the Bureau of Foreign and Domestic Commerce from $60,000 to $600,000; recruited and assigned commercial attaches to the ten most important world commercial centers; established district offices in all major U.S. cities to enlist local companies in the foreign trade effort; obtained a special appropriation to target trade expansion in Latin America; founded the National Foreign Trade Council, bringing together the most important U.S. exporters to lobby Congress for laws strengthening foreign commerce, and traveled the country on speaking tours to promote U.S. overseas business expansion. Robert E. Hennigan, *The New World Power: American Foreign Policy 1898-1917* (Philadelphia; University of Pennsylvania Press, 2002), 80-82; William H. Becker, *The Dynamics of Business Government Relations, 1893-1921* (Chicago; The University of Chicago Press, 1982), xii.

275   Among other things, Redfield was actively involved in shipping legislation, designed to create a U.S. merchant marine, and legislation carving out exemptions from the antitrust laws for cooperative business ventures in overseas markets. See Kennedy. *Over Here*: 304, 307; Becker, *The Dynamics of Business Government Relations*, 145-146; *Wilson Papers*, 35: 345n.1 (regarding a draft shipping bill prepared by Redfield and McAdoo); Letter, dated September 18, 1914, from Redfield to Wilson, *Wilson Papers*, 31: 454 (urging certain antitrust exemptions in aid of foreign trade).

these issues, Redfield stepped on toes, notably those of Secretary of the Treasury McAdoo and Secretary of State Lansing, each of whom was anxious to expand his department's role in the foreign trade arena.

Redfield also had to deal with one of the deadliest accidents in American history, one that fell within his department's responsibilities.

On 24 July 1915, the steamship *Eastland* was resting in its pier on the Chicago River, about to take 2,500 Western Electric employees out on Lake Michigan for an outing. Suddenly, without warning, the ship listed and capsized. In the ensuing panic, close to 1000 died, most of them crushed on the river bottom under the ship. The Steamship Inspection Service, responsible for ensuring the safety of steamships in domestic waters, was part of the commerce department. Redfield immediately went to Chicago and took personal charge of the department's investigation.

He had rushed, perhaps precipitously, into a political hurricane. The Chicago Federation of Labor sent a "most emphatic protest" to Wilson charging that Redfield's investigation would be a whitewash. *The Chicago Tribune* charged federal officials with corruption and called for Wilson to appoint an independent investigation. Wilson suggested the wisdom of such a course to Redfield, but Redfield charged ahead. As Wilson noted, in replying to criticism from one of Redfield's cabinet colleagues:

> I have myself come to the conclusion that Redfield had gone too far to justify me in insisting upon a substitute course of actions which might seem to discredit him...[276]

The Chicago newspapers pilloried Redfield. A *Daily News* editorial characterized him as having

> an abundance of egotism and a general feeling of complacency in which all things connected with his department are comfortably submerged like sardines in oil.[277]

The commerce department had to wrap up its investigation sooner than expected when Judge Kennesaw Mountain Landis, overseeing a separate grand

---

276   Letter, dated August 2, 1915, from Wilson to Josephus Daniels, *Wilson Papers*, 34: 56-57.
277   Letter, dated August 3, 1915, from Wilson to his Secretary Joseph Tumulty, *Wilson Papers*, 34: 65n.1 (referring to "confidential information" received by Tumulty and passed on to Wilson).

jury investigation, enjoined witnesses from testifying. Redfield returned to Washington, bloodied but unbowed.[278]

Wilson was re-elected in November 1916. The following February, Redfield hosted Charles and Mary Fuller at Wilson's second inauguration.[279] Redfield probably introduced the Fullers to the president, perhaps included them for a dinner in the White House, and made sure they attended the various inaugural functions.

Wilson's second term was largely occupied by the war and its aftermath. With the declaration of war, Redfield was forced to abandon his aggressive leadership on the foreign trade issue and pull in his horns. Instead of exploiting the preoccupation of the European powers with their own war, the U.S. was now a full participant with a new and overriding national objective: defeat Germany.

Redfield was not part of Wilson's inner circle on war matters, but as secretary of commerce and a member of the War Trade Board, he was deeply involved in the war effort.[280] An expert in machine design and industrial production, he was an active participant in the complicated wartime effort to create a U.S. air force where none had existed prior to the war.

Following the Armistice, Redfield tried once again to create a leading role for the Department of Commerce in U.S. trade policy. But the world had changed, and he was frustrated in his efforts. Trade policy had become much more complicated, more agencies had their fingers in the pie, and the U.S. faced the huge challenge of helping the weakened European nations get back on their feet.[281]

Redfield's service came to an end in September 1919. A front page article in *The New York Times* carried the news in bold type:

---

278   The Grand Jury proceedings were never made public, but they resulted in indictments which were later dismissed for lack of sufficient evidence. A special Chicago board of inquiry made a number of recommendations for improving steamboat inspection, which Redfield adopted and put before Congress, including review by a new board of naval architects to be created within the Commerce Department. Numerous lawsuits were filed against the ship owners and others, but nobody every recovered a dime.

279   The inauguration took place over two days: a private ceremony in the White House on Sunday, March 4, and the next day a public ceremony at which Wilson spoke to a modest crowd Wilson's speech was heard only by those present, since there was then no means of reaching a wider audience. In it, he emphasized U.S. neutrality and his policy of avoiding involvement in the European war. Less than a month later, on April 2, 1917, Wilson appeared before Congress and asked for a declaration of war against Germany.

280   Redfield's commerce department was responsible for acquiring from Russia large quantities of platinum used in the manufacture of high explosives; designing a manufacturing process for optical glass used in telescopes, binoculars, periscopes, range finders and camera lenses (before the war, Germany had been the sole source of optical glass); and developing the radio compass, vital for ship navigation. Redfield, *With Congress and Cabinet* (New York; Doubleday, Page and Company, 1924), 191-204; 207-212.

281   See Becker, *Dynamics of Business Government Relations*, generally.

"REDFIELD RESIGNS, WILSON ACQUIESCES."

Redfield explained that he needed to attend to his "personal affairs," and the president expressed "deep and genuine distress" at losing him: all probably true. The article suggested another angle. Early in 1919 Redfield, with Wilson's acquiescence, had established an Industrial Board within the commerce department that would set "fair" prices for steel, coal and certain other industrial products. The attempt to continue wartime price controls generated intense opposition. The attorney general flatly charged the board with acting in direct violation of the antitrust laws. The secretary of the treasury charged that "the entire process was fundamentally wrong." The charges were extraordinary in their vehemence. Redfield's resignation came shortly after Wilson ordered that the board be disbanded. [282]

After resigning, Redfield remained involved in politics as an adviser to John W. Davis, the Democratic candidate in 1924, and spoke out in support of active U.S. engagement with the rest of the world. In 1931, he received the gold medal award of the National Institute of Social Science "in recognition of his... bringing to the people of this country the realization that America cannot be isolated from the rest of the world."[283]

* * *

Charles Fuller got one more chance to realize his ambition to be a judge. In 1917 he received the Democratic Party nomination for justice of the Brooklyn municipal court. A committee of one hundred leading citizens, including Redfield, was formed to spearhead the campaign. The *World*, a Democratic paper, endorsed him as "The best Senator in either party from New York—Charles H. Fuller, of Brooklyn." The Citizens Union, a good government organization, endorsed Fuller but also endorsed his opponent, Ed Dougherty, noting that Dougherty "had served with distinction for 2 years." Charles Fuller did his best, but it was not to be. Priscilla wrote in her diary for November 7, 1917: "Father did not get elected."

282 *The New York Times*, September 6, 1919, 1 (unattributed article). Redfield and Wilson continued to maintain a cordial relationship until Wilson's death in 1924.
283 *The New York Times*, June 14, 1932, 21, Obituaries.

Charles Fuller's last campaign

By 1924, the Fullers' sons and daughters had all married into respectable Brooklyn families. Only Priscilla, the youngest, remained unmarried and living at home.

6. Eliot and Priscilla: Courtship, Marriage and the Great Depression

The morning of Saturday, February 16, 1924, Priscilla met her date, "Elliott Vessler," under the clock at Grand Central (it took her a while to get the spelling right). Years later, she recalled their "rather shy conversation on the way up to Stamford, feeling each other out." Her diary entries for their first weekend together gave no hint that Eliot was anything special:

> 16 February: Sat. Met at Grand Central at 9:30 to go to Forest Lodge Club near Stamford. Linzee King, Arthur Davis, Justine Sackett, Gibb Kissler, P.A.F & Elliott Vessler & Mrs. King. Got there at 11 & coasted & skied. In P.M. coasted, skied & skated & in eve. danced & played fool card games. Wonderful food & stunning house.

> 17 February "Sun. Dandy breakfast, long walk around reservoir & Elliott talked politics. Snow fight. Great turkey dinner. Talked, played bridge in front of fire & took short walk. Supper & left at 9. Home at 10:30. Fun!!

She also made her way into Eliot's little black book as "Pricilla Fuller."

He didn't waste any time. Priscilla's diary for the next weekend, February 23 notes:

> Lunch at Brossard [sic] with Elliott then to movies in N.Y. Walked down 5th Ave. & had tea at Schrafft's. Fun.

She still didn't know how to spell his name, and Eliot didn't have the field to himself. Donald Love had been aggressively courting Priscilla through most of 1923. On February 26 Don came to dinner and took Pris to see the hit musical, *Stepping Stones*.[284] Two days later: "Elliott" came in the evening and joined the family for a game of Mah Jongg—the Mah Jongg craze had hit the country and by 1924 everybody was playing it. The next night Pris went to a Packer-Vassar dance with Don Love. But two nights later "Elliott" was taking her for a walk on the Coney Island boardwalk, then to dinner at the Bossart followed by a movie at the Albemarle. On March 4, Don Love took her to a concert at Aeolian Hall.

On March 6, Pris noted that "Elliott & Ran came in eve and played Bridge and talked army." Since Eliot and Ran were veterans of the Mexican border and the war in France, they had a lot to talk about. On Saturday March 8, Eliot took her to lunch at the Bossart and a walk in the park, but she had another date for a dance at the Plaza Hotel that night. On March 9 she went to church with Don Love, but Eliot was there too. March 12 Don Love took her to see another Broadway musical: George M. Cohan in *Song & Dance Man*.[285]

Her next diary entry was June 7 (when she was very busy or going through a difficult time, she tended to neglect her diary): "Sat. Eliot & I took Hudson Boat up to West Point. Went all over the place, saw game with 7th Reg. Back on afternoon boat. Dinner on boat. Wonderful sail & day." In July she was still seeing both men. On July 1: "Eliot & I took a bus-ride. Fun." But on July 2: "Crescent Club by boat for dinner & danced with Donald L." On July 7: "Tennis in PM with Donald L. He stayed to dinner & all eve. Talked on porch." But the next day: "Hot. Went to Democratic Convention with Eliot in eve. Very exciting. Home at 2. Nobody nominated."

July 23: Don Love came to the house and spent the evening. But the next day Pris noted "Saw *White Cargo* with Eliot. Heel came off. Too late for Bossart." And the day after that: "Marine Roof at Bossart in eve with Eliot. Fine time talking & dancing." On Saturday, July 26, Don Love took Pris, her sister Ruth and Ruth's husband Lowell Shumway to the Crescent Club to see tennis matches, after which they all dined at the Fuller house.

---

284   Fred Stone (1873-1959) was one of the great figures in Vaudeville and Broadway. "Stepping Stones," starring Fred Stone, his wife Allene and daughter Dorothy making her debut in the theater, opened at the Globe Theater, Broadway, November 6, 1923 to rave reviews.
285   George M. Cohan (1878-1942) was a leading performer and song writer on Broadway. Among his hits were "Give my Regards to Broadway," "Yankee Doodle Dandy," and "Over There."

Priscilla in 1924

Pris was busy the next day: "Church at 7:30 with Donald & at 11 with Eliot." July 28: "Seagate by boat with Donald L. Dandy swim. Dinner & dance at Feltman's after. Fun."[286]

In August she was still juggling dates. On August 4: "Donald Love & I left at 8 A.M. & took the Hudson River boat to Newburgh. Lunch at Palatine & walk. Home by boat. Sang. Supper at Crescent Club & home at 11 P.M. Tired." But she spent the next few days with Eliot at the beach. On Thursday August 7: "Very hot. Eliot & I went to Long Beach in PM. Rained off & on. Dandy rough swim. Cooked supper under the boardwalk & home at 12. Nice talk on train." [287]

That fall, Priscilla saw either Donald or Eliot several times a week. On September 9: "Rain off & on. Met Donald for polo game but came home because of rain. Eliot came in eve. We went to Ruth's and made fudge." On the twelfth,

---

286   Sea Gate was the easternmost community on Coney Island. About two miles up the island at Brighton Beach was Charlie Feltman's Ocean Pavilion, "a gigantic restaurant-cum-entertainment center" which grew out of a clam shack started by a German immigrant in the 1870s. See Burrows and Wallace, *Gotham*, 1132-1136.
287   Long Beach is a strip of island just west of Jones Beach in Nassau County, Long Island.

Eliot came and sat on the Fuller porch and talked. The next day, a Saturday: "Great day. Met Donald at 1:30 & went to Westbury to see international polo: England 5 U.S. 16. Very exciting. Saw Prince of Wales. Crescent Club for supper." [288]

On September 15, she played tennis in the morning with Eliot, then more tennis in the afternoon with Don, who stayed for dinner. On the seventeenth, she spent the afternoon in the New York Public Library with Eliot looking up games to use in her job as supervisor of afternoon play at Packer. In the evening, they experimented with the games.

The next week she went to watch Don in a lacrosse game, with dinner and dancing afterward. On September 27, a Saturday: "Horse-back riding in Central Park with Eliot on his (104th) Artillery horses. Wonderful ride. He stayed to dinner." Eliot and Pris shared a love of horses and often went riding on dates; Don Love was a rider and a polo player, and she rode with him as well.

Nineteen twenty-four was an election year. Eliot was interested in politics and followed the campaign closely. On October 2: "With Eliot to Democratic meeting at Madison Sq. Garden. Heard Davis, Smith & Hylan. Good fun, esp D & S. Walked over B. [Brooklyn] Bridge." [289] On Election Day: "Eliot & I went to Long Beach & cooked wonderful steak. Great day. Home about 11 & watched election returns. Coolidge beat Davis...."[290]

November 9, Pris and Eliot went to early service at church and played twenty-seven holes of golf at Dyker Heights. On the fifteenth Pris noted, "Eliot & I to Richelieu for lunch then walked part way home. Cold & dark. Sat in library & talked rest of P.M. With Donald to Paul Whiteman in eve."[291] Years later, Pris recalled that long afternoon talk with Eliot:

> You're so smart, Darling to remember that we had an anniversary in November! Wasn't it the 15th, and wasn't that when you first told me seriously that you did love me????.... And you may remember what my answer was?????[292]

---

288   Westbury, on the north shore of Long Island, was and is a wealthy enclave of large estates, famous for polo.

289   John W. Davis was the Democratic presidential candidate; Al Smith, Democratic candidate for governor of New York State, and John Hyland, Mayor of New York City.

290   Calvin Coolidge, Republican, elected president in 1924; Al Smith, elected governor of New York State. Pris' Uncle Will Redfield was a close friend of John W. Davis, Coolidge's Democratic opponent, and gave campaign speeches in support of his friend and colleague from the Wilson administration.

291   Paul Whiteman, the "King of jazz," introduced jazz to mainstream audiences in the 1920s.

292   Letter, dated November 3, 1954, from Priscilla to Eliot.

On November 22, Don Love took her to the Harvard-Yale game. They sat on the Yale side in the rain and cheered Yale on to a 19-6 win. The day after that game: "Sun. Church at 6:45. Nap. Sunday school & church with Eliot.... He & I walked through Botanical Gardens. Sat in St. George.[293] Supper at Richelieu. Movies at Plymouth Church. Home & sat in library."

Pris and Eliot were in love. At some point, Eliot dug deep into his well of courage and called on Charles Fuller to ask for Priscilla's hand. In 1925, it was still expected that a young man would seek the formal approval of his young lady's father, but parental approval was no longer the potentially decisive obstacle it had been when Charles Fuller was courting Mary Webb back in the early 1880s. Eliot had to explain himself to a seasoned lawyer and prominent political figure. He must have been nervous. Fuller may have had doubts about Eliot's career prospects, but he would have respected his military service and Priscilla's wishes.

By September 1925, Eliot and Priscilla were engaged. George Vestner, who apparently had not been consulted, was not pleased. He wrote Eliot on September 22:

> My Dear Eliot. I rec'd your note and clipping and put off acknowledging same from day to day for the reason that while I was pleased to know that if it is to be—it is to a girl who is apparently worthwhile—yet I must add a word of regret that you should plunge into such engagement before your vocation in life is settled.
>
> As I have told you repeatedly success in this age more than ever before is determined by burning the midnight oil. With mechanics the right kind of a girl and early marriage is undoubtedly the proper thing, but with occupations such as yours, a job today and none tomorrow, it is a mighty precarious undertaking.
>
> As long as everything runs along smoothly, you will both be happy and contented, but let the pinch come along as it is bound to do, then the trial is hard and only the strong survive.

---

293 The Brooklyn Botanical Gardens were located in Prospect Park, a short walk from Pris' family home at 2 Tennis Court. The St. George Hotel and the newer Bossart were then the most fashionable hotels in Brooklyn.

Optimism is alright, but it gets you nowhere without backbone, energy and will power and the strength to avoid the road of least resistance. Success comes only to those capable of sacrificing the pursuit of pleasure for study and constant study only must be one's guide to attain any objectives.

It is for these reasons that I regret your engagement which calls for time which should be occupied to improve your mind.

Read the obituaries of any of our selfmade men and you will always find that their early life was always given up to business to the exclusion of everything else.

You have made your choice and I wish you both happiness. But at the same time I must express the wish that you will nevertheless find opportunity to so lay out your course that it will reach and lead to a safe haven.

Sincerely, Your father.[294]

George saw Eliot at twenty-eight without a college or professional degree, now in his third job since starting out in 1920, with an uncertain future and no savings to speak of, yet "plunging" into an engagement. Eliot was falling short of his father's exacting standards.

WSJ dinner, May 12, 1926. Eliot at front right table, third on left

---

294   Letter, dated September 22, 1925, from George Vestner to Eliot.

In the spring of 1926, Eliot had been a financial news reporter at *The Wall Street Journal* for three years. The evening of May 12, he appeared front and center in a large photo taken at a formal Dow Jones banquet held in the Crystal Room of the Ritz-Carlton Hotel: all the men in tuxedos, the ladies in their best dresses, the men, young and handsome, the ladies, young and pretty, a sophisticated and debonair group.

During the late 1920s Eliot traveled several times to Europe on *Journal* business, interviewing business executives during their long days at sea away from the office, while Pris worked as a secretary at AT&T, commuting by subway from Flatbush to 195 Broadway.

Eliot on board the *Aquitania*, ca. 1927

Golf in the 1920s

In 1929 Eliot and Priscilla had been engaged for four years. But Eliot's mother was the main woman in his life, and she had no intention of relinquishing that position without a fight. Ruth Vestner was a formidable adversary. Aside from that, Eliot and Priscilla were doing quite well: they were in love, they had good jobs, they were putting some money aside, and they were investing in the stock market. In 1929 the market was pretty exciting.

Lovers

The Fuller family, 1928: Pris, Everett's wife Gertrude, Ruth, Lowell,
Priscilla May, Everett, young Ev and Eliot

In October 1929 the Dow hit 343, up from 155 at the beginning of 1927.[295]Buying stocks and watching them go up was fun. *The Saturday Evening Post* printed a poem that captured the mood of the times:

> Oh, hush thee, my babe, granny's bought some more shares
> Daddy's gone out to play with the bulls and the bears,
> Mother's buying on tips, and she simply can't lose,
> And baby shall have some expensive new shoes![296]

It was a time when the possibilities seemed limitless. In 1927, Charles Lindbergh had been the first to fly across the Atlantic. There were exciting new technologies—radio, telephone, talking movies, automobiles—that were becoming profitable. The stocks of companies making and selling the new products—General Motors, RCA, AT&T, General Electric, Westinghouse, Wright Aeronautics, Curtiss—were soaring. Herbert Hoover, running for president on the Republican ticket in the fall of 1928, was full of optimism: "We shall soon, with the help of God, be in sight of the day when poverty will be banished from this nation." Optimism was in the air.

Only the older generation had any memory of the financial crises and depressions of 1873, 1893 and 1907. To Eliot and Priscilla, those events would have seemed as remote as the Civil War. It was all ancient history. While the market had its ups and downs, it seemed that every time the market took a step back it recovered and moved up to a new record. The course of wisdom, it seemed, was to buy good stocks and hold them. Market downturns were simply good buying opportunities. Impatient with the old measures, such as valuing a stock at ten times earnings, people willingly paid fifty times earnings for blue chips like General Motors and RCA. Eliot and Priscilla were swept up in a national mania.[297]

To those who studied financial history, it must have seemed that the Federal Reserve System, created in 1913 in response to the panic of 1907, now provided stability to the banking system that had not existed before. The central bank could provide liquidity as needed to forestall a banking panic. There was one problem with this assumption. The Fed was indeed using its tools in an effort to

---

295 The Dow-Jones Industrial Average, one among a number of measures of stock market activity, is the weighted average share price of a selected group of industrial stocks.
296 Robert Sobel, *The Great Bull Market, Wall Street in the 1920s* (New York; W. W. Norton, 1968), 127
297 See Allen, *Only Yesterday*, 290-320.

moderate speculative fever but with no discernible effect. The tail winds driving speculation were too strong.

Many experts believed a "correction" to the bull market was long overdue; some thought the correction might be severe and advised selling stocks, but the more commonly held view was that any market correction would be no more than a temporary blip. Irving Fisher, a prominent Yale economics professor, commented in the summer of 1929: "Stock market prices have reached what looks like a permanently high plateau." At the other end of the spectrum, Roger Babson in early September predicted that "Sooner or later a crash is coming and it may be terrific." Babson, going against the prevailing sentiment, was widely criticized. [298]

Eliot, a financial reporter and probably a small investor, would have encouraged Priscilla to invest in the market. Their fathers, with memories of 1893 and 1907, probably avoided the hot new technology stocks and felt safe, conservatively invested in railroad and utility bonds for their old age.

On Thursday, October 24, 1929, there were intimations of the predicted "correction." That day prices fell and continued to fall on Friday. The next week, "Black Tuesday" set a record for share transactions that lasted for thirty-nine years.[299] The bottom dropped out of the market as panicked investors dumped their shares for whatever they could get. Buyers were scarce and prices just kept falling.[300]

Following "Black Tuesday" and on into 1930 there was hope that stock prices might stabilize, that things might get better soon. The Federal Reserve was pumping money into the system.[301] Priscilla's Uncle Will Redfield gave a speech, reported in *The New York Times* with the headline "Brooklyn Banker Predicts Early End to Depression." According to Redfield, "No economic reasons can be found for the continuance of the prevailing depression." Redfield wasn't

298 See "Closed for the Holiday, The Bank Holiday of 1933" (publication of the Federal Reserve Bank of Boston), 4; John Kenneth Galbraith, *The Great Crash* (Boston; Houghton Mifflin Company, 1954), 89.
299 Sobel, *The Great Bull Market*, 138.
300 Brokers' margin calls helped propel the downward movement. It was common practice in the 1920s for investors to buy stock on margin. Typically, an investor would pay $10 to buy $100 worth of stock, the difference being covered by low interest credit from the broker. In 1920 a total of $1 billion in margin loans was outstanding. By the fall of 1929 that figure had increased to $8.5 billion. Buying on margin was a wonderful way to make money in a rising market, but once prices started to fall, brokers called on their customers to put up more cash. Failing receipt of the cash, the brokers immediately sold the stock which they held as collateral for the loan. A lot of this going on at once was instrumental in driving down stock prices.
301 Sobel, *The Great Bull Market*, 147-149.

the only prominent optimist.[302] But things did not get better; they got worse, much worse.

Eliot and Pris, along with millions of other Americans, lost their savings in the market, as the Dow dropped 25% in 1929, 34% in 1930, and 53% in 1931.[303] Businesses went bankrupt, borrowers defaulted, banks closed, unemployment climbed to nearly 25% of the workforce, demand for goods and services disappeared, and prices fell; the nation seemed to be caught in a downward spiral with no end in sight.[304]

In the spring of 1931 Pris was thirty-two. Her engagement was now in its sixth year. The Fullers must have wondered if this engagement was going anywhere. If they couldn't marry in prosperity, why would they marry in a Depression?

They almost didn't. Right up to the wedding, Priscilla wasn't sure she wanted to marry him. On the eve of the wedding, Ruth wrote her a frank letter:

Dearest Twin:

Better destroy this when read. I wonder if I could help you any to clear up any doubts you may have at this time.

I really think that getting married isn't the great big thrill it is cracked up to be in fiction. And I think we all expect and think we should feel more in that line than there really is. Don't try to analyze your feelings. Let them alone. This is all you need to think of—if you can feel now and then, or whenever you ask

---

302   See *The New York Times*, November 11, 1930, 39 (unattributed article). Redfield, who died in 1932, didn't live long enough to see the end of the Great Depression., which lasted until the Second World War. Most of the prominent political and business leaders of the day were predicting an early end to the market "correction" of 1929. See Allen, *Only Yesterday*, 340. A brief bull market during the first three months of 1930 seemed to support the optimism. But the market quickly reversed itself and continued its downward momentum.

303   From 300 on January 1, 1929, the Dow declined to 220 at year-end 1929, then to 164.58 at year-end 1930 and 77.90 at year-end 1931. Sobel, *The Great Bull Market*, 151, shows the decline in key common stocks during 1930-33. The stock market crash wasn't the cause of the Depression, but it was a leading indicator and market losses sharply diminished consumer confidence and buying power, which obviously affected business sales and caused bankruptcies and unemployment.

304   The unemployment rate rose from 3.2 percent in 1929 to 8.9 percent in 1930, 16.3 percent in 1931 and 26 percent in June 1932. See Gene Smiley, *Rethinking the Great Depression* (Chicago; Ivan Dee Publishing, 2002), 61, 67. It became fashionable among intellectuals to look to Stalin and Mussolini for communist and fascist models that might replace capitalism; demagogues like Huey Long of Louisiana, Father Coughlin and others fought for national attention with their own solutions to the crisis.

yourself, that you do want to marry Eliot why that's enough. I remember that was the way with me.... I was not just blissfully happy about everything....

You see, dear, I want to reassure you that if you shouldn't be feeling ecstatically happy and that everything was wonderful & blissful...well you are feeling as brides are more apt than not to feel. Try to relax and just think how nice it will be to go away for awhile into the country...and try, dearie, in your own particular case to forget all that is past—begin over again. We are all as keen for Eliot as if none of the past had been and are making a fresh start with him accepting him as the splendid man he really has proved himself to be.

I hope you don't think I'm intruding to write like this. I can remember so well how I felt before my wedding. Pretend romance and after awhile it will really be there. There's so much in the imagination. Make it work for you and not against.[305]

Exactly what was she supposed to put in the past and "forget?" Why was she being told to "begin over again?" Something had happened in their relationship, something that angered Pris and her family, something that caused Pris to have second thoughts about marrying Eliot.

The Fullers had probably seen Eliot as a questionable match for Priscilla from the start. They knew little or nothing about his family, except what Priscilla told them. Charles and Mary Fuller probably held rather conservative views of marriage, and may have raised an eyebrow or two on hearing that Eliot's parents lived separate lives. That Eliot had not gone to college would have set him apart from the men in Priscilla's family, and his various jobs on Wall Street might have struck Charles Fuller as lacking in substance. Added to all that, Eliot was German-American. Within the Fuller family there was considerable anti-German sentiment left over from the war. Priscilla undoubtedly would have defended her choice, but the family concerns may have planted seeds of doubt in her own mind. And then something happened that brought all those doubts to the surface.

---

305   Letter, undated and marked "private," from Ruth to Priscilla.

There is some evidence that Eliot had been involved with at least one other woman. A couple of letters, dated August 21 and 22 1930, from "Mary," written from The Chamberlin-Vanderbilt Hotel in Old Point Comfort, Virginia, suggest that Eliot and Mary may have had something more than a friendship. "Dearest Eliot...Just as I thought, it all seems like a dream, much too marvelous and much too disturbing to forget...I have been thinking of you such a lot.... I've missed you more than I could possibly tell you and am looking forward so much to seeing you in Sept...I dreamed about you last night....I have been thinking about you a lot since that Tuesday morning...When I look back on it all—well, it was just too glorious—I can't say another thing....Always, Mary."[306] It's conceivable that they spent time together during Eliot's two-week reserve service that summer in Fayetteville, North Carolina, and perhaps in August, when Eliot was in Virginia Beach, not far from Point Comfort. Priscilla was away that August in upstate New York and Dorset, Vermont.

The two letters from "Mary" offer a tantalizing glimpse into a private corner of Eliot's life in 1930. It may have been all smoke and no fire. That he kept the letters all those years says something—perhaps a reminder of what might have been, an option not pursued? Something kept him from just tearing them up and throwing them out.

Whatever doubts Priscilla may have had were resolved in favor of marriage. She and Eliot were married on May 28, 1931 at St. Paul's in Flatbush. They honeymooned in a cabin on one of the Rangeley Lakes in northern Maine. From the number of times they revisited Rangeley over the years, the honeymoon must have been a happy experience for both of them.

They returned to a one-bedroom apartment at 1911 Albemarle Street in Flatbush. Eliot had his job at the *Journal*, interviewing business executives as they arrived or departed by ship and writing a column on financial "shipnews." But his job hung by a thread. Every business in America was having trouble generating revenue and the *Journal* was no exception. Pris still had her job at AT&T, but even AT&T was facing the need to retrench.

Other members of the family had been hit hard. The market crash virtually wiped out Charles Fuller's retirement savings. Even supposedly safe investments, such as railroad and utility bonds, lost much of their value during 1929-33. Fuller also felt the impact of the real estate depression. He had put his big Flatbush house up for sale in 1929, valuing it at $40,000. But in 1930 real estate wasn't selling. Fuller finally sold it for less than $15,000, a stunning loss

306   Letters, dated August 20 and 22, 1930, from "Mary" to Eliot.

of value.[307] The Fullers moved into a small apartment a couple of blocks from their old home; even so, they needed financial help from Randolph, Everett, and son-in-law Lowell Shumway.

George Vestner owned 118 shares of Anaconda Copper Mining Co., probably a good part of his retirement savings. On September 3, 1929, with the shares selling at $162, George's holdings had been worth $19,116. In November 1932 those same shares, at $10, were worth $1,118.[308] Like many investors, George held on through 1930, 1931 and 1932, expecting the market to bounce back. When the stock hit $10, George's broker recommended he sell—precisely the wrong recommendation, as the market was about to take off and post a record rebound.

At the bottom of the Depression in 1932, Pris and Eliot lived seemingly normal, humdrum lives. They were caregivers to their parents. Priscilla's mother suffered from Aphasia (a brain disorder affecting speech); Eliot's mother was lonely and in need of attention. Evenings with friends were invariably in the home and alcohol-free (the sale of alcohol was prohibited); they played bridge, gin rummy, hearts, pinochle, poker, anagrams and Parcheesi. If they went out, it was to inexpensive places like Schrafft's, Child's, Drake's, the Automat, or Happiness. Eliot did manage to take her to the Marine Roof of the Bossart Hotel for dinner and dancing on May 28, their first anniversary. But an evening of dinner and dancing was the exception. The also listened to a lot of radio, still in its infancy: the comic Ed Wynn; Fred Allen; George Burns and Gracie Allen; Eddie Cantor, as he made his satirical run for the presidency, and the Metropolitan Opera, which began broadcasting in 1932.[309] The movies were also prime entertainment, and they were now "talking." Actors and actresses actually talked to each other on the screen—a seemingly miraculous step forward in film technology. Alone or with Eliot, Pris saw a lot of movies in the early thirties: *Secrets* (Mary Pickford); *Storm at Daybreak* (Kay Francis); *Another Language* (Helen

---

307   The 1929 valuation of $40,000 would be about $985,000 in current dollars. See www.measuringworth.com. Fuller loaned the buyer the purchase price of $21,000. That loan was the principal asset in Fuller's estate when he died in 1938. The next year his widow took $15,000 in full satisfaction of the mortgage. In short, the Fullers ended up taking $15,000 in 1939 for a house valued at $40,000 in 1929. The real estate market didn't begin to recover until long after the end of World War II.

308   In current dollars, the decline in value was from $240,000 to $17,000. .Presumably that wasn't the only stock George owned, but it's the only investment for which the record has survived.

309   The origins of radio go back to Marconi's first demonstration of controlled transmission and reception of radio signals in 1905, followed by years of financial losses as businessmen tried to figure out how to make money from it. With the entry of big companies like GE and Westinghouse, radio began to go public in the mid-1920s. The first radio broadcasts had come in the early 1920s. The Yankees-Giants World Series had been broadcast in 1923; the Democratic Convention in 1924. By the early 1930s, radio had become a major source of entertainment, as Broadway stars started appearing on the radio following disastrous seasons in 1930 and 1931. One of the questions in the 1930 Census was, "Do you own a radio?"

Hayes); *Berkeley Square* (Leslie Howard); *Night Flight* (Clark Gable); *Shanghai Express* (Marlene Dietrich); *Lady with a Past* (Constance Bennett); *Washington Masquerade* (Lionel Barrymore); *The Passionate Plumber* (Buster Keaston—"Not so hot"); *Huddle* (Ramon Navarro); *Westward Passage* (Ann Hardy); *Grand Hotel* (Greta Garbo); *As You Desire Me* (Garbo); *Love Me Tonight* (Maurice Chevalier); *Smiling Flora* and *Riptide* (Norma Shearer); *Too Busy to Work* (Will Rogers— "very funny"); *Rasputin* (all the Barrymore's—"Strong picture!"); *Little Women* (Katharine Hepburn); *Little Miss Marker* (Shirley Temple); *Sadie McKee* (Joan Crawford); *The Thin Man* (William Powell and Myrna Loy, twice); *The Girl from Missouri* (Jean Harlow); *I'm no Angel* (Mae West); *Mutiny on the Bounty* (Charles Laughton); and *Tale of Two Cities* (Ronald Colman). After one double feature, she noted "3 hours, too much movies!"[310]

In the spring of 1932, Pris was secretary to Jack Reese, a senior AT&T executive. Even mighty AT&T was suffering from the Depression as people were cutting back on telephone service. On May 7, she noted in her diary "Office closed Saturday from now on!" She was excited to have Saturdays off, but also probably concerned about her job. The AT&T office at 195 Broadway provided a good part of her social life. Friendships she formed at the office, cemented by daily lunches at local restaurants, lasted well beyond her working days, as did her friendship with Reese and his family. AT&T was more than just a nine-to-five job; it was a home away from home.

Most nights that spring she slept in her parents's apartment to care for her mother. On July 15, she took her parents to Grand Central Station where they boarded a train for a long vacation in Dorset, Vermont. In August she received a newsy letter from her father:

> This is a lovely spot. Nice old house with lots of books and old furniture. Mabel Gilbert runs the house—a very intelligent maid (about 34) graduate of Smith 1919. She is the boss and is assisted by her mother whose grandmother was a Fuller and a probable cousin away back....We have a nice large room. Two beds both very high up, so that a little step ladder would come handy, a nice easy chair and good light. I get mother to bed early where she reads with a good light beside her. I keep

---

310   As with the telephone, Victrola, and radio, the development of talking movies was yet another advance that radically transformed communications and entertainment.

my watch on D.S. [daylight saving] time so that I don't feel ashamed to go to bed when standard time says it is only 9:30.

The dining room is very pleasant: nice old china; everything very dainty and the food excellent. Dinner is fruit cocktail, meat and vegetables all on one large plate, a nice salad and dessert. Two other boarders (O.M.'s of course) have a separate table and after the recent babble at Harwood's it seems like a haven of peace.

We are now sitting out in easy chairs under some crab apple trees whose branches hang down low so that it is shady all day. I took my pre matutinal[311] walk this AM down to the beginning of Church St., just one mile. We don't go to the Cong Church. I went once but now we read our Prayer Book and Hymnal which does me more good than listening to the young man who preaches quite intellectually....

You can see from mother's letters that she is quite a different person from the pale invalid whom you saw off at the Grand Central on July 15. She can really be quite pert and sassy now & looks ever so much younger & fresher. I know we shall be happy here & it makes me specially happy to see her improving so much.

We use the Library a good deal and have read some good books and there are lots of books in this house, both solid and light. For a solid, I am enjoying a Life of Disraeli. I keep this going with novels in the evening.[312]

In the fall of 1932, Pris and Eliot began the search for a cheaper apartment. Most of October was devoted to apartment hunting, which was a frustrating exercise judging by her diary notations: "all day, no luck," "nice but expensive," or "nice, but taken." They found what they were looking for at 1803 Beverly at 18th Street, still in Flatbush. November 2 was her first night in the new

---

311   From the Latin matutinus, middle English matutyne meaning "of the morning." *Webster's Third International Dictionary*: 1395. Fuller was always a Latin scholar.
312   Letter, dated August 7, 1932, from Charles Fuller to Priscilla.

apartment; it wasn't quite what she expected: "Spent eve at apt. Couldn't do much because of cockroaches!"

That same fall, the presidential election shifted into high gear. Back in 1920, Charles Fuller had introduced Pris to young Franklin Roosevelt on the speaker's platform during a Democratic rally in Brooklyn. Now she had another opportunity to vote for Roosevelt. He had been governor of New York for four years and would be the Democratic nominee, running against President Herbert Hoover.

Her first diary reference to the 1932 election was June 30, when she reported that "Eliot sat up all night listening to Dem convention at Chicago. I was up almost all night," and the next day: "Roosevelt & Garner nominated for Pres & Vice Pres."[313]

They followed the campaign in the newspapers and on the radio. Hoover and Roosevelt made full use of radio to get their message out to the voters.[314] Pris liked what she heard from Hoover and Coolidge, but she also liked it when Roosevelt denounced Hoover's spending and big government policies.[315] Her diary entry for Election Day was brief:

> Election Day (Hoover-Roosevelt). El & I at apt. all day. Maude came in PM & cleaned up beautifully. Lowell called. To Aunt Lil's in eve. Lib & Luke there. Hearts & election returns. Roosevelt. Home early.

They got home early because the election was over early.[316] The next day *The New York Times* ran a big headline:

ROOSEVELT WINNER IN LANDSLIDE;
DEMOCRATS CONTROL WET CONGRESS[317]

---

313   The vice-presidential nominee on the Democratic ticket was John Nance "Cactus Jack" Garner, Congressman from Texas and Speaker of the House.
314   Eliot and Pris listened to Hoover at Des Moines (4 October), Coolidge for Hoover (11 October), Hoover at Cleveland (15 October), Roosevelt at Pittsburgh (19 October), Hoover (22 October), Al Smith for Roosevelt (24 and 29 October)and Hoover at Madison Square Garden (31 October).
315   See Arthur Schlesinger, *Crisis of the Old Order* (Boston; Houghton Mifflin, 1957), 433.
316   It was a Democratic landslide. Roosevelt received 22.8 million votes to Hoover's 15.7 million, Roosevelt carried thirty-nine states with 444 electoral votes, and the Democrats captured the House and the Senate with large majorities. See Charles and Mary Beard, *A Basic History of the United States* (New York; Doubleday, Doran, 1944), 455. Roosevelt ended seventy years of Republican domination, during which the Democrats had held the presidency for only twelve years.
317   The reference to "Wet Congress" meant that the newly-elected Democratic majority favored repealing Prohibition (those supporting Prohibition were "dry").

That the paper would headline "WET CONGRESS" speaks to what a big issue Prohibition seemed to be in 1932. The 1920 Constitutional amendment prohibiting the sale of alcohol had been honored largely in the breach. Prohibition had not stopped people from drinking; it just changed their drinking habits. Instead of going to a bar or restaurant for a drink, or buying a bottle of wine at the store, people "in the know" now went to "speakeasies." Behind an innocent-looking door and with the right introduction they could drink bootleg liquor all night.[318] Before Prohibition, bars were for men only; after Prohibition, the ladies joined the men in the speakeasies. The new "wet" Congress quickly passed the legislation that led to its repeal in 1933. Pris's diary records a brief history of the end of Prohibition, at least as it worked out in New York City:

7 Nov. 1932: Prohibition to be repealed.

26 Jan. 1933: To Bill Fine's office at 5 then to speakeasy "Charlies" on W. 46th St...Great cocktails.

14 Mar.1933: Beer bill passed in Washington

6 Apr, 1933: To 86th St. Hofbrau. Beer supposed to be in again at midnight. Home at 2:45.

5 Dec. 1933: Prohibition repealed at 5:30 P.M....Repeal evidently a success.

23 Dec. 1933: Macy's and to their wine store. Line half a block long waiting to get in.[319]

With the end of Prohibition, cocktails came out of the closet. By April 1934 Pris was describing a "between the sheets cocktail. Strong!"[320] Nothing surpassed the Martini in popularity. The following September she had several

---

318   Prohibition was a bonanza for organized crime, with huge profits to be made from smuggling illicit liquor into the country. It also led to increased violence, as gangs fought over turf. In effect, Prohibition criminalized the liquor business.
319   The "beer bill" permitted the sale of 3.2 percent beer in all states where the sale of beer wasn't prohibited by state or local law. The repeal of Prohibition on December 5, 1933 removed the Constitutional prohibition of the sale of alcohol, effectively leaving the regulation of alcohol to the states.
320   Sometimes referred to as "Maiden's Prayer," the standard recipe was (and is) equal parts Triple Sec, white rum, brandy and lemon juice (or some other fruit juice, such as passion fruit).

too many when she and Eliot went to Edge's for cocktails: "4 martinis's....Was I drunk!"

In March 1933, Pris noted "Big layoffs at office." At the same time, her boss asked her to take on extra work at the same salary.[321] And things were busy at the office. The Roosevelt Administration, through the new Federal Communications Commission, launched an investigation of the telephone monopoly and its pricing policies. She worked on the investigation. She had a job, she was busy, and there were benefits in working for AT&T. On May 27 there was a big office outing:

> Left at 8 & met Mr. Barrett at Atlantic Ave. He drove us out to Meadowbrook Park beyond Montclair where Transmission Dept. had picnic. Played golf with Mr. Jacobs. Sandwiches & then more golf, baseball, treasure hunt. Supper. Dancing & games. Home at 11:45. Fine day. Sunburnt!

Pris at her AT&T desk in the early thirties with the latest model telephone.

321   She worked on AT&T Annual Reports, FCC investigations, and the "Chicago rate case" (the details of which are mercifully lost to history).

Skiing at Buck Hill Falls, Pennsylvania, winter, 1933

In addition to her day job, Pris worked several nights a week for Miss Hart, her old English teacher at Packer and head of the camp at Silver Lake. Her diary for February 19, 1933 notes: "To Miss Hart's at 5. Dinner there & worked for her till 9:30 ($1.50!)." She wasn't thrilled. Even in the Depression, $1.50 for four hours of work was cheap.

When Roosevelt assumed the presidency in March 1933, the banking system was paralyzed. The banks had uncollectible loans on their books, they were short of cash, and their depositors were nervous. Because there was no deposit insurance, depositors were ready to race to the bank to get their money at the slightest hint of a problem. When a bank ran out of cash, that was it; the doors were closed. Early in 1933, Pris experienced the banking crisis first hand, noting "Serial Bldg Loan Bank won't pay any money. I have $75 there." Seventy-five bucks was a lot of money in 1933—probably her entire savings.[322]

One by one the states declared bank holidays, closing the state-chartered banks until they could be examined for soundness. On March 4, Roosevelt declared a national bank holiday. Priscilla's diary entries provide a glimpse of

---

322   In 1933, $75 was about $1,200 in current dollars. See http://www.measuringworth.com.

what was going on that week, but the news had to compete with the mundane details of her life:

> 4 March: Newsweek came. Bank Holiday declared & Roosevelt inaugurated. Mamie cleaned our apt & got dinner. Listened to [inauguration] ceremonies... Shopped & called on Ruth and Lowell. [323]

> 8 March: Office. El and I had lunch with Lib [good friend Elizabeth Hatfield]. She depressed over banks being closed...

> 13 March: Office, lunch with El at Child's...To Miss Hart's, supper and worked til 10. Met El & John Easton at Grand Central, they having been to Reg. meeting [reserve officers meeting, 7th Regiment]...Banks opened again.

With the banks closed cash was scarce, paychecks couldn't be cashed, church collection plates were empty, and people had to buy groceries or gas on credit. For only the second time in its history, the New York Stock Exchange closed, so no securities traded during the bank holiday. On March 13, banks that had been examined and found to be solvent were again open for business. Later in 1933, President Roosevelt signed legislation creating federal deposit insurance, effectively putting an end to the bank runs. [324]

Investors could look back on three and a half years of unrelieved misery in the stock market. It would have taken a brave soul to buy stocks that March. But from a very low base (the Dow was at fifty in early 1933) the market moved up, and continued to move up—sixty-seven percent for the year. Pris and Eliot followed the market closely; they didn't want to get burned again. But the market seemed to be recovering. In early 1934 she bought four shares of AT&T common stock. [325] Since AT&T was the biggest corporation in the country and a legal monopoly, she obviously considered the risk worth taking. Compared to a savings account which paid virtually no interest, AT&T securities paid a dividend and seemed like a good bet.

---

323   Pris' reference to a bank holiday was to the holiday called by New York State Governor Herbert Lehman. New York's holiday was quickly followed by Illinois, Massachusetts, New Jersey and Pennsylvania. The national bank holiday became effective March 6.

324   The Federal Deposit Insurance Corporation insures bank deposits. It was created in the 1933 Glass-Steagall Act, which separated commercial and investment banking. At first, deposits were insured up to $2,500, a limit that was almost immediately increased to $5,000.

325   *Priscilla's Diary*, March 15, 1934. A year later, she bought eight more shares at 108.

Even if the market looked a bit better, unemployment was still a terrible problem. Eliot, having lost his job at the *Journal*, tried selling securities on commission for Spencer Trask & Co. Priscilla's diary entries for March and April 1933 suggest that he was under the gun at work:

15 March: "Stock market opened again so El was too busy to come [to lunch]";

20 March "Nice dinner home with El. He stayed in all evening";

31 March: "El worked late (home about 1AM)";

20 April "Big day on stock market. Lunch alone. Met El for a minute at 5... He came [home] at 7:30."

Dorothy, Priscilla's older sister, had a husband who had given up looking for work. Dorothy supported them with her secretarial job in the city. Eliot's brother-in-law, Victor Bensch, lost his job and couldn't afford to pay the rent on his family's apartment, so the family split up. Vic's wife and child went to live with Eliot's mother; Eliot and Pris set up a cot for Vic in their living room. As Pris noted: "Chinatown for lunch. Dinner home. Vic there. He is going to stay with us for a while."[326]
A "while" turned into a year, and Vic was in the living room every night. When Eliot was away, Pris would come home, cook dinner for Vic, and the two of them would play gin rummy or pinochle. On March 15, 1933, Pris noted that she and Eliot couldn't go out in the evening because Vic was out with their only key. But he was family, and there was an obligation to help.
By April 1933, Eliot was again looking for a job, and on Wall Street there were none. Since the end of the war, he had been active in the army reserves; now he was attending reserve officer meetings at night. He and Pris discussed his "going off with the conservation army for several months." The Civilian Conservation Corps was one of the first measures to come out of the emergency session of Congress in March 1933.[327] The purpose was to create a peacetime "army," recruiting thousands of unemployed men and putting them to work on forest conservation: planting trees, preventing soil erosion, clearing forest roads and

326   *Priscilla's Diary*, March 9 1933,
327   Immediately after his inauguration in March 1933, President Roosevelt had called Congress into emergency session to deal with the economic crisis. The Emergency Conservation Work Act, creating the Civilian Conservation Corps, was one of the many pieces of legislation to come out of that session.

trails. The regular army was put in charge of establishing and running the CCC camps and sent out a call to reserve officers. Eliot jumped at the opportunity.

As it turned out, "several months" stretched into three years. Except for brief times when he was able to get home on leave, Eliot was away from June 1933 to January 1936.[328] In the CCC he was outdoors and doing what he liked. During the twenties, he would have turned up his nose at a first lieutenant's pay of $100 a month; he was making much more than that at the *Journal*. In 1933 any paying job looked good. Combined with Pris's earnings they could get by, even supporting Eliot's mother, and their two salaries put them in a better position than most people.[329] But they had to live separately: Pris in Brooklyn, Eliot in Montana and later Tennessee.

That summer, Eliot was assigned to CCC Camp 1223 in Red Lodge, Montana, deep in the Beartooth Mountains. In September, Priscilla took the train to Montana and stayed at Richel's Lodge near the camp.

Red Lodge, Montana, 1934

---

328 "Record of Assignments," Eliot N. Vestner personnel records (National Personnel Records Center, St. Louis, Missouri, Case Reference No. 2001-296-1569). He served from June 19, 1933 until January 14, 1936.

329 I would guess their combined yearly income was about $2,500 or roughly $40,000 in 2007 dollars.

CCC Company 1223; Eliot on right

She found time to write up her last two days at the Lodge:

17 Sept 1933: "Lovely day. El worked all AM & I lay out under pine trees. Early dinner then rode horses up the mt. & across the plateau. Wonderful ride. Back at the Ranch at 6. Supper. El stayed around all eve. & we read in cabin. Bed early."

18 Sept 1933: "Up early, nice long ride on Susie way up the canyon. El at Ranch for lunch. To Red Lodge for mail. Back & packed. Mrs. Richel kept us for supper. Left about 7. Drove to Billings.... Danced at Old Heidelberg. Train East at 12:20 AM.

She managed to snag a lower berth and, after passing through the Dakotas, Chicago, and Buffalo, arrived September 21 at Grand Central, 6:40 AM, in time for an early start at the office. Her comment: "Punk to be back in N.Y."

In October 1933, Eliot left Montana and took up a new CCC assignment in Clinton, near Knoxville, Tennessee. On February 20, Pris arrived at Penn Station to take the bus to Knoxville, but because of snow and wind the buses weren't running. She went to brother-in-law Lowell Shumway's office. Lowell arranged for a berth in the Pullman car and put her on the night train to Knoxville.[330] Eliot, his boss Captain Ordway, and Sandy, Eliot's great big shaggy dog of indeterminate breed, met her in the afternoon. After checking into the Hotel Andrew Johnson (where her mother-in-law was also staying), they drove twenty-five miles out to camp for dinner and a night of talking and bridge in front of a big fire.

The next day, they drove 117 miles through the mountains to Asheville, North Carolina, spending the night at the George Vanderbilt Hotel. Next day, they drove back to camp in a blizzard, arriving in time for a steak dinner and more bridge in front of the fire. That evening they had a big argument:

> Icy ride to K'ville at 1:30AM. I drove. Bus late so decided to take the train after Battle of Wills. Hotel Andrew Johnson at 2:30. Snow & rain.

She took the train the next morning and arrived in Washington at 1:30 AM, waited in the station for a "dinky little train" to Philadelphia, where she changed trains again and caught a 6:54 AM to New York. She arrived at eight in a snowstorm and without sleep but in time to start the day at AT&T. Her diary comment for that day was "Very sleepy." That evening, with her family, she fell asleep at the dinner table.

Working in CCC camps meant that Eliot was separated from his aging father. In the early thirties, Pris and Eliot had occasionally met George Vestner for dinner and a movie in the city. George sometimes invited Eliot to join him and his friends for a night of poker. On July 17, 1932, Pris described an outing with George:

> Put up sandwiches. Subway to Flushing.... Bus to Bayside Yacht Club. Mr. Moody & Mr. V. there. Rode down the sound in Mr. M's cabin cruiser. Anchored in Glen Cove & swam & ate lunch. Back to Bayside about 9. Great day. Sunburnt!

By 1934, George had retired from his law practice and was managing real estate. He had a girlfriend, the widow Plum, who raised turkeys and dogs

---

330   The Pullman Palace Car Company, founded by George Pullman, developed the sleeping car in the early twentieth century as a pricier alternative to sitting up all night. The new cars featured carpeting, upholstered chairs, comfortable sleeping berths and excellent service. The company hired African-Americans as porters.

and lived on the Shrewsbury River near Red Bank, New Jersey. But in March, George came down with pneumonia. Excerpts from Priscilla's diary during the week of 13 March 1934 describe George's final illness and death:[331]

13 March: M.V's [Mother Vestner]; Dad sick.

15 March: Called El about his Dad having pneumonia.

17 March: Dad Vestner died in eve....Tried to get El on phone & couldn't.

19 March: El on way home from Knoxville...knitted & radio. Didn't sleep because expecting El.

20 March: El home at 8; had breakfast with me. Uptown to Stephen Merritt funeral place. M. V. there.

21 March: To Flatbush for M.V. Flat tire in front of St. George. Breakfast there. To N.Y. for Dad's funeral...all had lunch at Child's."

Priscilla's diary captures a slice of life as it was in 1934: before antibiotics, pneumonia was often fatal, as it was for George Vestner; inability to get through on a long distance phone call was the norm rather than the exception; radio, the main source of evening entertainment for most people, was in its heyday; without air travel, it took Eliot all night by train to get from Knoxville to New York; Stephen Merritt's Funeral Home, long since disappeared, was one of the more fashionable funeral homes in the city; the St. George hotel in Brooklyn, with 2,632 rooms, was the largest hotel in the city, but in 1934 it was bankrupt and its lenders had foreclosed; getting a flat tire was more common when tires were less resistant to nails; Child's was then (but is no more) one of the country's leading low-priced restaurant chains, specializing in self-service cafeterias.

Five days later, they were on the train to Washington, with Eliot continuing on to Knoxville while Pris caught a 12:35 AM train back to New York. As she noted in her diary: "Not much sleep."

That August, Eliot was commanding officer of CCC Company 292, nine miles outside Coal Creek, Tennessee. His company was at work on the Norris Dam project,

331   Death Certificate, March 17, 1934, No. 7203 (New York City Municipal Archives). George Vestner died in the Postgraduate Hospital in New York City.

controlling soil erosion and clearing woods around the town of Norris, a new town constructed for the workmen on the dam. There is a large picture of the 150 men comprising Eliot's Company, the all-male-all white group lined up looking fit and tanned, with Eliot and his staff seated in chairs. As camp commander he was in charge, but he worked closely with the Tennessee Valley Authority and employees of the Forest and National Park Services who supervised the forestry and conservation projects. Eliot was thriving in the CCC. [332]

Lt. Vestner, CCC camp, Tennessee, 1935

332   As commander of Camp 292 he received a letter notifying him that "Your company has been given the rating of 100. This is a very fine showing and reflects credit upon your efforts." In operation from 1933 until the onset of war in 1941, the CCC was a great success. In addition to its major conservation projects, the CCC instilled military discipline in the men. When war came in 1941, the nation had more than a million men of draft age with CCC experience. Among its other accomplishments were: 3,470 fire towers; 97,000 miles of fire roads; 4,235,000 man-days in fighting fires; more than a billion trees planted; soil erosion projects credited with arresting erosion on more than 20 million acres; development of recreation facilities in national, state, county, and metropolitan parks; protecting wildlife habitat; stream improvement; building dams for generating electricity in rural areas; building drainage systems for agricultural land; and emergency work in floods, hurricanes, and other natural disasters. The CCC was a success.

Like the CCC, the Tennessee Valley Authority (TVA) was another Roosevelt initiative launched during the first hundred days of the new administration.[333] The Norris Dam project was part of the TVA's effort to harness the power of the Tennessee River and its various tributaries to provide cheap electricity to a large swath of the rural south, impoverished even by Depression standards. With the completion of the massive Norris Dam in 1936, Norris Lake was formed, displacing 3,500 farming families and the town of Loyston, which now lies at the bottom of the lake.

Survey team, CCC camp, Tennessee, 1935

On August 17, Pris went to her bank to load up on travelers' checks.[334] That evening she boarded the 6 o'clock Greyhound bus for Roanoke, Virginia. The next morning she wrote in her diary: "Seasick all night & a boil on my nose."

After a change in Washington, she arrived at noon in Roanoke, where Eliot was waiting for her in his well-seasoned Chevrolet. They stayed at the Roanoke Hotel and saw Jean Harlow in *The Girl from Missouri*. The next morning they drove up into the Blue Ridge Mountains to Blowing Rock and then to Linville. "Loved it so much we stayed. Eseeola Inn. Great place: tennis, swim, nap....

333   The TVA bill, signed into law in May 1933, created an independent federal government corporation, with broad authority over a forty-one thousand square-mile area including parts of seven states—Kentucky, Virginia, North Carolina, Georgia, Alabama and Mississippi. The TVA was created to improve navigation of the Tennessee River, control flooding in the valley, conserve forests and other natural resources, construct dams, and generate and deliver electricity to the people and businesses throughout the area.
334   At the time, traveling around the country wasn't much different from traveling overseas. There were no credit or debit cards, and banking was local. If they didn't know you at the bank, you could forget about cashing a personal check. Traveling from New York to Tennessee required cash or traveler's checks.

played tennis. Fine food. Bed early. Boil on nose." Despite that pesky boil, they had fun: golf and tennis, riding the trails, and in the evenings playing poker and bridge with new friends. The Eseeola was a gracious old inn, four thousand feet up in the mountains. The inn's least expensive accommodations were about five dollars a day including meals, golf, and riding.

From the Blue Ridge Mountains, they drove to Eliot's Coal Creek camp, where Pris helped with the bookkeeping and payroll. After she straightened out the books, they drove back to Roanoke and left the car, which now had 23,000 miles on the odometer and was on its last legs. They caught the night train to New York and accommodations were tight. As she put it, "Good sleep, both in upper!"

They had a couple of days together in New York. Her diary for September 5, 1934 notes: "At 5 El & I to Edge's for cocktails (4 martinis). Din at Ella Barbour's..... Saw Ann Harding in *The Fountain* at Music Hall & dashed to Penn Station where El took 10:50 train to Roanoke."[335]

While Pris lived alone in their Brooklyn apartment and commuted to Manhattan, Eliot's mother lived at the Hotel Arnold in Knoxville, close to his camp at Coal Creek. The mother-son arrangement irritated Pris, but sharing the Brooklyn apartment with her mother-in-law was out of the question. Putting Eliot's mother up at the Hotel Arnold was cheaper than renting a second Brooklyn apartment and it relieved Pris of one more family chore in Brooklyn: regularly visiting an unhappy mother-in-law. Even so, Pris found the mother-son relationship peculiar to say the least.

She was also frustrated and unhappy over her seeming inability to get pregnant. She knew they needed her job to make ends meet and a baby would be expensive, but she wanted to be a mother. At thirty-four, her time to have a baby of her own was running out. Living apart was not helpful.

Adding to her frustration was the summer heat, insufferable in a small Brooklyn apartment long before air-conditioning. She found ways to escape the heat—notably Craig House in Beacon, New York.

---

335   Ella Barbour's, an inexpensive midtown restaurant, was for special occasions; more often, dinner out meant going to the Horn & Hardart Automat in Times Square. The glass and chrome Automat was one of the earliest "fast food" places. Entire walls were lined with little windows and coin slots. Would Pris like the roast chicken, peas, mashed potatoes, and gravy? All she had to do was put three nickels in the slot, twist the knob, reach in, take out her hot dinner sitting on a china plate, pick up some silverware, and carry it all to a table. For coffee she would get a cup, place it under a fancy spout and put another coin in the slot. The spout would dispense exactly one cup of good coffee: hard to spend much more than fifty cents on dinner at the Automat.

A large gothic revival mansion set on sixty-four acres in the village of Beacon overlooking the Hudson River, Craig House was a very comfortable private hospital and Pris's sister, Ruth, was a heart patient there. It was no ordinary hospital. Along with excellent medical facilities, there was riding, tennis, golf and swimming, not to mention top quality food. It was a country club. Zelda Fitzgerald was a patient at Craig House while Ruth was there. Zelda's wire to her famous husband, Scott Fitzgerald, indicated the range of activities available at Craig House: "WOULD MRS OWEN PACK ALL MY CLOTHING INCLUDING RIDING THINGS, TENNIS AND GOLF CLUBS..." Later, she wrote: "All the beauty of this place must cost an awful lot of money and maybe it would be advisable to go somewhere more compatible with our present means." [336]

Craig House was indeed expensive, but where Ruth was concerned Lowell spared nothing. Most summer weekends, Pris would meet Lowell at his McCall Corporation office in Manhattan and the two of them would drive the hour or so to Craig House to visit with Ruth, play golf and tennis, and ride the trails overlooking the Hudson. The weekend of August 11, 1933 was typical of many:

> 11 August [Friday]: Met Lo [Lowell] at 5:30. Drive to B'ville. Dinner with Swan's. Then Lo & I drove up to Craig House at Beacon where Ruth is. Lovely little cottage. Slept with Mrs. Curley, nurse.

> 12 August: Watch Lo take golf lesson. Then played 9 holes. Very bad! Lunch, tennis with Dr. & Mrs. Morrison. Good tennis. Dandy swim in lovely pool. Good dinner at cottage. Sat out in front. Read. Milk nogs & bed.

> 13 August: Warm day. Lo had golf lesson, then we drove to Vassar. Dinner. Tennis in PM. with Mr. & Mrs. deRham (grandparents!) then a peachy swim in the pool. Rain all eve. Dr. Slocum stopped in for a short call. Milk & bed.

---

336   Zelda Fitzgerald was the wife of F. Scott Fitzgerald, the most famous American writer of his time. She was also a mental patient at Craig House in the spring and summer of 1934. See Jackson R. Bryer and Cathy W. Berks, eds. *The Love Letters of F. Scott and Zelda Fitzgerald* (New York; St. Martin's Press, 2002), 178, 180.

Golf, tennis, games of all sorts, were still an important part of Priscilla's life. Good and bad, she carefully noted her golf scores and whether she won or lost at tennis. Evenings with friends still revolved around games—bridge, poker, hearts, gin rummy, pinochle, the "ad" game, and beginning in 1936, the new game of Monopoly. But usually the game was bridge. After one evening of bridge, she wrote in frustration and anger: "Failed to bid a slam!"[337] She saved one Bridge joke ("Too Much Bridge") from the politically incorrect thirties that made her laugh:

> Yessum, dey pay good, but dat was de mos' rediklus place I'se
> eber been. Dey plays a game dey calls bridge, an' las' night
> dere was lots of fellows dere, and just as I was fixing to bring
> in de refreshments, I hears a man say to a woman, "Take yo'
> hand off my trick." I just pretty near dropped dead, when bless
> my soul, I hears annudder man say, "lay down, and let's see
> what yo' got." And then annuder lady says, "You got length,
> but you a'int got strength." Well, I just ups and gets my hat,
> 'cause I knows data place faint for me, and just as I was leaving,
> I hopes to die if a man didn't say, "Well, I guess I'll stop now
> as dies am de last rubber," and doggone if she didn't say, "Lay
> down your dummy and let me play with it." Norm, I's a lady,
> and I just couldn't stay deer.

In 1934 the Fullers finally left Flatbush for the suburbs.[338] On July 5, the family gathered at Ran and Margie's new house in Scarsdale to celebrate Charles and Mary Fuller's golden wedding anniversary—they had married July 5, 1884. Pris noted in her diary for September 17, 1934: "Father resigned from vestry [St Paul's] after 38 years." It was the end of an era for the Fullers. On September 26,

---

337 Contract bridge was born in 1925 when Harold Vanderbilt, on an ocean cruise, figured out the new variation on an old game—basically introducing the concept of the contract. In bridge, you score the most points by bidding (the "contract") and making a grand slam. It doesn't happen often, you have to have the right cards, you have to have the guts to go for it, and you have to win all the tricks, not losing one. A little slam is the same, except you can afford to lose one trick. Pris was obviously disappointed by her too cautious bidding.

338 Pris' sister Dorothy had moved to Bronxville in Westchester County sometime in the 1920s. Brother Ran bought a house on Heathcote Road in Scarsdale, next door to Bronxville, and moved out with his family in March 1934. Pris' sister Ruth and brother-in-law Lowell Shumway moved to a Bronxville apartment at 12 Meadow Avenue in September 1934, where Dorothy and Manny had their apartment. Lowell and Pris found an apartment for the senior Fullers at 64 Sagamore Road in Bronxville. After living with Lowell and Ruth for several months, Pris found a small apartment near her mother and father at 64 Sagamore and moved there later in the year.

Charles and Mary Fuller moved from Flatbush, their home since 1892, into a one-bedroom apartment at 64 Sagamore Road in Bronxville. That night the family, refugees from Flatbush, gathered for dinner at the Alps, Bronxville's premier dining establishment.

In the early evening of November 2, Pris had cocktails and dinner with her sister Dorothy at the Sherry-Netherland Hotel and barely made the train to Knoxville. This time, she spent a month at Eliot's Coal Creek camp, playing poker with the forestry men in the evening, and during the day helping Eliot with bookkeeping and payroll. She stayed in a cabin near the camp and returned to New York early on December 5: "Train in to Pennsy at 6:50 AM. Washed in station, breakfast there & to office. Long day."

By January 1935, Pris knew she was pregnant, adding one of her rare exclamation points to her diary note: "All O.K. for July!"

In the thirties, pregnancy meant forced retirement, a daunting prospect in a family that needed two incomes. By 1935 the economy had come back from its bottom, but prosperity was still a long way from what it had been in 1929, and Roosevelt was still taking radical steps to try and get the economy back on track. On February 18, Pris noted "Uptown for theater tickets for Mr. Reese at noon. Supreme Court upheld decisions in gold cases, making stocks go up." The "gold cases," a product of Roosevelt's steps to devalue the currency and take the country off the gold standard, were hot news.[339] But in the spring of 1935, the hot news for Pris was that she was pregnant.

On her last day at the office, the girls on the 17th floor of the AT&T building gave her a surprise luncheon. Messrs. Reese and Woodford gave her an

---

339   Gold was a big deal in 1935 .Since the late nineteenth century, the dollar had been linked to gold; holders of dollars were legally entitled to turn in their dollars for a set amount of gold; a dollar backed by gold was viewed as "sound money;" the U.S. and other western countries, were on the "gold standard." But adherence to the gold standard was regarded by Roosevelt and his advisers as exacerbating the Depression. In an effort to get more dollars into circulation and inflate the currency (the problem then was deflation), Roosevelt took the country off the gold standard, and after 1933 citizens could no long exchange paper money for gold. Roosevelt explicitly devalued the dollar by increasing the price the Treasury would pay for an ounce of gold from $20.67 to $35. That created a huge potential problem. Creditors invariably insisted on a "gold clause" in their contracts, entitling them to payment in gold or the dollar equivalent. The gold clause, included in virtually all debt instruments, including government debt and home mortgages, was designed to protect creditors against dollar devaluation—the very thing that Roosevelt had done. Now, with the dollar devalued against gold by about 69 percent, creditors were poised to invoke the gold clause and debtors—and there were far more debtors than creditors—stood to lose heavily. Congress, at the request of the president, abrogated the gold clause in all contracts, an action that was immediately challenged as unconstitutional. On February 16, 1935, after the close of the market, the Supreme Court announced its decision upholding the congressional action. It was headline news. The markets reacted positively, reflecting that corporate earnings and balance sheets would no longer be burdened by the gold clause. Creditors, of course, saw the value of their holdings reduced. See Randall Kroszner, "Is it Better to Forgive than to Receive?"(Paper presented to the Graduate School of Business, University of Chicago, November 2003).

inscribed silver plate and ten dollars cash (about $160 in current dollars). On March 19, she went back to Flatbush for a baby shower with old friends and Packer classmates.

In April, Charlton cautioned her about her weight: "Doc Charlton's at 9:15. He says I'm too fat and must diet (139)."[340] On July 26, she heard from Eliot that he was being transferred from Tennessee back to Fort Missoula, Montana. On August 4: "Hospital at 5 PM & El Jr. born at 11:55. Duff [Sister Dorothy] there...." She was in the Lawrence Hospital in Bronxville for twelve days, spent a week with her sister Ruth, and finally went home to 64 Sagamore on August 25.[341]

A month later Eliot was on his way home, a prospect that called for three exclamation marks: "Says he's coming home next week!!!" On October 10 she wrote: "Dashed down & had hair done in AM. El arrived at Camp Dix with CCC boys called in eve. Slick." It took Eliot until the twelfth to actually get home: "El finally came at 5:30! Dinner here at 64. Walk to stores in eve & ice cream. Father slept at Duff's." When Eliot came home, her mother took the baby, and her father moved down to Dorothy's for a few peaceful nights. Eliot was home and job-hunting, with Pris typing the letters and Lowell using his contacts. But with financial activities now heavily regulated and the stock market in the doldrums, Wall Street was not hiring, and it was no longer the exciting place it had been in the twenties.

Pris and Eliot took some time off and drove up to West Point with old friends to see Army beat Harvard 13-0. The days went by fast. I was christened on October 22, and on October 28 Pris wrote: "El off to Montana.... Took bag of baby's clothes by mistake but sent it back via Lowell. Bum to have him go." The next evening, Lowell took Ruth and Pris into the city to see *Top Hat* with Fred Astaire.

Christmas 1935 was quiet and depressing for Priscilla, with her husband three thousand miles away. In a letter written the evening of Christmas day, she gave vent to her loneliness:

> I'm in an ickety mood tonight, mad at everyone (except you & the Bunny) and mad at myself for being mad. I'm awfully tired of putting on a "front" all the time & want someone I can talk to truly without feeling disloyal to you—and you're the only

---

340   Priscilla's Diary, April 8, 1935.
341   During that first year, I was known variously as "baby," "El jr.," "bunny," and "bun." My official name was Eliot Noble Vestner Jr.

one I can do that with…I know all the things I have to be mighty thankful for and I'm a bad, bad girl![342]

That night, she went to midnight service with her father, and on December 28 she helped entertain a crowd of family—mostly Redfields and Fullers. Her only diary entry for New Year's Eve was "Getting a cold."

In January 1936, Eliot received notice that he was no longer needed in the CCC.[343] He immediately came home and resumed his job search. Once again he came up dry. But he was still in the Army reserves. Taking advantage of his Army contacts, he qualified for artillery school and left on February 24 for ninety days at Fort Sill, Oklahoma. His mother went with him. The Army was still his friend; but the Army kept him far away from home. Pris wanted to have another baby, but her obstetrician advised against it. Adding weight to the doctor's advice was their precarious financial situation.

Early in April, she got bad news from her mother-in-law: Eliot had "hurt" his back falling off his horse. According to army records, he had fallen while on a "hunt"; a military board found that the injury occurred "in the line of duty," which meant all his medical expenses would be covered.

Two days later, she received more details from her mother-in-law: Eliot had a broken back. He was in a plaster cast in the Army hospital at Fort Sill, about to be transferred to the hospital in Houston. She called him in the hospital and sent a telegram but got no reply. Finally on April 15, she noted in her diary: "Letter from El written by him!" She was fed up getting all her information from her mother-in-law. A year later he was declared physically unfit for duty and transferred to the inactive reserves. He spent the rest of 1936 and into 1937 recuperating; Pris got part-time secretarial work to pay the rent.

In 1938 she got more bad news. During the night of December 4, 1938, Charles Fuller suffered a cerebral thrombosis and died.[344] He died of the same sudden heart attack that had killed his own father, Humphrey Roger Fuller.

---

342 Letter, dated December 25, 1935, from Priscilla to Eliot.

343 Letter, dated January 10, 1936, from Office of Commander, Second Corps, to First Lieutenant Eliot N. Vestner, subject: "Relief from active duty with the C.C.C." With the 1936 election campaign starting up, Roosevelt was cutting back on expenditures, including the CCC—he wanted to defuse the issue of fiscal irresponsibility and mismanagement that the Republicans were using against him.

344 *The New York Times*, December 6, 1938, (Obituaries). He had long suffered from atherosclerosis.

Charles Fuller was seventy-nine when he died. Bishop John Wallace Gardner of New Jersey, former minister of St. Paul's in Flatbush, officiated at the service in Christ Church, Bronxville. "Charlie" Fuller was buried at Sleepy Hollow Cemetery, Tarrytown. Mary Fuller survived another fourteen years, to her ninetieth year, and is buried beside him.

For Eliot and Pris, 1938-39 were tough years. An old document tells the story of Eliot's search for work:

MEN'S CLUB OF THE REFORMED CHURCH OF BROXVILLE

RE: UNEMPLOYMENT

CASE NO. 11

The document describes the applicant: "AGE: 39; DEPENDANTS: wife, son and mother, EDUCATION: Elementary and High School." After listing the applicant's Army and work experience, Dr. John Powell, the minister, added a comment at the bottom of the page:

> He comes from an old New York family, and is a person who impresses one immediately with his courtesy and good character. He inspires confidence both as to his ability and soundness of principles, and I feel that he is very much worth helping.

In the fall of 1938, Eliot was forty, jobless and physically disabled; and he was hardly from "an old New York family." The following May, a judgment was entered against him in "Brooks Brothers against Eliot N. Vestner" for $137.78, an overdue bill never paid. He landed a temporary job with American Cyanamid in their public relations department, but there was no telling how long it would last. If Eliot and Priscilla were thinking about their future, and they surely were, they would have been scared: war looming on the horizon, a bad economy at home, no savings, and no pension aside from Social Security, from which they could expect no more than $500 yearly starting in 1962, a date impossibly far in the future.

Dad, amazed that he has a son, 1938

We lived then at 111 Sagamore Road in the Village of Tuckahoe. Tuckahoe was next door to Bronxville, but to the people who lived in Bronxville, Tuckahoe was Timbuktu—far away, physically and socially. I remember a few things from those years: the magic of that first Christmas when I was old enough to know what I was getting—a Lionel train set, complete with batteries, tracks, stations, and a real train; Sandy, our dog, lifting his leg against the Christmas tree and getting a good whacking for it; riding the little engine, just big enough for me, that Mom's old boss, Jack Reese, had set up on tracks that ran all over his backyard in Westport; Mom and I taking the night train up to Lake Placid, fishing on the lake early in the morning and catching trout, which Mom fried for breakfast (we stayed with the McNairs, friends from Bronxville, who were members of the Lake Placid Club).

In 1940, Congress authorized an expansion of the army and Eliot jumped at the chance. The examining doctor found Eliot unqualified, but he was overruled—the Army needed experienced officers.[345] On October 15, 1941, Lieutenant Eliot Vestner was placed on active duty and ordered to report to Washington. That November we moved from Tuckahoe back to Bronxville.

---

345   The examination report noted that "Examinee states he is not drawing...disability allowance from the U.S. Government." But that was not true; he was receiving disability for his back injury, and much later he would be required to pay back all the disability payments received since October 1941—a lot of money.

7. Second World War, Bronxville, New York

The war came Sunday, December 7, 1941. Bang! Just like that.

I was six. A small group of us kids were sitting around the radio in a neighbor's apartment listening to *The Shadow*, a weekly mystery program that had us all scared.[346] The program suddenly stopped and an authoritative voice announced that the Japanese had bombed Pearl Harbor. We didn't know much, but we had a pretty good idea that this was big and that our parents' lives, and therefore ours, would be affected.

That first winter Dad was stationed in Washington, D.C. We lived in an apartment at One Beechtree Lane, corner of Kensington Road, about half a mile from the Bronxville School. Our building was a big old brown wood-frame house, once the grand mansion of a wealthy stockbroker surrounded by gardens and acres of open land. In 1924, the mansion had been carved up into nine apartments, some of them quite small. We lived in one of the small ones: two bedrooms, a bathroom you could hardly turn around in, a kitchen, and a living room.[347]

In 1941 our days were marked by familiar rhythms: the Borden's milkman picking up our empty bottles and leaving fresh ones with thick layers of cream at the top; the Dugan's Bakery man with bread, muffins, and coffee cake; the iceman carrying a great block of ice in iron pincers for our icebox; the Gristede's delivery man with the weekly groceries. In the evening, we'd hear the bells of

---

346   The *Shadow*, one of the most popular radio programs ever, ran from July 31, 1930 through December 26, 1954. Never seen, only heard, the Shadow waged a weekly and inevitably triumphant battle against the forces of evil, closing with his signature deep-voiced, lines that never failed to send a tingle down my spine: "Who knows what evil lurks in the hearts of men? The Shadow knows."

347   Now there's no trace of the old manor house, demolished sometime in the sixties. All that remains is a park bench with a small plaque describing what was once there.

185

the Good Humor wagon, a distinctive white truck with a refrigerator filled with ice cream on a stick, with the smiling Good Humor Man dressed in white. A Good Humor—which might be chocolate with vanilla ice cream, chocolate with chocolate ice cream or toasted almond with vanilla—was a dime; but you could get a Popsicle (orange, lemon lime or raspberry) for a nickel. When he rang the bell, it was the signal for all the kids in the neighborhood to come out and line up. Even now, as I hear those bells in my memory, I can taste the Good Humor.

The Christmas Eve pageant was another fixture of life in Bronxville. Performed outdoors before a large crowd, initially on the hill in front of the Gramatan Hotel and later on the lawn in front of the Dutch Reformed Church across from the school, the pageant ended with everyone singing Christmas carols, and with the last carol, invariably "Silent Night," I could feel the excitement, knowing that in a few hours I would be opening presents under the tree. In those early years of the war, I believed in Santa Claus.[348]

Our family, with Skipper, in the apartment, at One Beechtree Lane, 1943

---

348   The famous old Gramatan Hotel, once a very fashionable hotel, sprawled over a hill overlooking the Bronxville train station. The hotel was torn down in 1972 to make room for new townhouses.

Dad managed to get home about once a month, and when he did our small apartment got even smaller. He was six feet tall, towering over Mom who was five-four, and carried himself tall and straight. When he was home, we'd go down to the school and he'd hit fly balls to me, or we might go down to fish in the "lake" in the park on the far side of town—it was actually a dammed up section of the Bronx River, but it looked like a lake to me. Dad bought me a rod and tackle, showed me how to bait the hook, cast the line, and reel it in very slowly to make the worm move but not too much. The fish were tiny: little perch and sunfish no bigger than your hand, but to a six-year old it was pretty exciting to catch one. I always had trouble taking the hook out of a squirming fish. When I tossed it back it would lie motionless for an instant, just to make sure it was really off the hook, before disappearing into the murky depths of the Bronx River.

The Army sent Dad's paycheck directly to Mom and she managed the money, a challenging task for her in 1942. That year, their end-of- month balance in the checking account dipped as low as twenty-three cents. Mom couldn't survive that kind of stress for long; in 1943 they borrowed $2,200 from the bank, and that gave them a cushion. She was meticulous in her household accounting, keeping track of her daily expenses in a little notebook. Whether it was a $5 weekly grocery bill, a 25-cent haircut, or a 10-cent magazine, it all went in that little book.

Dad was the disciplinarian. Mom might slap me if I talked back to her, but her heart wasn't in it. For Dad, spanking was a natural act. He was quick to anger and strong. I can hear him now: "Goddammit Eliot, I'll teach you to treat your mother with more respect!" followed by a good beating on my naked butt, usually with the flat side of a big wooden hairbrush. That was right in line with the conventional good parenting wisdom: "Spare the rod and spoil the child." It hurt, but I figured it just went with the territory.

If I got my nose bloodied in another fight with my friend, Hank Holmes, Dad was unsympathetic: "Eliot, when are you going to learn how to win a fight? When are you going to give him a bloody nose?" He offered me a dollar if I could honestly tell him I'd beaten Hank. He'd take me aside, show me how to use my left arm to defend myself, and get all my weight into a right-hand punch. But Hank was a tough little guy with an older brother, Stacy, and I was never able to claim that dollar. Dad liked Hank and admired his spunk, but he was chagrined that I couldn't beat him in a fistfight.

Dad's limited time at home was also taken up with visiting his mother, now in her eighties and living alone in a Bronxville apartment. Grandmother Vestner always complained about something, and the biggest item in the monthly budget was rent on two apartments—ours and hers.

187

Grandmother Mary Fuller, widowed in 1938, was also living in Bronxville. She was friendly, warm and gentle, but increasingly puzzled by what was going on around her, an early indication of the dementia that later took over her life. We knew the dementia was in full bloom when, one night sitting in her accustomed easy chair in Uncle Lowell's living room, she looked at Lowell's reflection in the window and asked what to her was a perfectly reasonable question: "Who's that little old man sitting in the tree?" She couldn't be persuaded that it was merely Lowell's reflection, and it bothered her to see that little old man sitting out there in the tree staring at her.

Ruth and Lowell lived at 12 Meadow Avenue. Ruth was largely bed-ridden, in line with the medical wisdom of the time that cautioned against exercise that might strain the heart. Ruth's favorite song was "My Hero," and Lowell was her hero. Lowell was a vice-president at McCall Corporation in the city. He needed that job to pay for Ruth's medical bills; McCall's, in line with most companies, did not provide medical insurance. I never heard him complain. Manny and Dorothy Swan, Mom's older sister, also had an apartment at 12 Meadow. Dorothy was no longer commuting to a job in the city and therefore no longer bringing in an income. Manny hadn't worked in years. Lowell was helping them pay their bills.

Lowell hosted summer reunions for the family at the Bronxville Field Club, bringing various Fullers and Shumways together to swim and eat club sandwiches. Uncle Everett Fuller's daughter, Priscilla, was just then starting in at William & Mary down south and rather glamorous, but I was too young to notice.

Cousin Pris, summer, ca. 1943

In his office, Lowell kept a chart behind his desk showing *McCall's* circulation against its main competitor *Ladies Home Journal*. If *McCall's* was on top, Lowell was a happy man. Lowell was a fierce competitor: in business, on the tennis court where he was exceptional, and on the golf course where he was average. His passion was tennis. He had a group—Bill Barber, Frank Stafford, and Blev Dunklin—that played doubles together every day for years at the Bronxville Field Club. You had to be good to play in that group.

Lowell's tennis group: Frank Stafford, Blev Dunklin and Lowell on the right.
The fourth, Bill Barber, took the picture

All the family gathered regularly for Sunday dinner, usually hosted by either Uncle Ran in Scarsdale or Lowell in Bronxville. Despite wartime rationing, they always managed to get hold of a turkey, a roast beef, or a big steak. Dad wasn't an enthusiastic attendee, but when he was home, we all went. The conversation was lively; neither Lowell nor Aunt Margie was shy about expressing an opinion, and Dad would speak up. Lowell usually had the last word, which didn't endear him to Dad.

Aunt Margie had a wide range of prejudices: racial, religious, and ethnic. She was a gifted mimic and not shy about speaking up. She didn't mean to be malicious, and she always had a twinkle in her eyes. Maybe she said things just to stir the pot. But her tongue wasn't always under control. She had never gotten past the last war, and she didn't like Germans. Dad, of course, *was* German. I think she got a kick out of teasing Dad; but there was an edge to her comments. She would say things like, "I just don't understand why we can't put all the Germans in a big concentration camp. We did it with the Japs, and I think it would make perfect sense. Everybody knows most of them are Nazis anyway." Dad would respond, "Margie, you don't know what you're talking about. Half the country is at least part German." But Margie wouldn't let go: "I know perfectly well what I'm talking about. We're at war with Germany. I think the FBI should do a better job of watching Germans in this country and keeping them out of responsible positions; maybe even put them in a concentration camp somewhere in Montana."

Later, going home, Dad would boil over, "Dammit Pris, who the hell does she think she is? Is she questioning my loyalty? What has she ever done for her country? She lives out there in her big house in Scarsdale and thinks everyone who's not a Catlin or a Fuller is trash. She's just a goddamn bigot!"

There was hardly anyone Mom loved more than Margie; they'd been close since they were girls. But rather than take Dad on directly, she tried to calm him down: "Dear, Margie was just teasing you. Maybe she took it too far. But she doesn't mean any harm; she's a wonderful person, and I really appreciate your spending time with my family." Mom always tried to smooth the waters.

Without Aunt Margie, family gatherings wouldn't have been half as interesting. She was one of my favorites—funny, smart, gracious, warm-hearted, and politically incorrect. Uncle Ran and Uncle Everett were highly intelligent, but they weren't outspoken like Margie. Everett's wife, Gertrude Gladding, was a charming and gracious lady from an old Brooklyn family. All the Fuller men, including Uncle Lowell, had Amherst College in common. They were an Amherst family; Dad was sick of hearing about Amherst.

During the first year of the war Mom worked as a volunteer at the Lawrence Hospital. I couldn't figure out what Dad did. Everything to do with the military was secret. Letters, movies, radio news, newspapers were all censored by the government's office of censorship, a wartime creation. Dad's letters home were bland and didn't tell us much. If he'd been more informative, the censors would have taken a razor to his letters. The alternative, of course, would have been to use the telephone, but long distance calls were expensive and the operator always listened in. Posters, prominently displayed, reinforced official censorship with warnings about what could happen if people talked carelessly.[349]

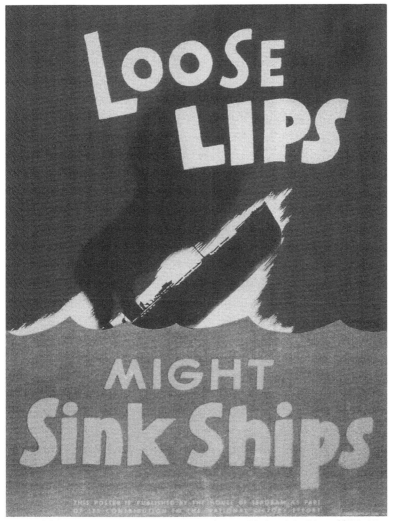

One of the most popular wartime posters (Courtesy, National Archives, 44-PA-82)

349   This became one of the most popular World War 11 posters, part of the government's extensive propaganda strategy to raise awareness of the potential consequences when seemingly innocuous information gets into enemy hands.

Even a seven-year-old couldn't ignore the war. On our radio, I got used to hearing the stentorian voice of H.V. Kaltenborn and the dramatic, rapid-fire delivery of Edward R. Murrow. In the winter of 1942, William L. Shirer said he thought the Germans could send a squadron of 150 bombers to New York with light bomb loads and still make it back to their bases in France. Their voices brought the war into our living room. I walked to school with my friend, Corny Crock, whose family had fled Holland in 1939 before the German invasion. Jenny, another neighbor, was an English girl who had been sent to Bronxville when the Germans started bombing London.

My First Grade drawings were mostly pictures of tanks and planes. At Christmas, Santa brought me toy soldiers, tanks, and artillery, so I could create my own battles. The toy soldiers were all made of lead, and they had a nice weight and feel to them. I'd line up the Germans on one side, the Americans and British on the other, and go at it. The games we played were games of good guys against bad guys: Americans against Germans or Japs; cops and robbers; cowboys and Indians. Sometimes I'd put on my Superman outfit, go into the woods, and pretend to be defender of good against evil. The world was divided into good guys and bad guys, and the good guys always won.

Shortly after Pearl Harbor, the Bronxville Office of Civilian Protection was established to organize air raid drills, and the warning siren became part of our daily lives. In school we had to crouch down under our desks and cover our heads. At home we had to quickly douse the lights, pull the shades and put up black curtains. If you had a light on, a warden with helmet and armband would come by, rap on the door and tell you to put it out.

At night searchlights scanned the sky for enemy planes, which we all learned to identify from government booklets: German Messerschmitts, Henkels, Focke-Wolfes, Dorniers, Stukas, and Japanese Zeros. Occasionally the civil defense people thought they saw actual German bombers, and the sirens would go off. But everybody assumed it was just another drill.

Rumors were going around about German submarines lurking off the coast sinking our ships; bodies of dead Germans washing up on beaches; German spies landing on the coast to carry out sabotage. We didn't worry too much; we all knew that J. Edgar Hoover and the FBI would catch any spies.

When Dad came home, we talked in general terms about the war. Much later, going through his old army records, I learned that he had been recruited by the Office of Strategic Services (OSS, later the CIA) and transferred to an OSS camp in Maryland, where he instructed officers preparing for missions in Europe in the finer points of sabotage.[350] The wartime head of the OSS was William Donovan, Dad's old regimental commander in the First World War.

Dad wanted to know what I was doing—specifically, how I was doing in school, how things were going with the other boys, and whether I was learning to "handle" myself. He bought me boxing gloves, taking me down to a local gym in Yonkers for boxing lessons. At home, he and I sparred in my new gloves. But he wasn't home enough to really push it and I had other things to do.

With the men away, women ran our lives (even if the men had stayed home the women probably would have run things). All the teachers were middle-aged women. Miss Julia Ann Markham was the principal of the Elementary School. She was a big woman with a strong personality. She ran the school, no question about it, and that went for parents as well as teachers and students. Florence Eagle ran The Gramatan National Bank and Trust Company. She probably wasn't even a vice-president, but to me she was "The Bank." I got to know Miss Eagle because Mom took me with her to the bank when she went to get cash, and Miss Eagle always kept a supply of lollipops on her desk. Mom and Dad had to take out loans from time to time, but Mom hated to do it and always viewed borrowing as slightly immoral. She liked to quote Polonius: "Neither a borrower nor a lender be."

World War II ration book

350   Certificate, dated October 1, 1945, "Eliot N. Vestner [has] honorably served the United States of America as a member of the Office of Strategic Services," signed by General Donovan.

Since women did the shopping, they had to cope with wartime rationing; everything that tasted good, like meat, milk, butter, eggs, cheese and sugar, was rationed, as were gasoline, rubber, steel products, oil, cigarettes, and other items that had a military use.

Each family got a ration book filled with stamps, with a prominent warning on the cover: "You could get up to ten years in jail for any violation of the rules of the Ration Board." There were different stamps for different items; you couldn't buy butter with sugar stamps. If Mom asked for something known to be scarce, she'd get the standard response: "Lady, don'tcha know there's a war on?"

Even with rationing, I don't remember being deprived of anything I really wanted. My wants were pretty simple: comic books, candy, and ice cream. If you wanted something bad enough—a good steak, for example, or an extra supply of gasoline—you could probably find a way to get it. Lowell always had meat on his table and gas in his tank.

Mom and I lived on what came out of cans: Spam, chili, chipped beef, chicken a la king, corned beef hash, tuna fish, and Boston baked beans. We ate creamed chipped beef on toast and tuna noodle casserole. I loved Hormel's canned chili con carne with beans. Our idea of a real Italian meal was Chef Boy-ar-dee's package of spaghetti, red sauce, and Parmesan cheese. Fresh vegetables were hard to come by unless you grew them in your own garden.

The village offered plots of land for growing vegetables. These were called "Victory Gardens." The idea was that if people grew their own produce it would reduce consumer demand, and more food could be channeled toward the war effort. Mom seized the opportunity, and we had our own Victory Garden.

We had fresh vegetables, but Mom boiled them to death. When she boiled asparagus, spinach and Brussels sprouts they were inedible; I couldn't keep them down. But she persisted. "Eliot," she'd say, "just finish up your spinach. Don't you want muscles like Popeye?" or "Eat your carrots, they're good for your eyes. If you ever want to be a fighter pilot, you've got to have perfect eyesight."

Friday was fish day. Mom was a devout Episcopalian and liked the idea of meatless Fridays. Fish was cheap, and that helped with the weekly food budget. I hated fish. At a restaurant, filet of sole—it tasted like milk of magnesia—was the cheapest thing on the menu. When Uncle Lowell took us out to dinner—and in Bronxville that was usually to the Alps or Town Tavern—Mom would automatically order the filet of sole. Lowell usually encouraged me to order steak, which cost about $2 at the Alps. Mom and Lowell usually had Martinis: one for Mom, three or four for Lowell.

Carefully tending the Victory Garden

One day I overheard Dad tell Mom that he thought we were living pretty high on the hog, courtesy of Lowell, while he was working his butt off in the Army down in Maryland. That didn't sit well with her, and they had one of their rare arguments, at least rare within my hearing range.

195

Gasoline, when available, was tightly rationed. If you drove on a summer weekend, you risked not finding any gas if you needed it. Most people were allotted no more than three or four gallons a week. Not everybody owned a car, and you couldn't buy a car during the war. We didn't own one, but Lowell did. He drove a big Oldsmobile and used to take us out to Jones Beach. The President of McCall, Marvin Pierce, probably drove a Cadillac. Oldsmobile and Buick were vice-president cars. That's how GM and Ford marketed their cars. There were starter cars, young executive cars, mid-level executive cars, senior executive cars, and CEO cars. Everyone knew his place in the pecking order. Nobody owned a foreign car, and certainly during the war none were available. I never saw a German car on the road. Nobody even envisioned a Japanese car; we all knew anything the Japs made was cheap junk.

I got a small allowance—too small. Dad thought I was a wild spender, throwing it all away on comics, like *Superman* and *Captain Marvel*. He laid down the law: I had to put 50 percent into savings. So I decided to save up and buy a war bond. Every week there was a big push to get people to buy war bonds. Bob Hope, Bing Crosby, Dorothy Lamour, all the big Hollywood names were urging people to buy bonds. For $18.75 you could buy a $25 "E" bond. After ten years, you could cash it in and get $25. That struck me as a good deal, because I didn't know any better. So I collected pennies around the neighborhood, took them to the bank for quarters, inserted the quarters in my savings bond book, added quarters that I managed to earn by helping an older boy deliver *Collier's* and *Saturday Evening Post*, nickels that the tooth fairy put under my pillow, the forced savings from my allowance, and eventually accumulated enough to buy a bond. That was pretty exciting. In ten years I was going to get $25 for my $18.75, and I was helping win the war.

When Dad was home we'd sit around the radio listening to Mel Allen (for the Yankees) or Red Barber (for the Dodgers) broadcast the ballgames. When we actually went to Ebbets Field in Brooklyn to see the Dodgers beat the St. Louis Cardinals 5-0 behind Ralph Branca, it was a let-down compared to the excitement of listening to Red Barber on the radio.

We were passionate about baseball. Most of the big stars, like Joe DiMaggio, were away in the war, but there was enough talent to keep the game going. I used to daydream that I was a great pitcher, writing down in neat columns my imaginary wins, losses, and earned run average for each year and adding everything up for my lifetime record, which always put me in the Hall of Fame. I'd do the same thing with batting averages: add everything, divide by the years, and produce my lifetime batting average, which always put me right up there with Ty Cobb. One day I looked up, and Mrs. Brown, the teacher, was standing over me staring at my numbers. "Eliot, *what* are you doing?" I didn't have a good answer. She reported to Mom that I was too consumed with living vicariously through my baseball fantasies; she said "it is his escape from real life."

I was a St. Louis Cardinals fan, and I listened to all their games. Dad was a Yankees fan; Mom liked the Dodgers. But I've always been a contrarian and I've always liked winners. The Cards were not from New York, they were winners, and they had Stan Musial. "Stan the Man," with his batting stance like a coiled snake ready to strike, was my hero.

After school and on weekends we played baseball (or basketball or soccer, depending on the season) every chance we got, choosing up teams on the spur of the moment. We also played stickball behind the school, drawing a chalk batter's box on the wall and using an old hairless tennis ball. Anything over the jungle gym was an automatic triple; over Garden Avenue was a home run. Mom used to come by the ball field one or two afternoons a week. She was afraid that if she didn't personally come and get me, I'd forget my piano lesson with Mrs. Marsters, who lived in a big house on a hill.

Mrs. Marsters would test me on drills: up and down, two octaves for every scale, both hands working together. That's not easy; it's like patting your head and rubbing your stomach at the same time. I didn't like the pieces Mrs. Marsters wanted me to play, and she wanted me to learn the music exactly as written. I wasn't interested in that, so I taught myself boogie-woogie by listening to Albert Ammons and Pete Johnson on old 78s.[351] I could listen to Ammons and Johnson for hours on end, which is exactly what I did when I was in bed with a bad case of pneumonia. Mom got so sick of listening to the boogie that she'd go for long walks. When Dad was home, he'd yell at me from the other room "Eliot, will you please shut off that damn Victrola!"

---

351 In the 1940s records were designed to revolve at 78 rpms. You got one song per record. Later, the music business developed records that revolved more slowly, some at 45 rpm (generally small records with a single song) and others at 33 rpm, which could hold four or five songs. The record store in Bronxville let us go into a booth and listen to records so we would know what we were getting. We used to spend a lot of time in those booths.

With my father, One Beechtree Lane, ca. 1942

When the war began I was in First Grade. When it ended I was in Sixth Grade. Since Dad was away most of the time, Mom was the one who met with my teachers. From the beginning I was a hard case. Miss Markham identified me early as a problem child. I still have a letter from sixth grade that Miss Markham made me write:

Dear Mom,

I have been fighting in the halls today and Miss Markham had me write this letter. I am trying to stop this foolishness but have not been succeeding. I will try not to do this again.

Love, Eliot

P.S. Mrs. Brown sent me into the hall to get my coat instead I picked a fight.

Markham had it in for me. "Mrs. Vestner," she would say in her authoritative voice, articulating every word, "we need your help. Eliot acts up in class, he fights with the other boys, and he's not working to his capability. He is quite capable of doing as well as Crawford Shaw." Crawford, a friend, was Miss Markham's gold standard.

Markham made it clear that Mom should "work on me" at home, and she did, monitoring my homework and making sure I did the work and understood it. She also drew on Kipling for inspiration. She could recite Kipling's "If" by heart, and I can still hear it:

> If you can dream—and not make dreams your master,
> If you can think—and not make thoughts your aim;
> If you can meet with Triumph and Disaster
> And treat those two impostors just the same…

Mom also worked on my religious education, making sure I learned my Bible, attended church, joined the choir (it paid a nickel a week), went to Sunday school, and was confirmed.

At Christ Church the minister's name was Harold Hohly. Mom liked Hohly, but not his assistant, Father Stone: "Stone, I can not stand. His mouth is always full of hot potatoes and he should really be a Catholic priest."[352] Whenever Stone was scheduled to give the service, she went to the Dutch Reformed Church to hear Dr. Powell. Powell was a great preacher, but the elders of the church decided he'd gone too far after he had divorced his wife, married "Miss Sweden", but then divorced her. It was the second divorce that got him fired. The rumor was she was crazy and had gone after the dignified Dr. Powell with a kitchen knife. She was quite a package: long blonde hair, gorgeous figure, riding a bike around town. Mom also grew to like Dr. Ditzen, Powell's successor. He was another great preacher.

One Sunday at Christ Church, early in the war, Father Hohly was giving the sermon. I was sitting with the boys' choir up in the stalls, where we all tried to look serious. It was hard to keep a straight face, but if we didn't, we risked a sharp look from Mr. Owen, the organist and choir master. This particular Sunday Father Hohly was getting all worked up, thundering about our loss of

---

352 Catholicism baffled her. She noted "I'm reading an awfully interesting little book written by a Rabbi, called 'What the Jews Believe,' having just read a book written for Catholic teenagers about Catholicism. I feel more kindly towards the Jewish faith! I just don't understand the Catholics…." Her Puritan ancestors would have said "Amen" to that.

values. He was moving around in the pulpit, his voice reaching a crescendo. All of a sudden he whipped out a copy of *Life* magazine with the picture of Rita Hayworth, kneeling on her bed in a satin slip. He held it up for the congregation to see, a vivid example of moral degeneracy in our time. After the service I went home, found our copy of *Life* and just feasted on that picture of Rita Hayworth.[353]

Rita Hayworth, a young boy's fantasy (Bob Landry, 1941/MPTV.net)

---

353 The 1941 photo of Rita Hayworth, then twenty-three, taken by Bob Landry of *Time/Life*, was one of the most popular "pin-up" photos of the Second World War.

In Dad's absence, Mom had to deal with some serious disciplinary issues on her own. I had begun stealing items from F.W. Woolworth's (the local five and dime store) downtown on Pondfield Road. Largely, it was the excitement of getting away with something. When Mom found out, she was horrified, and marched me down to see the manager.

"Go on," she said, "Tell him what you did." I confessed to stealing candy, a jack knife (which I handed over), and a few other things. The manager looked at me: "He's a fine boy, Mrs. Vestner. I'm sure he won't do it again." Mom was furious. She expected more from the manager. She marched me out of there and straight home. She called Uncle Lowell at his office in the city. I knew I was going to catch hell. That night Lowell came by and talked to me "man to man." He was grim as death and wanted to know why I'd done it, but I had no good answer. He stood close and made me look him straight in the eye; his eyes were ice blue. He really chewed me out. He said I'd better smarten up, and warned me if I ever did anything like that again he personally would see that I'd have good reason to regret it. The interview was over and I was dismissed.

After that, the thrill of stealing lost its charm. It took a long time for my relationship with Mom to get back to normal. I knew I'd failed her, not because of anything she said, but because in my heart I knew I'd done wrong and disappointed her.

Towards the end of the war, at Mom's insistence, I started going to Miss Caroline Covington's Dancing Classes. Dad thought it was a waste of money. Covington's was a local institution for learning manners, proper behavior, social poise, and respect for authority. We had to dress up; boys and girls had to wear white gloves. The mothers were pressed into service as greeters in the receiving line. Caroline Covington herself was a large- bosomed woman in her early fifties with ramrod posture. When she wanted your attention she clicked her little cricket. If she called a dance, and all the boys headed for a few girls leaving the rest sitting there, the cricket went off—click, click, click—the music stopped, she took boys by the arm and not so gently steered them in the direction of the "wallflowers." Occasionally she reversed it so the boys could share the experience— the prettiest girls invariably made a beeline for one or two guys with the rest of us all too obvious wallflowers. We were getting a taste of our own medicine.

When the discipline broke down, she'd click us back to order. One evening we were all standing around listening to Covington explain a point of etiquette. Suddenly someone let out a long fart. For an instant it seemed this was going to be a fart without an owner. There was some nervous giggling. Covington pretended she didn't hear it. Then with everybody looking around to see who did it, one boy turned beet red. Poor Billy—better him than me.

* * *

Dad was having some success in the Army. In 1942, he was promoted to captain and the next year to major. By late 1943 the Army was focusing on the postwar world, organizing the occupation of Japan and Germany, recruiting and training officers for occupation duty. In early 1944 he was accepted for civil affairs training. He studied civil administration and Japanese culture and language at the University of Virginia and Harvard. Mom and I went up to Cambridge to visit him. He was like a kid in a candy store. As a boy he had dreamed of going to Harvard, and there he was, living the dream courtesy of the U.S. Army. The first thing he did after finishing at Harvard was order a Harvard chair.

Dad in Harvard Yard, winter of 1944

At about the same time, Mom started sending me to summer camp. She thought the experience would do me good (and perhaps give her some free time). My first experience was Camp Greystone just north of Brewster, New York, where I broke my arm chasing another boy. Doctor Colley set the arm, but he couldn't get it straight, and it stayed crooked. After that I went to Camp Dudley in Westport, New York, where I learned to swim by getting pushed off the dock into deep water. It was at Dudley that I got my mouth washed out with soap. Adults were always saying, "Watch your language, young man, or I'll wash your mouth out with soap," but you never expected anyone would actually do it. One afternoon I used a word that the counselor found offensive. He gave me a sharp look and asked "What did you say?" So I repeated it. He yanked me out of my cot, took me outside, handed me a small bar of soap, and said "Chew." It tasted awful. My mouth was so sensitive I couldn't eat without pain for twenty-four hours. After my first year at Dudley, they didn't want me back, but Lowell took the head of the camp, "Chief" Beckman, to lunch at the University Club and persuaded him to give me another chance.

The afternoon of April 12, 1945, we learned President Roosevelt had died that morning. Everything stopped: flags were lowered, stores closed, and people mourned openly on the street, even in Bronxville, which had voted 81 percent for Dewey in the 1944 election.[354] I was ten and Roosevelt had been president my entire life. I had, of course, heard from people who had never liked FDR; Lowell for example. To me, he was God. I couldn't imagine anyone stepping into his shoes. But I was only ten; what did I know?

That same April Dad was ordered to the Presidio of Monterey on the California coast, the first leg of his next assignment to Japan. The three of us took the Canadian Pacific Railroad across Canada. People weren't flying then except for the military, and we had to get permission to take the train; the trip had to be related to a military purpose.

We boarded the train in Montreal, ate, slept, woke up and stretched our legs in Thunder Bay on Lake Superior; then nothing to do but look out the window, read, sleep and eat, while the train sped through woods and lakes, wheat fields then plains stretching to the horizon, until on the fourth day the Rockies, starting out as a speck, got bigger and bigger until we finally pulled into the Banff train station, surrounded by big mountains. We stayed a few days at the gigantic Banff Springs Hotel, hiked in the mountains around Banff and Lake Louise, and then

---

354   Anne Curtis Fredericks, "Election Fever in Bronxville: 1936," *The Bronxville Journal*, Vol. 4 (2009): 64, 71, including a table showing the Bronxville vote in every election 1920-2008 and a picture of Mom's cousin, Humphrey Fuller Redfield, with the caption "The Man Who Voted for Roosevelt."

spent a week at the Diamond Cross Ranch about forty miles west of Banff, where we rode horses, fished, and ate venison steaks around an outdoor fire. Dad talked with the owner, Mr. Starkey, about buying that ranch. It was his idea of the good life. But he was dreaming; neither he nor Mom was ready to put all their money and then some into a ranch in the middle of nowhere.

We re-boarded the train and continued to Vancouver, then down to Seattle and real life. With wartime accommodations scarce, all three of us slept in one double bed in a cheap Seattle hotel that smelled of stale beer, piss and vomit, It was a big comedown from the Banff Springs Hotel and the Chateau Lake Louise.

At the end of the trip, Mom and I moved into a garage apartment with a hotplate for cooking in Carmel-by-the-Sea, a quaint little village near the Monterey peninsula, known mainly for its Spanish mission and beaches. Dad was stationed at the Presidio, a short distance away.

Carmel was surrounded by open country, farms and ranches. Mom and I spent several weekends at a Carmel valley ranch, taking long day trips on horseback through the valley. On the beaches there were a few surfers. Occasionally we'd see divers in the water looking for abalone. For twenty cents at Bluett's Creamery in Carmel, I could get a milkshake, so thick I had to use a spoon. We had nothing like that back in Bronxville. To me, age ten, that was California living.

* * *

Dad's flight to Japan left Hamilton Field (in the San Francisco Bay area) on August 20, 1945. Only three weeks earlier, we had been planning the invasion of Japan, the cost of which in lives lost would have been extraordinary. Then in rapid succession we dropped the first atomic bomb on Hiroshima, the second on Nagasaki, and the Japanese surrendered, all in the space of a couple of weeks. It seemed unreal; we were so used to war and to the prospect of a long and bloody invasion of Japan. Suddenly it was over.

Dad flew in a C47 with a top speed 220 mph. His flight orders show fuel stops in Hawaii, Johnson Atoll, Kwajalein, Guam, Pelieliu (in the Carolinas), and Manila. The final leg of his trip was the flight to Atsugi Airfield outside Tokyo. He landed there shortly after August 26, 1945, part of the advance guard of the U.S. occupation and among the first Americans to set foot on Japanese soil after the surrender on August 15.

Those first Americans to land in Japan didn't know what to expect. How would the Japanese react to an American occupation? Violent elements in the

Japanese military were not reconciled to the surrender, and there had been at least one attempted revolt by hotheads against the Emperor's order. With almost three million armed Japanese soldiers, the first Americans to arrive were utterly at the mercy of Japanese good will.

Dad's Tokyo office was in the Dai Ichi building, which became General MacArthur's headquarters. He worked in the economic affairs section, specializing in banking matters, including liquidation and recapitalization of Japanese banks and corporations. For part of his time in Japan, he was assigned to the Amatsuyi ball-bearing factory, helping management restore the factory and put it back in business. From his photographs, it's possible to piece together some of his experiences during that year in Japan: his living quarters in Tokyo; brochures from his favorite hotels in Kyoto, Kobe and Osaka; photos he took of famous tourist destinations: Himeji and Osaka Castles; Atami, a Japanese seaside resort near Tokyo; shrines and gardens in Kyoto and Nara; the menu for an eleven-course dinner by the owner of the Amatsuyi Factory that included "dried cuttlefish" and "Fried food (Hiroshima Vegetables)" [!]; photos of Christmas and New Year's parties with the owner, his family and staff of the factory, the American officers towering over the Japanese. There were also photos of a bare-breasted female Japanese pearl diver, and one picture of an attractive young Japanese woman with the name "HanakoWatanabe" inscribed.

Mt. Fujiyama, Tokyo Bay, 1945

205

Surrender ceremony at Yokosuka Naval Base, August 28, 1945, showing former Japanese
commander and senior officers retiring after the American flag is raised for the first time in Japan

The Ginza, Tokyo's main shopping center, fall of 1945

Celebrating Christmas at the Amatsuyi ball-bearing Factory, Tokyo. Dad, second American on left

At the time, Dad's Japanese experience was a blank page—the Army kept a tight lid on all information about the occupation. Mom and I continued to live in Carmel until October 1945, when we returned to the East Coast. That Thanksgiving, we went into the city to watch the huge parade down Fifth Avenue: soldiers in neat formation, music, tanks, and guns; battleships and carriers in the harbor. The troopships were now unloading thousands of returning veterans every day; fathers, long absent, were coming home, the stock market was moving up, and Bronxville was changing.

The father of a friend in Bronxville came home and resumed his stock brokerage business on Wall Street. Within days, it seemed, they had moved from their little apartment just above ours into a big new house on the other side of town. His dad was suddenly driving a bright yellow Cadillac with tail fins. New houses began to pop up on Young's Hill where we used to play cops and robbers in the summer and toboggan in the winter. At some point in 1946 I was invited to a friend's house to watch a ballgame on one of the new TV sets— tiny screen, everything in black and white, and the pictures a little fuzzy. It was amazing. You didn't have to buy tickets and go all the way to Ebbets Field to see a Cardinals-Dodgers game; you could watch it in your own home! But TV seemed like a toy, not serious business, and it wasn't as good as listening to Red Barber and Mel Allen on the radio.

After the war we began to think of girls differently. Girls started organizing parties. Parties made me anxious; I had very little social self-confidence (not being invited was much worse; then I would sit home and agonize over why I wasn't invited). As soon as we got to a party, the boys went to one side of the room, the girls to the other. Somehow, we started pairing off. But it wasn't easy. The first time I got up the courage to ask a girl out on a date I could hear a whispered conversation at the other end of the phone. When she came back on the line, the answer was "my Mom says I can't." You never forget that first rejection.

Later, I summoned the courage to ask another girl for a movie date. Her mother and mine were good friends, and her mother said okay, provided mine went along. Mom was discreet enough to sit in the back of the movie theater. As far as sex was concerned, forget about it. We might hold sweaty hands in the movies or even dance cheek to cheek, a pretty daring move, but that was it. Dmitri Boidi, whose parents owned the Alps restaurant, did his best to educate me and other guys my age about sex; certainly our mothers weren't about to do it. Mom figured Dad would talk to me about it, and he clearly preferred to leave it to her. It just fell between the stools. Dmitri, a year older, knew everything. Where he picked it up, I don't know.

Bronxville was a great place to grow up. You could walk or ride a bike everywhere in the village. I don't remember any school buses, and most mothers didn't drive their kids to school. There wasn't much violence—except one Halloween a group of fourteen-year-olds stole my bag of candy, the entire night's collection. The movies were all clean as a whistle. If you said "hell" or "damn" in front of an adult, you were in trouble. That's not to say it was all perfect. It wasn't. I was living proof that the kids in Bronxville weren't always "good"; some of the things I did then, I'd just as soon forget.

Dad came home in June 1946, bearing souvenirs: a Japanese officer's pistol, an officer's dagger with a small chrysanthemum, symbol of the Emperor; two intricately carved, samurai swords; some antique Japanese scrolls; a "Happy God," carved from solid ivory. He explained that you rub the big belly of the happy god for good luck. He also brought back some Japanese cigarettes. I snuck a pack from his desk and tried one. It was awful, and after that I never thought about smoking another cigarette.

* * *

In the fall of 1946 Congress, responding to the Cold War, had authorized an increase in the permanent officer corps, and the Army had solicited applications from reserve officers. Dad desperately wanted regular Army status and the assurance that he could stay in until retirement age. He applied, but the competition was intense; his application was rejected, and his appeal denied.

He tried to avoid another overseas assignment, arguing that his ailing mother needed him. But with his long experience in the Army, he shouldn't have been surprised when the Army assigned him to Berlin. On September 25, 1947, he sailed on the *Alexander*.

8. Postwar Germany, 1947-1952

Berlin, like all of Germany, was divided into four occupation zones: U.S., British, French and Soviet. Because of its geographic location deep inside the Soviet zone, ground access was restricted and controlled by the Soviets. In 1947, Berlin was a hot spot in the Cold War.[355] Surrounded by formidable Soviet military forces, the city was a vulnerable outpost that could be easily overwhelmed.

Dad was assigned to the engineers. He also served on Army court martial panels, including a three-member board set up to investigate the mysterious disappearance of millions of dollars worth of Army property—there was a thriving black market in American military equipment, cigarettes, coffee, chocolate, liquor, and other American products.[356] In December 1947, he was transferred to Heidelberg, the new U.S. Army headquarters for Europe.

May 1, 1948: Mom and I arrived at the Brooklyn dock to board our ship bound for Germany. It seemed to me that the *Jarrett M. Huddleston* was a big ship. In reality it was rather small, and in a few days it would seem very small, nothing more than a toothpick, out there in the North Atlantic.[357]

---

355 When did the "Cold War" begin? Probably with Churchill's speech at Westminster College, Fulton Missouri, March 5, 1946, in which he noted "the indisputable fact" that "an iron curtain had descended across the continent" from "Stettin in the Baltic to Trieste in the Adriatic." With President Truman in the audience, he called for an alliance of the Western democracies to counter the Soviet Union. The speech was roundly criticized as a "call to war." A year later, President Truman asked Congress for funds to assist the Greek government struggling against a Communist-led insurgency. On June 5, 1947 Secretary of State George Marshall, speaking at Harvard, announced the Marshall Plan to provide substantial funding for European recovery. The Soviet Union denounced both initiatives and the battle lines were drawn. See David McCullough, *Truman* (New York; Simon & Schuster, 1992): 486-490; D.F. Flemming, *The Cold War and its Origins* (New York; Doubleday 1961), 1: 433-476.

356 A court-martial board is a board of officers established to preside over and decide trials of military personnel charged with a crime under the Military Code of Justice.

357 The *Huddleston,* built in 1942 at the Richmond Shipyards, Richmond, California, was first known as the Samuel F.B. Morse. Taken over by the Army Transportation Corps in 1944, she was modified to carry troops and dependent passengers. She measured 418 feet long, fifty-seven feet wide, and thirty-seven feet deep, with four decks, and was capable of averaging 10.5 knots.

On board and ready to leave for Germany

Army band playing 'Now is the Hour' as we leave

The family came to the Brooklyn dock to say goodbye. Ten minutes before departure the loudspeaker came on warning visitors to get off the ship. The gangplank went up, the horn sounded, we eased away from the dock, and the army band played one of the great tear-jerkers of the 1940s: "Now is the hour, when we must say goodbye...." The dock slowly disappeared, the music faded, and the *Huddleston* moved out into New York Harbor.

Our "ocean liner" was built for stability, not speed. We were in for a long voyage. Mom and I were assigned to separate bunkrooms: one for women, the other for "men" seven and older. She was worried about our being so far apart; in particular, that we were assigned to separate lifeboats.

There were several hundred passengers, many of them under ten. Mother was in a bunkroom with sixteen women. My bunkroom, with accommodations for fifty-two, was located deep in the bow. When I finally got down there most of the bunks were taken. But I found an empty one, put my stuff on it, and climbed back up to the main deck by way of a steel ladder, a walk down a narrow corridor, another steel ladder, another corridor, then a third ladder. If the ship went down at night, none of us in that bunkroom would survive.

When I went back down to get something there was a man in my bunk and my stuff was in an upper bunk. *"Hey buddy, get your ass out of there. That's my bunk!"* was what I wanted to say. But I didn't. So I slept on top. My bunk was

213

about six feet long and maybe two feet across. I could touch the ceiling above me; my head touched one end, and my feet were firmly planted against the other end. I got up and down by ladder at the end of the bed. Every morning, sick or not, we all had to get up and out of the bunkroom by 8 A.M. to make way for the cleaning crew, followed by daily inspection.

At regular intervals the loud speaker announced, "Attention all passengers; mothers watch your children." At first all the mothers scrambled to find their children, but after a few days they relaxed. For exercise we walked around the ship on the upper deck. There was an open space in the bow with deck chairs in case the sun came out. For entertainment there was a lounge, all plastic and linoleum, a ping-pong table and an old piano securely nailed to the floor. In the lounge everybody smoked.

Late that first afternoon, as we moved out past Sandy Hook, New Jersey, the city slowly receded into the distance. In the evening, all that remained of Manhattan was light on the horizon. The next morning, there was nothing but the steel gray Atlantic Ocean, the wind, the sound of waves beating against the ship, and the peculiar manic laughter of seagulls.

Meals were tightly organized. We were assigned to the second mess and our times were 8:15, 12:15, and 5:15. The food was okay. It was a functional dining room, with tables and chairs bolted to the floor. After dinner there was usually a movie, and always bridge, poker, and canasta. Every night the loudspeaker went off at 11: "Now hear this, now hear this. It is 2300 hours. All lights will be put out and quiet will prevail," followed by the mournful sound of a trumpet playing Taps. In the morning, the speakers came on just before seven: "Good morning folks. It is now thirty seconds before seven o'clock. The temperature is fifty-six, and the weather is overcast, like the bridegroom at a shot-gun wedding."

We eased into shipboard routine. On the bulletin board in the lounge a daily weather report was posted, and there was a map showing the East Coast of the United States, the Atlantic, and Europe. The *Huddleston* was represented by a dot; each night the dot moved imperceptibly closer to Europe. We were averaging about nine knots.

The weather quickly turned nasty. On our second day I made the mistake of looking at one of the portholes in the dining room, with the horizon moving up and down. I couldn't take my eyes off that porthole, mesmerized by the moving horizon. I could feel the food in my throat trying to get out. Towards the end of the meal I excused myself, raced up to the deck, leaned over the rail, and gave up my dinner to the ocean. "Feeding the fishes," they called it. I had lots of company. There was no cure for seasickness and no escape. As one of the stewardesses in Mother's bunkroom put it, "It's all in getting your inner ear tubes used to it, dearie."

We ran into serious North Atlantic storms. With high winds and heavy rain, we had to stay inside, and if we walked anywhere we had to hold on to something to keep from falling or sliding. The dim bulbs hanging in the narrow corridors would swing wildly. A glass on a table would slide back and forth and, if not caught, hit the floor and shatter. The ship creaked and groaned as it hit first one wave then another—standing in the stern, with a tight grip on the rail, it was like riding an elevator up and up and suddenly down. Every time it went down I felt as if I'd left my stomach hanging in midair. But standing out there was the only way to breathe fresh air.

Mom was no help: "Bun, dear, I know you're miserable, but try to pull yourself together. Think how lucky we are: a free ocean cruise to Europe, courtesy of the government." I didn't think we were lucky to be on this miserable boat in the middle of an Atlantic storm.

She and some other ladies found a German scientist on board who gave them German lessons. Weather permitting, the ladies sat around in their deck chairs, bundled up in warm blankets with hot cups of tea, reading, practicing their German, and telling one another their life stories. But for me, the little dot on the map was moving too slowly.

Life boat drill on the *Huddleston*

After ten days or so the sun came out. Then one day we saw the coast of Ireland, no more than a speck on the horizon. That night, with an English pilot on board, we were in the Channel headed for the North Sea.

Mom was worried about hitting a North Sea mine left over from the war—the North Sea had been heavily mined by the Germans. The captain, too, was apparently concerned, because we crawled at a snail's pace past Holland toward Bremerhaven, the principal German seaport. The last issue of the *Huddle*, the ship's daily newspaper, reported what was going on in the world as we approached Bremerhaven. The hottest news was the war in the middle-east: the Jews in Palestine had just proclaimed the new State of Israel, Arab armies were attacking on all fronts, and the U.S. had asked the UN Security Council to order an immediate cease-fire by Jews and Arabs. In other news, the White House announced successful testing of new atomic weapons in the Pacific. We arrived at Bremerhaven on May 19, exactly nineteen days after leaving Brooklyn. It felt good to walk on land.

My Father met us at the dock, and we boarded the train for the overnight ride to Heidelberg. The redcaps at the station and the waiters in the dining car were all German; the passengers were all American, French or British. As we headed south, evidence of war was everywhere. There was hardly a whole building standing in the cities we passed through—Bremen, Hanover, Kassell, Frankfurt, and Darmstadt. Apartments and office buildings were sliced in half, the insides exposed, or reduced to a pile of rubble. Passing through one city, it appeared that everything had been destroyed except the huge cathedral, now an empty shell, its windows blasted out. People were at work clearing the rubble: women wearing work pants, men wearing remnants of old German army uniforms stripped of insignia, the men often missing a leg or an arm.

Early the next morning we arrived at the Heidelberg railway station. Heidelberg, an ancient university city without factories or major military facilities, had been one of the few German cities to escape damage. But the city looked tired and shabby: shops with empty windows or the windows boarded up, buildings in need of fresh paint, pot holes in the streets, prewar trolleys jammed with people dressed in prewar clothes.

My father's car and driver met us at the station and drove us to our new home at 40 Bergstrasse, a large solidly built three-story house. We had the entire first floor, which included kitchen, dining room, living room, sun porch—there seemed to be room for a ping-pong table—two bedrooms and two baths. The apartment opened onto a small garden. Another military family occupied the second floor. The house had belonged to a prominent local banker named

Eisenbeis before it was requisitioned for U.S. military personnel. Herr Eisenbeis had moved to smaller digs on the other side of town.[358]

Hannah, our twenty-seven-year-old German maid, was there to greet us. She was gaunt and her dress hung loosely. She wasn't pretty; she had a strong face with deep set eyes and a prominent jaw, and she was painfully anxious to please. Despite the efforts of the German scientist on the *Huddleston*, Mom and Hannah couldn't understand each other. What Hannah thought was English made no sense to Mom; what Mom thought was German made no sense to Hannah.

On their first day together, Hannah stood with an armful of bed linens and unleashed a torrent of German at Mom. Trying desperately to figure out what Hannah was saying, Mom thought she was complaining about the quality of the bed linens, so she patted her on the back and in her best German reassured Hannah that her husband would take care of everything when he got home. But Hannah wasn't cheered up. When Dad heard what Hannah had to say, he explained that she was describing the war years, the loss of her parents, and the problem of finding a man in postwar Heidelberg. There wasn't much he could do about that. Over time Mom and Hannah improved their communication skills, and Hannah proved to be honest, loyal, intelligent, and hard-working. The two women, from very different backgrounds and cultures, developed a close friendship that lasted far beyond our time in Europe.

Our new home at 40 Bergstrasse

---

358   My parents visited with Herr Eisenbeis and his family. When I returned to Heidelberg in 2001, "Eisenbeis" was still the name on the door.

Hannah, with Rudolph, our gardener

The streets of Heidelberg were filled with Americans and Germans going about their business. Traffic signs were in German and English. German cops directed traffic under the watchful eye of an MP. Every now and then the cop would stop traffic so that a green Chevrolet could speed through. Those green Chevrolets carried little flags with stars on them, making it very clear that there was a general inside. The *Hauptstrasse* (main street), lined with shops, was narrow, winding, and invariably crowded. Cars and buses attempting the Hauptstrasse had to slowly negotiate their way through a sea of pedestrians and bikers.

For news, we relied on *The Stars and Stripes*, the official army newspaper. Everything in the paper had to pass Army censorship. Sometimes you could get Army news on the radio. The telephone was okay for local calls, but all calls went through an Army operator. A transatlantic call was awkward and expensive, the connection uncertain. The call had to be placed first with an operator. *If* it went through, the operator would call at an appointed time—maybe eight hours after the call was placed. In our family there were no transatlantic calls. If something important happened in the States, like a death in the family, we got the news by Western Union telegram.

In the spring of 1948, the German economy was moribund. The shops had little to sell; people purchased food by riding a bicycle into the country and bartering with a farmer, trading household items and work for fresh vegetables and perhaps a little meat. The currency was worthless, and American cigarettes would buy anything (Dad used his cigarette ration to buy a nice German hunting rifle). Germans—boys and grown men—fought over a butt casually tossed in the gutter. Ragged, hungry-looking men would come to the door looking for something to eat, and Mom would always feed them. Years later, she recalled:[359]

> At that time the war had been over only a couple of years and the Germans were really in a terrible state, which I won't go into because that means getting involved in matters of war-guilt and retribution and subjects that are certainly too immense for me to discuss. But it's not good to see, anywhere, children going around in winter with pieces of wood tied on their feet for shoes and wearing little, thin coats or shawls. Every day, time after time, our bell would ring and there would be someone maybe very very old or very very little, asking for just a bit of food. We kept coffee and cocoa and peanut butter sandwiches going all the time and I hope I can honestly say that most of us never shut the door on anyone. I remember one tiny, thin boy who always appeared with his little violin and while I made him a sandwich he would play for me. When you open the door on a cold, wet morning and see there, maybe a young man, thin and ill-looking, with the remains of soggy shoes on bare feet, you don't say to him "you started the war" and slam the door in his face. You just give him a cup of hot soup and a sandwich and hope he'll decide that Americans are

---

359   Text of a talk by Priscilla Vestner, probably to the Effingham Women's Club, Effingham, New Hampshire, of which she was a member from 1957 to 1969.

really good people in spite of all the propaganda he'd been fed
to the contrary.

Hannah, by habit and necessity, was thrifty. After making our morning coffee, she saved the used grounds to make her own coffee the next morning. Nothing in the kitchen was discarded. All the leftovers from the dinner plates—the
stuff we called "garbage"—went up to her apartment to make another meal.
When Mom discovered what was going on she made sure Hannah had a good
supply of food, including fresh coffee.

We had never lived better: car and driver for Dad; large comfortable apartment with maid, cleaning woman, and Rudolph the gardener. Food, liquor and
cigarettes, though rationed, were readily available and cheap at the U.S. Army
Commissary and PX. We could see first-run Hollywood movies at the Casino,
the big officers' club at the army base on the edge of town. Dad also brought
home German war movies which we watched in our living room. Those movies,
filmed during the early days of the war, were the exact opposite of the wartime
films and newsreels we had seen back in Bronxville, when we always won and the
Germans were the bad guys. Now everything was reversed. The *Wehrmacht* was
on the move against a background of breathless reporting and stirring music.
German soldiers were handsome, friendly, and courteous; the local crowds were
enthusiastic, throwing flowers at the triumphant Germans.

Bergstrasse (Mountain Street), our street, was on the side of the Neckar
River opposite the Heidelberg castle, which sprawls over the mountainside high
above the old city with its narrow streets and ancient university. The river splits
the city down the middle. Near our house there was a path leading up to the
Philosofenweg (Philosophers' Way), a woodland trail winding around the mountain for miles high above the river before disappearing into deep forest. From
the path, the views across the river to the old city and castle are magnificent.

My father was area engineer, responsible for making sure everything
worked: electricity, phones, water, and heat. If a water main burst, he was on
the job. Colonel Feeman was Dad's boss. My parents spent a lot of time with the
Feemans, at their house or ours. They seemed to be good friends, but Feeman
apparently resented Dad's personal relationship with Feeman's ultimate boss,
General Clarence Huebner, Commander-in-chief of all U.S. forces in Europe.
I can only speculate on the source of Huebner's fondness for Dad. They shared
a common background: neither had gone to college; they had both served as
enlisted men on the Mexican border in 1916; and they had both worked their

way up in the Army without benefit of having gone to West Point.[360] In any event, Huebner's preference for dealing with Dad rather than Feeman put Dad in a tight spot. In the Army, if a three-star general tells you to do something, you do it, no questions asked. But it was Feeman, not Huebner, who filled out Dad's annual efficiency report.

Heidelberg, showing old bridge and castle

Over the course of that first year, Mom developed a life for herself in Heidelberg. She worked with a local charity delivering food to the most destitute Germans; she was on the board of the Heidelberg Women's Club; she joined a book group; she was a room mother at my school (chaperone for parties, ferrying us to basketball games, meeting with teachers); she was active in the PTA, the German-American Women's Club, and the Engineer Wives (who put on an engineers' lunch or dinner every month). She studied German at the university, joined a German music group, and developed a circle of German friends.

Mom and Dad were travelers and explorers, and for them Heidelberg was a base for exploring all of Western Europe (Eastern Europe was closed, sealed off from the West with barbed wire, searchlights and heavily-armed guards). Shortly after we arrived, Dad took us down to Strasbourg, formerly German but

---

360   Huebner received his officer's commission in 1916. His rise during the First World War was meteoric. Starting the war as a lieutenant, he ended it as a colonel and regimental commander in the First Division, with two distinguished service crosses and a silver star for bravery. In the Second World War, he commanded the First Division, leading it through North Africa and on Omaha Beach in Normandy. He rose to corps commander, and eventually to commander-in-chief of all U.S. forces in Europe until his retirement in 1950.

221

now a French city about 150 miles south of Heidelberg. To go there we needed U.S. Army orders and a French Army authorization for the days of our visit, and those documents were scrutinized at the border.

Strasbourg 1948: our restaurant Kammerzell, with prewar Mercedes in foreground

That first night we ate at the best restaurant in town, Kammerzell, which occupied the ground floor of one of the oldest buildings in Strasbourg. There were six of us: Dad, Mom, three officers from Dad's army unit, and me. We had a private room: waiters coming and going; soup out of a silver tureen and the biggest steak I'd ever seen, a Chateaubriand, surrounded by fresh vegetables—not out of a can and not the over-cooked, soggy kind we used to have at home. All I wanted then was steak, the bigger the better, and that was the best I ever tasted. All through dinner waiters were pulling corks and keeping the glasses filled with wine—I was permitted one glass. There were seconds on everything. The cost of that dinner at Kammerzell was trifling; the dollar was king and everything was cheap.

Dad was inspired, and when we got back to Heidelberg he arranged for us to have our own cook. He had visions of gourmet dinners and perhaps thought he was doing Mom a favor by relieving her of kitchen work. Hans reported for duty and became part of our entourage. Before the war, Hans had been a sous-chef at the Hotel Adlon, the preeminent hotel in Berlin. For his first meal, he served tuna fish in a remoulade sauce, a warm-up for things to come. When Mom realized Hans had used two whole cans of tuna for a first course she was horrified. A can of tuna was an entire meal. Two cans, just for starters, was extravagance on a grand scale. She straightened Hans out politely and quickly. Poor Hans; he wouldn't get the chance to really show his stuff. After a couple of months he left for greener pastures. Dad may have thought he was doing Mom a favor, but she couldn't deal with an out-of-control food budget. She regained control of the kitchen and never gave it up.

In June 1948, we witnessed the beginning of an economic miracle when the American, British, and French occupation authorities launched a coordinated program of currency reform in their zones. Currency reform, like everything else in occupied Germany, was driven by the U.S. authority under the High Commissioner, John McCloy. The Soviets had been given the option to participate but declined. On June 18, 1948, the new "Deutschmark" replaced the old Reichsmark. Before the reform, a suitcase full of Reichsmarks might not have been enough to buy a loaf of bread. As a result, people bartered for food, and food was scarce: virtually no meat, butter, eggs, coffee, or fresh vegetables; nothing but bread and potatoes, and even that was hard to come by.

As a result of currency reform, the Germans could turn in their old and worthless Reichsmarks for something of value. It wasn't all good news, especially for families with their life savings in Reichsmarks, who could only get one new Deutschmark for ten old Reichsmarks. But at least they received something of value, and the new Deutschmarks (in the form of crisp new bills) were pegged at about four to the dollar. Along with the new currency, most price controls were lifted, rationing eliminated and taxes reduced.

Overnight, the pace of commercial activity picked up. Shops with empty windows, shops with boarded-up windows, suddenly came alive, their shelves miraculously filled with goods for sale. The effect was immediately visible on the Hauptstrasse, and shopping began in earnest. Currency reform was like a jolt of electricity to the economy.

The Soviets denounced currency reform as divisive and threatened to retaliate. On June 24, 1948, they made good on their threat and blocked all rail, highway, and water access to Berlin.[361]

A few days later President Truman ordered a massive airlift to keep the Western sector of Berlin supplied with food and fuel. At first that was seen as a stop-gap measure, and it seemed entirely possible that the Soviets would run us out of Berlin, which they easily could have done, but that might have precipitated a Third World War.[362] Over the course of the winter and into the next spring, airplanes flew in and out of Berlin around the clock and met the needs of the city.

As the weeks passed and June turned into July, the airlift seemed to be working; it demonstrated to the isolated Berliners that we would not abandon them. The Soviets didn't attack our planes, but they continued to block the land routes to Berlin and nobody could predict how the situation would play out. Everyone we knew was anxious; sooner or later, virtually every evening, the talk around the dinner table would turn to Berlin and the risk of war. Berlin may have been a ten-hour hour drive from Heidelberg, but the Soviet *zone* was only sixty miles away. If the Soviets decided to move into West Germany, they would be in Heidelberg in less than two hours.

The Army distributed detailed instructions marked "RESTRICTED," including warning signals ("five (5) blasts of local warning sirens, each blast of one (1) minute duration with an interval of one (1) minute between blasts..."), local assembly points, and a short list of items that could be carried (blankets, warm clothing, etc.) by air to Spain.[363] We were all acutely aware that things could happen very quickly, and evacuation might not work as planned. As it turned out, the Berlin airlift was successful and the blockade was lifted in May 1949.

---

361 See Flemming, *Cold War*: 507-509, for a discussion of currency reform and the blockade.
362 As we now know but didn't then, Stalin was too cautious to provoke a war with the West. He wanted to get us out of Berlin, but without a war.
363 "INFORMATION AND INSTRUCTION FOR NONCOMBATANTS IN THE EVENT OF EMERGENCY," Headquarters, Heidelberg Military Post, 1 January 1951 (updated from earlier bulletins).

That summer of 1948, blockade or no, Dad took advantage of his thirty-day leave and we drove all over Europe —France, Belgium, Holland, Denmark, Switzerland, Austria, and Italy. But we couldn't just get in our car and take off. Everything had to be authorized in writing. If we were entering France, we needed a stamped and signed permit from the French army. Italy had a similar requirement. The Swiss required a special entry permit, with a prominent warning against taking photos of any Swiss military installation. Every country had some special requirement, and it took time to assemble the necessary permits and visas. Once granted, the authorizations were good only for the days specified. Crossing a border was always slow, as the border guards carefully inspected everything, especially the documents. On one trip to Austria, Mom noted, "Trouble at Austrian border as my visa had expired. Finally, ok." There was no such thing as spontaneous travel around Europe.

We spent a week in Paris at the Hotel Astor. The bill for five nights, with breakfast, was the Franc equivalent of about $43. Dad took us to the Folies Bergere—the bare-breasted French version of the Radio City Music Hall Rockettes in New York. Mom thought I was too young; Dad thought it would be "educational." It was. I'd never seen bare breasts before and that night there were a lot of them, all firm and perfectly shaped. Mom was embarrassed. Later that week, they took me to the Louvre for some culture, which was probably Mom's idea. I spent most of my time racing down long hallways and through large rooms, the walls covered with paintings, searching desperately for a bathroom which, as in a bad dream, I could never find. The Louvre could have used some of those public toilets that seemed to be located on all the streets of Paris.

From Paris we drove to the Normandy coast. It had been only four years since the Allied landing on D-Day and the area was littered with the twisted and rusting reminders of battle: beach obstacles, gun emplacements, empty concrete pill boxes. In contrast, the cemeteries were neat and orderly, with fields of white crosses, all in perfect formation. We visited Deauville, an elegant prewar seaside resort, and Mont St-Michel. An island off the coast accessible by causeway, Mont St-Michel rises straight up from the ocean, dominated by its thirteenth century Benedictine abbey and church, crowded with narrow streets that wind steeply up to the abbey. We ate dinner at La Mere Poularde; I can still taste Madame Poularde's omelets, cooked in a long-handled pan thrust into a roaring fire on a damp, chilly evening—and most evenings were damp and chilly.

225

D-Day relic: German pillbox on the Normandy coast

The original Madame Poularde and her omelet pan

The Swiss border and the Swiss city of Basel were within an easy day's drive of Heidelberg. All through Germany, France, and other European countries you could see the impact of war, but not in Switzerland. The Swiss houses were neat and tidy, the shops full, food plentiful, the people well-dressed, and everything expensive compared to the rest of Europe.

When not traveling I went to school, starting September 1948, in the Eighth Grade at the Heidelberg Dependents School. All the kids my age were "army brats" and they all seemed to know one another. The school was a short walk from our house. The principal was Mildred Linck from Battle Creek, Michigan. The school board was all military, headed by a colonel. Of the twenty teachers, fourteen were women. Six were German, all with prewar degrees from Heidelberg, the Harvard of Europe. The Americans came from all over: Iowa, Washington, Tennessee, California, Georgia, South Dakota, Connecticut, Nebraska, Pennsylvania, Kentucky, and one from Brooklyn, New York.

In the winter of 1949, we drove south from Heidelberg to Berchtesgaden, where the main attraction, apart from the spectacular mountain scenery, was Hitler's *Berghof* (mountain house), situated high above the town in Obersalzburg. One entire side of the large living room was floor-to-ceiling glass facing a range of mountain peaks. His tea house (the "Eagle's Nest") was another four miles up a precipitous road on top of Kehlstein Mountain.[364] At the end of the road, carved out of solid rock in 1937, an elevator inside the mountain rose smoothly to the granite house at the summit. In 1949, the Eagle's Nest was a sinister place. Only a few years before, it would have been crawling with SS guards in their black uniforms.[365]

Garmisch, another mountain village in the Bavarian Alps, larger than Berchtesgaden, had been the site of the 1936 winter Olympics. The stadium ski jumps and slalom course all looked new, as if they had never been used. We hiked in the mountains around Garmisch and took the cog railway and cable car up to the top of the Zugspitze, at 9,700 feet the highest mountain in Germany. We made the drive down into the Bavarian Alps several times a year to Berchtesgaden, Garmisch, and other places like Chiemsee and Lake Constance. It was easy to get there from Heidelberg, and Dad loved the mountains.

---

364   The Berghof was destroyed by the German government in 1953, so that it would not become a Hitler shrine. The Eagle's Nest was constructed in 1938 and presented by the Nazi party to Hitler on his birthday, April 20, 1939.

365   "SS," which stands for "Schutzstaffel," literally "Protective Echelon," was the security and military arm of the Nazi party, its insignia twin lightning bolts (runic spelling for SS).

Immediately after the war, Americans had been prohibited from "fraternizing" with Germans. By the time we arrived, there was a lot of "fraternizing:" American soldiers with German girlfriends, attractive and intelligent women, far beyond whom those same guys might have been able to attract back home. There was a shortage of young German men, and the survivors were either wounded or just plain defeated. In spite of all the fraternizing, there was still a clear social segregation. The local golf course was off-limits to Germans, as were the tennis club, swimming pool, and all the various American social clubs. Most Americans preferred to socialize within the large American community. The Army base on the outskirts of town was a small American city; the "Casino" served excellent food (steak dinner with shrimp cocktail for $1.25) and offered current movies from the States, as well as regular bridge, canasta, and bingo with prizes. The old Heidelberg castle on the hill overlooking the city had been turned into another swankier officers' club, and one of the grand old mansions along the Neckar River had been turned into the "Macogen Club," for majors, colonels and generals.

My parents were active within the American community. As a director of the Heidelberg Women's Club, Mom organized and led a group of forty army wives to Vienna and a night at the opera. She also helped organize the weekly dinner parties at the Heidelberg castle for the engineers. She and Dad gave dinner parties (usually followed by games, home movies or slides and at least one scavenger hunt), went to dances, and played cards, tennis, and golf with their Army friends.

Unlike most of the American Army families in Heidelberg, my parents developed a large circle of German friends, all cultured and civilized, invariably better educated than we were and good company, able to converse in English on a wide range of topics. If the subject came up, their German friends would have made it clear that they had no use for Hitler. But of course no German in his right mind would admit to an American that he had ever admired Hitler or been an enthusiastic member of the Nazi party, so who knows what lay beneath the surface? My parents treasured those friendships and took their friends at face value.[366]

---

366   De-nazification panels were established by the allies; individuals who had been Nazis were examined, starting with a personal questionnaire followed by investigation. The resulting decision could result in permanent loss of employment. The process was criticized as naïve and meaningless. Few if any Germans under investigation admitted they were serious Nazis; friends provided glowing character references; and Germany, as a practical matter, couldn't function if the six million former party members were excluded from the workforce. See Robert Erikson, "Denazification at Gottingen," presented at the International Commission for the History of Universities Colloquium, Oslo, August 10-11, 2000 (arguing that, however flawed, the process served a beneficial purpose).

Mom, showing off her new suit from Vienna

Dinner party with army friends, 1950

Mom and German tennis group; left to right, Frauen Plock, Vestner, Henrici, Ruschia and Diekraut

Dad, his secretary Lisa Ritter, and German friends; they're not about to run out of beer

Mom and her German friends went off on trips and on at least one occasion had too much to drink, as on January 14, 1949, when Mom wrote: "Drove Frau Ruschia & Edith across the Rhine to buy Pfalz beer in Mosheim. Too much 'tasting'...Awfully sick."

Her adjustment to Germany was relatively easy. For me it was harder. I was an unusually tall fourteen-year-old and an easy target. Downtown one day, I passed three older American high school guys in jeans, shirt collars turned up, ducktail haircuts, cigarettes hanging out of their mouths, leaning against a wall. "Hey Annabelle, come over here. You're a piece a shit, d'ya know that?" I didn't say anything. "Let's hear ya sing—sing for us." I tried "Near You," and my voice cracked. They couldn't stop laughing. I walked away. "Hey, where the hell d'ya think your goin'? Come back here. We're not finished." I just kept walking, but they grabbed me, pushed me up against a wall, and beat me. When I came home that night I was a mess. Dad wanted to know who did it, but I wasn't about to tell him. That would have guaranteed more of the same.

I occasionally ventured into the teen canteen, the official hang out, mainly for the older American high school kids. One of the regulars was Norm Schwarzkopf, with his ducktail haircut and turned-up collar—that was the cool look (much later Norm, minus the ducktail, was the four-star general who commanded all the troops in operation "Desert Storm").

Mom was on the board of the PTA, and she had a mission. The school didn't offer Latin, and she thought that was a big mistake. Failing to get the school to offer Latin—Miss Linck, the principal, patiently explained that it was a "dead" language and of no use—she tried to line up some other mothers to hire a Latin teacher for an extra-curricular course. But she couldn't interest enough of them.

Her larger concern was that we teenagers were isolating ourselves from the surrounding culture. Here we were, living in a famous old university town, our teachers were mainly American, we studied American subjects in English, we played sports only with other American kids, and we associated only with other Americans. And, of course, we got into trouble—for setting off firecrackers late at night in mailboxes (big noise), tossing cherry bombs off the bus on the crowded Hauptstrasse, or leaning out the bus and swiping the hat off a German's head. She was upset and frustrated that we were acting like spoiled Americans, oblivious of other cultures. She thought there ought to be more emphasis on learning German, more school visits to German cultural sights, and some exchange programs with German schools. She ran into a brick wall. None of my friends were particularly interested in reaching out, so of course I wasn't either. Associating with German kids wasn't cool. She thought we were missing the opportunity of a lifetime. Of course she was right. Years later, speaking before a group of women in New Hampshire about her German experience, Mom still felt the frustration over her inability to broaden my cultural horizons:

> If you'll excuse me for being personal, I think I can safely say that our own boy was fairly typical of the twelve and thirteen-year-old youngsters. They attended a school run by the Army since, of course, there were no facilities in the German schools for teaching English-speaking boys and girls. We parents were very deeply distressed by the fact that our children formed a tight little group, determined to live just as Americanish lives as they possible could in that foreign country.

> Instead of realizing the opportunities and advantages of living with a foreign people, they resented everything German. And you can understand that when you realize that from the time these young-sters were five or six years old, all through those very formative years, we had been at war with Germany and they had heard nothing in their homes but stories of German atrocities and hatred. To them all Germans were stupid and cruel. We had practically to bind and gag our own boy to get him to go off on trips with us ...

> I remember one time our boy was invited to spend a weekend in Berlin with a friend of his who was the son of General Maxwell Taylor. We weren't too happy about putting him on the train for an overnight ride to Berlin through the Soviet Zone (Americans could ride in to Berlin only at night, with the window shades on the Pullman cars pulled down). But Tom Taylor had visited with us and we didn't feel we could say that we were "afraid" to let our boy go to him. Besides which we knew it would be educational for the boy to see Berlin. When he came home we asked him to tell us all about conditions in that interesting, besieged city, and much to our disgust he said that he and Tom had spent the entire weekend inside of a gymnasium shooting baskets.[367]

---

367   Talk to Effingham Women's Club by Priscilla Vestner, sometime in the 1950s.

She escorted our basketball team to Berlin in the spring of 1949 and made sure we saw all the sights I had missed during my visits with Tom Taylor. She made sure we didn't spend all our time in a gym. Berlin was still a destroyed city, with hollow buildings and piles of rubble. Mom took us to see the Olympic stadium (site of the 1936 Olympics), the Brandenburg Gate, and the Soviet war memorial, with the big T-34 tank and the Soviet army guards who didn't look a day over sixteen and probably weren't. When we got too close, he aimed his gun right at us and we backed away in a hurry.[368]

The Reichstag, home of German parliament in the 1920s, later headquarters of the Luftwaffe In 1948 it was a burned out hulk

I was fourteen in 1949. Sex was a hot topic among the guys my age and rumors were flying. Fred, with his pompadour, upturned collar, and cigarette hanging out of his mouth, was the very definition of cool. Rumor was that he was "getting it" regularly from his seventeen-year-old girlfriend. That just amazed me. It was beyond my imagination. I was absolutely clueless and scared of girls, so I poured all my energy into basketball. A bunch of us were always in the gym at the big Army base. Maybe we wouldn't have played so much if we were operating at Fred's level. But we weren't, so we had a pretty good basketball team.

---

368   Getting to Berlin wasn't easy. Trains from the West could run only at night with shades drawn, and the Soviet border guards were brusque, demanding, and slow. Traveling by car, one risked getting shot (or so we thought). One time driving to Berlin, Dad stopped the car so he and I could relieve ourselves. In midstream we heard shots and high-tailed it back to the car.

Dad tried to make me into an athlete. He arranged golf lessons, but that was a frustrating sport, especially with the unforgiving golf clubs we had in 1949—tiny woods with persimmon heads, thin-bladed irons, and golf balls that never seemed to get off the ground. He pushed me to go out for the football team and I did, until I broke my middle finger and had to go around with a six-inch cast on it, much to everyone's amusement. He recruited an Army sergeant with track experience to make me a better quarter-miler. In the spring, the sergeant and I would meet at the track three or four days a week. He was tough, forcing me to do one quarter mile after another, holding his stopwatch, always pushing. I'd finish what for me was a fast quarter, ready to take a break; he'd tap me on the shoulder: "Do it again, and this time put something into it!"

Franz Zielmann, the tennis pro at the club, gave me tennis lessons. I was pretty good, but the German ball boys my age could always beat me. After a match on a hot day we'd down three or four bottles of Royal Crown Cola. One day Dad took us to watch Baron Gottfried von Cramm play a top American in an exhibition match. The American—Earl Cochell—was a Californian and ranked number ten in the world. He appeared in the latest fashion—white shorts and tennis shirt. Von Cramm, who had been one of the top players in the world before the war, wore long white pants and a dress shirt with collar—the standard pre-war tennis fashion. In 1939, Von Cramm had gone five sets with Don Budge in the deciding match of the Davis Cup, but war and ten years had slowed him down. He still gave Cochell a good match.

Mom was determined that I continue with piano lessons, and hired an unemployed German concert pianist. The poor guy was dressed in rags; judging by his appearance and smell, he had no place to take a shower. After each lesson, Mom sprayed pine scent around the piano. He was a drillmaster, but I had no interest in classical music—too much precision and practice. I felt sorry for him; he probably would have had a promising career but for the war. He was gently let go and Dad arranged lessons from Lottsie, leader of the jazz combo at the Macogen Club. Lottsie taught me how to play "Stardust," "Two Sleepy People," "As Time Goes By," "Smoke Gets in Your Eyes"—a whole repertoire of pop.

Dad's new 1948 Chevy, Hannah behind

On our next trip, summer of 1949, we picked up our new Chevrolet at the port in Hamburg ($1,550) and drove north through Germany to Copenhagen. Dad wanted to stay at the D'Angleterre, the best hotel in town but it was booked solid. We found a pension out of town, where we all shared a double bed. We couldn't get out of there fast enough, and drove into the city for breakfast on the veranda of the D'Angleterre under its gaily-colored awning. I have a warm memory of Copenhagen, and Tivoli, its great amusement park, but the only detail I remember was Davidson's sandwich shop, which served about two-hundred varieties of *Smorrabrod*, open-faced sandwiches: caviar, tiny shrimp, smoked salmon, eel, raw beef, anything you can imagine, artistically designed on a thin slice of homemade rye bread, usually (but not by me) washed down with a cold Tuborg beer or, in Dad's case, Aquavit. From Copenhagen, we took the ferry to Sweden, and drove up the coast to Bastad, staying at an inn that Mom loved. As she noted in her diary: "Very lovely inn. Dinner by the shore. Must stay here longer!" Unfortunately, her "very lovely inn" is no more.

Stockholm was a two-day drive, and there we stayed at the Grand Hotel, which to me was the height of luxury. We explored Stockholm and the surrounding area— Town Hall, Drottingham Castle, the Archipelago,

235

boat trip through the canals, and dinner at Operakallaren, a famous old restaurant in the late stages of faded elegance. And then we were off to Oslo.

On the road to Oslo; 424 kilometers to go

During our long driving days, I would ask Dad to stop while I got out and went for a run. He thought I was nuts. He liked to go in a straight line as fast as possible. When I asked him to stop he'd throw up his hands, and say, "What now? Can't you just sit and relax like a normal person?" But with coaxing from Mom he'd pull over, I'd get out, put on my running shoes, do stretches, then he'd drive a couple of miles down the road and wait, fuming about the time we were wasting.

We always carried extra gas, just in case

Oslo was a full two-day drive across Sweden with an overnight in Karlstad. We arrived in Oslo at the Grand Hotel after midnight, but it was still light; it could have been four o'clock in the afternoon, except the streets were deserted. The next day, I swam off the beach in water crawling with jelly fish. My parents wouldn't go in; I don't know why I did. Mom's diary describes the rest of the trip through Norway and back to Denmark better than I can:

> Mon. Left Oslo at 11. Beautiful ride through mts. & by rivers to Geilo at 6. Dinner & night at Dr. Holmes Hotel. So lovely & so late! In eve. Climbed small mt. & waited while El & Bun went way up. <u>Very</u> nice place.

Tues. Left Geilo after breakfast. Long weird ride over high plateau to Eidfjord for ferry at noon. Picnic by fjord and lovely boat ride of an hour.... Bergen for late dinner...

Wed. Shopping, lunch up on Mt. in Bergen. Took boat, lovely trip all P.M. Arrived at Stavanger and drove all night along fjords and over high mountains. Deep snow. Slept an hour in car by a lake. Needed no headlights, no darkness. [We drove all night because Dad couldn't find our inn]

Thursday. Arrived Kristianstad 8:30 A.M. after all night drive. To hotel & all to bed. El & I up at 12 & went around town. Took night boat to Denmark. Sat on deck all night. Nice crowd of people, but too many.

On the ferry from Norway to Denmark, Mom sat up all night on deck because she was terrified of the North Sea, believing, correctly, that it was full of left-over mines from the war.

On that long trip through Scandinavia, I learned something. Before, it was all one lump—"Scandinavia." After, the countries and people were quite distinct: Denmark, flat, dairy country, friendly people; Norway, remote, mountainous, the people rather taciturn; Sweden, prosperous, sophisticated, the people, proud even to the point of appearing somewhat self-righteous (or so it seemed to me). Perhaps the Swedish attitude reflected the fact that Sweden had been the only Scandinavian country to avoid German occupation during the war.[369]

Later that year, Mom traveled with a friend through Switzerland, Austria, Italy (Cortina, Venice, Pisa and Florence), Monaco and France (Nice and Cannes). Dad joined the two ladies halfway through the trip. They ate very well and probably saw much more, certainly in the way of museums, palaces and cathedrals, than if I had been along. But I envied them going to Italy and the South of France—I liked to eat well too.

The next year, 1950, Mom and I returned to Bronxville for a two-month visit, departure and return dates explicitly noted on our orders. We sailed on the *Alexander Patch*. It was a rough trip, but this time we had a new pill to take

---

369 In 1949, Sweden stood apart from the other Scandinavian countries; unlike Denmark, Norway and Finland, Sweden had maintained wartime neutrality, but at the price of making certain concessions to the Germans, and like Switzerland, had profited from the war.

for seasickness, Dramamine, and our own cabin with private bath. The trip took nine days. Our third day at sea Mom noted: "Left Southampton at 1 PM. Rough weather. Felt fine so didn't take pill at night. Sorry for that..."

Ruth's heart condition had worsened. Beautiful and gentle as always, Ruth was now almost completely bedridden. Lowell devoted his non-working hours to taking care of her. Mom had to clean out our old apartment at One Beechtree Lane, which now seemed impossibly small, and give it up. She and Dad didn't know where they were going to be when they returned to the States and there was no point in continuing to pay rent on the old apartment; but they hated to give it up because it was their only "home." Left alone in Heidelberg, Dad was unhappy and complaining. He was stuck with the job of duty officer, and had to spend a long weekend at the office. In a letter, Dad shared his acute discomfort with being caught in the middle between General Huebner and Colonel Feeman:

> We have a new officer a Major O'Brien, who is playing the favorite for the moment. My work goes along as usual. I had a nice talk with the General [Huebner] last Saturday and his dealing direct with me is somewhat embarrassing, particularly when I have to inform Feeman about the contents of his complaints. I know he [Feeman] hates me for it.[370]

He complained about his "overactive social life": late nights of bridge, canasta, poker, movies, bingo, cocktails, and dinner out with friends. He didn't get much sympathy.

Back in Heidelberg, we were off on another trip, this time to England, Scotland and Ireland. We left on June 14 and returned June 31. England at the time was still suffering from the war, and certain kinds of food—milk, eggs, butter, and meat—were in short supply. Mom shopped in London and we hiked in the English Lake District and the Trossachs in Scotland. As with our Scandinavian trip, I learned that geography is much more specific and diverse than I had imagined. What I had assumed was one country—Great Britain—was at least three and possibly more. We picked up a hitchhiker in Scotland and couldn't understand a word he said; it was a different language. Scottish geography, mountainous and remote, was very different from England, with its carefully-tended landscape. While the English seemed reserved, the Scots were

---

370 Letter, dated May 11, 1950, from Eliot to Priscilla.

even more so. In contrast, the Irish were outgoing, friendly and hospitable, while showing no love lost toward the English or the Scots. What seemed to tie it all together was golf.

Mom teeing off, Royal County Down course, Newcastle, Ireland, June 1950.

In her diary, Mom recorded our last day—a long one:

Sat. Left Dover 12:40 A.M. Dunkirk at 3:30 A.M. Up, then Coffee. Off & waited for French customs until 6:30. Brussels at 11:30. Lunch. Across Belgium to Aix-la-Chapelle & into Germany Bad Homburg at 9:40 & grand steak dinner at Ritter Park Hotel. Heidelberg at 1:15 A.M.

Later that summer we drove down to Liechtenstein, one of a number of trips we made to that small country (sixty-two square miles), almost invisible between Austria and Switzerland. There's not much reason to go to Liechtenstein, except for spectacular mountain scenery, great skiing, superb food and very discreet private banking.

Most weekends we drove down to the Black Forest. Badenweiler and Baden-Baden were elegant prewar spa towns just beginning to recover their old magic but still affordable for an American with dollars. Baden Baden, with its baths, the Brenner Park Hotel, and the Baden Baden Golf Club, was an easy two-hour drive from Heidelberg on the Autobahn. Constructed in the thirties by Hitler, there was nothing like the Autobahn in the United States, and wouldn't be until the construction of the interstate highway system after 1956.[371]

On the road to Lichtenstein

---

371   The Autobahn was the world's first limited access high-speed road network. Begun under the Weimar Republic in the early thirties, with the Nazi takeover in 1933, construction became a top priority, providing over one-hundred thousand construction jobs and helping the country recover from an economic depression.

The German Autobahn about 1950"

In the winter, we skied in St. Anton, Austria—deep snow and sunny skies. At least that's how I remember it. Mom tried skiing and got depressed at how terrible she was, so she and Dad dragged a sled four kilometers from St. Anton to St. Christof's on the Arlberg Pass. It took them hours, but after some hot rum they coasted home in fifteen minutes, getting in just ahead of an avalanche which would have buried them. When the avalanche hit, they were sitting beside a fire in the Post Hotel having tea.

St. Anton, winter of 1950, Dad and Me

Although the Second World War was recent history, Dad was still wrapped up in the First World War. That was his war. One day he and Mom got an early start and drove to Baccarat, France, about sixty miles south of Strasbourg, where Dad had his first taste of German artillery, poison gas and battlefield death. Mom noted one evening—and I'm sure there were other such evenings: "Capt Benson came & he and El refought World War 1. Headache."

In the spring, Mom encouraged me to think about going back to the States. She was concerned about the quality of the academics at Heidelberg High and thought I would benefit from the "discipline" of a New England prep school, like Kent or Exeter. I chose Andover, took the exams, and was accepted with a small scholarship. Dad grumbled at the expense, but Mom had her way. It was good for everybody: Mom got what she wanted, I got the school I wanted, and Dad got me out of Heidelberg so that Mom could go with him to his new post in Orleans, France, where the Army had established subsidiary headquarters for Europe.

Orleans was on the Loire River, about 116 kilometers from Paris; its claim to fame was Joan of Arc, who saved the city from the English in 1429. Moving there was not what Dad wanted; but the year before, he had passed up an invitation by General Huebner to take a position in Garmisch. Garmisch was a beautiful town in the mountains and Huebner was trying to be helpful. But Dad didn't want to leave Heidelberg.

General Huebner, retiring Commander-in-Chief, U.S. Army, Europe, and Mom at a dinner party

243

When the general returned to the U.S. Dad was at the mercy of several colonels who didn't like him, resented his relationship with Huebner, and engineered his transfer out of Heidelberg. Maybe there were other factors: maybe Dad was just getting stale in his job. Who knows? But he blamed his transfer on those colonels out to get him.

From Orleans, Dad had to drive about seven hundred kilometers coming and going to see us on weekends, bumping along on French country roads through little towns and villages. After the long drive, he wasn't always in an easy, relaxed mood, and sometimes things got ugly between us. One day in Heidelberg, I thought he was being a little rough on Mom and I said so. The next thing I knew we were in my room, I was on the bed and he was on top, giving me a good beating and a bloody nose. I was almost six feet tall, but he was a lot stronger, and he was furious. I said, "I'm never coming back to this house!" and stormed off. That lasted for about four hours, until dinnertime.

Dad was miserable in Orleans. He described it as "the most uninteresting city I have ever been in. Not a thing to recommend it except an historical past." He was sitting at a desk, nothing to do. "As to work, I have been designated as Civil Affairs Officer but have received no orientation on what I am supposed to do. Consequently, I am sitting idly by awaiting security clearance, which is apparently required before I can have access to secret material. It is a most discouraging period.... I struggle to look busy and keep awake but it ain't easy."[372] He was tempted to use the time to travel, and he did take a long weekend in Tangier, where he went to a bull fight, but otherwise he had to stick around Orleans to avoid trouble.

In his free time—and he had a lot of free time—he played bridge, poker and bingo with friends, played the slot machines at the officer's club, watched first-run movies from the States, and went into Paris to his favorite bistro, Chez Mercier. Walking to his Paris hotel from the Latin Quarter one night, he reported that "at least twenty street walkers propositioned me. Quite an education."[373] But he was frustrated and bored; his career was going nowhere, and he was worried about the immediate future. How much longer could he stay in the Army? How much longer would they be able to stay overseas? He expected that any day relations with the West German government would be normalized, and when that happened, Americans in Germany would have to live on the local economy: no more free housing, cheap maids, gardeners, and cooks.[374]

---

372 Letters, dated July 5 and July 11, 1951, from Eliot to Priscilla.
373 Letter, dated August 7, 1951, from Eliot to Priscilla.
374 Letter, dated July 16, 1951, from Eliot to Priscilla.

I returned to the States for good in September, 1951. Mom moved out of the Heidelberg house and into Dad's one-room quarters in Orleans.[375] On October 1 they drove their by-now-old 1948 Chevy to Bremerhaven (they had put almost 50,000 miles on it in two years) and picked up their new 1951 Pontiac Catalina coupe, an upgrade that cost $2,535. They were loyal GM customers.

Their time in Europe was rapidly winding down and they scrambled to take advantage of it. Mom took daily French classes in Orleans. On her fifty-second birthday, October 7, 1951, they drove to Chartres, spending the afternoon in the Cathedral and "prowling" the old town. Dad took her to dinner at the Hotel du Grand Monacle and, dissatisfied with their hotel room, changed it "for a very fancy red, plush and gilt one," which Mom thought looked like a room in a French whorehouse. They loved Paris: walking, window-shopping, buying at the flea market, sightseeing, eating at little bistros—their favorite was still Chez Mercier. From Orleans they took day trips along the Loire, poking around little villages and visiting places familiar to Dad from the First World War

In November 1951 they took their last big trip, a long one through France and Spain. On the way to Spain, they stopped for dinner at La Pyramide Chez Point, a Michelin three-star restaurant in Vienne, France. Under owner-chef Fernand Point it was then regarded as the best restaurant in Europe. Mom described their dinner in her notes:

> Pate de foie gras, hare pie, mussels in crème and pastry shells, thrush pate, chicken in cream sauce and haricots verts, choice of cheeses; dessert—pots of chocolate, five-layer chocolate cake and ice cream. Cost: 1750 francs--$5 a piece: no menu; stuffed; on to Valence for the night (11 PM).

They entered Spain at the border near Perpignan, picked up their Spanish visas, hard to get from the Franco government, and continued to Barcelona where their guide took them to a "crumby hotel," which they quickly abandoned. Accustomed to eating at six, they had to dine on Spanish time in Barcelona—nothing open before nine. Their late dinner at Casa Soli was a comedown from Le Pyramide: Mom had lobster while Dad ordered a local fish dish that she described as "gruesome."

---

375   Mother kept handwritten notes of her days in Orleans and their last travels together in Europe, covering most of 1951. Her notes are the source of information for their last year in Europe.

The next day they took the night boat from Barcelona to Majorca, where they hired a driver and his 1924 Chrysler to take them out to Cabo de Formentor, where they lunched at the elegant Hotel Formentor overlooking the ocean. Returning to Barcelona, they picked up their car and drove down the coast to Valencia, where they met an American who steered them to "a terrible eating dive." Fleeing back to the "dreary and dirty" Hotel Metropole, they had a dinner that was "all olive oil." Glad to be rid of Valencia, they drove south to Puerto Lumbreras, where they stayed in a "lovely Parador, like a Hollywood Hacienda," and had dinner with a couple from Vermont with a son at Exeter. A night in a parador was fifty Pesetas. Since the Peseta was then worth about 2 cents, the paradors were a good deal for traveling Americans.[376]

Granada was the high point of the trip. There, they stayed at the Spain's premier parador, the Parador Nacional San Francisco, located within the grounds of the Alhambra.[377] They were able to spend a morning, undisturbed, in the Alhambra, with its geometric designs and rectangular reflecting pools.[378] They met a Greek couple who persuaded them to go out in the evening to watch the gypsies sing and dance. Before they knew it, they were buying wine for the gypsies and dancing with them. The Greeks were used to it; Mom and Dad were not. The gypsies got free wine and Mom got a bad headache.

From there they drove over the mountains to Gibraltar, Algeciras, Cadiz, Seville (where they stayed at the grand old Alfonso XIII), and Madrid, where they spent days touring the city and surrounding countryside. They returned to Orleans via San Sebastian and Biarritz. Their Pontiac, with 3,000 miles on it, was no longer new.

They had seen Spain, but had they? Mom's diary was typically simple and factual: where they went, where they stayed, what they saw, where and what they ate. But neither she nor Dad spoke Spanish, so they missed the opportunity to meet people and get a sense of what Spain was really about in those years: an impoverished country ruled by a repressive dictatorship, with reminders everywhere of its bloody civil war, a country very different from the rest of Europe.[379]

They returned to the States the following January 1952, when Dad took up his new assignment as Post Engineer at Fort Slocum, New York. From their

376   The Spanish paradores were developed starting in about 1926, usually reconstructed from old castles, monasteries and mansions in areas of cultural interest or natural beauty.
377   The parador was constructed on the remains of a fourteenth century mosque, later converted to a Franciscan convent.
378   The Alhambra, built during the fourteenth century, was the residence of the Muslim rulers of Spain until they were forced out in 1492. .It is Spain's most famous example of Islamic architecture and a major tourist attraction.
379   See, for example, Gerald Brenan, *The Face of Spain* (London; Penguin Books, 1950).

new quarters, they could hear the big band sounds from the old Glen Island Casino, just offshore from New Rochelle, where the Dorseys and Glenn Miller had played in the thirties. Bronxville was a twenty-minute drive.

By the winter of 1952, the family had shrunk. Dad's mother was dead; Mom's two sisters, Ruth and Dorothy, were dead: Ruth in 1950; Dorothy in the late fall of 1951 from a sudden heart attack. Lowell was still going strong. Brother Ran was still in Scarsdale; Brother Everett was still in Woodbury, New Jersey.

9. Getting Educated in the Fifties

On a crisp September day in 1951, Lowell drove me from Bronxville to Phillips Academy, Andover. He left me at Adams House with Jack Hawes. Hawes was the no-nonsense housemaster of Adams House, where I would live for the next nine months.

When I arrived at Andover, most of the boys my age had been there for two years. All the cliques had been formed and were well-established.

In November I received my first Andover report card: "F" in English, "F" in German, "D" in Physics, "D" in Math, and "B" in piano (at least I could play the piano). Dad wrote to John Kemper the headmaster, a West Pointer and retired Army colonel, who replied:[380]

> It isn't surprising that Eliot may think he is not adjusting too rapidly. Any youngster in his first few weeks might well feel that way. Actually, he is probably doing a lot better than he thinks...
>
> His instructor attributes the failure in English largely to poor earlier training. He says Eliot started out having a little difficulty accepting ideas as possible when they differed from his preconception, and presenting his ideas in writing.

Kemper's reply may have appeased my parents, but I was screwing up. Walter Gierasch assigned a lot of short papers, and mine came back with his comments, obviously scrawled in anger: "What on earth does this mean?" "Is this statement based on anything?" "Have you even read the book?" "Didn't

---

380   Letter, dated November 16, 1951, from John M. Kemper, Headmaster, to Major Eliot N. Vestner.

anybody ever teach you grammar?" With only seven in the class, there was no place to hide. Gierasch, dry and sarcastic, wouldn't let me off the hook, bringing me into every discussion with an unerring instinct for cutting through a superficial response and making me look stupid and unprepared. It seemed that the other guys in the class were all brilliant and I was the loser. Of course that wasn't true, but that's how it appeared to me at the time. At Heidelberg, I aced English. But this first Andover English class was an entirely new and terrifying experience

In Heidelberg, basketball had been my sport. I thought I was pretty good. In my daydreams, I was the star and nobody could stop me. Unfortunately, there was a real world out there with other guys, who were more talented and equally determined to make the team. And so on a raw damp day late in November I saw my name posted on the varsity cut list. I played on the JV team that season.

In the dorm one evening, I got into a fistfight with a boy who knocked my eyeglasses into my face, giving me a bloody cut beside my right eye. I had to go to the infirmary to get it stitched up. Every time the doctor brought his needle towards my eye, I thought he was going to stick it in my eyeball. I also made the mistake of mentioning my fear of snakes, probably in the course of some late night bull session. So one evening, about to go to sleep, I had the feeling there was something in the bed with me; and of course there was—a four-foot black snake coiled up at the foot of the bed. The other guys were all listening at the door, and came in as soon as they heard the commotion. I jumped; the snake slid off the bed and escaped through a crack behind the radiator.

I didn't think things could get worse, but they did. I was put on probation for "too many cuts," mostly for being late to class or missing breakfast.

I seemed to have a problem with rules, and Andover was a strict and formal place governed by rules. We could get a "cut" (basically, a demerit) for anything: late for class, walking on the lawn, skipping breakfast, or just being in the wrong place at the wrong time. We could be expelled for smoking or drinking; we had to wear jacket and tie to class and meals (I learned to tie a quick bow tie while running to 7:30 breakfast, where a faculty member took attendance); afterward, promptly at eight, we had compulsory chapel. We had classes all morning, and of course you couldn't be late or missing without a written excuse. We had compulsory athletics and usually a class late in the afternoon. We could not be out of our dorm after nine, and if we were and got caught, we could get several cuts or even probation. Teachers and students addressed each other as "Mister."

Dad, shocked by my seeming disregard of the rules, wrote to Bill Bennett, one of the Deans:[381]

> Dear Mr. Bennett:
>
> I am in receipt of your notice dated 2nd December, informing me of my son's unexcused cuts for the fall term.
>
> I very much regret that Eliot's record in this respect is not free from any infractions and I will certainly discuss with him the need for immediate improvement in his attendance habits.
>
> While there is no excuse for failure to meet all school commitments on time I fear that with my boy Eliot, getting up in the morning is one of the most difficult adjustments he must make but that he will make it, I am sure.

"Not free from any infractions"? My father always stopped short of calling a spade a spade. I had nothing but infractions; I was the infractions king. Now on probation, I couldn't leave campus, couldn't walk downtown for a soda, and had to report every evening to Jack Hawes. I could lose my scholarship, even be expelled. It was a long winter.

In the spring of 1952, I was still kidding myself that I could run the quarter-mile. I was supposed to run in a JV meet against the Harvard freshmen JV. When I saw what I was up against, what little confidence I had just drained away. They seemed like big guys, and I didn't want to face coming in dead last, way behind everybody else. I slunk back to the dorm and went to my room. When I didn't appear for the race, Jack Hawes, who assisted with the track team, made a bee line for my room. He was furious: "What's the matter with you, Eliot? Were you afraid of the big bad Harvard freshmen? What did you think they were going to do, eat you?" I deserved it. In his report for the year, Hawes had this to say:

> As I look back upon my close association with Eliot this year, I think that he is certainly one boy about whom it may well be said, 'he is his own worst enemy.' Punctuality and an orderly

---

381   Letter, dated December 12, 1951, from Dad to William Bennett, Assistant Dean of Students.

approach to his school life have upon occasion been conspicuous by their absence. When it comes to a choice between rushing into things blindly and planning things carefully, Eliot can almost always be counted upon to do the former. He has not yet learned to appraise on personal grounds any new and different situation.

I wanted to go to West Point and make a career in the Army. At least, that's what I thought I wanted. During the summer of 1952, Dad and Uncle Lowell were working on getting me an appointment to West Point through Bronxville congressman Ralph Gwinn, one of the most conservative Republicans in the Congress. In his recommendation, Lowell described me as "bright without being brilliant, athletic without being a star athlete, a good all-around boy without being outstanding." Lowell, an honest man, must have thought long and hard before he wrote that.[382]

My father decided I needed to do some work on my eyesight to pass the Army physical. He arranged for me to see a man on Staten Island, a specialist in helping candidates for West Point pass the eye exam by learning to read the shadows on the chart. Even if you couldn't clearly see the letters you could make an educated guess by "reading" the blurs. Dad thought it was worth a try. I made quite a few trips to Staten Island on the ferry and practiced at home. After taking the civil service exam in Yonkers and a preliminary physical, the congressman gave me an appointment as first alternate.

Senior year at Andover passed quickly. Hawes said he'd give me $50 ($387 in current dollars) if I went through the year without a cut. I almost took his money; my luck ran out in the spring when my housemaster, Guy Forbush, gave me a cut on a technicality (I wonder if Hawes had a hand in that?). As to West Point, I passed all the exams but one; the eye exam. I took it twice, flunked it twice. Getting turned down for West Point was disappointing, but my parents figured it was just as well; they didn't think I had the discipline for an army career. They saw me breaking rules right and left at Andover and figured that if I happened to get into West Point I wouldn't last long.

That winter, Mom's mother was clearly near the end. Mary Everett Fuller had become a gentle, senile and white-haired old lady of eighty-nine who didn't know where she was or who was talking to her. She died in Bronxville on January 6, 1953, five days short of her ninetieth birthday. Her life had spanned the

---

382   Letter, dated August 19, 1952, Lowell Shumway to Congressman Ralph Gwinn.

period from January 1862, when the outcome of the Civil War was in doubt, to January 1953, with Ike in the White House and the U.S. on top of the world. The family gathered for the funeral at Christ Church, and Mary was buried beside Charles, at Sleepy Hollow Cemetery, Tarrytown, New York.

I hated Andover. But I have to admit, the teachers were very good. W.M. Sides, my math teacher senior year, had an unruly shock of white hair, intense eyes, quick nervous movements, and no tolerance for inaccuracy. At his early morning class he entered the room with a long flexible stick, which he cracked on the table whenever he got an inaccurate response. He never hit anybody, but that sharp cracking noise early in the morning was like a double shot of caffeine. Walter Gierasch, unpleasant as he was, forced me to improve my reading and writing. Another admirable character was George Grenville Benedict, dean of faculty. We called him "G squared." Tall, lean, and usually in a three-piece suit, Benedict had rectitude and integrity written all over him. You wanted him on your side. Mom and Dad maintained a lively correspondence with Benedict, who gave them a careful appraisal of my college chances:[383]

> He has applied to Amherst, Princeton and Yale (this omits West Point from consideration, and apparently Eliot is quite certain his eyes will rule him out there...). I understand that Eliot will go to Amherst on March 16 with his uncle and that I am to receive a prompt report from Mr. Wilson [Amherst Dean of Admissions] as to his estimate of Eliot's chances of admission. Disregarding any family connections there, I should regard Amherst admission chances as about 50-50, but I shall know more a little later.

In 1953, college admission was much tougher than before the war, and we all felt the competitive pressure to get into a top college. Dad offered Dean Benedict his own appraisal of my character:

> I have no illusions about Eliot. I believe he is an average boy, possessed with perhaps more than the average confusion of a boy turning to manhood. In fact, if I admit to it honestly, I can see many of the traits of my own boyhood coming to life again. Being in the army I do not like to hear of, nor do I appreciate, Eliot's non-conformance to the simple rules of school or self-discipline....

383   Letter, dated February 19, 1953, from G.G.Benedict to Major Eliot N. Vestner.

In light of my record, I don't know how Dean Benedict explained me to the gate-keepers at Amherst, Yale and the other places to which I had applied. But Benedict was a formidable figure and, God bless him, he applied himself to the task.

As I finished Andover, I failed to notice something strange, though it didn't seem strange to me at the time. There were no girls and there wasn't a single female on the faculty (there were rumors that certain elderly unmarried males on the faculty were "homosexual," but I had no idea what that meant). We lived in a male society, and most of us would continue to do so through four years of college; we had only the most superficial contact with girls. In 1953 there was a natural order to things. Boys went to Andover, then to Harvard or Yale; girls went to Abbott, then to Smith or Wellesley. Boys engaged in serious sports, girls didn't. After college, boys went on to serious careers; girls married and raised children. Boys earned the money; girls stayed home. Those were the immutable facts of life. Everybody was aware of the civil rights issue, but nobody considered that the status of women, and the limited options available to a young woman, was a civil rights issue. It was right there, staring us in the face, and we didn't see it.

Thanks to Dean Benedict, I was accepted at Yale and Amherst and chose Amherst. Amherst actually sent me a rejection, but the Amherst Dean of Admissions said it was "by mistake." I don't think that happens very often.

It was June 1953, and I needed a summer job. As Post Engineer at Fort Slocum, Dad used his contacts to get me a four-week job with the I.W. Kamp Construction Company, which was building a gas station in New Rochelle. I lifted big cement blocks up to the guys on the second story. Occasionally, they'd let me work the drill, which kicked and bucked. I couldn't handle it, and they had a good laugh watching me try. I was their gofer—7-up, cigarettes, coffee, anything else the guys on the job wanted. In the hot summer sun the guys always wanted 7-up. "Hey pussy, three 7-ups over here."

All they talked about was sex, sex and more sex. I got a kick out of it; but most of it was just bullshit. They laughed at me and told big stories in graphic detail about all the sex they were getting just to watch my reaction. I tried to be sophisticated, but they saw right through me. I was just a dumb naive white boy. They got a kick out of telling me about "real life." At home after work I flexed my new muscles in front of the mirror.

In the fall of 1953, I went to college. My first night at Amherst I was walking across campus. When the clock struck nine. I jumped and ran to get back to my dorm before the final stroke. But then I stopped. This was college; I could stay out all night if I wanted!

That fall I should have studied more, but there were too many distractions. Getting a date was time-consuming and frustrating. I roomed with three guys in James Hall and we were cramped for space. Most of the time I was dead broke. Mom was on the receiving end of pathetic letters, describing how I lived for a week on ten cents and pleading for money, "at least enough to buy some food downtown to keep in my room & to take care of my laundry..." Money was always a big issue between Mom and me. She alternated between sympathy, occasionally sending me a few bucks, and lecturing me on the need to live frugally and pay my bills, including my share of the car insurance.

The first two years of college passed by in a flash. Wasted? Maybe not entirely wasted. I did the work and passed the courses, but I was just going through the motions. I did okay in physics and math, history came easily, but it was freshman English that really got to me. Messrs. Walker and Gibson presided over my small English classes, and they devoted an inordinate amount of time to my pompous, heavily clichéd, ungrammatical, and seemingly never-edited writing. They must have been deeply depressed by what they saw.

We had to write two or three short papers each week in response to very specific and simple questions. This was not a normal English course—we read no poetry, novels or plays; it was more of a course in composition, but not entirely. We were forced, most of us for the first time, to think about a question from the standpoint of our own experience and write about it. There were no "right" or "wrong" answers, and for class discussion the instructor would mimeograph examples from student papers.

For our first paper, the instructions were crystal clear:

(a) Select an occasion when you appeared by name in a newspaper or in a photograph appearing in print. What was said about you? Or, how did you look? (b) Did you think that the words were the right words to use about you, or that the photograph did you justice? Explain yourself.

Mr. Walker circled half my first page and wrote: "Omit. This is...off the point of the assignment." On the back of my paper he wrote "Reread the assignment. This paper reduces to

Q: An occasion? A: Last spring
Q: What did you look like in the photo? A: (No answer)
Q: Did the photo do you justice? A: yes, more than justice
Q: Were the words the right words? A: (No answer)
Q: Explain. A: (No explanation)."

I hadn't read the assignment; I'd written the paper without thinking about the questions posed. In other words, I was doing just what Jack Hawes had said about me at Andover—going off half-cocked. On another early paper the instructor wrote, "Re-read the assignment. The idea is NOT to use examples. This I repeated in class, 3 times." Why couldn't I do what most people do every day: read and follow simple instructions?

For another early paper, the assignment was to describe what we had been told about Amherst before we came and, now that we were "on the spot," describe it. Here is my response, with Mr. Walker's marginal and not so marginal comments in brackets:

The work at Amherst is both long and hard. [**How hard? What does this mean? Does this mean you work 2 hrs a day, 6 hrs, what? Try to be as specific as possible.**] There is always something [**What?**] going on to eat up one's [**write abt yourself in this section**] time. The food is excellant [**Sp**] and their [**Stop doing this! This is a bad error. Try not to do it again. THERE=a place. THEIR=possessive.**] are alot of good men, especially in the Freshman class.

Walker's comments took up more space on the page than my essay. If he used as much time and ink on every other student, when did he find the time to sit down to dinner with his wife and kids, let alone write the scholarly articles required if he was to advance from instructor to tenured professor?

In a typical assignment that first semester we were asked to define "photograph" and discuss whether a photograph could be said to convey "the whole story." A number of assignments were raising questions about the "whole story" and who gets it: Eyewitness? Reporter? Photographer? The good students were able to write coherently about perspective and suggest that maybe there's no such a thing as the "whole story." It's an interesting point: if it's all a question of perspective, are all perspectives equal? Or do some tell more of the "whole story" than others? And how do you differentiate among perspectives? Forcing a discussion of those questions was an excellent way to transform narrow-minded freshmen into broad-thinking, tolerant citizens. But I wasn't up to it—I wasn't even close.

At one point, I argued that a good newspaper account gives the "whole story" because the reader can imagine he is really at the scene. Walker's comment: "& this is better than <u>being</u> at the scene?" At the bottom of the page he wrote: "I find this confusing & incomplete. There may be some gd. ideas here, but I can't find them." And when I said in the next paper that a camera catches the whole story as it really was at the instant the shutter is snapped (I must have forgotten I'd said the same thing about a news account), Walker's comment was "You don't say <u>what</u> 'whole story' you're talking about." At another point, he seemed to agree half-heartedly with something I said, but not with any enthusiasm: "Well, yes.....I suppose so. But this doesn't get at anything very fundamental does it?"

Another typical assignment required that we go to the library in search of a book and describe the process of finding it. I wrote about how I "located" the card in the index, "looked" at the card and, as a result of what I saw on the card, "found" the book. Walker's comments: "<u>How</u> did you locate the card? What <u>method</u> were you using when you 'looked' and 'found'?" He was obviously trying to get me to think about what I was doing and to choose specific words as opposed to generalities. But I still didn't get it. Sure, I "located" the card, but how?

The next semester, Professor Gibson took over from Mr. Walker. I asked Gibson to move me from the back to the front, thinking that would improve my chances—the people up front seemed to be doing better in class discussion. His response: "The average grade of the front row was 75, of the back row was 81 (excluding your grade. Including yr. grade it was 79.5). What do you say abt this?" Everything was more complicated than I imagined.

On one of my papers, I described an official weather observation as "more accurate" than my own observation, and used words like "accurate" and "better" several times. Gibson wrote: "What does this mean?" and "You keep saying this, but what does it mean?" At the bottom of the paper, he wrote: "A maze of undefined words."

When I failed as usual to follow the instructions and copy the assignment, Gibson scrawled at the top of the paper: "AGAIN, please copy it <u>exactly</u>; <u>all</u> of it." Was I genetically incapable of following simple instructions? At the end of

257

that paper he wrote, in utter frustration: "Who is yr audience for this paper? Do you know anyone in the world who would understand it? I think you are talking to yourself. I can't follow it at all. What are you trying to say here?"

Spelling, grammar, clichés, sloppy thinking—everything I did made Walker and Gibson grind their teeth. On one paper Walker had written, "Between two complete sentences you need either a CONNECTIVE WORD or a PERIOD or SEMI COLON. Do you want a bk with some examples in it? I can give you one." Gibson plaintively wrote at the bottom of a paper: "Do you ever proof-read?" In a later paper: "Proofread! I keep telling you this."

Those poor guys must have been completely frustrated; here they were, teaching at a top college with their own scholarly careers to worry about, and they had to spend time on this stuff? They should have been teaching us litera-ture and poetry, right? I don't think so. What they were doing was just what I needed—to be hit over the head with a two-by-four every day, all the easy assumptions, illusions, fuzzy thinking, and sloppy, clichéd writing knocked out of me. I was a piñata, with Walker and Gibson flailing away, trying to get the thing to open up and spill its contents.

After a year of getting beaten up in English, I spent the summer of 1954 as a busboy at the Otesaga Hotel, a Treadway Inn in Cooperstown, New York. Busboys were the sludge at the bottom of the pond. The waitresses hated to share their tips with us, but they had to if they wanted their tables cleaned and set. The hotel served pretty good food to the guests, but they fed us early from a big bucket, usually chicken a la king or spaghetti and sauce. I was always hungry, and I was always horny for one of the waitresses, a nice girl with a sen-sational body who finally got tired of my groping and dumped me. In July Mom drove up for a visit. I had complained about my boss. He was the headwaiter, Baldwin, and we hated him. He never smiled and he was a tough boss in the dining room. Mom took Baldwin on as a challenge. One day she caught up with him when he was out walking and coaxed him into a conversation. He poured out his life story to her. He'd lost a son in an airplane accident—after the son had survived fifty-two bomber missions over Germany in the war—and a young daughter to meningitis; he'd had to deal with tragedy, unimaginable to me. He said he was pleased with the boys and girls working in the dining room that summer and liked us. I was stunned. All my easy assumptions about the boss went down the drain.

Mom never got around to Mr. Merrick, manager of the hotel and the big boss. He was one mean SOB, and gave me a hard time when I told him I was leaving early, despite the contract I'd signed, which committed me to stay until September 15. That created a moral dilemma for Mom. She really got worked up over the issue in a letter to Dad, who was on assignment in Korea: "I'm concerned about Eliot! I do so much want him to do the right thing and not be a 'quitter'—and yet I know boys at his age need a little chance to unwind the tension now and then...I guess after this he'll be careful before he signs another contract. Live and learn!" Wrestling with the dilemma consumed the better part of two letters to Dad. She finally threw up her hands: "This is one of those times when I wish you were here to talk things over with!"

I had pledged a fraternity and moved into the fraternity house in the spring of 1955. The DKE house was a Greek mansion on a hill. I shared a living room and bedroom with two other guys. I was a DKE only because they had asked me to join; I wasn't their first choice, and they weren't mine. I was chosen to be the DKE representative on the House Management Committee, but that was a no-win proposition: DKE was notorious for partying and bad behavior. On weekends, there was always a keg open in the basement bar; Martinis, Manhattans, Whiskey Sours, French 75s—you name it—were available upstairs. Girls were often in rooms behind closed doors during the week, though that was strictly against the rules. Like everybody else, I had girls over on the weekend from Smith and Mt. Holyoke, but I never got anywhere. Drinking was easier. One evening after three or four Martinis, I collapsed into the bushes outside the house and just slept it off.

I left the DKE house after a year, moving into a single room in Valentine Hall. Friends in Chi Psi, the Fuller fraternity, invited me to be a social member and I accepted.

When I started at Amherst, I intended to take a five-year engineering program: three years at Amherst, two at MIT. Going into engineering was my parents' idea. Second-year math put an end to that. Having done well in calculus my first year, I signed up for differential equations. With the results of three tests, I dropped it like a hot potato and that was the end of engineering. For years I had a recurrent nightmare in which I was on my way to a final math exam; I had neither gone to classes nor read the book, and I could never find that exam room.

So much for the first two years of college. The summer of 1955 I woke up. *The Razor's Edge*, by Somerset Maugham did it. The central figure, Larry Darrell, was a young aviator in the First World War. After the war he came home to Chicago, rejected a conventional career and marriage to his rich girlfriend, chose to live plainly and simply, and travel the world in search of answers to fundamental questions about God and life. That just fired me up. I returned to college with a thirst for reading and understanding.

I spent the year in a history honors section, but towards the end of the semester I got in trouble. My thesis advisor, a specialist in European history, loved it when I told him I'd write my honors thesis on Heinrich Heine. Now I had second thoughts: Why spend senior year struggling with nineteenth century German poetry? I mean, what could be worse? I told him I wanted to switch and write about Sir Walter Raleigh, an Elizabethan literary and historical figure who had caught my imagination—I thought Raleigh would make a terrific thesis topic, combining poetry, literature and the romance of exploration and discovery; much better than Heine. The professor dropped me from the honors program as "not serious."

I knew I'd regret it at graduation when I'd be listed for an ordinary degree without honors—Mom would certainly notice that—but now I didn't have a thesis hanging over my head, and I could take the courses I wanted to take from great professors, like Alfred Kazin on great books—Dostoevsky, Stendhal, Austen, Dickens, and Tolstoy, Caesar Barber on English poetry, and Ben DeMott on the modern novel.

Robert Frost was giving readings at the College. I bought a collection of his poetry and gave it to Mom on her birthday. She asked if I could get Frost to autograph it. An English professor made the arrangements. I went to Frost's room at the Lord Jeffry Inn, introduced myself, and we settled down for a conversation. I was nervous, but he was easy to talk to. We talked about my courses and the poetry I was trying to write. I handed him the book and told him Mom was a great fan of his. He asked her name and wrote a personal inscription. Then he started leafing through the book. "Ah," he said, "this is the first I ever wrote." He made a little notation, "First I ever wrote, R.F." Turning the pages, he looked up: "Here's the first I was ever paid for," and he duly noted, "First I was ever paid for. R.F." Every time I open that book, I recall that Amherst afternoon, when I was young and full of dreams and a famous poet was kind to me.

10. Korea and the Home Front, 1953-1955

In the fall of 1953, as I began my first year at Amherst, Mom and Dad packed up, moved out of their quarters on Fort Slocum, and took the train to Seattle. There, Dad boarded a ship which arrived October 22 in Pusan, a major port city at the southern tip of the Korean Peninsula.

Three years earlier, Pusan had been the scene of bitter fighting, when it appeared the North Koreans might drive us into the sea. But when Dad arrived, the fighting had stopped, thanks to a truce with the Chinese. But it was a fragile truce, in effect only since July 26, and both sides were on alert.[384] In 1953, the U.S. Army had two missions: build a defensible line at the border, and help South Korea rebuild its roads, bridges, railways, airports, and lines of communication, all of which had been destroyed in the war. Dad, assigned to the Army's civil affairs section, was engaged in the rebuilding effort.

He lived in cramped, rat-infested quarters with other officers, forty of them sharing an outdoor latrine. He hated Korea: hot, muggy summers with biting insects; bitter cold winters; the landscape scarred by war; the cities, towns, and villages wholly or partially destroyed; the people mired in bleak poverty. He described the country as "desolate." To Dad, the Koreans, with "customs and habits unchanged in the last two thousand years," presented a stark contrast to the "modern, intelligent and thriving" Japanese. His pessimism reflected his own state of mind. Now fifty-seven, he wasn't happy to be there.

---

384   North Korea had invaded South Korea on July 25, 1949 and seemed on the verge of victory. But with full U.S. commitment to the defense of South Korea, the North Koreans were driven back, and U.S. forces advanced deep into North Korea toward the Chinese border. That triggered massive Chinese intervention, and by 1952, U.S. and Chinese forces were bogged down in a stalemate near the North-South border at the 38th Parallel. That was an election year, and Dwight Eisenhower, the Republican candidate, promised that if elected he would go to Korea. He was elected, he went to Korea, inspected the situation on the ground, and decided the United States should negotiate with the Chinese for the best terms it could get to end the war. The result, after contentious negotiations punctuated by renewed fighting, was the truce of July 26, 1953.

Dad in Korea

Washing day

Old woman laughing with gold teeth

Dad and Buddha, at Nara, ancient capital of Japan

He was on the move, by jeep over bad roads or in small planes. Off duty, he played bingo, slots, bridge, and poker; ate bad food and drank too much. Dad described his army colleagues in Korea as "hungry wolves" on the prowl for women, to which Mom responded, "If we gals can get along without men for a spell I don't see why they can't get along without girls!" Sending home a detailed description of what he was doing, he told Mom to cut it up into little pieces when she finished reading it. Unfortunately, she followed instructions.

He seized the opportunity to see more of Japan. In 1946, he'd spent a year in Japan with the occupation; now he could see old friends and revisit familiar places: Tokyo, Osaka, Nara, and Kyoto.[385] He loved Japan, and to Mom's horror, seriously considered taking a position there with the Army, bringing Mom over, and extending his time in Asia by another year.

We had to find a place to live. Lowell offered to share his Bronxville apartment with its two spare bedrooms. The rent-free arrangement made financial sense, but Dad was always suspicious of Lowell's relationship with Mom.

Mom and Dad wrote each other almost every other day.[386] Only her letters survive. They had agreed to destroy all their letters, but Dad could never bring himself to destroy anything of hers. She had no problem getting rid of his letters: she always did what she said she was going to do. Her letters, never meant for prying eyes, speak to their relationship, their concerns, and life as it was in the fifties.

Because her letters respond so clearly to Dad's concerns—she was always quick to pick up on the slightest nuance of his mood—it's easy to figure out what was on his mind: getting up in the middle of the night and finding the latrine, getting sick from Korean bugs, eating bad food, the grimness of life in Korea, concern about Mom's life in Bronxville.

Dad didn't want advice, and he didn't like Mom's lectures; she was free with advice and pep talks: "Dearest, I do realize it's hard & I just want you to throw yourself into this new experience with a will & get all you can out of it by putting all you can into it...." That was Mom's philosophy of life, pure and simple, but Dad never really bought it. He liked to complain and wanted a sympathetic ear. He also wanted gossip; he wanted to know everything Mom was doing and spending, and he expected her to seek his approval—prior approval

---

385   By the end of his time in Korea, he'd acquired a large collection of Oriental artifacts. Mom tried to discourage him from buying too much stuff, but without much success.

386   All quotations are from the approximately 350 letters Mom wrote during the period September 1953 to March 1955 when Dad was in Korea.

if possible—for everything. Anxious to meet his demands and avoid his anger, Mom tried to satisfy him, but sometimes it got on her nerves.

She reported every item bought or sold: a $7.82 receipt for a thrift shop sale; $10.37 for anti-freeze and gas; $14.95 for a dark blue dress at Best & Co, a long-defunct clothing store. In December 1953, she described the shoes she had bought with money Dad sent her for Christmas: "I have bought from you to me for Christmas the most wonderful pair of shoes! They're British Brevets, soft, good looking and with a heavenly crepe sole. They make me feel as if I had wings on my feet. To tell you ALL as I seem to have to do, they cost $16.95 at Altman's."

She wanted to work but needed his approval. "My Dear...would you object very much if I looked around for some part-time work?" Two months later: "I feel more and more that I want some kind of part-time job, Pet. And I'm inquiring around. I'm frittering my time—and I want the extra cash!" She reported on her work at the election board: "Tuesday I had an awfully good time at the Election Board.... You didn't really mind my doing that did you, Pet? I hope not...the nicest people do it in Bronxville. It was a 6 AM to 7 PM stretch & I was home before 8." She assured him that "I'll never never sell magazine subscriptions...so DON'T WORRY!" And she assured him that she would find "something very genteel."

She found the work she was looking for at the Bronxville School. "At school they said the psychiatrist wants some outside typing done by someone who is 'Adult' and 'Discreet' and they recommended me! He's a Dr. Harris and I picked up some work from him this morning—four pages only. He's a mere child, I imagine just out of college, but very nice. I felt like patting him on the head and saying 'Don't worry, dear boy, I'll keep your little secrets.'"

She tried to feed his appetite for gossip about their old post, Fort Slocum. Admiral Binford was retiring as Commandant, and Mom went into the city with Mrs. Binford and several other wives: "I had never really seen Mrs. Binford away from parties and groups before the other day.... She's nice and rather cute.... And she's so used to having her every word hung on by a breathless audience that I don't see how she could help being spoiled.... I bet she'll have a lot to learn when she starts living a civilian life." [387]

---

387   Binford, a vice-admiral and winner of the Silver Star and Navy Cross, was a Second World War hero. On his retirement as Fort Slocum Commandant, the *Herald Tribune* described his early encounter with the Japanese: "Twice, in the earliest stages of the war, he led a thin strand of over-age destroyers out of pockets between crushing forces of Japanese warships that outnumbered and outgunned his own force in the Java Sea." At the end of the war, he was commanding the cruiser *Miami* off Japan.

The new Commandant at Slocum, Colonel Munford, was bad news. After lunching with the ladies at the *Bird & Bottle*, she reported, "The Munfords are creating dissension. Mary Munford always seemed to put her foot in her mouth." Reporting on a conversation with Myron Barrett, one of Dad's friends at the Post: "Myron said that after the Munfords leave there won't be anything to talk about..." Later she reported, "All the men are working like mad, I guess with Col. Munford's efficiency reports in mind."

She attended a luncheon on June 2, 1954 for sixteen ladies at the Fort:

> There certainly is a strong undercurrent of tension among the ladies over there now.... Mary Munford is so sensitive and misunderstood, but somehow I like her.... Very fancy lunch... The chocolate cake had been put away in the freezer. Helen [the hostess] had to cut it out in the kitchen where no one could see her (except Jean and I who were helping) because the cake was marked 'Happy Birthday, October 31, 1953'—and she didn't want anyone to see how old it was. After lunch we all sat and watched TV as the Army-McCarthy trials were on and everyone stays glued to that.

She dropped in on her friend, Edith Kraft, wife of Colonel Kraft: "She was up in bed, but very cordial and seemed glad to have me come in. 'Jeemsy' called out from his room, but was dressing so I didn't see him. They apparently have separate rooms—I'd hate that! And was the place a mess!!"

Screw-ups were part and parcel of army life, and Mom reported on one at a retreat marking the retirement of Colonel Kraft:

> They presented Kraft with a citation and had the first Army band there. There was one hitch.... I guess poor Maj. Moses will get called down for it. All the troops were at attention and the band sounded retreat and we all looked toward the flag and there wasn't a single MP there. Suddenly the doors of the Mess Hall flew open and out dashed the MP's on the double. They fired off the cannon and set the grass on fire and had to stamp it out and finally get themselves grouped around the flag pole for the national anthem....

With a new commandant in place, it was time for the Munfords and Krafts to leave. But in the Army, nothing goes according to schedule: "The Munfords pulled out officially yesterday & the ferry was held up 20 minutes because Col. M. couldn't find Mrs. M.! The Krafts are supposed to be out of their quarters but aren't & there is much muttering about them…"

All the gossip had Mom wondering: "Is anyone ever really happy, satisfied and contented and enthusiastic about his job in the Army? Do you believe there really are more gripes in the Army than in other businesses?"

Dad, of course, had his own gripes and was so discouraged that he said he would "welcome a separation from the service." Mom was appalled: "You can see that your practical old Prissy is worried when you say that you would 'welcome a separation from the service!' Civilian life is rough—one is so <u>unprotected</u>— nobody really gives a hoot whether you sink or swim." That's not really what Dad wanted to hear.

Dad was fifty-seven; he could be retired from the Army at any time. Mom wanted him to stay in another year or two, long enough to complete twenty years of active duty and qualify for a pension, but that wasn't entirely within his control. She wanted to understand their retirement options—he obviously had kept her in the dark. She put some questions to him:

> My Dear, I want you to think the matter of your future out carefully your own self. Of course I've always been a great one for security, haven't I? I realize there's a strong possibility of your being out of the Army any time, Pet, and whatever comes you'll find me cheerfully prepared for, I promise you that…. Tell me, Pet, because it's not quite clear in my mind; just what would be the difference in retirement benefits between (1) staying in till 60, (2) officer curtailment any time before then, and (3) not having your category renewed? Not that I care too much one way or the other, but I'd just like to have it clear in my fuzzy mind…

He may have answered her questions and put her concerns to rest in one of his letters that she destroyed. Then again, he may have been too embarrassed to say "I don't know."

Mom was a ruthless economizer. Traveling with a friend, she was pleased that their room for the night cost only $4. She was also pleased that by washing her own hair she could keep the cost of a permanent at Bruno's to "$1.50 and no tip!" She reported a car repair bill of $48, which she went over carefully with the repairman, finally throwing up her hands: "Who knows if everything was necessary? I don't." She spent a week in November 1953 at the Singer Sewing Machine School, so that she could hem and repair her dresses at home. At the end of 1954, she compiled a detailed financial report for Dad and blamed herself for spending too much and not saving more.

Investing was predictably a source of conflict. Mom and Dad disagreed on stocks versus bonds. Although not against buying AT&T bonds, Mom had been burned by the 1929 stock market crash and was never willing to go as far as Dad would have liked:

> Darling, I must be the world's worst wet-smack to you when it comes to buying stock! I didn't mean to ignore your suggestions.... But you know how I am about stock, Pet. I'm sure you have good ideas, but it's just not in me to go ahead. I'll admit that even if you were here I'd probably be overcautious. That back-log of bonds gives me the most comfortable feeling...more than stocks would, for which I'd be scanning the Exchange every day. The only plunge I ever did take I took at the most unfortunate time in history so I guess I'm a case of once bitten, twice shy.

Usually anxious to avoid conflict, she was ready to do battle on matters of principle, which included joint tax returns and financial aid applications to Amherst. In January 1954, she wrote,

> I'll put this letter with the Income Tax folder that came for you, Pet. Please imagine I'm sitting beside you when you make it out! What I really mean is, remember our dividends and savings accounts and, well, just remember that we have to sign our names to any statements....

Later in May, she had to submit a scholarship application to Amherst and didn't have time to send it out to Korea for Dad's signature. Dad wanted her to put in a number for rent, but since they weren't paying rent she refused to do it. Dad didn't mind cutting corners if he could pay less tax or get a larger scholarship out of Amherst. His theory was: if everybody else is doing it, I'm a fool if I don't. But for my mother, what "everybody else is doing" was irrelevant—she wouldn't cut him any slack and that infuriated him.

Mom had a keen eye for my shortcomings: "a well-known tendency to exaggerate," "doesn't seem to be able to make up his mind ahead of time about anything," "tries to go in all directions at once," "flies off without knowing what it's all about," etc. She reported a conversation with Mrs. Howard Patterson, the mother of one of my friends, who was impressed that I had gotten in to Amherst: "She said Eliot must be very bright, which I denied. I don't honestly think he is, Hon...." She thought the Army would be good for me: "We must follow up that National Guard thought with Eliot. I do want him to have some military training...I'm glad he has no thought of trying to avoid service."

She took advantage of every educational opportunity. Describing a Christmas party we went to in 1953, she told Dad, "I just turned him loose & left him alone because I think it's good for him to have to make small talk with strange females." The next November, she described another learning experience, this one on her favorite topic—money:

> The boys had a perfectly wonderful time Friday night and yesterday at the Army-Navy game...He and Bob Keiter learned something Friday evening that we could have advised them on till the cows come home but they'd never have learned without personal experience I guess; that is, that it costs money to play around New York! They both said "Never again!" They loved the Victor Borge show, and that was all right, but they found taking the girls to dinner first and some place afterwards was too much.

Dad was angry that I wasn't saving enough money, that I was too consumed with girls and not burning the midnight oil (forgetting, of course, that his father had expressed the same exasperation with him in 1925), and that I didn't write often enough, complaining that "communication with Eliot is a one-way street." Mom was quick to defend me, always careful to concede that I fell far short of perfect and that I certainly needed to do better but that in general I was okay.

Mainly, he was angry over my use of the car—"Ponty" as Mom called the family Pontiac, the car that had been new for their last European trip in 1951.

Ponty was a member of the family with its own personality. Dad considered Ponty "his" car, which technically it was. He thought I drove it too much, that Mom was too soft on me, and that I didn't pay my fair share of the expenses. Mom defended herself: "if the car isn't being used why shouldn't Eliot drive it?" She explained how access to a car was necessary for a boy in college, that a boy was expected to take his date out in a car, and while Mom and Dad were perfectly happy riding the subway when they were dating back in 1924, that didn't work in 1954. In one letter, Dad apparently had taken a hard line and Mom responded:

> Darling, I don't think it <u>unusual</u> for Eliot to ask if he could go off for a couple of days in the car. Of course I said no & that was that. But you can't blame the boy for trying! I know for a fact that there's constant friction in any home with two generations of drivers, but we'll just have to work it out with respect & consideration the way thousands of other families do... And please, Pet, don't say to him 'as long as you're under <u>my</u> roof you'll do as I say,' because nothing will drive a spirited boy to leave home quicker than that.

College was another bone of contention. Dad thought college boys had too much freedom. He saw college as a joy ride for the privileged few, four years of "wine, women and song." As evidence, he sent Mom a copy of a highly critical article from *Newsweek*, to which she responded at length:

> I read that article in *Newsweek* about college youngsters and it wasn't pleasant, was it? As far as Eliot being exposed to drinking, smoking, etc. goes, Hon, I don't know how we can stop that, do you? Of course you and others your age were exposed to all that a little later in our day. He's just got to build up character—and I do hope he is... I'm torn between a desire to help and advise him, and a realization that he must make his own mistakes and learn good judgment himself. You made your mistakes, I imagine, and came through all right!

Later, she pleaded with him, "El dear, you mustn't be so pessimistic about young men and college—please. Believe me, those boys do study.... It isn't a matter of 'wine, women and song,'" But I don't think he ever changed his mind.

Mom gave Dad a detailed explanation of my grades, arguing that I could "grind" out higher grades but that other things in college—girls, for example, and friendships—were important too. She was a great believer in "well-roundedness." Watching me study Economics during Christmas vacation, and hearing that I was going back to school two days early to study, she worried: "I love his being so ambitious academically, but is it normal???"

She reported on fraternity rushing in the spring of 1954 and fraternity initiation the following fall, acknowledging that it had all been a terrible distraction. She felt I had acted "stupidly" in putting all my eggs in one basket, and that the entire fiasco (not getting into my first choice) was "a lesson in judgment and diplomacy" for me. Her family had a long connection with Chi Psi at Amherst, and Mom believed fraternities served a useful purpose, instilling values like loyalty. But Dad wasn't convinced. He thought their reputation for wild parties was richly deserved. Mom vigorously defended them, explaining that "Eliot would really be a queer if he didn't want to join one."

She described an Amherst football weekend. "Honey, I had the very best time at Amherst with Bun.... In fact he was most flattering all weekend. He kept saying he could easily 'fix me up with a date.'" But she assured Dad that college boys had no interest for her. Later that weekend, she and Lowell met my date from Smith, and Mom explained to Dad that "Bun had picked [her] from a picture in the Smith freshman book...."

She took advantage of every opportunity to drive me to and from Amherst, usually with two or three other boys from Bronxville. Invariably eavesdropping on our conversations, she reported them in detail to Dad. She was surprised at how "serious" we were about everything, from basic values to girls to school-work. She also used the information to educate Dad about the realities of college life in the fifties.

At Amherst she stayed with her good friends, Warren and Ethel Green. Warren, Professor of Astronomy, taught at Amherst and Smith and was known as the "Globe," a reference to both his shape and area of expertise. He and Lowell were fraternity brothers (Theta Xi), and Lowell, who was on the House Management Committee, responsible for oversight of the fraternities, was also a frequent guest of the Greens.[388] The committee, fourteen busy men, would convene at Amherst to debate such cosmic issues as whether to allow girls in the fraternities on Friday evenings.

The Greens took Mom to parties, where she had a chance to meet and talk with faculty and their wives. Her take on academic life was that it was like life on

---

388 Lowell was awarded the college's medal for eminent service at the 1954 commencement, which was also his fortieth reunion for which I tended bar.

an Army post, only more so because "it must really get on their nerves to live, not for a few years, but for maybe a lifetime in such a close community." The Greens' house was my home away from home. Ethel Green gladly put up my out-of-town dates, fed me milk, cookies, and orange juice, and gave me advice on girls. Warren helped me with math. Mom described a morning at the Green's to Dad:

> I'm sitting at Warren Green's desk here in Amherst & the sun is
> pouring in & the house is filled with cooking of an apple pie &
> I have an 11 hour sleep behind me, and I wish you were here!
> I drove Eliot, Ben & Carl Andrus up yesterday.... All the boys
> are worried about their physics. Warren says the physics prof
> is a 'cruel marker & is out to get the freshmen.' Eliot spent at
> least 5 hours on his physics on vacation....

Most of us were scared of our "physics prof," Arnold Boris Arons, and with good reason; six weeks into freshman year, most of us were flunking it. But when Arons spoke at Parents' Weekend, Mom was like a giddy teenager, writing in her diary about his "spell-binding" speech.

Those were her main concerns: Dad, family finances, and me. But her letters also describe life as it was in 1954. Lowell's apartment was short on new technologies, although Mom did note that "the man from the Telephone Co. has just been here changing over to a dial phone, tho' we won't start dialing before June...." That was a real technological breakthrough. Before the dial phone, every call was initiated by waiting for the operator to come on the line, and then giving her—and it was invariably "her"—the number.[389] Most people in Bronxville had the new toys that were just hitting the market: dishwashers, TV's, bedroom air conditioning units, but Lowell wasn't having any of that. He had his housekeeper, Mrs. Fitz, to wash the dishes; evenings he spent working on McCall and Amherst matters, and Mom was happy to read, write, or listen to Fulton Lewis Jr., Elmer Davis, and Edward R. Murrow on the radio. When Mom visited her brother, Everett, and his family in Woodbury New Jersey, she was impressed that they had a TV, but wondered, "When does anyone get time to read?" As for air conditioning, Lowell hated the very idea of it.

The cars around Bronxville were all American, mostly General Motors models, Mom and Dad, of course, had "Ponty"; Lowell had an Oldsmobile; wealthy

---

389 You could get the new dial phones in one color-black-and there was only one telephone company-AT&T a national monopoly. The advantage was that it was all so simple.

friends had Cadillacs and Buicks. Mom and Lowell went to the big GM auto show in New York and she was dubious about what she saw: "Of course, the new autos are splendiferous, but I wouldn't trade Ponty for one of them. They all have those great broad snouts and fish tails in the back."

Bronxville was a wealthy community, and she observed the signs of wealth around her: "At Mrs. Pullen's funeral... I could, without turning around, reach out & touch 6 mink coats. I tho't the lady in front of me at least had on a plain cloth coat like mine, then she stood up & threw a gorgeous mink stole around her. It was certainly an accumulation of middle-aged wealth...."

Those were the Eisenhower years. In one letter, she noted: "Of course I read the *Tribune* now so the present Administration doesn't appear in such a mean light. I don't know about the Republicans, but I do like and trust Eisenhower." Later, she wrote: "I like Eisenhower and think he's a 'good' man.... Remember I've been exposed to a big dose of the *Herald Tribune*! What paper should I read to get good, sensible facts on the other side?" Presumably, Dad suggested *The New York Times*. Even after getting the "facts on the other side," Mom remained an Eisenhower fan, as she noted in a November 1954 letter: "I still think Eisenhower is a grand President and feel that he does things because he thinks they're right and not to benefit anyone in particular." Dad shared his thoughts about U.S. policy in Asia. He felt we were making a mistake with our commitments to Korea and Vietnam, and he complained that nobody in the U.S. was paying any attention to Asia.

He was dead right. Despite Mom's assurance that "the Indo-China problem is very much in all of our minds here," Indo-China was out of sight and out of mind. Few Americans were paying any attention either to Korea or Vietnam, where the French in 1954 were getting beaten by Ho Chi Minh.[390] The hot political news in the U.S. was the Army-McCarthy hearings in Washington,[391] as Mom noted: "Of course, everything here is buzzing with the Army-McCarthy trial. Everyone is glued to it on the TV all day long...."

---

390   Ho Chi Minh was the leader of the Vietnamese Communists. The Geneva Conference, on July 21, 1954, recognized Ho's defeat of the French by dividing North and South Vietnam, enabling the French to withdraw from a losing war. Unfortunately, this was only a step in a long and painful war, with heavy U.S. involvement, leading to the final unification of Vietnam in 1975.

391   The hearings, which opened on April 22, 1954, came as a result of Senator Joseph McCarthy, Chairman of a Senate committee investigating Communist infiltration in government, browbeating army officers all the way up to Secretary of the Army, Robert Stevens. The Army was put on trial. But the Army's special counsel, Joseph Welch, succeeded in turning the hearings into a trial of McCarthy, and when they concluded on June 17, McCarthy had been made to appear for what he was—a blustering bully. The hearings received extensive television coverage and attracted a rapt nationwide audience. See Stephen E. Ambrose, *Eisenhower, The President* (New York; Simon and Schuster, 1984), 163-168; 186-189.

Lowell provided the fluff in Mom's life. He enlisted her in mixed doubles tennis outings at the Bronxville Field Club—but she had to reassure Dad that the tennis wasn't too "strenuous." In the evening, Lowell often took Mom and me, if I was home, out to dinner at the old Alps or the new Trianon, where the French chef offered, among other things, "pommes soufflé" and "sweetbreads Eugenie." He occasionally took her into the city to the theater (his secretary could always get tickets for anything): *Kismet*, *Prescott Proposals* with Katherine Cornell, *South Pacific* (twice), and *The Caine Mutiny Court Martial*. One evening Mom, Lowell, and sister-in-law Margie ran into Harry Truman:

> Last night Lowell took Margie and me on a real bat. We went to see *The Girl in the Pink Tights* after having a theater supper at the Waldorf, in the same dining room with Harry Truman, Bess, Margaret and a boyfriend. It was very exciting seeing them sitting there and applauding when the band played the Missouri Waltz. Harry was beaming.

She saw just about every movie that came out in 1953-54 and usually had an opinion. She thought "Liz Taylor is beautiful, but I'd love to see her smile and laugh and get pepped up." She gave *Mr. Hulot's Holiday* a bad review: "The stupidest movie I've ever seen." She took a friend to the movies at Fort Slocum to see *The Flame and the Flesh* with Lana Turner and exclaimed, "Boy was it a hot show! The audience was mostly GI's and their comments and hoots and whistles were worth the admission price."

Dad didn't like to hear that Mom was having fun. His suspicions were enflamed by an unfortunate letter from a good friend, Helen Wood, who tried to assure Dad that Mom was looking well and enjoying herself. Helen went a bit too far and said, "tongues were wagging" about Mom and Lowell. Dad hit the ceiling and Mom went into overdrive:

> I have your letter of the 5th, and Honey I want to just send you a short line to say that HELEN WOOD IS A DOPE!!! I can't imagine her writing you as she did. I'm not blooming, but am trying to keep myself in good shape for your return— and life is not a bowl of cherries here at all…. Now please, my Darling, don't give Helen W.'s letter a thought. I was so mad I showed it right to Mrs. Fitz and she was amazed and

said 'I always thought Mrs. Wood was intelligent, but that's just plain stupid.' Can I trust you, Pet, not to think anything more about it....You do believe me, don't you? I can't bear to think of anything coming between our love and trust for each other. Again—HELEN WOOD IS STUPID. And no tongues are wagging.

She managed to scrape him off the ceiling, but only temporarily. Later, after we got back from a trip to St. Simons Island off the coast of Georgia with Lowell (Lowell was giving me a chance to work on my tennis for the spring season at Amherst), she must have received a real stinger, and she had to pacify him again:

> Pet, I know you're generous enough not to mind the good times I write about. If you weren't that way, they wouldn't be 'good times' to me. The 'cocktail parties, evenings of bridge, theater, exclusive night spots and winter vacationing in Georgia' have all been spread out over about 7 months—but they do sound like something when listed like that, don't they! Don't worry, Darling, most of the time life flows along in the well-known groove here....

Dad's resentment stemmed at least partially from his unhappiness in Korea and frustration with his Army career. He had been awarded a Bronze Star. Mom was thrilled and, of course, wanted to show his medal to all her friends and family and get an article about it in the *Bronxville Review Press*. But Dad wanted to keep it quiet. Mom was angry:

> First, let me tell you how thrilled I was to have that Medal. I don't know when anything has made me prouder—I actually had shivers when I saw it. And the citation is simply fine, Darling. Your 'unusual ability, outstanding initiative and constant devotion to duty' aren't news to me, but it's mighty good to have those traits recognized. I'm awfully sorry, and a bit mad at you, Sweetheart, for doing anything that might stop publicity from getting into the Bronxville papers. That would have given me a great big lift. Hecky, I know how wonderful you

are and I just want everyone else to see it too! Of course I have
to concede to your wishes and won't do anything about it, but
I'm twitching.

He wouldn't give her the satisfaction of showing off the medal. He saw it as
a consolation prize. He'd been led to believe he would be promoted to colonel,
but it never happened. Mom responded, "You're a five star general to me," and
pressed him to find out why he'd been passed over for promotion. "Isn't there
anyone willing to go to bat for you?" He tried, but couldn't pin it down. He
wrote letters up the chain of command at the Pentagon, but nobody was able or
willing to answer his question. Someone had blocked his promotion, but who?
And why? It was a frustrating end to his army career.

My father finally came home the first week of February 1955, and reported
to Fort Belvoir, Virginia, his last Army assignment. Mom got a secretarial job
in the Pentagon.

II. Freedom, New Hampshire

Summer, 1955. I was a counselor at Camp Quinebarge, Center Harbor, New Hampshire. Center Harbor is a small town at the western end of Lake Winnipesaukee. There were several of us from Amherst and a guy not from Amherst who we called "the General." Every night I'd hear the General shifting gears in his green MG as he drove back to camp from across the lake where he had a girlfriend. God was I jealous! I had my own car. It was the first I ever owned, a green 1948 Plymouth coupe which had cost me $275, a loan from Lowell over Dad's objections (Dad had made it clear: no car, and I should rely on the "transportational facilities" of the camp). Mom kept asking me to please drive over to Freedom, New Hampshire, a small town about forty miles north of Center Harbor, and visit Elizabeth Hatfield, her old Packer schoolmate from Brooklyn. She was encouraging Mom and Dad to move to Freedom, and she had some houses she wanted to show them. So I arranged a visit.

Freedom town center, 1956

Mrs. Hatfield showed me several houses. She favored one in particular, small and in need of repair but with a fair amount of land. The house next door—the "Rogers farm"—was also for sale, but we both thought it too big and expensive. When my parents came up to look for themselves, they fell in love with the big house and bought it in the fall of 1955 for $20,000. They borrowed $15,000 at 4 ½ percent from the Amoskeag Savings Bank.

Buying that house was an act of faith. To be sure, the economy in 1955 looked pretty good: inflation was less than zero (actually prices had gone down a bit), the unemployment rate was around 4 percent, the stock market was up, reaching levels not seen since 1929, and consumers, their confidence at an all-time high, were in a buying mood.[392] But the Cold War was still going strong, and memories of what happened to real estate values during the Great Depression were still fresh. Eliot and Pris knew all too well that good times could turn sour in a hurry. They took the gamble. They emptied their bank accounts, sold their bonds, cashed in their life insurance and acquired what must have seemed to them a crushing mortgage debt. It was a risky move.

Dr. Alfred Rogers of Brookline Massachusetts had acquired the farm in 1925. Before that the house and land had been known as the "Towle farm," and had been in the Towle family since about 1820 when Lovell Towle, son of Amos Towle, one of the town pioneers, built it.[393] Rebuilt in 1845, and again by Dr. Rogers in the 1920s, the house could sleep ten comfortably. It came with forty acres, an attached barn complete with all the old farm implements, a beach and a boathouse on Loon Lake with a wooden Oldtown canoe. It was located two miles east of Freedom village on the old Portland Road heading toward Kezar Falls, Maine and eventually Portland.

Dr. Rogers had already sold acreage around the lake to a local partnership, and hundreds of acres of woodland to the Kennett Lumber Company, which retained an easement across my parents' new property. Bob Kennett, a big friendly man, assured Dad that the easement, to haul timber from the woods back of the house, was just a formality. Years later, when the Kennett company decided to harvest trees from the woods behind the house, that easement became a serious issue. But in the fall of 1955 everything was friendly and business was done with a handshake.

392   *The New York Times*, January 3, 1955 (unattributed article), 41. At 4.09 the 1955 misery index—the sum of the unemployment rate plus the inflation rate—was the second lowest on record for the period 1948-2009. See <http://www.miseryindex.us.> (last accessed March 20, 2010).
393   On July 12, 1965, Mom and Dad received a visit from old Mr. Philbrook, age 93, who had worked on the farm for Joseph Towle as a teenager in the 1880s.

It was their first house: a two-story colonial, white with green trim, a large eat-in kitchen, living room with fireplace, dining area, library with fireplace, "sun room" filled with books, five bedrooms, five bathrooms, a big old barn and a basement with a cupboard holding jars of preserved fruit picked long ago. There were neglected gardens behind the house, and Mom went to work meticulously planning exactly where everything would go. Beyond the stone wall marking the gardens, a hill rose and disappeared into endless woods. At the edge of the woods there were two cabins that Dr. Rogers had built for his children, each complete with bathroom and kitchen.

The stone foundations of old Freedom lay half buried in the woods behind the cabins. Freedom, incorporated in 1831, had once been a much larger town. The 1860 census reported 917 residents.[394] In those days there were tanneries, a saw-mill, a machine-shop, small factories making beds, carriages and furniture, and various retail shops. The Ossipee Valley Ten-cent Savings Bank was in the center of town; the E.P. Towle General Store was next door. There was a Baptist Church, a Christian Church and a district school. By 1956 the population had dwindled to 315; there were no factories, no retail shops and no bank, and the Baptist Church was long gone. Freedom Village had shrunk to just a few buildings: the Freedom Christian Church, a town hall, a post office, "Margie's" lunch place, a one-room school house, a small library, its hours dependent on when the librarian, Avis Goss, was available, and Whitaker's General Store.

* * *

On February 29, Dad officially retired with typical Army ceremony: a real parade, with band, color guard, reviewing stand, master of ceremonies, ambulance and a "medical aidman provided by commanding officer." They weren't going to take any chances with the old guys. Afterward, Lowell hosted a family party for Dad at the Shoreham Hotel in Washington. The Army packed and moved everything to Freedom.

April 2, 1956 was a bitter cold and snowy night. Mom, Dad, and I spent it at the Presidential Inn in Conway, New Hampshire. The next day we drove the fifteen miles to Freedom. The town was blanketed in snow; we had to dig our way into our new home. That same day, Jimmy Howe, with the oil company, came

---

394 Before its incorporation, Freedom had been part of Effingham. Effingham was founded by people moving north from Hampton on the New Hampshire seacoast. But with migration from Maine, the town became divided by culture and religion. As a result, North Effingham split off and was incorporated as the town of Freedom in 1831.

and turned on the furnace, and Harry Wormstead, the plumber, came and turned on the water. A couple of days later the furniture came and we were in business.

Dad's favorite place was the barn workshop with power tools of every description. He spent hours in that shop, making cabinets, tables, chairs, cribs, and bookshelves. He was good with his hands, and he happily worked all over the property: repairing and screening the west porch, repairing the cellar beams under the first floor, painting a quarter of the house and barn each year, tearing down and rebuilding the boathouse, installing bathroom tiles, wallpapering every room in the house, and solving plumbing and electrical problems. He also gathered cow manure from the field for the garden, mowed ten acres of lawn every week, chopped wood, shoveled snow and chipped ice off the roof, paths and driveway; built a stone wall separating the front lawn from the road; re-created and planted the vegetable garden, and cut the hay in the upper field with the big old tractor that had come with the house. He was like a kid on that tractor.

Mom worked the flower gardens; baked and cooked for family, guests, potluck suppers, and community club suppers; took on painting, wallpapering, and other repair projects; helped Dad clean up the beach on the lake; cleared walking paths through the woods; kept their finances, and did their income taxes. Mom was also a volunteer and a joiner; there was hardly a local organization that didn't reap the benefit of her energy and goodwill.

She brought her upbeat approach to life in the country. No matter what happened, the days were "nice days" or "lovely days." Evenings out with friends or visiting family were always "fun." She was enthusiastic about their new friends in Freedom; she still got excited when she won at bridge, invariably noting in her diary "we won!" or "girls <u>creamed</u> the boys!" She just got a big kick out of winning at anything. When she was angry, her usual expression was "oh hecky!" When she said that, you knew she was mad—usually at herself.

In retirement Dad mellowed a bit. He was kind, cordial, and polite, but still a serious person with a temper. Years later one of his Freedom friends, interviewed for an oral history of Freedom, described him: "Eliot was a charming man, a little bit on the formal side, a little bit gruff, but when you got to know him he proved to have an excellent sense of humor"[395] That's not a bad description. He had a temper which usually erupted when I was around. When he got mad, "God Dammit" would shake the house. He didn't like his routine interrupted, and he'd get angry if I came in late for dinner, and he didn't mince words

---

395   Interview of Chilton Thomson by Joan Grossman, November 2002, included in a collection of interviews comprising an oral history of the town (available at Freedom Town Library).

when he got angry. He didn't like house guests messing around in the kitchen, which is why he was always up early to make breakfast. If I was home and he heard a noise in the kitchen, he'd be in like a flash to see what I was up to.

He became a country squire. When they went out or entertained at home, which was often, he always wore one of his Brooks Brothers sports jackets, a dress shirt, tie, pressed pants, and freshly shined shoes. Lowell called him the "Duke." Mom also took pains with her clothes. She was more budget conscious than Dad, but she was pleased with herself when she knew she looked good, as in her diary note for August 27, 1964: "At 6... to the Turners—Nice crowd. Wore my new black Peck & Peck dress."

Social life in Freedom was mainly in the home: dinners, bridge and canasta, games like charades. There was nothing going on in the town—no movies, no bars, no restaurants, nothing. If Mom and Dad went to the movies, they drove the half hour to the North Conway drive-in. For dinner out they had to drive to the Eastern Slope Inn in North Conway, Edge Hill Inn in Tamworth, or to Kennebunkport where they could get a lobster dinner for a buck.

Mom could make a little go a long way, and she no longer boiled her vegetables to death. She had become a good cook. She really put her shoulder to the wheel when it came to dessert: rum chiffon pie, coffee Bavarian cream, Spanish cream, chocolate cake, mocha chiffon pie, Boston cream pie, bisquit tortoni, apple pie, cherry pie, baked custard, floating island, chocolate pudding with whipped cream, chocolate pecan pie, crepes suzettes, chocolate peppermint cake, zabaglione and crème brulee, featured in the new *Fanny Farmer* cookbook. At some point the doctors at Pease Air Force Base in Portsmouth began checking their cholesterol, but if my parents ever received a warning about diet—and I suspect they did not—it had no discernible effect.

* * *

Freedom was a mix of old-timers, newcomers and summer people. You might have lived in Freedom for thirty years, participated in town meetings, served on local boards and committees, but if you came from somewhere else you were a "newcomer" or "flatlander." If you only came for the summer, you were "summer people." Summer people were good to have around because they put money into the local economy, such as it was. Mom and Dad's good friends were mostly flatlanders and summer people.

Luke and Lib Hatfield lived a mile down the road heading toward the center of town. They had been best friends with my parents since the old days in Flatbush. Lib, a Packer classmate of Mom's, had gone on to Vassar after Packer. Luke was a mining engineer who spent most of his career in Bogotá. Luke and Dad were friends largely because of their wives.

Howard and Alice Turner came to Freedom from Washington, DC. Turner, a retired air force major general, had flown Henry Stimson back and forth to Europe and the Pacific during the war.[396] Whenever my parents had the Turners over for dinner, the conversation would eventually get around to politics. If I took issue with any of their observations, the general would give me a hard look and Dad, embarrassed, would say, "Eliot, you don't know what you're talking about." Turner was far to the right of Dad and probably a John Bircher.[397] Dad may not have agreed with him, but even in retirement he wasn't about to challenge a general.

Nelson ("Skrow") Works was from an old Freedom family, but he was also a New York banker. After losing his job at Marine Midland bank, Skrow and his wife, Glad, had retired to Freedom in the seventies. A history buff who founded the Freedom Historical Society, Skrow was big, blustery and highly intelligent. You couldn't discuss history or politics with him, because he knew everything. Every conversation turned into a lecture. Like many of my parents' Freedom friends, he loved guns, and used to keep a Thompson submachine gun under his bed "just in case."

David Dutton was our local doctor. A graduate of the Harvard Medical School with a Boston practice, David decided to move to the country where he could indulge his twin passions: fishing and golf. David never shared the exact location of his favorite fishing places.

Charlie and Mab Owen were from Storrs, Connecticut, where Charlie was Chair of the English Department at the University of Connecticut and a well-respected Chaucer scholar. Charlie and Mab were among the few liberals in a very conservative town. Charlie was an indefatigable hiker. He and I, usually with one or more of his children, hiked all over the White Mountains.

Mrs. Alexander Thomson was the *grande dame* of Freedom. A formidable and charming woman, Mary Moore Thomson had served as president of West-

---

396   Stimson was Secretary of War during World War II.
397   In the 50s and 60s the John Birch Society was an extreme right-wing organization, strongly supportive of Joe McCarthy's efforts to root out Communists or suspected Communists in all walks of life. Robert Welch was the founder.

ern College for Women during the war years. She had the nicest house in town and entertained royally.

There were also families who were actually from Freedom: Abbotts, Allards, Godfreys, Mayhews, Nasons, Thurstons, Millikens, Libbeys, Davises, and Meserves, among others. The old families pretty much kept to themselves and closed ranks against the summer people and the newcomers. Many of the old-timers were hardworking, diligent and thrifty types. Jesse and Bertha Nason ran a general store outside of town on the way to Effingham Falls; Spike Mayhew was a successful local builder. Margie Allard ran "Margie's," where you could get a burger or sandwich, while George ran the dump. George kept an eagle eye on the things people were throwing out, and he was quick to take his pick of the trash: reusable tires, pots and pans, clothes, an old radio or clock, perhaps an old black-and-white TV set. He always had several fires going, and the place smelled of burning rubber. Sometimes George got too close to the fire. On April 11, 1963, Mom noted, "George Allard burned his pants off at the dump." The dump was a good place to pick up local gossip. Two or three times a week Dad hauled a load of trash in his tractor and stood around chewing the fat with the other men.

The *Carroll County Independent*, a weekly newspaper, included a column of news for each of the local towns. A sampling from the Freedom column for 1957, written by an old-timer, provides a glimpse of what was then considered "breaking news":"

> Mr. and Mrs. Kenneth Libbey and Mrs. Lulu Philbrick were in Rochester last Saturday afternoon shopping.

> Mr. Melvin Watson who has been confined to the house was out and had a short auto ride last Tuesday. Melvin has got along very nicely and free from colds by staying in where it was warm the last few months.

> Vern Ramsdell has traded his pickup for a new Ford Pickup.

> Mr. Ernest Leavitt and sisters Addie, Melloon and Elsie Thurston spent last Sunday afternoon at Mr. and Mrs. Wesley Millikens.

> Mrs. Lulu Philbrick has had an oil furnace installed in her home.

> Verne Ramsdell was in Bethel Maine on Monday.

The next year, the Freedom columnist reported on an event that excited a fair number of Freedom residents:

> 25 Apr: There was quite a lot of excitement in the village last Saturday evening about 6:30 when a large Light Bulb was seen in the sky over Freedom Village square by many people and the different ones were in great wonder as to what it was and just what was going to happen. It was last seen going East, a relief to know it had gone and maybe it was a weather balloon.

Occasionally old-timer resentment would bubble to the surface, as when a wealthy summer resident began buying up old houses in town and tearing them down or renovating them. The Freedom columnist, in a rare departure from her normal reporting of comings and goings, gave vent to that resentment:

> 14 Nov. 1960: We of the old folks of which there are a few old-timers as we may be called that now feel very badly in seeing a perfectly good house in the square being torn down. It was the house beside the road and many a good time has been enjoyed by us old folks when we were young. Some may remember when it was built by the late Arthur Merrow who always lived there. ..Last year [it was] sold to Chilton Thomson and now it is only to be thought of making a big change in the square. The barn is to be made into garages for his tenants.

Life in Freedom was personal and up close; there wasn't much privacy. The telephone was on a party line, and someone usually listened in on conversations. Mom wrote warning me to be discreet: "It was good to hear your voice Thursday evening. The first time the phone rang I imagined Bobbitt Healey was asleep, woke up suddenly & grabbed the phone thinking it was her ring, before dad got to our phone. Undoubtedly, being awake, she had a good time listening in on our conversation."

Fred, the Fuller Brush man, came by several times a year with his brushes and cleaners.[398] Mom liked him and always bought something. They bought

---

398   The Fuller Brush Company, started in 1906, relied on superior brushes and a door-to-door sales force that was entirely dependent on what it sold. The "Fuller brush man" became a popular figure, usually welcomed by housewives interested in seeing what new household items he had to offer. In 1948 Red Skelton starred in a popular movie: *The Fuller Brush Man.*

fresh fruit from Schlosky, the fruit peddler. If they wanted eggs or chicken, they went to Dan Lord's farm. If they needed a doctor, they called Doc Dutton and he would come right over ("right over" is perhaps an exaggeration).[399] Bill Rich, their insurance agent, would drop by several times a year to have a drink and talk insurance. When they needed to update the car registration or drivers' licenses, they simply went over to see Betty Godfrey, a neighbor and town clerk, who did all that.

* * *

When I came home on vacation, Dad and I would usually get into a long dinner-table argument about some political issue: civil rights, the budget, or perhaps universal health care, Mom adding her thoughts, always carefully phrased to calm the waters. Dad was all for stormy seas. The precise issue didn't really matter; he just loved a good argument. And when Lowell visited, he always joined in and tried to back me into a corner or catch me in a logical inconsistency. That really gave Lowell a big kick, watching me try to squirm my way out of his trap. He tried to keep a straight face, but you could tell he was pleased with himself. For Lowell, trapping a cocky college kid in an inconsistency trumped any political issue. Arguing politics at the dinner table probably made Dad and Lowell feel young again.

They had moved to Freedom just in time for the 1956 election. In August, Mom noted: "El & I up till 1AM listening to Democratic Convention nominating Stevenson." That November, they both voted for Eisenhower.[400]

In 1960, they watched every one of the three Nixon-Kennedy debates. Since they didn't own a TV, they depended on their friends. Sometimes their friends brought the TV to them. On October 7, 1960, Mom's birthday: "Lib & Luke came for cocktails & roast beef dinner. Lib brought choc. cake…. Luke brought his TV & we all listened to Kennedy-Nixon debate." The vote in that room was Nixon 4 Kennedy 0. Mom's diary entry for Election Day: "El & I voted for Nixon (vs. Kennedy). In eve to Lib's & watched returns. Kennedy won about 2 A.M. "Nixon swept Freedom, 170 to 54.

New Hampshire held the first presidential primary during election season, and the Republican primary in 1964 was hotly contested. On January 23,

399 In her diary for February 3, 1961 Mom noted: "In bed all day with a very sick headache. Doc Dutton came at noon with morphine but it didn't work…came in eve. Meperidine & Demerol worked."
400 In 1952 Adlai Stevenson, Governor of Illinois, was the Democratic candidate for president. Dwight Eisenhower was the winning Republican candidate. The 1956 election was a rematch between Stevenson and Eisenhower. Eisenhower won easily both times.

Mom noted, "To Hitching Post [Center Ossipee] where we met Mr & Mrs. Goldwater & heard him answer questions." On February 29: "El & I drove Lib to Conway to coffee hour at The Presidential Inn for Rockefeller & his wife. Shook hands." Then on March 10:

> Heavy snow. Town meeting day. Went at 9 AM & was ballot clerk. There until 11:15 PM. Pres. Primary: 1. Lodge, 2. Goldwater, 3. Nixon, 4. Rockefeller.... Albert Godfrey beat David Perry for Selectman....[401]

On July 14-15, they stayed up until 2 AM watching the Republican convention. On Election Day, Mom served as ballot clerk from 10 AM to 10 PM, with time out for oyster stew at lunch. She noted that 248 voted out of 280 registered, and Freedom voted overwhelmingly for Barry Goldwater over Lyndon Johnson.

The annual town and school meetings were big events. Mom noted some of the items that came up at the meetings:

> 10 Mar. 1959: El & I walked in AM to School mtg as we had a flat tire. Mr. Davis picked us up. Article to join 4 towns in a co-operative school was defeated. Over at 3 (I was re-elected Trustee).

> 8 Apr. 1960: In eve to Town Meeting to decide on town buying a grader. Much talk. Motion defeated 56-34.

> 14 Mar. 1961: Town meeting, there all day as a Ballot Clerk.... Town voted to buy grader.... I was re-elected to 3-yr. term as Trustee.

Town meetings attracted a big audience, a good portion of the year-round population. There were other local institutions that drew people together: Sunday service at the Freedom Christian Church, suppers put on by the Community Club and the General Store.

---

401   Henry Cabot Lodge, former U.S. senator from Massachusetts, had run as Richard Nixon's vice presidential candidate in 1960 and devoted time and energy to campaigning across the border in New Hampshire in 1964.

The Freedom Christian Church was non-denominational. George Davidson was a superb minister who also taught social studies at Kennett High School in Conway. In the spring, Mom's church discipline weakened a bit—but only a bit—and her diary contained a few Sunday entries along the lines of "Worked in the garden with El instead of going to church." Dad, never much of a churchgoer, could occasionally be persuaded to put on his best Brooks Brothers sports jacket and tie and escort Mom to church. In May 1957, the Freedom columnist for the *Independent* felt it necessary to issue a reminder: "Several town folk missed church service last Sunday by failing to set their clocks ahead an hour Saturday night. You need to be on the 'alert' in this day and age."

The weekly Community Club suppers typically attracted about fifty people, and started early so there'd be time for entertainment: bingo (three cards for a nickel) or a movie, provided the operator could make the projector work. One evening, following a "delicious" baked bean supper, a Dr. Rube demonstrated hypnotism, as reported in the *Independent*:

> He asked for volunteers and several responded and his ability to hypnotize was accepted by some. To demonstrate more clearly, Mrs. Albert Godfrey was under his influence and it was proven it could be done.

From time to time, Mom was a member of the Community Club Supper Committee. For October 11 1960, she noted: "made 150 meat balls for Community Club supper." In the spring of 1964, the committee decided to raise the supper price from $1 to $1.25. The price increase met resistance. After only twenty-two showed up for dinner—about a third of the usual attendance—the committee backed down and reduced the price to a buck (a quarter was important money in Freedom). Attendance picked up again.

Dad, to his regret, became deeply involved in the Freedom General Store. In the spring of 1956, the store was owned and operated by Bert Whitaker. It was "Whitaker's General Store," a convenient if limited source of groceries and along with the dump a good place to pick up gossip. Whitaker's best product was his "Store Cheese," a big wheel of Vermont cheddar under glass.

Whitaker's Store, Freedom Old Home Week, August 1957

In the late fifties, the food business around Freedom was getting more competitive. There were two new stores in the area: Steve's convenience store on Route 25 heading toward Kezar Falls (Steve also sold guns and adult magazines), and Abbott's Grocery, also on Route 25 but heading in the opposite direction towards Center Ossipee. Whitaker started feeling the pinch, from the competition and the numerous Freedom deadbeats that he carried as "accounts receivable." He finally put the store up for sale. Dad and other local men endlessly discussed the issues: to put money into a losing operation? To let it go to an outsider? To just let it go, period? The idea of Freedom town center without a general store was unthinkable. So they formed "Freedom Store, Inc." and bought it for $19,000 in the fall of 1959. Dad was a small investor, probably a *very* small investor. After the sale there was a big farewell party for Bert and Elsie Whitaker, followed by a meeting of the new owners at the Vestner home.

Dad agreed to serve as treasurer and supervisor of the store. He hired a manager, Bill Savard, but spent hours every day taking inventory, purchasing supplies, pricing goods, paying the bills, managing the bank account, updating the income statement and balance sheet, and supervising Savard. Within the year, Savard was fired and Dad was running the store on a day-to-day basis. Buying your food at the store was a patriotic duty. After one Community Club supper Mom noted that the supper was good "but all mad because food was not bought at the store." It probably came from Abbott's.

288

Dad worked seven days a week on store business, but it never paid for itself and needed periodic infusions of capital. By March 1961, he was sick of it. He and Mom completed a final balance sheet and financial statement and turned the operation over to Luke Hatfield. But things only got worse. For years Dad continued to work at the store as needed. That store just stuck to him like tar; he couldn't get rid of it.

* * *

Summer was the main attraction in Freedom; winter was another story and a very challenging time, with short days and long nights, temperatures in the neighborhood of twenty below—sometimes forty below—and long stretches when it snowed and snowed, and the stuff piled up so high you couldn't get out of the house. The summer population dwindled to a few hardy souls, some of whom handled winter by drinking themselves into a stupor every night. But Mom and Dad loved winter; they loved the cold; they loved the crunch of snow underfoot on a cold moonlit night, walking the two miles to the Hatfields's house for an evening of bridge and then walking back. They loved to put on snowshoes and walk through the woods, as on February 18, 1958: "Lovely, deep snow. Temp 0-15 below.... After lunch El, Lib, Luke & I snow-shoed across Bennett's field to the woods. Deep." The cold outside also meant a blazing fire in the fireplace, a thick steak grilled on it, and a cozy evening at home.

The Vestner home in the dead of winter

In the winter my friends and I invaded their privacy and put their patience to the test. In a March diary entry, Mom noted:

> Hank Holmes phoned re spending the night here with his girl. Made guest beds, stew, Spanish cream, etc. El & I sat up by the open fire waiting for him. Also El Jr. was supposed to phone from Boston. Hank & Linda Bartholomew (Smith freshman) came at 3 A.M. Both very nice.

The next day they still hadn't heard from me.

> Gave Linda & Hank a late breakfast & they left for skiing. Expecting call from El Jr. so in all day. Finally in eve after phoning Lowell, called Ken Hayes (Police) & got reassurance from him.

I finally called at 7:30 A.M. the next day and brought them another houseguest.

In February 1961, I brought a group of seven to the house, including my then girlfriend Betty. Mom had to impose some discipline that weekend:

> February 6: El Jr. & Betty slept late, then took the car to N. Conway to ski…Dinner…. El Jr. & Betty sat up too late (2:30)

> February 7: Lovely day. El Jr. & Betty slept late. We talked "House Rules" over breakfast…. They snow shoed all PM… Rather early bed.

What she really meant by "House Rules" was "please don't stay up all night making out in the living room, which is right under our bedroom." But Mom would never put it that bluntly. She just danced around the point.

We skied at Mt. Cranmore in North Conway with its innovative new "ski-mobile": $2.50 for the regular line and $4 for the short line. After a day of skiing, there was always a good fire going in the fireplace (Dr. Rogers had left a twenty-year supply of cut wood that filled a shed by the barn). After dinner, Mom would lead us in games, like charades or Guggenheim, my favorite.[402]

---

402   In "Guggenheim," you start off with a little chart with a five-letter word across the top and five categories down the side. The idea is to move down each column, selecting a word for each category starting with the letter at the top of the column. A timer is set, and when it goes off, everybody stops. Then you go around the room, giving points for each word, the maximum points going to whoever has a word that nobody else has. The game rewards verbal dexterity and creativity.

The furnace always seemed to give up the ghost just when they needed it most. That's when it was important to have a good relationship with Jimmy Howe. On 12 January 1961, Mom noted:

Home at 10 P.M. & found that the furnace had gone out. Jimmy Howe came from Kezar Falls & was here until about 12 fixing it. Very cold.

Sometimes several bad things happened at once, as on 24 January 1961:

Minus 15 degrees. Lib & I went to Tamworth & had tea with Mrs. Marjorie Harkness.... Home & found furnace dead. Phone also dead & El ran the car into a snow bank..... Lovely stars.

Well thank God for the stars. Poor Jimmy Howe had to come over from Kezar Falls again.

Winter was hell on the car, and in January 1959, they had a particularly rough time with "Ponty." On January 17, Mom wrote, "Very icey weather. On the way home turning into our driveway, we smashed the front right headlight. Finally got in by spreading sand." They drove to Portland a couple of days later to buy a second-hand headlight. On the way home, "muffler & exhaust pipe dropped out of Ponty." The next day they limped over to White's garage in West Ossipee to have the second-hand headlight put on. Apparently White didn't have a muffler, or more likely, the muffler he did have was too pricey, because on February 13, they were driving over to Portland to get a new muffler at Sears.

Four days later, Dad took the car to Walker's Garage in Kezar Falls to have the new muffler installed. Three days after that, on a very cold morning, they couldn't get it started: "Kenneth & George Allard came to help but no go." Later, Kenneth came back with two other men to. They couldn't get it started either, so they all trooped into the kitchen and chewed the fat for a couple of hours as Mom served up coffee and coffee cake.

After a long winter of car problems, they finally sprang for a new car, a Chevy Bel Air—"Blue & lovely." But aside from car problems, there wasn't much going on in the winter beyond Community Club suppers.

Winter was quick to come but slow to go. Some years it snowed well into April. But there came a time when the snow was gone, the ground wet, the temperature slowly rising above freezing, and the black flies stirring in their winter hiding places. That was "spring."

In early spring, Mom and Dad started working the garden. They had to wear netting, cover up their arms and legs, and keep a smudge pot going, the smoke providing a temporary deterrent to the black flies. The black flies were a terrible scourge, and Mom was in favor of any pesticide that would get rid of them.[403] In the flower garden, the Japanese beetles were the enemy, but the thumb-size golden spiders, glistening in the morning sunlight, hundreds of them, took their share of beetles. Each spider had at least two beetles in storage, wrapped in white, little mummies. You had to be careful because those golden spiders could bite.

Mom and Dad, early 1960s

Deer, woodchucks, rabbits, and raccoons—even an occasional bear—ravaged the vegetable garden back of the house. Dad built an electric fence, but the woodchucks were formidable adversaries and they burrowed under the fence. Dad would get up early in the morning and station himself in a chair by the

403   On April 10, 1963, Mom and Dad went with the Hatfields to the University of New Hampshire in Durham for a symposium on gardening. Obviously thinking about black flies, Mom noted: "Good talk on pesticides by Dr. White Stevens of Cyanamid refuting Rachel Carson's *Silent Spring*." As far as Mom and Dad were concerned, controlling the black flies and mosquitoes was a very high priority.

barn door with his army assault rifle, watching for the first sign of a woodchuck. Sitting there in the stillness of early morning, his mind may have wandered back to June 1918, on the line at Luneville- Baccarat, watching for Germans. He got a few woodchucks, but it wasn't easy. They knew when to duck and run. But at least they weren't firing back at him.

In the spring the cows reappeared in the big field across the road. Dad had a deal with Ralph Smith and later Ralph Brooks: they kept their cows in the field and maintained the fence. The cows created a picture- perfect view, and Dad got a free supply of cow dung. But sometimes the cows got out. In May 1957, Mom noted, "The cows got out of the West pasture & we had quite a time finding them. Got Mr. Smith over & he located them down near the village [about two miles down the road]." Another time we all woke up in the middle of the night to loud and strange noises around the outside of the house. It sounded like an army division mobilizing in our yard. About half a dozen cows had gotten loose and were foraging around in the garden.

When the weather warmed up, Mom and Dad would walk through the woods to the lake in the early morning, take the canoe out, and explore the heavily wooded shore for loons, hawks, beaver, fox, and deer. Then after working all morning up at the main house, they'd bring a picnic down to the lake, nap in the sun, and take a swim. The lake water was clear, cool, and drinkable. Our sand beach always needed work, especially pulling the water lilies and cleaning up the leaves and pine needles accumulated over the winter. Sometimes in pulling that gunk off the bottom, a water snake would suddenly pop up and swim off, as alarmed at seeing me as I was him.

Loon Lake in the spring, Green Mountain behind

293

Summers were packed with guests arriving and leaving: Lowell and his second wife, Katherine; Mother's brothers and their families, which now included grandchildren; Mom's cousin, Humphrey Redfield, and his wife Amy; Dad's sister Marj and her husband, Vic; and countless friends who would arrive from Tennessee, Virginia, New York, New Jersey, Connecticut, England, Germany, and other places. Mom tried to organize a Fuller family reunion once a year in the summer, a time for cocktails, big steaks cooked on the grill, rich desserts, photos, family slide shows, and lots of reminiscing about the old days in Flatbush.

Mom, flanked by her brothers, Ev (left) and Ran

Freedom Old Home Week was the major event of the summer, launched on a Saturday around the 15th of August with the "Old Home Week Parade." The local camps—particularly Cragged Mountain—put up imaginative and well-crafted floats, and there were prizes for the best. Sunday was the "Old Home Week Church Service," followed by the "Blueberry Social." The week was filled with sailboat and canoe races on the lake, a big beach picnic, a day of land sports, an auction, bean suppers, spaghetti suppers, eating contests—who can eat the most blueberry pie in fifteen minutes?— bingo, a masquerade, a square dance, and the International Camp dance. There was a "Firemen's Lobster Supper," with two big lobsters, corn, steamers, and pie for $2.50, and a beauty pageant, open to girls fourteen to nineteen, to crown "Miss Freedom," the winner entitled to wear the crown until the next August.

Even in summer, systems occasionally broke down. On Sunday September 20, 1959, with a house full of guests, the water pressure gave out. The next day Harry Wormstead came over and found a dead rat in the well. The weekend of October 3, with another house full of guests, the water gave out again. On Monday, Mom noted, "no water at all, so we all went to Margie's for breakfast—9 of us." Harry Wormstead came and "fixed it." But old Harry wasn't done. The water gave out the next day and the next. Each day Harry came over and "fixed it." The last day, while Harry was "fixing it" for good, Dad took his guests over to Province Lake for golf—and presumably to use the facilities.

Toward the end of August, the summer heat gave way to crisp cool days when everything seemed clean, clear, and sharp. The woods turned yellow, red, orange, gold. It was a time to walk in the woods and pick mosses and berries for terrariums, which Mom composed and handed out at Christmas. Mom and Dad hiked the local trails—Prospect, Green, and Foss mountains. Foss in particular offered a spectacular view of Mt. Washington and in season was covered with blueberries. But like black flies in the spring, the hunters came out in the fall. Mom kept a supply of bright red hats to wear for walks in the woods, because the hunters shot at anything brown that moved.

My parents continued to travel, but at a slower pace, and Mom continued to keep detailed records of expenses. Every day on the road she noted the mileage, time of departure, each stop for gas, including location and cost, lunch, snacks, time of arrival at destination, dinner, motel, including location and cost. She was obsessive about keeping track of things.

They drove east along the Maine coast, out to Prince Edward Island and Cape Breton, Canada; north to the Rangeley Lakes in Maine and the Connecticut Lakes in New Hampshire; south to New York, Washington, Virginia, and Florida, and southwest to Arizona. As Mom's brothers retired and moved south, she and Dad had to extend their trips. On March 29, 1964, they dug the car out of deep snow and left Freedom for a long southern trip to visit Fullers in Richmond (Pris and Mac Downs and their kids) then on to more Fullers in Naples, Florida, where Mom's brother Ran took everybody down to the as-yet-undiscovered Marco Island to look for shells. After Naples, they drove up through Georgia and the Smoky Mountains to visit Dad's old CCC campsite outside Knoxville. Then up through Kentucky to Cincinnati to visit Mrs. Thomson. They didn't get back to Freedom until late on May 6, after stopping for oysters and scrod at Proctor's in Peabody, north of Boston. Mom's notes on gas, tolls, lunch and mileage for that trip must have filled a book, but they saved on lodging by staying with friends and family, and when that wasn't available, by staying at the officer's club on the nearest military base. But occasionally the base was full and they had to put in at a cheap motel, as in Virginia:

> Tried to get room at Ft. Belvoir but no luck. Settled on 2nd rate motel on Shirley Hwy near Alexandria...In to Washington for dinner...Back to motel. Put in some 100 watt bulbs which made it better.

They got back home in time to resurrect the garden, and get ready for another summer of cocktails on the porch, fresh corn and tomatoes, steak on the grill, Freedom Old Home Week, and houseguests.

Freedom seemed to be a picture-perfect town. But scratch the surface and Freedom was no different from any small New England town: friends who were alcoholics, bringing misery to their wives and families; the nice local handyman, reeking of stale beer and poverty; dilapidated old houses with rusted cars dotting the yard, people sitting on the porch drinking beer and staring out at the world; neighbors drinking themselves through the long winter; occasional house break-ins; nasty boundary line disputes. Some or all of that was occasionally a topic of conversation in the house, but it was all part of living in Freedom, and for my parents, life in Freedom was good.

* * *

From 1955 on, Mom diligently recorded the main events in my life as seen through her eyes, starting with their visit to Amherst on May 12, 1957 to try and figure out what I was planning to do after college:

> May 12, 1957: We met Eliot at the Library. Parked by the War Memorial & talked about his plans for summer & fall. He wants to study for M.A. in English at U. of Michigan. Took him & George Moses to dinner at The Lord Jeff.

> *Dad thought going to graduate school to study English was a waste of a good college education. Mom harbored doubts about teaching as*

a career, at least for me. In her family there were plenty of lawyers and businessmen, but not one teacher. George Moses, a close friend and classmate, intended to study for the ministry in Scotland.

May 13, 1957: Eliot & I had a good talk with Prof. Copeland about El Jr.'s desire to study next year at U. of Mich.

Copeland, whom I did not know, assured them what I planned to do was "normal."

September 10, 1957: El Jr. left at 2:20 with Lowell...on his way to U. of Michigan.

Lowell drove me from Boston to Ann Arbor. After Amherst the size of Ann Arbor, especially the football stadium, was a shock.

December 23, 1957: Heard that Ben Symon & George Moses were killed in auto accident in England.

Two of my closest friends at Amherst, they were studying for the ministry at the University of Edinburgh in Scotland. Ben and I had grown up together in Bronxville, while George became a close friend at Amherst. It was an irreparable loss.

April 12-14 1958: On Thruway to Buffalo.... Reached Ann Arbor at 10:30. Dinner at German restaurant and to the student union for the night.... To El Jr.'s apartment at 5. Drinks & very good dinner.... El Jr. joined us for breakfast, then had to go to classes.

My basement apartment at 325 East Jefferson, shared with two other grad students, was shabby and cheap. We drew straws to see who would do what and I drew cooking, which became a life-long passion. During 1958, I had a teaching fellowship and taught freshman English. I had a dumb football player in class, and the athletic department leaned on me to pass him. I also had to deal with a case of plagiarism by two girls who should have known better.

June 9, 1959: Bill Lane came at 4. At 5 came El. Jr. from Ann Arbor. Drinks on the sun porch....

After two years in the PhD program at Michigan, I was home waiting for the results of my law school applications. Bill Lane and I had roomed together at Michigan. Seeing a limited future in teaching English and observing how Bill's father, a lawyer in Columbus, Ohio, loved his work and lived well, inspired me to go to law school. I may have loved reading and studying fulltime, but that was a luxury I could not afford, or so it seemed to me.

September 10, 1959: Telegram came from Columbia offering $1,200 scholarship.

Hallelujah! I needed as much help as I could get, and $1,200 amounted to full tuition for my first year.

September 12, 1959: Met El. Jr at Columbia. He had talked with Ass't Dean, trying to decide between Columbia and Michigan.

I finally decided if I was going into the "real world," no better place to start than New York City. Lowell agreed to lend me the money I needed for the first year, and drafted a promissory note for me to sign. That fall I met a girl and couldn't keep my hands off her. I tried to rent a room so we could have some privacy and approached a nice old Jewish landlady who had a room to rent. She looked me up and down: "Why do you want an apartment? You want to bring your girlfriend up here? You should be ashamed of yourself! You should be in a dormitory, studying!" And that was that.

December 6, 1959: El & I met El Jr. at John Jay Hall (Columbia), all to St. James (Union Theological Seminary) to hear Reinhold Niebuhr....

Niebuhr, one of the great theologians of the last century, was a spellbinding speaker. I went over to Union to hear him whenever he spoke.

18 April 1960: El & I drove in to Columbia & went to class with El. Jr. Prof. Reese on torts. Very interesting....

Willis Reese, tall and skinny (he looked like a praying mantis) was our Torts Professor.

One day Reese called on me. I stood up. He asked a general question about one of the cases. When I gave my answer he screeched at me: "Oh! Oh really, Mr. Vestner, surely you don't believe that?" Everyone was laughing. I replied "That's what the case says." "Oh! So it does. But do you like the decision, Mr. Vestner? Does it thrill you?" I hadn't really thought about whether I liked the decision or not and mumbled a non-committal answer. "Mr. Vestner, speak louder so I can hear you. Did you say you liked the decision? Did you say it was good law? Why would you say that?" Our one-sided dialogue went on for minutes—which seemed like hours.

June 2, 1960: El Jr. left at 9 in Ponty for N.Y. & his summer job doing research at Columbia for Prof. Goebel on Alex Hamilton....

The research and writing for Goebel's book on Hamilton's law practice was interesting, but Goebel was a cranky taskmaster. I had a key to his office, and his deep leather sofa was a good place to make out after midnight when the guards stopped making their rounds.

October 31, 1961: El Jr. phoned & said he has taken position for next year with Debevoise, Plimpton & McLean in N.Y.

I was lucky to line up a job so early. The Debevoise firm had a reputation as one of the best firms in the city. I didn't have the foggiest idea what they did. I never considered whether or not I actually wanted to practice law; I didn't travel outside New York to interview with firms in other parts of the country; I didn't consider the merits of a large versus small firm; and I passed up an opportunity to clerk for a judge. I just took the job that came along, because I didn't want to have to worry about it all year.

June 3, 1962: I borrowed dress from Lib to wear to El Jr.'s graduation.... El & I...went to Columbia Law School where we watched El. Jr. get his law degree from Dean Warren.

Amen.

12. The Sixties

For Mom and Dad, the sixties started on a high note: they loved their new home in Freedom, they were in good health, they had achieved a measure of financial security, they took pleasure in each other's company, and they were no longer quite so worried about me. In September 1962, I was about to begin my first real job—as an "associate," the lowest rung on the ladder at the law firm of Debevoise, Plimpton & McLean.

The firm occupied several floors in the ITT building at 320 Park Avenue. We were across the street from the Seagram Building, a breathtakingly beautiful bronze skyscraper, tall, straight and elegant, a masterpiece by Mies van der Rohe. Looking up at the Seagram Building, I was proud to be living and working in New York City.

That September, Bob Riggs, John Davenport and I, friends from Amherst and Columbia, all of us new lawyers starting out in the city, decided to room together. We found a two-bedroom apartment at 200 East 84th Street for monthly rent of $228, or $76 apiece. As an inducement, the landlord gave us two month's free rent.

The supply of apartments in the city actually exceeded the demand, and landlords were desperate to fill their buildings. New apartment buildings were going up all along Third Avenue, displacing the seedy bars and tenements only recently exposed to sunlight, after the city tore down the old elevated railway that for years had run along the avenue from downtown Manhattan up into the Bronx. There were still bars, but many were being upgraded to attract young professionals. Our apartment was only a few blocks from East 86th Street, the heart of old "Yorkville," which used to be German but was now a mixed bag. A few old German places were still around, like Kleine Konditorei, Forrester's, the Hofbrau, Cafe Mozart and Kramer's bakery.[404] But the Germans, who had moved from the Lower East Side to Yorkville in the nineteenth century, were moving out of the city.

Shortly after moving into our new apartment, the three of us threw a big party, figuring it would be a good way to meet some girls. We invited everyone we knew. My assignment was to buy the cheese. I told the guy at the cheese store we were expecting about one hundred and how much cheese should I buy? He cut a sliver and handed it to me. "That's an ounce. Do you think everyone will eat an ounce?" I thought sure, and bought 100 ounces—about six pounds. We had over one hundred people; we polished off all the liquor, but hardly made a dent in the cheese. We were eating that stuff for weeks and eventually had to throw some of it out. The cheese guy had taken me to the cleaners. Lesson: a little cheese goes a long way.

Keeping that apartment clean was a challenge. Our building may have been new, but the cockroaches loved it. Coming home at night we'd roll up newspapers and turn on the kitchen light. Hundreds of bugs would freeze for a split second then scatter in all directions. They were fast and shifty, but we got our share. No matter how many we killed they kept coming back. I guess they figured it was worth the risk.

Before reporting to work, I went to Paul Stuart and bought a dark blue pin-stripe suit with vest for $98, black shoes, black socks, white shirts, neckties, and, of course, a hat. I showed up for work in my new three-piece suit and hat, just like every other lawyer in the firm. But the younger lawyers soon stopped wearing hats, and the older partners grumbled about "declining standards," meaning we weren't wearing hats, some of us had gone to law schools other than Harvard and Yale, and at $7,200 a year we were overpaid.

The firm had hired ten law school graduates in 1962. It was an intensely competitive group, which included two former Supreme Court law clerks. My future at the firm looked bleak. After seven or eight years of eighty-hour weeks, no more than one or two would make partner. I was one of three new associates from Columbia Law School crammed into a single office. We were green and clueless.

At some point during my first week at work one of the partners, his name was Bob, called me into his office. He gave me my first assignment: he wanted a memo on an issue concerning trademark law, about which I knew nothing. That didn't seem to faze him. And he wanted it first thing in the morning. I spent all night

---

404   Back in the mid-nineteenth century, the Germans had crowded into "Kleine Deutschland," a large German city within a city that occupied a large chunk of the Lower East Side. As new immigrants arrived toward the end of the century and new apartments were constructed around 86th Street, the Germans moved uptown, so that the Yorkville area became another "little Germany.

in the library, quickly learning that the firm operated on a twenty-four hour day. Typists were on call to type and re-type all night. Promptly at 10 AM, I presented my memo. Bob put his reading glasses on, briefly scanned the memo, asked a few questions, and then dismissed me—all in the space of a few minutes.

Having flunked the bar exam on my first try, the firm was kind enough to give me time to study and in the winter of 1963 I passed. But passing the exam was only the first step. I then had to go before Judge Bruce Bromley, senior partner at the Cravath firm, who represented the character committee. He looked like a judge, and his eyes bored right through me. I felt that no matter what I said he would see right into my soul, see the truth, and find me wanting. Somehow I passed the character committee and was sworn in as a member of the New York bar, March 25, 1963.

That spring, Charlie, a litigating partner, asked me to help him defend a client, First National City Bank, in a lawsuit brought by the beneficiaries of a trust set up in 1929 with high quality railroad bonds. The trust value, initially large, had shrunk to a pittance by 1962. A big part of the problem was that the bank held the bonds all through the thirties, finally selling them at a substantial loss in 1943. My job was to draft the brief and make a convincing case that the trustee had acted prudently by continuing to hold the bonds.

I researched old newspapers, magazines, and economics journals to understand what knowledgeable people were saying and doing during the early years of the Depression. Not surprisingly, they mostly believed the 1929 market crash was a temporary market "correction;" that the economy, was fundamentally sound, and that the economy and the market would quickly bounce back. The conventional wisdom was to hold the bonds of seemingly solid companies rather than sell at a loss. That wisdom held through three years of steadily falling prices. By the time prices hit bottom, it was too late to sell except at a whopping loss.[405]

Fortunately, we had good records. We could show that the trustee met regularly to assess the situation and consult other investors and industry experts; that the trustee regularly considered data on the railroads and the market for railroad bonds; and that other institutional investors similarly decided to hold their railroad bonds through worsening conditions. Viewed from a 1962 perspective, everything was clear: there were fundamental problems with the railroads that were not going away, and of course the trustee should have sold at the first sign of market weakness in the fall of 1929 and built up a strong cash position.

---

405 Weekly Letter of the Harvard Economic Society, January 18, 1930: "the severest phase of the recession is over."

But the trustee wasn't required to be clairvoyant; the trustee wasn't even required to be smart. It was enough to show that the trustee was diligent and followed the crowd. The diligence of the trustee, of course, was of small consolation to the beneficiaries of the trust.

I loved digging into the past, marshalling facts to support an argument, and writing a convincing brief. Of course there was more to litigation than that; you also had to be quick on your feet, which I wasn't.

The firm encouraged *pro bono* work, and I took on some legal aid cases. In one, my client had been convicted of armed robbery. I took the conviction up on appeal and lost in the Appellate Division by a 3-2 vote. That gave me the right to appeal to a higher court. I argued my one and only case before the seven judges of the Court of Appeals in Albany, the highest court in the state, and won it by a 4-3 vote. But I won it on a technicality, so I'm not sure if my work, which resulted in someone who had probably committed a crime going free, was a net benefit or loss to society.

As beginning lawyers, we worked most nights, breaking around seven for dinner. Dinner was usually at the Brasserie in the basement of the Seagram Building, open all night every day. If I was alone I could sit at the counter, get a good steak, and be out of there in half an hour. Some of the lawyers with grander tastes went to places like Henry IV, and didn't hesitate to put dinner with wine on the client's tab. But if you were working for Francis Plimpton, Rod Perkins, or Asa Rountree, you'd be lucky to take a fast walk at nine or ten o'clock over to Hamburg Heaven on 51st Street for the house specialty.

The firm had an annual outing at a club in the suburbs, like the Piping Rock Club in Locust Valley, Long Island, where we played tennis, golf, or both. Francis Plimpton, an Amherst alumnus, occasionally recruited me for an Amherst-Harvard doubles match. Those outings could be hazardous. At cocktails one evening in the early sixties one of the senior associates, trying hard to make partner, deep in conversation with a partner's wife, bit into a cherry tomato and shot a bright red stream of juice onto the lady's sheer white dress. She was a good sport about it.

After several years of general legal work, including a year spent trying to evict poor old Mrs. Howell from her Greenwich Village apartment (she was a half-blind, middle-aged lady who stopped paying rent because she didn't like how the landlord maintained the building), I began to drift toward private placement financings, the firm's most reliably profitable business representing insurance companies.[406]

---

406 Loans by insurance companies to businesses are called "private placements" because they are structured to qualify for the private placement exemption under the Federal securities laws. Otherwise, the borrower would have to submit to the long, complicated and costly registration process, required for all public offerings of securities.

I never really got the hang of the private placement business. Early on I was negotiating terms of a deal with a senior associate at Sullivan & Cromwell. He kept talking me out of a point that my boss, Bill Everdell, felt was important. Everdell would explain the issue to me, but I just didn't get it. I'd go back to the other lawyer and he'd patiently explain why my arguments made no sense. So I'd give in, but then Everdell would explain his point once again and back I'd go into the fray, with the same result as before. Everdell finally threw up his hands and negotiated the point himself. There was only so much he could do with this stupid associate.

One of the partners I worked under had a real temper. Let's call him "Hank." One time I had spent all night at the printer's, proofreading a prospectus due to be issued the next day. The printing firms tried to make life easy for young lawyers by serving up free liquor and food. But even one Scotch could dull your ability to spot a typo buried in dense legal language. I came into the office next morning straight from the printer and found a message on my desk to report immediately to Hank's office. I smelled trouble. He held up the Prospectus, opened to page 35, with a big red circle around the single typo I'd missed. He was livid. A hundred pages of fine print, and there I was, getting yelled at for one lousy typo that nobody would give a damn about.

Another time Hank and I were working late at night on a document. Suddenly he threw his pencil at me: "God dammit Vestner, when are you going to learn how to write?" He was quick to anger and quick to let it pass. We finished up after midnight and walked over to the Brasserie for a very late dinner.

* * *

On 28 August 1963 two young women, Emily Hoffert and Janice Wylie, who lived on the Upper East Side not far from our apartment, were murdered. It was shocking. We all knew in the abstract that these things happened, but we never thought they happened to people like us and so close to home.[407] We hadn't thought much about the dark underside of city life. We were young, naive and invulnerable. The Wylie-Hoffert murders were headline news until the fall of 1963, when the most shocking event of all took the headlines, one that spelled the end of our innocence.

---

407   A man was arrested and charged with the crime, and the Brooklyn police felt they had an airtight case based on a confession. The newspapers lionized the police for their brilliant work. But it turned out they got the wrong man. Careful detective work by the Manhattan DA's office later exonerated the arrested man and led to the eventual conviction of another man, a drug addict who lived in the same neighborhood as the two young women.

I had voted for John Kennedy in 1960, but he didn't get me all fired up. His press conferences were great theater, and he was very quick and witty on his feet, but he was a frustrating president: sometimes outstanding, as in the Cuban missile crisis, other times too cautious, as on civil rights. In October 1963 I saw him up close. I picked up my date at Smith and took her to Amherst to hear Kennedy speak at the dedication of the new Robert Frost Library. We stood as the president entered the packed field house and the band played "Hail to the Chief." It was a thrilling moment. As he walked to the platform, he passed no more than two feet from me; I could have reached out and touched him. John McCloy, chairman of the board of trustees, stood up and announced "Ladies and Gentlemen, the president of the United States!" Kennedy gave a graceful speech on the value of a liberal arts education. He was only forty-six, young and seemingly fit. Looking back on it, the whole thing seemed quite informal; the security was not at all obvious. A month later he was dead. How could that be? I had trouble understanding it. One crazy guy with a gun and the Secret Service, with all its resources, was unable to protect the president?

Everybody my age or older remembers that day—November 22, 1963. We were all glued to the radio and television. It was unbelievable; we all assumed that sort of thing might happen in other countries, but not in the United States (we shouldn't have been so shocked; Presidents Lincoln, McKinley, and Garfield had been assassinated, and serious attempts had been made on both Roosevelts and Truman).

* * *

By the mid-sixties I had moved and was living with Bob Riggs in a basement apartment at 25 Charleton Street in the heart of Greenwich Village, with its cozy bars and cheap restaurants. I was dating a girl in the chorus of *Fiddler on the Roof*, meeting her at midnight and trying to get to the office on time in the morning. I thought that was cool, until I started falling asleep at work. New Yorkers tend to be street smart, but I wasn't. One night, a nice-looking guy whispered to me from a doorway: "Hey, buddy. I'm from Boston, and I've lost my wallet. Can you loan me money for a bus ticket back home?" He had a good story so I gave him fifteen bucks for a bus ticket (about $100 today), took his name and phone number, and gave him a card with my address so he'd know where to send the money. When I told this to my girlfriend that same night she just shook her head: "You are so naïve." She was right. I'm still waiting for my money.

Mom continued to give me advice on a range of issues. She was worried about their expenses in Freedom:

> Darn it, our typewriter has to go to the repair shop just when I feel an urge to talk over all sorts of matters. Will you bear with me? Having the typewriter gone over is just another must which I don't know how we are going to manage this month.... We had to buy a new tire for Chevy, an installment is due on the car insurance as well as on Blue Shield and Bankers Life & we'll be getting Gil's bill on the Ford; Ugggg.

But she also drilled down on my situation in New York:

> Believe me; we do realize what you are up against financially.... I think your chief concern now is to keep yourself from making any additional commitments that will mortgage your income.... Pass up anything that you can't reach right into your pocket and pay cash for. I'm pretty sure that your outstanding obligations consume practically your entire income. You must get those paid off and not make any additional commitments, Eliot.[408]

She suggested I pass up any vacation travel and come home, describing how I could expect to spend my vacation in Freedom:

> Do you know any strong young man who would like a part-time, outdoor job in N.H. for a couple of weeks in August? Not just anyone—you know our specifications!

> This work is not weeding, Dad can take care of that, but it doesn't leave him time to take care of the extras that are necessary to keep a place from looking shabby and rundown, i.e.

---

408   Letter, dated June 12, 1964, from Priscilla Vestner to Eliot Jr.

1. He hasn't had time to do his yearly painting of 1/3 of the house

2. He has to lay a new roof on the house

3. Up at the cabin there is a new growth of small trees and underbrush that needs cutting and carting away

4. The pine grove and pool could be a beauty spot, but ditto

5. The lake property is a valuable asset, but it needs attention, clearing of underbrush, building a dock, finishing painting the boat house—which I did ¾ of last fall—mending the tar paper roof.

That is That!

Proof that I did some work around the farm

She also weighed in on civil rights. In the summer of 1964, a time when the civil rights movement was in full bloom, with lunch counter sit-ins, marches, bombings and killings, I volunteered to go to Mississippi as a lawyer handling civil rights cases. Mom was worried. She argued with me by phone and letter in June 1964:

> You say you are planning to spend most of your vacation in Mississippi (HOT)—Here is how we feel about that, my dear—perhaps we are wrong?

> 1. You must now weight every move you make that might be a blot on your record;

> 2. Is this plan not only sanctioned, but actually encouraged by your firm? You would have to be terribly cautious not to do anything which would give possible adverse publicity to your firm.

> 3. The local people in Miss are going to resent the intrusion of 'foreigners.' They will be over-ready to beat up and jail at the least—or even at no—provocation. Driving a car down there, under your circumstances, would be inviting an attack on, and destruction of, the car. We would be highly resentful if South-erners or Westerners piled into New Hampshire to take over our local courts.

> 4. Shouldn't any violations of Federal law be handled by Fed-eral persons, not by imported dissenters?

> 5. Even granted that the issue at stake (civil rights) is consid-ered a right issue by all of us, if you feel this issue strongly wouldn't the wisest and most expedient action be to do something about it here in the north? People in the south may justifiably feel we have no right to barge in and clean

them up while we have such questionable conditions here at home.

Please consider these points.[409]

She needn't have worried, but then if she hadn't she would not have been the mother I knew. Had there been an unmet need for lawyers, I would have gone; but there were far more applicants than places. It was like applying to Harvard. My friend Steve Williams, a lawyer with a record far superior to mine, was accepted and did go. He later told me how he felt about driving around Mississippi at night on lonely back roads with his New York license plate—like having a target on his back.

In late 1964, a friend took me to a meeting at Senator Robert Kennedy's New York office. Kennedy had just won election to the U.S. Senate despite charges that he was a "carpetbagger" from Massachusetts. There were a lot of guys my age in the room, brainstorming how to get Orin Lehman's congressional campaign against John Lindsay back on track. Kennedy was there in his shirtsleeves, sitting on the front of his desk, asking questions, and inviting anyone with an idea to speak up. One guy asked Lehman's campaign manager a pretty good question: "Why should I vote for Orin? What can he do for me that Lindsay can't?" Lehman's guy fumbled the answer. Kennedy said if he couldn't answer the question any better than that, Lehman shouldn't be running. I was impressed. He was quick, had a good sense of humor, and seemed to be a real person without a trace of self-importance. I began working for him part-time.

And then I got engaged. Mom was tired of trying to be nice to the girls I brought to Freedom, and she worried about my life in Greenwich Village surrounded, as she imagined, by predatory homosexuals. Her excitement shows in her diary entry:

> 26 September. Lovely day. Penny & El Jr. climbed Mt. Shaw. They got home about 5 & we had a chopped meat dinner. They left about 6 & Penny drove El Jr. to the Boston airport. He phoned at 12:45 to tell us he had asked her to marry him! We are very happy about it. Didn't sleep!

---

409   Letter, dated June 18, 1964, from Priscilla Vestner to Eliot Jr.

Elizabeth ("Penny") Gwin and I were married, January 1, 1966, in Trinity Church, Boston.[410] Before the wedding, I had a quiet conversation with my father in the dressing room. He gave me some advice, which he later put in a letter:

> When occasion arises where simple conflicts create tension, don't let it get under your skin and try to never say things that you will later regret. The worst thing I can think of in married life is the tendency to create scars that are hard to heal. I realize that this is not a one way problem, but I do know that in some ways you are like me a little selfish in having your way and a bit quick tempered. Try to count ten before saying anything that will hurt....

I should have listened to my father, who spoke from experience.

Penny, who had been with the Museum of Fine Arts in Boston, got a job working for Tom Messer, director of the Guggenheim in New York. We moved into the basement apartment at 25 Charleton Street which Bob Riggs had graciously vacated. One morning, after a week of pneumonia, I collapsed in the bathroom. The doctor put me in St. Luke's Hospital with hepatitis, where I languished for the better part of a month: weak, gaunt, unshaven, and useless, a fine excuse for a new husband.

About eighteen months after getting married, I hosted a bachelor party for Riggs in a private room at the University Club and got home rather late. The next morning, August 4, 1967, was my thirty-second birthday. I was barely asleep when Penny woke me with some hot coffee and we were off to the hospital. Late that night, Doctor Todd came out of the delivery room, took me aside and in his very deep voice said, "Congratulations Mr. Vestner, you have a baby girl." As Mom recorded in her diary for August 4:

> Tried to reach El. Jr. all day to wish him a Happy Birthday but no answer. I stayed around the house. About 4:50 he phoned to say that we have a grand-daughter, Alice-Lee!

---

410   Penny's parents were Sam and Betty Gwin of Boston. Sam Gwin was descended from Gwins who had long lived in Greenwood, Mississippi. Elizabeth ("Betty") Thomas' family came from Baltimore. Orphaned at a young age, Betty and her sisters were raised by their aunt, Alice-Lee Stevenson of Boston.

New grandmother, new mother and new daughter: Penny with Alice-Lee and
Mom leaving the hospital

That fall the three of us moved out of the city and into our first house at 23 Deepwood Hill, Chappaqua, New York; a small colonial on two acres in a wooded section of town.[411] We had a big black retriever, Whitney, who loved it there: rabbits, deer, and skunk. For some reason, whether it was the size of the place, the layout, or our decorating skills, we never got that house so that it felt right. To make a garden out back I dug stones out of the earth until my back went into spasm and we had to call an ambulance to take me to a hospital. It was a Catholic hospital, and one day a priest paid me a visit to give me last rites until he realized he had the wrong room and made a quick and silent exit. So I don't have happy memories of that house on Deepwood Hill.

It had all happened so fast: marriage, fatherhood, new house in the suburbs, big mortgage, and now a long commute. Was that really me? It was all too predictable. I was doing the same things other people did, including not making enough money to cover my monthly bills, which I sorted into three piles: pay now, next month, possibly some day. I managed my three-hour daily commute

411   The purchase price was $45,000. Thanks to my friend Virgil Conway, who had gone from the Debevoise firm by way of the New York State Banking Department to become executive vice president of Manhattan Savings Bank, the bank gave me a 6 percent $34,000 mortgage, more than twice my salary. Penny furnished the down payment with money she had received from her very generous father.

by reading books like Macaulay's *History of England* and Gibbon's *Decline and Fall of the Roman Empire.* Other guys slept, read the paper, worked, played cards, drank or talked; but I could be different by reading Macaulay and Gibbon. I couldn't wait to get into those books; I loved that stuff.

Carter Burden, who worked in Senator Kennedy's New York office, asked me to draft a speech that Kennedy could give to a group of New York environmentalists. The subject: a federal interstate compact to manage the natural resources in the Hudson River Valley. I was working on it late one night at the office. Around midnight Carter, dressed in his tuxedo and fresh from a party with his new wife, Amanda Paley, dropped by to take a look at it. Amanda sat patiently. In the morning I took it over to Kennedy's office and Jeff Greenfield, his principal speechwriter from Washington, went over it, adding some good ideas and rhetorical flourishes. I reworked it again and the speech went to Kennedy.

The morning of the speech, Carter and I went up to Kennedy's apartment. As we sat down I started to explain the speech but Kennedy cut me off, flashing that toothy smile of his: "I know, I read it." We talked over some of the ideas in the speech. He asked crisp questions and wanted short answers. He had no tolerance for long explanations. Later that day, he gave it as scheduled on a cruise up the Hudson sponsored by the Scenic Hudson Preservation Council. There were about two hundred people on board. On his way to the front of the room, Kennedy spotted Penny and me. He came over put his arm around her, gave her a big smile and said, "Your husband did a great job for me and I appreciate it." At that moment I would have charged through a brick wall for Kennedy.

There were several more assignments, mostly on environmental issues. At the time I was actively involved in conservation: through the bar association and through a land trust that several of us had organized in Northern Westchester to acquire land and hold it for conservation purposes. I produced a memo recommending how Kennedy might position himself on a range of environmental issues. One of my sources was David Sive, a leading early environmentalist who became a good friend. I was asked to co-chair a committee on environmental issues for Kennedy with Allen Gussow, a Hudson River artist, a project interrupted by Kennedy's decision to run for the presidency in the spring of 1968.

Vietnam was the hot issue driving his decision. It was also the main topic of conversation among the younger lawyers at the firm, with deep divisions between supporters of Senator Eugene McCarthy and Kennedy. We interrupted work to sit around in an empty office and talk about it; we wrote what we thought were brilliant letters to the editor at *The New York Times*, who obviously didn't share our opinion. Few, if any, of our letters got published. Passionate in our outrage at the war and contempt for Lyndon Johnson, passionate in our allegiance to McCarthy or Kennedy, we were a microcosm of what was happening throughout the nation.

Mom and Dad regularly came to New York, to retrace their footsteps and to visit with old friends, like the Munns, brother and sister, who had lived on lower Park Avenue since the late 1920s. There weren't many of their old friends left. They loved to put on their walking shoes and tramp all over the city, window-shopping and observing, rarely buying. They generally bought food and ate in, avoiding the restaurants as too expensive. One night they went to Asti, and Mom was clearly concerned about the bill: "Italian dinner which we could just pay for & wonderful opera singing waiters."

In the summer of 1967, the three of us met for lunch at Wolf's delicatessen on lower Broadway. We ordered the best of Wolf's: thick-stuffed hot corned beef sandwiches, cole slaw, pickles and Dr. Brown's Cel-Ray soda. The conversation turned to politics, as it usually did with Dad. He didn't like Kennedy: "With your job, Eliot, you don't have the time to waste, and what would it do to your reputation in the firm if it were known you were working for Kennedy?" Dad was trying to keep me focused on what was important, and he assumed that being known as a Kennedy Democrat was not a good career move. Mom, who probably felt the same way, approached the subject differently: "El Dear, you've obviously thought about this, and we'd like to understand better why you feel so strongly about Kennedy?" I made the case for getting out of Vietnam, Dad rolling his eyes, Mom putting on her best earnest face. They didn't like the way the war was going, "but we can't just get out, we have to honor our commit-ment; if we don't, we'll lose a lot of respect in the world." To which I would reply "Dad, we've already lost respect because of what we're doing in Vietnam, How many lives is it worth to go on, and to what end?"

I struck a raw nerve by saying that Kennedy was the nation's best hope for dealing with the race issue. My parents believed that civil rights should be a matter for the states. They were more concerned with avoiding civil unrest in the South than enforcing civil rights. I passionately favored federal enforcement of the civil rights laws; the hell with the states. I remembered the Emmett Till case, and I remembered, when I was a young boy, my father yelling at a black man on our train going through Virginia because the man had been using the men's room reserved for whites while I waited outside desperate to get in.

That summer of 1967, Francis Plimpton returned to the firm, having served as Adlai Stevenson's Deputy at the UN. He gave me his old squash racquet ("one Amherst man to another") and asked me to go over an article he was writing, deploring the increasing disregard for the rule of law at the UN. He said he wanted my reaction to the article. I took him at his word and said I thought the United States was itself in violation of the U.N. Charter with our military action in South Vietnam and that it was unseemly to criticize other countries when we were arguably the biggest violator. Plimpton dismissed my arguments as superficial and made it clear he hadn't asked me for substantive advice. Later, as president of the Association of the Bar of the City of New York, he led a march of lawyers to Washington to protest the war.

Later that year, Sam Gates called me into his office for my first performance review (after five years!). Gates was a very senior partner. I had never worked for him and never been in his office. When we passed in the hall he rarely acknowledged my existence. But now I was in his office, the focus of his undivided attention, and I had a sick feeling in my stomach. He got right to the point. "Eliot, I don't think you're cut out for the law. Have you thought about government?" He figured if you couldn't make it in a law firm, you could always work for the government. The meeting was short. After recovering and thinking it over, I decided to do two things: work hard to redeem myself at the firm, and look for another job.

A friend had left the Debevoise firm the year before to enter a graduate program at Harvard in Arabic studies. He recommended me, and I spent a day interviewing at Harvard but decided that was not for me. In 1968, it was hard to see where years devoted to Arabic studies would lead. I interviewed for Lyndon Johnson's price control commission, but didn't like the job they offered. A position in the legal department of a big oil company was another option, but I didn't see that as a future. David Sive recommended me for the executive director position at the new Natural Resources Defense Council; I really wanted that one, but another guy got it. I talked with investment banking firms—Lazard, Lehman and Goldman Sachs—but I was not cut out to be an investment banker. There were a lot of possibilities, but finding the right one wasn't easy.

Finally, Virgil Conway, a Debevoise alumnus put me in touch with Frank Wille, New York State Superintendent of Banks. Frank, looking for a special counsel, offered me the position at a much higher salary than I was making at Debevoise and I took it. I liked what Nelson Rockefeller was doing as governor, I wanted to try public service, and Frank's description of the job, especially his apparent focus on getting the banks involved in rebuilding the inner city, was appealing.

Mom was embarrassed when I sent her the press release announcing my new position. She thought $24,000 was a huge amount of money to pay a thirty-three-year old (it was three times what Dad was making when he retired), and she couldn't understand why such personal information should be public. I explained that the taxpayers, who were paying my salary, were entitled to know.

Before starting my new job, I got a call from Tom Johnson, head of Kennedy's New York office: could I go out to Indiana to work on the primary? That would be the first primary of the Kennedy campaign and they were looking for volunteers, though they'd be willing to give me $100 weekly for living expenses. We agonized over the weekend of 31 March. We had a baby and a mortgage and I had a new job, but here was an opportunity to fight full-time for what I believed in. I felt an emotional connection to Kennedy. And what an adventure it would be! I regretted not having gone south for the civil rights fight. Was I going to regret not going out to Indiana? The answer was yes. Mom noted in her diary entry for Sunday, March 31, 1968:

> El Jr. phoned to say he was accepting job in N.Y. State Banking after turning down offer to work for Bobby Kennedy. Pres. Johnson gave talk on T.V. at 9 on Vietnam & announced he would not run for Pres.

That was a big day, capped by Johnson's dramatic announcement. In all the years since, I haven't come close to feeling the excitement of that weekend, when I was called to be part of something larger than myself.

There was a lot going on in the spring and summer of 1968. On April 4, Mom noted: "Martin Luther King shot in Memphis." That was followed by riots in major cities and a student takeover of the Columbia campus. On June 5, Mom noted "Lovely weather. News early in A.M. of the shooting of Rbt. Kennedy in Los Angeles. Very sad." Then the next day she wrote: "Bobby Kennedy died & we watched T.V. off & on all day."

As I walked to my office on Church Street the morning of 6 June, I was in tears, much more upset than I had been over John Kennedy's assassination. This one was more personal, closer to home. What had seemed so predictable and orderly in the early sixties now seemed unpredictable and chaotic. With King and the two Kennedys assassinated, anything could happen. We were living in a country that I didn't understand, and I saw no hope for the future. I went to a meeting of people who had worked for Kennedy organized by Steve Smith, Kennedy's brother-in-law, but without Kennedy's charismatic presence it all seemed aimless.

In June, we left Alice-Lee in Boston with Penny's parents, Sam and Betty Gwin, and set off on a month-long trip to Yugoslavia, a collection of disparate nationalities—Bosnians, Serbs, Croats, etc—united under the dictatorship of Marshall Tito.

316

Having left Debevoise and not yet started in my new job, I had thirty-days, I had never been to Yugoslavia, and it was cheaper than going to France or Italy.

We drove down the Dalmatian coast, visiting the island of Hvar with its scent of rosemary and lavender; met some people from Czechoslovakia who invited us to visit, and drove inland over precipitous mountain roads to Mostar with its minarets and old bridge. Our rented Volkswagen broke down just outside the city. I walked into town and found a lawyer in his office with a big picture of John Kennedy. He arranged for the car to be towed and fixed—an overnight job for several mechanics—and the next morning, over an elegant breakfast of coffee and fresh fruit, he hesitantly presented me with a bill that translated into $24. I tried to keep a straight face; he could have charged four times that and it would have been a bargain.

Opatja, an old resort, lies at the head of the Adriatic. The pro at the tennis club arranged for me to play tennis with Jarka, a Czech girl who played good tennis. She invited us to Prague. Now we had two invitations so we decided to go to Czechoslovakia, which was then experiencing a brief opening to the West under Communist Party boss, Alexander Dubcek. At the airport in Prague the authorities insisted on putting us up with a good communist couple, but that didn't work out, so I called Jarka and we stayed with her for ten days. From Prague, we drove up to the mountains on the Polish border, where we hiked and got picked up by the secret police, who accompanied us to the farmhouse where we were staying and grilled the lady of the house until she was in tears, wishing she had never laid eyes on us. We flew out of Prague the day before the Soviet tanks rolled in and crushed the Dubcek regime. As Mom noted in her diary entry for 18 August:

> Lovely day.... Alice Lee very good & adorable. El. Jr. & Penny due home from Czechoslovakia at 6. Their plane stacked up over Kennedy for 2 hours. He phoned from the airport at 8. Joy! They got home about 10:30 & were we ever happy to see them! Had a beef & kidney stew. All to bed about 12.

* * *

Frank Wille, my new boss, wanted to get the banks involved in rebuilding the inner city, a popular concept in the aftermath of the urban riots of 1968 (triggered by Martin Luther King's assassination). We had high-level luncheon meetings at the New York City banks—the food was always good—and the bankers

317

were interested and seemingly well intentioned. But the effort went nowhere; the problem was simply too big, and the bankers had their own business to attend to.

Frank now had me on his payroll and must have wondered what to do with me. He asked me to draft a bill regulating credit bureaus, which I did after doing some quick homework on the business. But I drafted that bill, which may still be on the books, with only the most limited understanding of the credit bureau business. Frank then suggested I take on the job of drafting consumer protection legislation for the governor. That was a big project. To understand the issues, I called on bankers, retail finance experts, and consumer activists. I had to get up to speed fast. Labor support was critical, so I had to go over each bill with Dr. Ludwig Jaffe, Research Director of the New York AFL-CIO. We argued endlessly. Jaffe thought I was no better than a shill for the banking industry. He forced me to accept a lot of changes I didn't want to make, and then I had to defend the changes to the governor's counsel. He was tough.

Ludwig and I became friends. He loved a good argument and so did I. And he probably liked the idea of having a "capitalist" to spar with. He was an extraordinary man, clearly overqualified for his job. Before the war he had been a judge in Poland, his native country. He left and came to this country in 1939. A committed socialist, fierce in his opposition to the free market system, he was also very well read. He loved classical music and good food. His favorite place to meet was Luchow's, the great old German restaurant at Fourteenth Street. We'd sit down to a German lunch—sausages and sauerkraut or sauerbraten always with a beer— and I'd ask him about his former life in prewar Poland. What fascinated me was how this distinguished intellectual came to be working for the unions. He was a man of deep and strongly held convictions about politics and society; he was passionately socialist and reserved a special place in hell for Josef Stalin. The Jaffes had an apartment on Cabrini Boulevard at 160th street, an old-world Jewish enclave. My wife and I went to a dinner party there one night, the only Gentiles and "capitalists" in the room. Ludwig and his wife were gracious hosts, but we were clearly outsiders in this tight-knit group of Upper-West-Side socialists.

The governor introduced my ten consumer bills as the centerpiece of his consumer protection program. After a lot of back and forth with certain legislators, five of them passed and were signed into law. In Albany, there are three people who count: the governor, the senate majority leader (usually an upstate Republican) and the assembly speaker (usually a New York City Democrat). When those three agree on a bill, it moves through the Legislature at lightning speed and within hours it's on the governor's desk for signature. In signing a bill into law, the governor typically used multiple pens, presenting them to those

318

responsible for the drafting and passage, usually nicely framed with a copy of the cover page of the bill. I received five framed pens, and felt pretty good about it.

Frank suggested I go up to Albany and introduce myself to Harry Albright, pointing out that I owed my job to Harry, the governor's appointments secretary. All appointments to senior positions had to pass through him. He was an interesting guy: warm and personable, but very quick to size up the person he was with, and there was no such thing as idle conversation: Harry always had an agenda. As the governor's chief talent scout, he had to make sure that the people appointed were qualified, posed no risk of embarrassment, and that the appointments didn't cause a problem with local Republican leaders, who looked at all high-paid state jobs as their private property. In other words, there had to be a damn good reason to appoint a Democrat like me. But unlike most politicians, Rockefeller didn't care if you were Democrat or Republican or neither. Harry hired a lot of Democrats, for which he took the heat from the party loyalists.

In the fall of 1970, President Nixon appointed Frank Wille Chairman of the Federal Deposit Insurance Corporation. Frank asked if I was interested in going to Washington with him, but I said no (even if he was serious, I was a registered Democrat then and the Nixon people would have told Frank to forget about it in no uncertain terms). Frank's replacement, Bill Dentzer, couldn't wait to get rid of me to make room for a friend. I needed to land a new job, fast, and once again Harry Albright came through.

The governor had put Harry in charge of coordinating the state's drug abuse programs and Harry asked me to help him, I jumped at the opportunity. That fall, Rockefeller was running for a third term as governor. Teenage drug abuse, and what if anything the state was doing about it, was a big issue in the campaign. The Legislature had appropriated hundreds of millions for drug recovery; Harry's job was to cut through bureaucratic red tape and get the money to the most efficient programs. The governor didn't want pickets lined up outside his elegant Fifth Avenue apartment. He wanted visible action and he wanted it fast.

Our office was in a town house that Rockefeller owned at West 55th Street. Some of the Rockefeller people, who had been working on drug and other social problems for years, wondered out loud exactly what qualifications I brought to the table: a fair question. But Harry thought I contributed something, and that's what counted.

Harry had become a very important person in my life. He had been a partner in the leading Albany law firm when Nelson Rockefeller hired him in 1964. The governor valued Harry for his intimate knowledge of Albany and State government, his intelligence and his keen political instincts. But Harry had another quality that enabled him to survive among the sharp-elbowed people who surrounded the governor: superb social agility. The governor, usually charming, was also demanding and unpredictable. Harry knew how to give him what he wanted, and he had a talent for getting things done without stepping on toes. Harry didn't make enemies, he made friends and allies. He did it by always presenting a smile and an optimistic outlook on life, by carefully cultivating relationships, lining up support before delivering a recommendation to the governor, doing favors for people, remembering birthdays, offering graceful condolences or congratulations. He did it by paying attention to all the little details that make a difference to people. And he did it without sacrificing either his intellectual or his personal integrity.

During my first week as Harry's assistant, the Reverend Timothy Mitchell of the Ebenezer Baptist Church in Flushing and two other ministers—all big men—came into our office. They sat down at the conference table and accused us of doing nothing. They leaned across the table, stuck their long fingers in our faces, used four-letter words, pounded the table, and made it clear they could call out demonstrators and cause a lot of trouble in the campaign. The ministers had formed an organization to fight teenage drug abuse. They used their size to intimidate and they were pretty good at it. We guided them through the tedious bureaucratic process for getting more state funds. They weren't interested. They just wanted the money, and out job was to get it for them. Were they legitimate? Or were they conning us? Did all that money go where it was supposed to go? We tried to keep track of it; we inspected their books and their facilities; they seemed to be legitimate and we treated them as if they were. I would like to think at least some of the money was used to get kids off drugs and go straight.

We also worked on other things. Harry served as Rockefeller's liaison to Senator Charles Goodell's campaign to retain his Senate seat. Goodell, a liberal Republican and vigorous opponent of the war in Vietnam, was the incumbent. Appointed by Rockefeller to fill Robert Kennedy's seat, he was running against Jim Buckley, a conservative, and Richard Ottinger, a liberal Democrat. It was a vicious campaign, splitting the liberals right down the middle. Buckley, pro-war and a Nixon supporter, slipped in.

Rockefeller easily won re-election in November 1970, beating Arthur Goldberg. Goldberg, with superb credentials on paper—former supreme court justice, secretary of labor, and UN Ambassador—came across as a stuffed shirt. This was his first political campaign, and he had taken on one of the great politicians of our time. The last week of the campaign a little paperback biography of Goldberg, not at all flattering, suddenly appeared all over the place, and it was free; you didn't have to go to the bookstore and buy it. Later, it turned out that the book may have been financed by Nelson's brother, Laurence—a case of overkill that could have backfired.

* * *

In the winter of 1967, Mom and Dad drove west, through North Carolina, Tennessee, Mississippi, Louisiana and Texas, visiting friends, staying at military bases or cheap motels, some good, some bad, ending up at the Triangle T Ranch outside Tucson, where they hiked, rode horseback, and drove down into Mexico.

Mom riding, Arizona, May 1967

On their way home, Mom made a last visit to her brother Ran, who died that April. Her brother Everett had died two years earlier.[412] She'd been close to her brothers, and their deaths must have affected her more deeply than she ever said. But Mom was a stoic, and she kept up her cheerful optimism even while losing her parents, her sisters, and now her brothers.

In February 1968, they flew to Tucson. It was Mom's first time on an airplane, and she probably clutched Dad's hand for the whole trip. In Tucson, they stayed with Mrs. Thomson, the grand lady of Freedom. There, they had their own guest house with private pool and a view out over the Santa Catalina Mountains. They flew back to New York in April and stayed with us in Chappaqua. Mom was relieved when Alice-Lee remembered her.

In the fall of 1968, Mom went to Doctor Dutton in Freedom complaining of a bad back. He gave her a shot of Demerol. Weeks later and still hurting, she went to the Portsmouth Naval Hospital, where the doctors added nothing to the diagnosis. Finally, she went to Dr. Dan Ellis at Massachusetts General Hospital in Boston. After more tests, Ellis told her she had kidney cancer. The cancerous kidney was removed, and she returned home to Freedom.

On 20 July 1969, she noted in her diary: "El & I sat up till 12:30 & saw the men walk on the moon." That summer Alice-Lee, age two, tried Loon Lake for the first time.

When fall arrived, her days of gardening and hiking were over. Her natural optimism gradually gave way to a realistic appraisal of her health. Dad did not want to face the facts, so the two of them probably had some difficult conversations. On November 4, she was back in Mass General for another operation. Her diary entry for that day was her last:

> After lunch went to the operating room (general anesthetic) & Dr. Wilkins cut a large lump off the back of my hand. Had to sew the skin together. Back to my room at 4 PM. El left about 5 for the Gwins. Heard Nixon's speech on Vietnam at 9:30. Rather a rough night.

---

412 Everett Webb Fuller died August 12, 1965 in Richmond, VA, survived by his wife, Gertrude Gladding, daughter Priscilla Downs, son Everett Gladding and six grandchildren. Randolph Mercein Fuller died April 6, 1967 in Naples, FL, survived by his wife Margaret Catlin, sons Randolph Mackenzie and Robert Catlin, and two grandsons. There is more detailed information on the family in Appendix 2.

Alice-Lee tests the water in Loon Lake

Her cancer had spread, and she was offered the option of radiation treatment which she declined. Her last weeks were spent at home. Her pain was relieved by morphine, and Dad was taking care of her on a fulltime basis. He nursed her, cooked the meals, and did the laundry. He was devoted to her, day and night. By early November, she could no longer speak coherently (it's very disturbing to hear someone you love, someone you knew as a smart and articulate person, babble unintelligably). On November 15, Doc Dutton came and gave her a double dose of morphine. We drove her to the hospital in North Conway and she rested her head on my lap in the backseat, sleeping peacefully. She died in the hospital without regaining consciousness.

George Davidson, the minister of the Freedom Christian Church, conducted her memorial service on November 22. Words cannot express the overwhelming sense of loss I felt during the service; the tears came as if the dam had burst. Late that afternoon, Dad, Lowell, and I buried her ashes in the cemetery overlooking Loon Lake as I read from the Book of Common Prayer: "Whosoever liveth and believeth in me, shall never die."

13. Public Service

January 3, 1970: My father was staying with us in Chappaqua, New York. It was a very cold night and I couldn't start the car, so I borrowed his and drove Penny to Columbia Presbyterian Hospital in Manhattan. That night, Charles Fuller Vestner was born, named after his great-grandfather, Charles Humphrey Fuller. When we brought Charlie home, Alice-Lee was excited to have a new playmate, but Charlie wasn't much fun, the excitement faded, and one day Alice-Lee took her mother aside and said it was time to take Charlie back. Penny explained that Charlie was here to stay.

No longer under the daily pressure of full-time care-giving, my father had given in to excruciating back pain. My doctor told him he had cancer of the spine and put him in Doctors' Hospital, a rather luxurious place on the upper East Side of Manhattan. He was fatalistic: if he died, okay; if he survived, okay. But the doctor had given him a premature diagnosis; he didn't have cancer, and over several weeks his back began to heal. When he walked out of the hospital leaning on a cane, I didn't know if he was relieved or disappointed. For the first time he seemed lost, uncertain what to do next.

After a few weeks with us in Chappaqua, he packed his car and drove south to Tennessee, west to Arizona and north to Montana, where he had spent so much time in the thirties. Along the way he visited old friends and widows of old friends. Later, he took off for Europe, traveling through Italy, Germany, Austria, France, Portugal, Spain, Holland, Denmark, and England. He never stayed long in one place. He was at loose ends: lonely and on the move. We kept track of him through postcards with cryptic messages of where he was and where he was going—he never took up more than a small part of the space on the back of the card.

That January I arrived at a fork in the road. Penny and I had flown to Boulder, where I interviewed for a teaching position at the law school. I had a close friend on the faculty there, and the Dean had made me a generous offer: Assistant Professor, teaching constitutional law. I also had an offer to go on

Governor Rockefeller's staff as a special assistant, based in Albany. In either case we would have to sell our Chappaqua house and move. My wife was flexible and would have moved to Boulder, though her family was in Boston and her heart was on the East Coast. The West was unfamiliar territory, physically and culturally. Dad was traveling, but I talked at length with Lowell who encouraged me to take the position with Governor Rockefeller and I did. I just didn't have the fire in my belly for a teaching career.

My new job sounded more important than it was. But it was a great opportunity to get involved in some interesting public issues. Harry Albright was still my boss and my friend, and if I hadn't had Harry as boss and friend up there in Albany, I would have been eaten alive by the sharks.

Harry Albright in action

Harry and I had adjoining offices on the second floor of the State Capitol, an immense Victorian-Gothic building with turrets, chimneys, dormers and gargoyles poking out in all directions.

Once a thriving city strategically situated on the Erie Canal, Albany was now a one- industry town, dependent on the state government and its thousands of employees. Downtown Albany was dead. Old department stores like Wheeler's, once thriving, had closed; there were a few seedy hotels which catered to legislators and lobbyists; the restaurants had seen better days, and the grand old Union Station, which from 1900 to the 1950s had been a busy railroad terminal at the city center, sat lonely and abandoned. The trains didn't even come into Albany; they stopped across the river in Rensselaer.

Of all the issues that Harry and I worked on, three stand out: health care, Attica, and the Scott Commission.

The governor asked Harry to chair a task force on health care, so I became an instant health care "expert," much to the annoyance of the professionals who ran the state health department.

From 1967 to 1971 Nelson Rockefeller had unsuccessfully recommended passage of a pioneering state universal health insurance law. By 1971, it was clear that only the federal government could afford to finance universal coverage. It was also clear, to us at least, that Medicare and Medicaid, by pouring increasing amounts of public money into an inefficient delivery system based on free choice of doctor and fee-for-service payment, had contributed to rising health care costs. The health care profession opposed changes in the delivery system. Despite opposition, we managed to get two major bills through the legislature: one encouraged the formation of prepaid health care groups (better known as HMOs) to provide comprehensive care for a fixed monthly fee; the other created the new profession of "Physician's Associate," capable of providing a wide range of routine medical services. The point was to alleviate a shortage of physicians and free up the physician's time for the more serious problems.[413] In Washington, President Nixon had proposed his own comprehensive health care bill and Congress was considering it. We were under the illusion that there might be a major break-through in health care reform.

Harry asked me to substitute for him as the featured speaker at a convention of oral surgeons at the Otesaga Hotel in Cooperstown. The subject was health care. Standing at the podium looking out over the crowd, I knew I was in

---

413   See Harry W. Albright, Jr. and Eliot N. Vestner, Jr., "Prepaid Health Care Legislation in New York," Albany *Law Review*, 36:3 (1972), 488-503.

trouble. The men were in black tie, the ladies in their best dresses, everybody was drinking up a storm, and dinner was being served. The last thing they wanted to hear about was health care legislation. They just wanted a couple of funny stories. But they were kind and gave me a good hand.

In August 1971, everything stopped as we focused on the most shocking event in recent New York history. From the moment the inmates took over Attica State Prison until the state troopers were called in and the bodies of forty-three hostages and prisoners carried out, Attica was front-page news. News reports highlighted the issues of race (the leaders of the revolt were Black Muslims), leadership (Rockefeller was heavily criticized for not personally going to the prison and overseeing the negotiations), and the harsh, sometimes brutal, conditions in the state prison.

When it was over, an investigating commission was established under Dean Robert McKay of the NYU Law School. I wrote a "history" of the event for the governor to use in preparing testimony. I studied everything, including hours with state police ballistics experts tracing the trajectory of every bullet fired when the troopers recaptured the prison from the inmates. The paper, which ran to seventy-five pages, later became known as the "Albright-Vestner" report. Eight years later I was called as a witness to testify in a Rochester court room in the lawsuit brought by the families of the dead prisoners.[414]

From Attica we moved directly into the war between Rockefeller and Mayor John Lindsay of New York City.[415] In the winter of 1971, Rockefeller and the Legislature created a "Commission to Study the Governmental Operations of New York City." Stuart Scott, a New York City lawyer, was appointed chairman. Scott was not prepared for the intensely political atmosphere surrounding the commission. This was not to be a disinterested academic "study"; it was to be a story with a villain (the mayor), a lady in distress (the city), a white knight (the governor) and a happy ending (major change in the structure of city government).

The commission got off to a slow start and immediately came under political attack. Senate Democrats charged that it had been set up "in the stealth of night when nobody was looking;" the mayor called Rockefeller "a tool of Nixon,"

---

414   The lawsuits dragged on and were finally settled in 2000, with the State paying $12 million to the families of the dead prisoners and the same amount to the families of the dead hostages.

415   The conflict between the governor and the mayor became intensely personal during the New York City garbage strike of 1968. When Lindsay made wage demands on the sanitation workers' union, the union went on strike and garbage piled up all over the city. Rockefeller finally moved in and settled the strike. Lindsay accused the governor of settling "at the public's expense." The governor, stung by the public charge, felt Lindsay was grandstanding at his expense.

the commission "a political hatchet job" aimed at damaging his candidacy for president, and retaliated by setting up his own commission to investigate state government. *The New York Times* chastised Rockefeller for "fatally undermining the commission's objectivity" by his attacks on the mayor. Lindsay's people were hard at work in the Legislature, and it appeared that the commission might be starved for lack of funds. Rockefeller, frustrated, asked Harry to get it back on track. Harry and I immediately began commuting daily from Albany to New York, in one of the state's small planes or bouncy helicopters.

We reviewed the academic studies lined up by the commission staff. There was an inherent contradiction: people with strong academic credentials were proceeding on the assumption this was to be an objective "study" of city government. Others, like the governor, knew what changes they wanted and saw the commission as a vehicle to achieve them.

Harry and I addressed three problems: focus, money and personnel.[416] Getting the money the commission needed to operate was a struggle with the state budget division. Authorizing a commission is easy; funding it is hard. As to personnel, Harry skillfully eased out the commission's top staff, replacing them with people more attuned to the governor's wishes. Steve Berger, the new director, was perfect: tough as nails, politically savvy and intellectually rigorous. He knew exactly what Rockefeller wanted, and proceeded to sharpen the focus to a single issue: could New York, a very large and diverse city, really be governed entirely out of city hall?

London was the model. Rockefeller, who had visited London many times, was an enthusiastic student of London city government. He was deeply impressed that London was divided into hundreds of self-governing districts operating under a relatively weak mayor. If it worked in London, why not New York?

Ed Costikyan, a partner in one of the city's top law firms and a former leader of the New York City Democratic Party, assisted by Professor Maxwell Lehman of NYU, produced a massive paper for the commission that challenged the structure of city government and recommended sweeping changes, notably taking power from the mayor and distributing it among numerous little city halls all over the city, each with its own constituency, each empowered to deliver a variety of local services.[417] Not everyone was in love with the idea of

---

416   Oscar Ruebhausen, senior partner at the Debevoise law firm, was actively and constructively involved as Special Counsel to the Commission.
417   Edward N. Costikyan and Maxwell Lehman, "Restructuring the Government of New York City," presented to the Temporary Commission to Make a Study of the Governmental Operations of the City of New York (15 March 1972).

decentralizing city government. Professor Wallace Sayre of Columbia, probably the preeminent authority on New York City government, wrote a paper for the commission concluding that London was not a good model for decentralizing New York City government. He followed that up with a scathing critique of decentralization on the op-ed page of *The New York Times*.[418]

Not surprisingly, the Scott Commission, after public hearings, adopted the Costikyan-Lehman recommendations, which Rockefeller whole-heartedly supported. We drafted a bill creating a "Charter Revision Commission" for the city; it passed and was signed into law. No hearings, no deliberative process: Done![419] The voters later approved a revised city charter, and a controversial era of decentralized city government ensued.[420]

In the spring of 1972, the governor fired Bill Dentzer and appointed Harry superintendent of banks in his place. Harry asked me to be his first deputy. I hesitated. We'd settled in Albany. It was home, Alice-Lee was enrolled in the excellent Albany Academy for Girls, and I was reluctant to return to the Manhattan rat race. I asked for a commitment from the governor that I would succeed Harry as superintendent, and with that commitment I accepted Harry's offer.

In August 1972, we sold our Albany house and moved into an elegant old Victorian set high above Grace Church Street in Rye, New York, about thirty-five minutes from the city. When I discovered the house had once belonged to my old Amherst professor, Henry Steele Commager, I wrote him and told him we had put up bookshelves and that books were once again a visible part of the house. He wrote back:

> As you have guessed, we lined the walls with bookshelves; the new owners who hated books pulled them all down; I am delighted that they are going up again.

---

418   Wallace S. Sayre, "Smaller Does Not Mean Better, Necessarily," *The New York Times*, April 8, 1972, Op-Ed. Among other things, Sayre argued that governing the city through numerous little city halls, dominated by local factions and with limited public information, would actually suppress voter participation and empower the most aggressive local factions. Sayre, with Professor Herbert Kaufman of Yale, wrote *Governing New York City: Politics in the Metropolis* (New York; W.W.Norton & Company, Inc, 1965). Other critics saw decentralization resulting in more costly and less effective delivery of public services.

419   I was responsible for producing the bill, with major assistance from Judge Milton Alpert, an expert on municipal law, and Bernie Richland, the city's Corporation Counsel.

420   The balance was later restored by strong mayors like Ed Koch, Rudy Giuliani and Michael Bloomberg. "Decentralization", which sounded so good in theory, didn't work as well as we thought it would.

Every morning a little before six, I walked down the stone steps past our big copper beech tree to the street and then to the station in time to catch the 6:14 to Grand Central. That fifteen-minute walk was a high point of my day, especially under a full moon. Evenings, we all sat down to a rather late family dinner and talked over the day. Charlie later offered his recollections of my work hours and those nightly family dinners:

> I remember enjoying the conversation and stories you had when you got home, about intrigue at the office, or politics or whatever was going on in NYC at the time....Occasionally, you'd take too much food and mom would say 'leave it to the growing boy' or something like that. You'd add too much spice to the chili and Mom would react. I remember you cooking a lot, especially on the weekend. Alice-Lee cooked, mom cooked, seemed like everyone cooked. Eating and cooking were big family pastimes....

> I remember you worked long days, getting up at like 5:15, taking the train to work, getting back at 8 PM, sitting back with jalapeno peppers, cheese and crackers and a beer. It always seemed like you got up in the middle of the night. I can't imagine working the hours you did...

The kitchen, where we spent a lot of time, was a source of pleasure, in a good meal, good wine, and good conversation. But it could be a source of friction, when conversation turned to argument or anger. The kitchen was where the kids did their chores, often reluctantly. It was also the coldest room in the house, so we bought a little Swedish stove which could provide terrific heat and also smoke out the house when I didn't properly fire it up.

Charlie's recollections of life in Rye include bribery for school-work and athletic achievement. I paid him and Alice-Lee a buck for an A, subtracting one for a C. When they were very little, I took them to the tennis courts and paid a penny for every ball they returned over the net. Charlie was more aggressive in chasing those pennies, with the result that he took up tennis and Alice-Lee took up swimming. I was a part-time father; their mother did the hard work in raising them to be serious and responsible individuals.

* * *

As first deputy, I had administrative responsibility for the seven-hundred-person state banking department. The core of the department was the unionized bank examiner force numbering about four-hundred. They examined a wide range of financial entities: large commercial banks, distinguished old savings banks, finance companies, and the little check cashers that operated all over Harlem.

We had no sooner settled in when Rockefeller's executive assistant, Anne Whitman, prevailed on Harry to put Tom Stephens on the payroll at a fairly senior position. I was surprised. Who was he? What were his qualifications? Harry said "Don't worry. This is something we've got to do, and it'll pay off." What a pleasant surprise. Tom, nearing retirement, was a treasure. Born in Ireland, a lawyer and political activist, he had served in the Eisenhower White House as special counsel to the president. Without a big ego, he was down-to-earth and funny. Among other things, Tom had created the "Thomas E. Stephens White House Art Collection" by sending paint-by-the-numbers kits around to top Republican officials and hanging the results in the White House, including an Eisenhower original. Tom, who had planted tomatoes in the Rose Garden, came out to our house in Rye one evening and showed me how to plant a vegetable garden. He and Len Hall, former chairman of the Republican Party during the Eisenhower years, used to sit around in my office before monthly meetings of the State Banking Board (of which Hall was a member) and swap old war stories. As far as they were concerned, Eisenhower was a great president, no question about it. Tom stayed with us for about a year.

I was still a registered Democrat, but that didn't last long. Shortly after the 1972 election, Harry, George Hinman and I had lunch. Hinman was a close adviser to Rockefeller and a prominent figure in the Republican Party. He suggested it might be more useful to my career if I registered as a Republican, so I did. There was no reason for me to be a registered Democrat. I had been a contributor to the Governor's Club since 1968 (a de facto condition of my job), and I had actually voted for Nixon in the 1972 election, based on his opening to China, which I thought took courage.

One day I got a call from a reporter for the *New York Post*. He said: "Are you aware that Marine Midland has loaned money to the Erie County Democratic Committee? Do you think they should be making those loans? What do you guys think about that?" Harry was away so I had no comment. But he pressed me: "You mean you have no comment on something within your responsibility that's a violation of the law?" I said, "We'll look into it." He hung up, seemingly satisfied.

Next morning I heard from the governor's press secretary, who called my attention to the *Post's* morning edition. There it was on page two, in big bold print: "STATE BANKING DEPARTMENT LAUNCHES PROBE OF ERIE COUNTY DEMOCRATS." In the article itself I was accurately quoted, "We'll look into it." You could call that "launching a probe"; it certainly makes a better headline. The guy at the *Post* had used a classic reporter's ploy: make the source feel like a fool for not being responsive. I'd screwed up, made a careless comment to a reporter, and deserved what I got: a good chewing out.

It was obvious that the banking industry was changing fast, but we didn't have a clue as to how fast or in what direction. In fact, we were very minor figures in a financial revolution that would play out over many years with huge consequences. Everything that later came to be taken for granted started then: ATM's, money market funds, adjustable rate mortgages, the market for mortgage-backed securities, the explosive growth of credit card debt, nationwide and worldwide banking, derivatives, swaps, and their increasingly complex variations. The competitive pressures of the 1970s were sweeping away the Depression-era regulatory structure, designed to build a fence around traditional banking and make it a dull and unexciting business.

The big New York banks were all expanding overseas, opening branches in Europe, Asia and Latin America. Harry and I decided we had better open an office in London so we could examine the European operations of our state-chartered banks. Bernie Gassman, the head examiner, and I flew to London and spent a week clearing our new office with the British regulators, renting office space, hiring local staff, and selecting the examiners who would move from New York. The British regulators were low-key, and seemed to regulate with a wink and a nod, or perhaps a raised eyebrow. It all seemed very informal and casual. But during our time in London a major British mortgage lender failed, the publicity reflected badly on the regulators, and they started moving toward a more formal system like ours.

I was invited to lunch by the chairman of Barclay's. It was an eye-opening experience for a guy who normally had a cheeseburger for lunch. The chairman had a private dining room. Promptly at noon, about ten of us were served sherry and hors d'oevres were passed. The guests included the British Ambassador to China, the financial reporter for *The Times*, and six or seven senior bank officers. Barclay's at the time was seeking regulatory approval for a major acquisition on Long Island (we subsequently turned them down, which created a fair amount of anger in London), and the conversation at my end of the table was about the U.S. banking situation. We sat down to a fish course with white wine, a meat course with red wine, a cheese course and brandy. We adjourned promptly at two. I had to go back to the hotel and sleep it off. The Barclay's bankers presumably went back to work, though I don't know how.

Responding to the increasingly competitive banking situation, the Nixon administration had conducted a study of the financial markets and made recommendations to Congress in 1972.[421] But Congress was slow to act. For Harry and me, the choice was to sit on our hands and do nothing, or try and shape events in New York. It was much more fun to do something, so we organized a committee on financial reform—known as the "Albright Committee."[422] Harry was the chair; I was the director, and we recruited bankers and academics. Our recommendations were designed to peel away regulatory restrictions on the banking business so that banks could compete more aggressively for funds. Perhaps our most controversial recommendation was to transform the state-chartered savings banks from strictly mortgage lenders into full service consumer banks offering ATM facilities, checking and consumer credit. The point was to give those specialized home mortgage lenders a chance to hold on to their customers against competition from commercial banks and mutual funds, like Fidelity. The small upstate commercial banks, very influential in the Legislature, fought that tooth and nail, but what they were fighting was change, and change, for better or worse, was inevitable.

The big news in 1974 was "Watergate." President Richard Nixon was impeached and resigned; Gerald Ford became president; Nelson Rockefeller became Ford's vice-president; Harry Albright went to Washington as special counsel to the vice-president; Lieutenant Governor Malcolm Wilson succeeded Rockefeller; and I was appointed New York State superintendent of banks. I liked Wilson, but he wasn't around long. He lost the 1974 election to Hugh Carey.

The New York Times, which never missed an opportunity to poke fun at the Legislature, reported on my first encounter with the members of the Assembly Banking Committee:[423]

> Assemblyman George A. Cincotta of Brooklyn beamed as he introduced a visitor to his Committee on Banks: "The Superintendent of Insurance—I mean, of Banks, Mr. Zetner, whose office is always open to us."
>
> "Actually it's Vestner, Eliot Vestner," the visitor said.

---

421   *Report of the President's Commission on Financial Structure and Regulation* (December, 1971)
422   *Report of the Superintendent's Advisory Committee on Financial Reform* (N.Y. State Banking Department, March, 1974).
423   *The New York Times*, January 22, 1975 (Business Section).

"How do you spell that, Eliot?" asked Assemblyman Hyman M. Miller, Republican of Fayetteville.

"E L I O T," Mr. Vestner replied.

Mr. Vestner shook hands with the 21 committee members present, told them his address and telephone number, and headed for the door. "I have a bill in to reduce the salary of the Superintendent of Banks," Assemblyman Stanley Fink, a Brooklyn Democrat, said in a stage whisper as soon as the door had closed.

As superintendent I also served as chairman of the state banking board, and Cincotta leaned on me to lower the state usury rate, then 6%. Legislators like Cincotta, wittingly or unwittingly, confused the usury rate with the market rate. They publicly argued that lowering the usury rate would lower the going rate on mortgages. That's just political baloney. Lowering the usury rate below the market rate simply makes it impossible to finance the purchase or sale of a house. Who's going to lend money at below-market rates? Nobody. When the board refused to lower the rate, Cincotta was furious: "Those dirty bastards.... I really expected them to lower the rate a quarter of a percent," Cincotta said. "We asked Eliot Vestner at a hearing last month to show us some good faith, to show that the board could lower the rate as well as raise it.... That economic stuff is just a lot of bull."[424]

There were a few perks in my new position, like use of a limousine and driver. When Dad came to visit, he got a big kick out of watching ex-boxer Slim Williams drive up in the big black Buick and hold the door for me as I climbed into the huge back seat area. With a reading lamp, the back seat was a mobile office. Lowell and Dad liked to remind me that it was all temporary and that someday I'd have to earn my salary in the real world, where guys my age didn't get to ride in big black limos.

From the end of 1973 through 1974, the U.S. experienced its worst financial crisis since the Great Depression. [425] The stock market was in the

424 *Newsday*, April 11, 1975 (Real Estate Section).
425 The stock market dropped 45 percent from the end of 1973 through 1974; inflation reached an annual rate of 12 percent. There was a new twist to this one. The middle-eastern nations restricted oil production, driving up prices and reducing the availability of gasoline. That produced long lines of cars waiting for gas that might not be available at the pump.

tank, inflation was on the rise, there was widespread unemployment, and the price of oil was going through the roof. Dad was unaffected. He was sailing along up in Freedom with his Army pension indexed to inflation, a 4 percent fixed rate mortgage, free health care and cheap groceries at Pease Air Force Base over in Portsmouth. But for most people, those were tough years.

Harry asked me to draft a memo for the vice-president with suggestions for how President Ford might frame domestic economic policy proposals in his 1974 State of the Union address. It seemed to me that a national crisis called for bold presidential action, so I plowed ahead with recommendations for a tariff on imported oil, increased federal gas taxes, standby authority for gasoline rationing, tax incentives to encourage use of smaller economy cars, a new RFC to provide capital to businesses that couldn't raise money in the markets, etc. [426] My over-heated memo was addressed to the wrong audience. We were supposed to be giving advice, not to Nelson Rockefeller, but to a Midwestern Republican president. I don't think my suggestions ever got past Harry, whose political instincts were far superior to mine. If Rockefeller had proposed any of the things I suggested, Ford's chief of staff, Donald Rumsfeld, would have cut him off at the knees, something he was itching to do anyway (Harry described Rumsfeld as "the meanest SOB he had ever run into").

As prices and interest rates rose, there were major bank failures, notably the Franklin National Bank on Long Island. The savings banks that we regulated were in a terrible bind. Their chief source of income was their portfolio of long-term fixed rate mortgages; their chief expense was the interest rate they paid on their deposits. With revenue fixed and the rates on deposits rising fast, they were losing money and deposits. A number of banks were in serious trouble, and mortgage lending in New York State dried up.

I worked with Harry on a proposal to the vice-president, suggesting that upwards of $6 billion could be injected into the national home mortgage market by enabling pension funds to buy mortgage-backed securities—at the time

---

426 "RFC" stands for Reconstruction Finance Corporation, a government entity first set up in the early years of the Depression to provide capital funds to industry and purchase troubled assets. A newer version was set up during the 1990's to buy failed S&L's and sell them to investors.

the funds held virtually no mortgage investments. Federal action was required, and we outlined the necessary steps in our memo.[427]

At the state level, I drafted a bill and lobbied for legislation that would permit banks to offer variable rate mortgages. A March 1975 article by Owen Moritz in the *Daily News* reported my efforts:[428]

Banking Chief Prods Albany
Seeks Aid for Consumers, Housing

Banks Superintendent Eliot Vestner has called for state action to encourage banks to invest in housing...Vestner had these proposals...

--That a variable rate mortgage be established—the rate to reflect the state of the economy—in contrast to the present fixed-rate mortgage...with controls to insure that rates did not rise precipitously over a given period.

In the winter of 1975 the "UDC crisis" was front-page financial news. As banking superintendent, I also served as a director of the Urban Development Corporation, created by Rockefeller in 1968 to spearhead construction and development of low-and middle-income housing. Rockefeller had recruited Ed Logue from Boston to run it. Logue, taking advantage of generous federal housing subsidies, made UDC a powerful public corporation with billions of dollars in on-going projects.

By the time I came on board, Logue was gone and UDC, overextended, was in deep trouble, its income insufficient to complete unfinished projects and pay its bondholders. Governor Carey had established a negotiating team under Dick Ravitch to get the big New York City banks to extend credit to UDC, but the banks wouldn't act unless the state legislature put up the money to make good on UDC's obligations to its bondholders. The Legislature wouldn't do anything until the banks committed themselves. It was a game of chicken.

---

427 There was a growing demand for high quality fixed income securities, and the investment banks were meeting that demand by creating new mortgage-backed securities. How did that work? The banks originated the mortgages and sold them to the investment banks or the federal mortgage agencies, who transformed them into the high quality fixed income securities demanded by the market, a form of modern alchemy called "securitization." The key point of securitization was to isolate the payments from a group of mortgages, usually through creation of a separate company, called a "special purpose vehicle," and dedicate those payments to the investors who held the securities.
428 *Daily News*, March 31, 1975, 17.

The directors elected me "acting chairman." Working with counsel, we made it our first priority to keep the business going and let the bonds go into default. Inevitably there came a day when, after paying the costs of the business, we didn't have enough left to pay the bondholders. We defaulted and prepared for bankruptcy. That caught the attention of the Legislature. After the usual political back and forth, the governor and his negotiating team were successful in getting the Legislature and the banks to put up the money to keep UDC solvent and make the bondholders whole. The Debevoise firm was outside counsel to UDC. Mike Goff, the partner on the account, wrote me a nice letter:

> I have been 'singing your praises' around the office for the superb way you have handled the UDC situation. I think the minutes…clearly show that the directors acted responsibly under almost impossible circumstances. This was in no small way due to your leadership, and all of us here are very proud of you![429]

* * *

Later in the spring of 1975 Bernie Gassman, our chief examiner, came to me with evidence that a savings and loan institution with uninsured deposits was in bad shape. I called in the owner, but he dismissed our findings with a wave of his hand. When I pressed him, he threatened me with his connections in the Governor's office. He was arrogant and nasty. After another unproductive meeting I arranged for a quick and private auction of the bank, went to court that night, seized the bank, changed the locks, put a team of examiners in to go over the books, and by morning there were signs outside directing depositors to their new bank. I turned evidence of fraud over to the Manhattan DA, who obtained an indictment, but the jury acquitted him. He sued me for $50 million, but the suit didn't go anywhere.

One day, a high-level delegation of Soviet officials came to my office. Big blustery guys, they said the Soviet Union intended to establish a branch of the Soviet State Bank in New York City and informed me they had received a green light from the state department. They needed my approval; their body language said that was a mere formality, a quirk of our strange system of government. But New York law required a showing of "reciprocity,"

---

a concept they found hard to grasp. They would have to show that a U.S. bank could operate in the Soviet Union with as much flexibility as the Soviet branch would enjoy in New York. In 1917, the then new Soviet government had closed the Moscow branches of Chase and Citibank and confiscated their property. At a minimum, the Soviets would have to return the confiscated property or pay compensation and permit some kind of U.S. banking presence in Moscow. When I told them that, they were surprised and disgruntled. Yuri Ivanov, head of the Soviet State Bank, and two of his deputies, came back to my office and forcefully argued their case. I asked if Citi and Chase could open branches in Moscow; they replied "Of course not! There is no room in the Soviet system for any bank independent of the State." Later, they submitted a long memorandum on the Soviet banking system, and returned to argue their case again. When I turned them down, they complained to the state department, but to no avail.

My days in government were numbered. Friends in the banking industry were trying to get Governor Carey to appoint me to a full term. One of the members of the banking board advised me to position myself as a defender of the state's regulatory authority against federal encroachment—a possibly valid point but without much sex appeal. I tried that at the New York State Bankers Association annual convention. The speech was okay; there was a lot to be said for avoiding a concentration of regulatory power in the federal government, and the *American Banker* gave me a nice write-up. But I was a Republican holdover under a newly-elected Democratic governor, and a speech wasn't going to save my job.

On the last day of the bankers' convention, Eliot Richardson was the featured speaker at dinner. I sat next to him and he was charming. I looked over and noticed he was doodling all over his pad, so I told him my wife was a great fan of his and that she would love that doodle signed by him. He signed it and gave it to me. When he stood up to speak, he started out in good form, but then he began slurring his words and repeating himself. He was a national hero for his role in Watergate; he was considered a possible candidate for president; he was addressing about six hundred bankers, all decked out in black tie, and he was drunk. It was embarrassing. People began to get up, walk around and leave, and a low murmur began to rise from the audience. He finally stopped and sat down to perfunctory applause.

It was time, as Dad kept reminding me, to get a "real job." I submitted my resignation and Carey graciously responded:

Dear Eliot:

It is with severe regret that I accept your resignation as Super-intendent of Banks. I am aware that your service to the State of New York over the past seven years has not only brought distinction to you as a public servant, but has been to the benefit of the citizens of our State. I also wish to express my personal appreciation for the way in which you met your responsibilities during these early days of my Administration. You have my best wishes for the future, and again my thanks.

\s\ Hugh Carey

14. Lowell & Eliot

In the summer of 1975, I left government and took a job at the Irving Trust Company. Gordon Wallis, the Irving chairman, warned me that I would have to get used to taking the train and subway to get to work, just like everybody else. At Irving, only the chairman and president got to ride around in a limousine. He had a thin smile on his face and he was kidding me, but there was a message: don't come in here thinking you're a big deal, because you're not.

* * *

August 4, 1975, was my fortieth birthday. It was hot—only in the evening did the temperature drop below 100. Uncle Lowell, eighty-two, came to the celebration that Penny had organized at our house in Rye, sat on our porch, listened to the music, watched the dancing, and spent the night. Lowell loved a hot night without air conditioning and that's what he got. I looked in on him when he was sound asleep. Lying on his back, barely breathing, Lowell looked like a very old man.

Over the next four years, I spent a lot of time with Lowell, on the phone or over lunch at the Playboy Club in midtown Manhattan. Neither of us was interested in the waitresses, dressed up like bunnies, but the London broil was good, and we could find a quiet corner table and talk. He was a good listener, and he had a wealth of experience that I could tap into. There was a lot going on in my life, personal and professional, and I shared it all with Lowell.

For some reason, I didn't go to Dad for advice the way I went to Lowell. Dad meant well, but when I talked with him about a problem at work he would say "I'm sure everything will turn out well," or "You've got a lot going for you, just remember that." Lowell would want to know who the people were, what they were doing, what I was doing, and he might say "I don't think you're going about it the right way," and then tell me what I should do. I might disagree, but we'd have an intelligent discussion of the precise thing I was dealing with.

On April 12, 1979, I got a call from the superintendent of Lowell's building. He had gone into Lowell's apartment and found him dead on the floor from a massive heart attack. He died instantly, exactly what he wanted.

Lowell had no children and I was his executor. After he died, I sorted through hundreds of unopened letters, bills, and checks all unopened and piled up on his kitchen table. I cleaned out his apartment and arranged for a funeral service at the McGrath Funeral Home in Bronxville (he had left explicit instructions: no church service). So we held a memorial service for him in one of McGrath's cold, impersonal rooms with a young minister who knew nothing about Lowell and his life. I should have delivered a eulogy to the small group gathered for the service, but didn't. I blew it. So here it is, years too late.

Lowell was born, 1894, New Brunswick, New Jersey, to Florence and Edgar Shumway. His father was professor of Latin and Greek at Rutgers University. His older brother, Waldo, a star at Amherst College, was national fencing champion and Phi Beta Kappa. Lowell graduated from Amherst in 1914. There, he was a top classics scholar; a 165-pound tackle on the Amherst football team in an era when Amherst played Harvard, Dartmouth, and other Eastern football powers; and twice runner-up at the New England Intercollegiate tennis championships, losing a five-set final each time to his Amherst teammate.

Once Lowell met Mom's older sister, Ruth, he moved fast and they were married in March 1918, at St. Paul's Episcopal Church in Flatbush. Lowell served in the First World War as a lieutenant with the 77th Infantry Division, but to his regret he never made it to the front in France.

After the war he worked briefly at National City Bank, followed by a thirty-year career at McCall Corporation, retiring as vice-president for Circulation in 1959. His boss was Marvin Pierce, father of former First Lady Barbara Bush. He held leadership positions in various business organizations including his favorite, the National Better Business Bureau. Honest to a fault, he didn't suffer fools gladly, and he didn't always tailor his opinions to please his audience. That probably cost him at work. He loved his job and didn't retire willingly. When the financier, Norton Simon, acquired McCall in one of the early hostile takeovers, he made it clear that the time was ripe for Lowell to retire.

At six-two, strong and wiry, he was a physically imposing man and a terrific athlete. He was always a superb tennis player with an unquenchable thirst to win.

342

When I was on the tennis team at Amherst and Lowell was in his early sixties, a friend and I challenged him and Bill Barber, to a best of three sets match. I played the backhand side. Lowell kept serving deep to my backhand. I wondered why, since that was my strong side. Without thinking, I kept moving inch by inch to the left. Then at a crucial point in the third set, Lowell put a perfect serve right down the middle line. I was caught flat-footed. All I could say was "Nice shot!" Lowell, who loved taking cocky young college kids down a peg, looked like the cat that had just swallowed a very tasty bird. He and Barber won the match.

He also played a fierce game of squash into his eighties, until one day he cracked a rib running into the wall of the squash court at the Bronxville Field Club. He loved golf and was an enthusiastic golfer. He played with the old hickory sticks and thin-bladed irons, and had a funny swing: slowly, slowly, and then bam! Not smooth, but usually effective. On the course, he was a stickler for the rules: Play the ball as it lies, no mulligans and no gimmees. He made me putt everything, even inches. Mom was the same way. It was very exacting playing with them. Lowell and Mom were a couple of Puritans on the golf course.

He had a rigorous intellect, and I had to work hard to hold my own with him when we argued politics. He was a solid Republican who believed in a balanced budget and limited government. He had no use for Roosevelt, Truman, Stevenson, Kennedy and the rest. I was an ardent Democrat, but Lowell thought I would eventually turn Republican when my tax bill got to a certain point. He was right.

He was, above all, a great human being. He cared for his wife, Ruth, all through her years of heart problems—his medical bills must have been astronomical, but he never complained; He provided a home for Mom and me during the eighteen months Dad was in Korea; he supported his brother-in-law Manny Swan, who couldn't earn a nickel; he supported his mother-in-law, Grandmother Fuller; he took care of several elderly widows around Bronxville who had nobody else to watch over them, and he lent me the money to go to law school when, without it, I couldn't have gone.

He held our family together, hosting family reunions, visiting cousins, nieces and nephews up and down the coast. He believed in family.

Lowell and Dad shared a lot of memories, and during the seventies they visited back and forth. Dad always felt a rivalry with Lowell, perhaps a touch of envy. He always kept Lowell at arm's length, which is sad because they shared so much history.

* * *

After traveling around Europe for a year, Dad finally came home in 1971. As a grandfather, he was much mellower than the father I had known when I was a kid. The kids called him "Grumpy Grampy." They didn't have a clue how rough he could be back in the forties and fifties when he was a father with a young son.

Alice-Lee, Charlie and tractor

Dad, Alice-Lee and Charlie

When I left government in 1975 Dad was relieved that I finally had a "real job". He worried that given the uncertainties of politics, I'd find myself suddenly out on the street with no job. But he was also worried about my family life. Once, when he came to visit us in Rye, he took me aside and asked how things were going at home. I said "fine" and left it at that. But things weren't "fine," though I was unwilling to see that. So I brushed him off. I just didn't feel like confiding in him. He saw that we had all the material things, but he also saw the tension in our marriage, the trouble bubbling under the surface. He gave me the opportunity to talk about it. I envied the life he had lived with Mom: a seemingly simple life without material abundance, a life in which the bank balance had periodically dropped below $10, but a life brightened by a deeply loving marriage. At least that's how I saw it then. But who knows about anyone's marriage, except the participants, and sometimes even they don't know. In the seventies, with Mom long dead, I could still feel the glow of their marriage, comparing it unfavorably with my own. We could have talked about that; we could have talked about what's really important, instead of our usual banter about politics and job. But we didn't. When I was promoted, he assumed I'd be president of the bank one day. He was at that happy stage of life where he could believe his son had a great future and would be a roaring success, and he would never be disappointed because he wouldn't be around for the final act. He may have been pleased when I told him about the promotion, but he was worried about me; he was worried because he knew me better than I realized.

That same year, he experienced three major events in his life. We celebrated his seventy-fifth birthday (believing him when he said he was born in 1900, which was off by three years), he made the final payment on the mortgage he and Mom had signed back in November 1955, ceremoniously burning the cancelled mortgage note in the fireplace, and he got married.

His new bride, Margaret ("Molly") Kovaleski Cunningham was a widow living in Freedom. Molly was the sort of person you either liked or disliked; there was no middle ground. She was a number of things: Polish, smart, tough, pushy, earthy, suspicious, protective, and even sexy. As a young woman she had had a career in Boston and New York, first in advertising and later, as an editor at *Vogue*. She was a survivor; she wasn't warm and cozy. In Freedom she stepped on a lot of toes, and as a result had as many enemies as friends. As for children, she was tolerant but generally regarded them as a nuisance. She and Dad cared for each other, and that's what counted.

Dad and Molly had a good time. Molly refused to fly, so they sailed to Europe on the *Queen Elizabeth*, visiting all the old places Dad had known from his past. The *Queen Elizabeth* was their idea of heaven—lots of people their

345

age, endless food and drink, fast and safe. When they weren't traveling back and forth to Europe they spent summers in Freedom and winters in Pinehurst, North Carolina, where Molly owned a small condominium. It was a nice life.

In 1981 my father lost his oldest and closest friend, Donald Munn. Donald and Dad had been friends since they were young men starting out in New York City after the First World War. A regular presence in our family, Don gave me an authentic St. Louis Cardinals uniform on my birthday in 1944. I've never forgotten the excitement of that gift. I put it on and pretended I was Stan Musial. He also used to take us out to play golf on the local Westchester courses. His game, easy and relaxed, was for me an unattainable goal. He could tease Dad and make him laugh, probably the only person who could do that. Mom and Dad always visited Don and his sister at their Park Avenue apartment when they were in New York; the Munn's were a precious link to their past. But in 1981, Dad was struggling over Don's death. In Mom's final days, Don Munn had made the trip to Freedom to stay with Dad and comfort him. But now Dad had a guilty conscience for not having visited Don in his last days, and he was drafting and redrafting a letter to Don's companion, a woman who was also an old friend. He couldn't figure out how to explain his absence.

Always vigorous, Dad was now walking less and staying indoors more. His emphysema got worse and he became a virtual invalid. Molly's role shifted from lover and companion to nurse. Thank God for Molly. I was absorbed in my own career and family and wasn't much help. We tried to get Dad to record his life on tape; we got a little bit out of him, but not much.

He died the afternoon of March 2, 1983, in the eighty-sixth year of his life in the sunlit library of his home in Freedom. I held his hand as he struggled for breath. To ease his anxiety, Molly crushed a sleeping pill and fed it to him with some water. He gave me a look as if he wanted to say something, but whatever was on his mind passed in an instant. His eyes closed, his breathing slowed, and then stopped. Later, strangers arrived, zipped him up in a rubber bag and took him away. When their big black car was still in the driveway, I felt like calling out, "Wait a minute; he and I still have some things to talk about." We buried his ashes next to Priscilla in the little cemetery overlooking Loon Lake. They're together now, as they had been together from that morning of February 16, 1924 when they met under the clock at Grand Central.

Reflections:

Priscilla and Eliot were so different, I sometimes wonder what brought them together and kept them together. Priscilla, raised in prosperity and sheltered in the bosom of a large and loving family, was outgoing, sunny and optimistic, with a strong religious faith. Every night she would kneel by the side of the bed, hands folded, and silently whisper her prayers to a God she believed cared about her and how she conducted her life. While she prayed, Eliot would be deep into a good book. He was raised in a broken family and then by a needy and demanding mother; no religious faith; a loner, consumed with his own ambitions and disappointments; quick to anger, occasionally impulsive in his judgments and impatient with details. Exposed at a young age to war, the rough and tumble of army life, and life in a foreign country, he was the more worldly and sophisticated of the two; but it was hard to tell what made him tick.

As different as they were, each seemed to meet a need in the other. Priscilla wanted a man she could lean on, and Eliot was that man. Even when he was physically absent on army business, he was a strong presence in her life; there was nothing bland or wishy-washy about him. Skilled with his hands, he was a renaissance man around the house: plumber, electrician, carpenter and painter. He was also physically strong and protective. If anybody had broken into their house in Freedom, he would have hauled out his army carbine and shot him between the eyes. No hesitation. Priscilla, with great social skills, tended to ameliorate his awkwardness and make it easier for him to be with other people. She was an avid listener, expert at drawing people out. She had empathy. She saw the subtle gray tones of things while he tended to see black and white, at least until she convinced him otherwise.

They also had a few things in common. They were both penny-pinchers; they loved the outdoors—riding, hiking, camping, gardening; they shared an

347

unquenchable thirst for travel; they both relished evenings at home alone, with a fire in the fireplace and good books to read. They were comfortable with each other and didn't need company. Though the world around them changed dramatically during their lifetime, they both remained Victorians at heart. Reading *Portnoy's Complaint*, Priscilla wondered if Roth ever wrote anything free of "what we Victorians call dirt."

I was their only child, and to some extent they survive in me. Like Eliot, I am impatient, quick to anger and driven by my own internal demons, some of which he might recognize. Jack Hawes at Andover hit the nail on the head when he said about me: "he is his own worst enemy." How true. Like Eliot, I am also selfish, which my wife, who is from a large family, describes as "only child" behavior. Like Priscilla, I am frugal, worry about money, make lists, and tend to be hard on myself. I did not inherit my father's plumbing, electrical and carpentry skills; nor did I inherit Priscilla's sunny disposition or her religious gene, a gift from her Puritan ancestors. All too often, I've fallen short of her standards for personal conduct. I suspect Eliot did too. She struggled mightily to improve the men in her life, a frustrating and thankless task.

Our family today is a fraction the size of the family that once surrounded my mother, and her family was only a fraction the size of the family that surrounded her ancestor, Thomas Fuller. When Thomas died at ninety-six in 1773, he was surrounded by hundreds of children, grandchildren and great-grandchildren. Thomas, in turn, had been only one of eleven children of John and Mehitable Fuller, and they all lived in and around East Haddam, Connecticut. In those days, it would have been rare for a Fuller to go into town and not bump into brothers, sisters, cousins, nieces and nephews.

A couple of things have happened to shrink the family. When Fullers moved off the farm, the need for children to serve as unpaid labor ceased and the cost of raising a large family increased. When it was common for children to die young, a large family ensured the survival of at least some of the children. In the late eighteenth century, Andrew and Elizabeth Mercein had twelve children, but only two reached adulthood. Later in the nineteenth century, only two of the Redfield's five children reached adulthood. With a declining rate of infant mortality, parents with only one or two children could increasingly count on those children reaching adulthood. The growth of the contraceptive industry in mid-nineteenth century almost certainly contributed to the shrinking family. Thus, the first six farm generations of Fullers produced an average of nine children; two nineteenth century urban generations averaged five; the twentieth century generations have averaged less than two.

There aren't many Vestners around, at least in my neck of the woods (I suspect there are a fair number of Vestners somewhere out in California), but there are still a lot of Fullers, Redfields, Merceins, Webbs and Dwights. Increased mobility has scattered family from coast to coast and beyond, and who knows where they all are. Family no longer comes naturally; now we have to work at it.

There are no U.S. presidents, industrial titans, great artists, actors or comedians in our family. They were all ordinary middle-class strivers, sober and serious, self-educated or college-educated. But they and many more like them made this country great. They were farmers, clerks, lawyers, soldiers, businessmen and public officials. They worked hard, supported their families, and persevered through tough times.

Eliot and Priscilla exemplified those values. Laid off on Wall Street and unable to find work in the depths of the Depression, Eliot used his army contacts from the First World War and embarked on a military career, starting with the Civilian Conservation Corps in 1933 and ending with service in Korea. Priscilla worked to help support the family during and after the Depression. They were physically separated for most of fifteen years from 1933 to 1948, their future was always a source of deep concern, and they didn't have a home of their own until they retired. That was probably not the life Priscilla envisioned when she married Eliot in 1931, but she put her heart and soul into it. They may have had grand dreams in the twenties when anything seemed possible; but they had to play the cards they were dealt. In the end, they achieved what in the depths of the Depression had been beyond their wildest imagination: a gracious home of their own in the country and a secure retirement. And in the intimacy of their marriage, they never lost the spark that had brought them together in 1924. They did well.

APPENDIX: 1

Fullers: Puritans, Separatists, Plymouth, Barnstable, Connecticut and Brooklyn—1575-1877

Priscilla's ancestors were original settlers of Plymouth Colony in the winter of 1620, the first permanent English settlement on the New England coast. Edward and Samuel Fuller were the sons of Robert and Francis Fuller of Redenhall, Norfolk; they were born in 1575 and 1580/81, respectively. William Bradford was the son of William and Alice Hanson Bradford, of Austerfield, Yorkshire, and he was born in 1589/90.

The Bradfords and Fullers were self-described "yeomen" and proud of it. Yeomen, a cut below "gentlemen" in the English pecking order, were merchants and landowners, the hardworking and prosperous backbone of England.

Born into moderately prosperous land-owning families, Bradford and the Fuller brothers as young men became deeply committed to an illegal religious sect and were forced to flee England and live as exiles in Leiden, Holland. They could have lived in comfortable manor houses, farmed familiar lands, and led respected lives in rural England, but they chose otherwise. What drove them? Why give up friends, family and the comforts of England for exile in Holland and then, in 1620, cross the ocean to the unexplored wilderness of New England? What part did Priscilla's ancestors play in the establishment of Plymouth?

When Bradford and the Fullers were growing up, Elizabeth was Queen, Shakespeare was a popular London playwright, and Catholic Spain was a superpower threatening England with invasion. Within the English church, there was bitter conflict between the Anglican establishment and reformers influenced by the teachings of John Calvin of Geneva, who sought to strip away all rituals, hierarchy and other vestiges of "Popery" and restore the church to its original simplicity. The reformers were called "Puritans," a term neither meant nor taken as a compliment. Bradford and the Fullers were Puritans.

The conflict within the church came to a head in about 1565 over the issue of vestments. The rules required that ministers wear vestments in church. The Puritan ministers refused, claiming that vestments set the minister apart from his congregation and symbolized the Catholic concept of the priesthood. Elizabeth instructed her bishops to enforce the rules. Leading Puritan ministers who dared to speak out for reform, or who refused to observe Anglican practices (such as making the sign of the cross, kneeling at the communion, observing saints' days) were summoned before church commissions and stripped of their right to preach.

Puritan ministers were typically scholarly university graduates who expected their congregations to be serious students of the Bible. They spoke plainly but eloquently, certain that theirs was the only path to salvation, a comforting message in a time of great turmoil and instability. Their eloquence, learning, and conviction appealed to intelligent young men looking for something deeper than the rituals of the established church

As Puritans, Bradford and the Fuller brothers believed that, at the beginning of time, God had chosen the few that would be saved and ascend to Heaven (the "elect") and the many who would be damned to an eternal life in Hell. But who were the elect? How could one tell? Leading a good and virtuous life was something to strive for, perhaps evidence of election; but by itself no guarantee of salvation. What mattered was "saving faith," a gift from God. Puritan theologians attempted to guide their congregations on how to detect "saving faith," how to distinguish between the illusion and the reality of saving faith. They struggled to devise tests to determine if a person was blessed with saving faith and therefore a "saint" destined for Heaven; not easy, since the gift of saving faith was admittedly a private matter between the individual and God.[430]

---

430   Edmund S. Morgan, *Visible Saints, the History of a Puritan Idea* (New York; Cornell University Press, 1963), 67; Francis J. Bremer, *The Puritan Experiment, New England Society from Bradford to Edwards* (Boston; University Press of New England, 1995), 15-28.

Bradford and the Fullers were students of Bible, especially the Old Testament, who measured their conduct against Scripture. They looked askance at theater, music, and other forms of entertainment as tools of Satan. They lived a God-centered life. They prayed to God and thanked Him for the good things in their lives. If things went poorly, that was because God was angry, or God was working things out in a way that was beyond their understanding, or it could be the work of Satan, always finding ways to insinuate himself into human affairs.

Bradford and the Fullers went beyond Puritanism; they were also Separatists. While most Puritans sought reform within the established church, the Separatists considered the established church hopelessly corrupt and formed their own congregations, chose their own preachers, and dispensed with virtually all sacraments and prescribed forms of worship. One Separatist in 1611 described the difference between Separatists and Puritans:

> The former doe both hold and practice the truth, and separate themselves from the contrarie. The latter have the truth in speculation onely and either dare not or at least doe not practice it.[431]

Separatist ministers were chosen by the congregation and could be dismissed by the congregation. That was unusual in a time when religion and everything else was hierarchical. The congregations were also exclusive and careful in admitting members—they had no wish to associate with the ungodly, and anyone not a Separatist was by definition "ungodly." A prospective new member had to satisfy the congregation that he or she understood and accepted Scriptural truths, had a reputation for good behavior, avoided the ungodly, and was prepared to enter into a covenant to walk in the way of the Lord whatever the cost.[432] As it turned out, the cost was high.

As Separatists, Bradford and the Fullers separated themselves from the English church and from normal social life. Bradford faced the "wrath of his uncles" and the "scoff of his neighbors." The Fuller brothers probably faced the same

---

431   Morgan, *Visible Saints*, 30, quoting from Mr. Henry Barrowes Platform (1611), 141.
432   One early covenant used the words "to walke with the rest; and that so longe as they did walke in the way of the Lorde, and as farr as might be warranted by the word of God," Morgan, *Visible Saints*, 28. Bradford described the covenant as joining "into a church estate, in the fellowship of the gospel, to walk in all His ways made known, or to be made known unto them, according to their best endeavours, whatsoever it should cost them, the Lord assisting them." *Bradford Journal*, 9

intense social pressure to conform.[433] By defying the law and holding religious meetings outside the established church, the Separatists were outlaws. In effect, they denied the power of the Crown to dictate the form and content of religious worship. At a time when the divine right of the monarch was accepted wisdom, that was treason. Separatists risked imprisonment and execution.[434] And yet, they persisted; they were prepared to give up everything, including their lives, "to keep a good conscience, and walk in such a way as God has prescribed in his Word." [435]

Bradford, thoroughly steeped in the Bible by the age of twelve, began attending meetings of the small Separatist congregation in Scrooby, about twelve miles from Austerfield.[436] There may have been a Separatist congregation in Norwich, ten miles from Redenhall.[437] If Bradford could walk or ride twelve miles to hear Richard Clyfton preach to the Separatist congregation in Scrooby, the Fullers could have easily covered the ten miles to Norwich.

While life was risky for Separatists under Elizabeth, it was worse under her successor, James. A staunch defender of Anglican orthodoxy, James cracked down on the Separatists. Bradford recalled the situation many years later:

> But after these things...they were hunted and persecuted on every side, so as their former afflictions were but as flea-bitings in comparision of these which now came upon them. For some were taken and clapped up in prison, others had their houses beset and watched night and day, and hardly escaped their hands; and the most were fain to flee and leave their houses and habitations and the means of their livelihood.[438]

---

433   "Nor could the wrath of his uncles, nor the scoff of his neighbors, now turned upon him...divert him from his pious inclinations..." from Cotton Mather, "Life of William Bradford" in *the Ecclesiastical History of New England* (London, for Thomas Parkhurst, at the Bible and Three Crowns, Cheapside, 1702), www. pilgrimhall.org/bradfordwilliamMagnalia.htm.

434   See Bremer, *John Winthrop*: 58 (Separatist leaders Henry Barrow and John Greenwood were arrested in 1587 and executed in 1593).

435   Cotton Mather, "Life of William Bradford."

436   The Scrooby group met at Brewster's manor house under the leadership of Richard Clyfton, their minister, and his successor John Robinson. Before going to Scrooby, Robinson had served in a parish near Yarmouth in Norfolk County, about twenty miles from Redenhall. The Fuller brothers may have been exposed to Robinson when he was at Yarmouth; exposure to the eloquent Robinson could have persuaded them to become Separatists if they weren't already.

437   Robert Browne, a major early influence in the development of Separatism, had founded a Separatist congregation in Norwich about 1581. That congregation may have been active when the Fullers were young men. See Morgan, *Visible Saints*, 18.

438   *Bradford Journal*, 10

The Scrooby congregation, including Bradford, escaped to Holland in 1608 and eventually settled in the university town of Leiden under the leadership of their pastor, John Robinson.[439] At some point Samuel Fuller became part of the Leiden congregation, later joined by his brother Edward with wife and children.[440]

Holland was a Protestant country and, in 1609, a safe haven for English religious dissidents. But how long would it remain a safe haven? Only recently, the Dutch had fought Spain to a standstill, gaining a twelve-year truce that would expire in 1620. During those truce years the Separatists were able to live, work and maintain their congregation in Leiden. But their employment opportunities were limited (mostly to the weaving and dyeing trades) and they had other concerns.

With the expiration of the Spanish truce in 1620, there was some risk that Holland would again come under the Spanish thumb, in which case the Separatists and other Protestants in Holland would be rounded up and executed. They also feared the very tolerance that allowed them to live and worship as they pleased in Holland; they feared losing their children to the temptations of the Dutch secular melting pot. In other words, they had religious freedom in Holland; what they really wanted was to create their own religious community in which theirs would be the only religion. They were self-righteous and they were intolerant.

They saw the uninhabited coast of America as an opportunity to spread the Gospel, and the unexplored new continent as the "promised land."[441] They believed they were in the hands of God doing His work. But they were human, and they weren't blind to the prospect of acquiring land and achieving prosperity.

In 1620, there was abundant information available on the New World. The Spanish had long ago established themselves in North and South America and the French were busy exploring the Northeast. Not until 1584 did Sir Walter Raleigh establish the first English settlement, on Roanoke Island just inside

---

439 *Bradford Journal,* 17, n.2. The congregation initially settled in Amsterdam, but decided to move to Leiden, which granted their application February 12, 1609. George Willison, *Saints and Strangers* (H. Wolff, N.Y. 1945): 60, places Fuller in Amsterdam by 1608. Fuller was later part of the Leiden congregation. Their first pastor, Richard Clyfton, preferred to remain in Amsterdam.
440 See George Willison, *Saints and Strangers* (New York; H. Wolff, 1945), 60, suggesting that Samuel Fuller was a member of a Separatist congregation in Amsterdam before the arrival of the Scrooby Separatists, and that he joined the Scrooby congregation in Leiden when the Amsterdam Separatists split up over doctrinal differences.
441 *Mourt's Relation:* 12

the Outer Banks; but that settlement disappeared without a trace.[442] The Separatist leaders in Leiden knew all about Jamestown, established in 1607 by the Virginia Company as the first permanent English settlement on the East coast. The Virginia Company tried to recruit them to settle in Virginia.

Establishing a permanent settlement on the Atlantic coast was a risky proposition. On Roanoke, most of the settlers had been victims of either starvation or hostile Indians; Jamestown had barely survived—during the first year 66 of 104 settlers died, mainly from disease. All other attempts north of Jamestown had failed, notably the 1607 Popham settlement at the mouth of the Kennebec River in Maine, which lasted one year through a very cold New England winter.[443]

Weighing the options, the Leiden Separatists decided to settle near the Hudson River, then regarded as within Virginia, but far enough from Jamestown to effectively insulate them from the Jamestown (and Anglican) authorities.[444] To raise the money to pay for the voyage, they sold their possessions, pooled their resources, and negotiated financing from a group of London investors. The investors, putting up cash and looking to squeeze profit from a risky venture, imposed hard terms.[445]

On July 22, 1620, the group set out in the *Speedwell* from Amsterdam bound for Southampton, England. Bradford, writing many years later, described them as "pilgrims:"

> So they left that goodly and pleasant city which had been their
> resting place near twelve years; but they knew they were pilgrims, and looked not much on those things, but lift up their

---

442   The Separatist leaders may have been familiar with Thomas Harriot's *Briefe and True Report of the New Found Land of Virginia*, published in 1588. In 1589, Richard Hakluyt published *the principall navigations... of the English nation,* a comprehensive study of all the English coastal explorations up to that point. Hakluyt's book played a major role in publicizing the commercial opportunities for England in the New World.

443   Popham was abandoned when the head of the settlement, Raleigh Gilbert, had to return to England to assume his inheritance. There was no leader among the remaining settlers, so all returned with him, much to the chagrin of Sir Ferdinando Gorges, sponsor of the expedition. Gorges also attributed the failure to a frigid New England winter.

444   See *Bradford Journal*: 28-29. In 1596, after another of his voyages, Raleigh published a glowing description of Guiana as a possible settlement. The charter of the Virginia colony included Manhattan and Long Island (which the Dutch also claimed by virtue of Henry Hudson's 1609 exploration of the river named for him).

445   A joint stock company would be formed; each share in the company would be worth ten pounds; each settler would receive one share; all land and property would be held in common for seven years, at which point everything was to be divided, reduced to cash and distributed according to shares. During the seven years, the settlers would have to work full time for the venture and could own no property or housing. In effect, it would take them seven years of servitude to pay for their passage.

eyes to the heavens, their dearest country, and quieted their spirits.[446]

They intended to sail to America on two ships: the *Speedwell,* to be used for fishing and coastal trading, and the larger *Mayflower.* But after leaving Southampton, the *Speedwell* sprang a leak and was forced to return. Her passengers were then loaded onto a very crowded *Mayflower,* which left Southampton on September 6 with 101 passengers: tailors, merchants, wool combers, weavers, sawyers, hatters, and one "cooper," John Alden.[447] The Pilgrims comprised less than half the passengers; the rest were fortune-seekers recruited by the investors. Among the Pilgrims, William Brewster, who had attended Cambridge, was the only one with a university education. With their pastor, Robinson, staying behind in Leiden, Brewster, as the ruling elder of the church, was their de facto pastor.[448]

During the long voyage, the Atlantic storms cracked a main beam, a potentially fatal disaster that could have sent the Pilgrims to the bottom of the ocean. A passenger had brought a "great iron screw" from Holland, apparently for use in a printing press. They used it to raise the beam back into place and the ship was saved.[449]

The *Mayflower* finally reached Cape Cod on November 9, 1620 (more than two months after leaving England) and immediately turned south toward its intended destination—the Hudson River. Two days later, faced with dangerous sailing conditions, they turned back to a safe anchor off Provincetown.[450] They lacked legal authority to settle in New England (their patent was for Virginia), and some of the "strangers" were making mutinous speeches, refusing to

---

446   *Bradford Journal,* 47. The Leiden group didn't refer to themselves as "pilgrims." Bradford, writing years later, used the biblical reference to "pilgrims" and it stuck. Henceforth, the Leiden Separatists will be referred to as "Pilgrims."
447   A "cooper" was a barrel maker. That was important because by law any ship leaving England with wooden barrels was required to return with an equal number.
448   *Bradford Journal*: 179. Robinson, who died before he could join the Pilgrims in Plymouth, was an exceptional individual whose moderating influence might have softened the hard edges of the Pilgrims. See Philbrick, *Mayflower,* 162-163. It was not until 1636 that the Plymouth church had a satisfactory minister. They rejected John Lyford, sent by the investors; a Rev. Rogers, brought over in 1628, was sent back, Bradford noting that he was "crased in his braine."
449   *Mourt's Relation,* 25; *Bradford Journal,* 58-59. As Bradford described it, without the "great iron screw" they would have been forced to turn back.
450   *Bradford Journal*: 60. Was there a Dutch plot to keep the *Mayflower* away from the Hudson? The editor, Samuel Eliot Morison, states "there is no basis in fact" for the theory that the ship's master was bribed by the Dutch. Morison, thoroughly familiar with the waters around the Cape, takes Bradford's explanation—that the *Mayflower* was forced by dangerous sailing conditions to turn back to the Cape—at face value.

recognize anybody's authority.[451] Faced with chaos, Bradford and the other Pilgrim leaders drafted a short and simple agreement for their governance and got it approved by enough men, Separatists and strangers, to make it stick. The signers by consent established a government and agreed to submit to "just and equal laws." [452] The agreement avoided a mutiny, enabled the group to impose order on a chaotic situation, and thereby served its purpose.

But the Pilgrims faced a daunting prospect. It was winter; they had no shelter outside their ship, and the captain was anxious to get rid of them and return home; the long voyage had left them with few provisions and no prospect of getting more until spring, and their only information about New England was Captain John Smith's description and maps of the coast. In Bradford's words:

> they had now no friends to welcome them, nor inns to entertain or refresh their weather-beaten bodies, no houses or much less towns to repair to... what could they see but a hideous and desolate wilderness, full of wild beasts and wild men? ...What could now sustain them but the Spirit of God and his grace?[453]

They found a good harbor and land for settlement at "Plimoth," so described on John Smith's map. The land had recently been an Indian settlement, but a plague that swept up and down the coast had wiped out the Indian population. Instead of finding thickly settled communities, the Pilgrims found little evidence of Indian life. During their first winter, the Pilgrims lost half of their number to sickness. The survivors faced severe challenges: Indians, who even in reduced numbers could have easily slaughtered the small Pilgrim group; near famine conditions, and angry investors in London. Priscilla's ancestors, William

---

451   During the long voyage the legal landscape had changed. On November 3, with the *Mayflower* at sea, a Council for New England (including the indefatigable Sir Ferdinando Gorges) had been granted jurisdiction over an area from present-day Philadelphia north to the Gaspé Peninsula and "from sea to sea," a grant strenuously opposed by the Virginia Company. Whether the Pilgrims settled on the Hudson or north of the Hudson, they were now in "New England." Their Virginia charter was no longer valid. They had no charter to settle in New England, but were soon granted one by the Council.

452   *Bradford Journal*, 76; *Mourt's Relation*, 26-28. Governance by consent was something the Separatists were used to; they elected their own pastors, and this was one of the things that had set them at odds with the Anglican authorities in England. The Mayflower Compact was far from democratic. Not all the men and none of the women signed the document. See Stratton, *Plymouth Colony*: 141-153, for a discussion of governance in the Colony. See also Letter, dated July 1620, from John Robinson to William Bradford, *Bradford Journal*, 368-370, containing Robinson's views of governance.

453   *Bradford Journal*, 62; *Mourt's Relation*, 31-47, provides a day-by-day account of these first explorations. While the *Mayflower* was anchored off the Cape, Bradford's wife, Dorothy, fell overboard and drowned. Later in 1623 Bradford married Alice (Carpenter) Southworth, who arrived that summer on the *Anne*. Alice had been married in Leiden to Edward Southworth, who died.

Bradford, Myles Standish, John Alden, and Dr. Samuel Fuller, led Plymouth Colony through the challenges of its early years.

William Bradford: Bradford was annually elected governor for most of the years 1621-1657. Bradford's leadership was critical to the success of Plymouth. Managing Indian relations was his first challenge.[454]

The local tribe, the Pokanokets (Wampanoags), saw the Pilgrims as useful allies against the powerful Narragansetts, the Pokanoket's enemies. Separated by language and culture, Pilgrims and Indians needed an interpreter. By a stroke of good luck, Squanto appeared on the scene. An Indian who had learned some English, he was immensely helpful to the Pilgrims. Bradford, with the other Pilgrim leaders, negotiated a treaty with the Pokanokets that kept the peace for fifty years.[455] When the Narragansetts delivered a snakeskin with arrows, Squanto explained to the puzzled Pilgrims that it was a challenge. Bradford promptly returned the snakeskin, loaded with powder and bullets. The Narragansetts chose not to call Bradford's bluff.

Bradford faced another serious challenge with the investors who had financed the Mayflower voyage.

By 1623 it was clear that the terms of the agreement were too onerous, particularly the requirement that all property be held in common for seven years. Common ownership of everything wasn't working. People were disgruntled; some worked hard, others didn't, and food production was inadequate, leaving the colony in danger of starvation. To remedy the situation, Bradford and the other leaders distributed an acre to each man, who was allowed to keep what he produced for his family.

---

454   The Pilgrim attitude toward the Indians was practical—they were, after all, vastly outnumbered— but underlying their practical approach were assumptions common to Europeans at the time. In his journal, Bradford described America as "vast and unpeopled,... where there are only savage and brutish men which range up and down, little otherwise than the wild beasts of the same." The Pilgrims, like most Europeans, just did not regard the natives as "people." They assumed that King James possessed the legal authority to establish English settlements anywhere in America. They recognized that France, Holland, and Spain made similar claims, but the notion that non-white "savages" could lay a superior claim would have seemed preposterous. Land not occupied and ruled by a "civilized" Christian country was deemed "uninhabited," ripe for settlement and commercial exploitation.

455   Squanto had been kidnapped, sold into slavery, escaped and ended up in the custody of Sir Ferdinando Gorges in Plymouth, England. He had made his way back to the New England coast in 1619 on board Captain Thomas Dermer's ship and, on Gorges' instructions, was released. According to Dermer, Squanto's entire tribe had been virtually wiped out by the plague. See *Mourt's Relation*, 60-62; Letter, from Thomas Dermer to Samuel Purchas, published in Samuel Purchas, *Purchas His Pilgrimmes* (London, 1625); *Bradford Journal*, 79-81.Philbrick, *Mayflower*, 120. 130-34.

It was a courageous decision, but the investors reacted sharply. They charged Bradford with violating the agreement; they charged that the Pilgrims were "negligent, careless, wasteful, unthrifty," spending their time in "idleness..."[456] They tried to use their influence in Parliament to undermine the colony and its leaders. Bradford had clearly made more enemies with the decision to distribute land. But private ownership, even of one acre, proved a much-needed stimulus for increased food production.[457]

The investors severely tested Bradford's leadership in 1624. One group of investors, determined to make major changes in Plymouth, sent over a preacher, the Reverend John Lyford, to serve as pastor. Lyford was no ordinary pastor. He and his co-conspirator, John Oldham, both of whom had arrived on the *Anne* in 1623, secretly gathered accusations against Bradford and the other leaders. The accusations reflected a certain amount of discontent within the colony. Lyford and Oldham included their accusations in letters addressed to influential people in England.

An alert Bradford got aboard the ship that was to carry the letters, seized and copied them, and called a public meeting of the entire colony. Confronted with their accusations, the accusers backed down, were discredited, and banished from the Colony.[458] Lyford's disgruntled London supporters saw Bradford's actions, not as a justifiable defense of the Colony by a strong leader, but as further evidence that Plymouth was being run as a tight little religious community, intolerant of those who "in all points, both civil and religious, jump not with you..." But the Lyford episode was a challenge that could have destroyed the community.

Myles Standish: When force was required, Bradford relied on Myles Standish. Standish had not been part of the Leiden congregation. Probably from Lancashire, England, with experience as a professional soldier in Queen Elizabeth's army, he was described as "short, stocky, with red hair and beard and a

---

456   *Governor William Bradford's Letter Book* (Bedford, MA; Applewood Books, reprinted 2001), 4 (letter, dated December 18, 1624, from four investors to Bradford).

457   *Bradford Journal*, 120-121 Relations with the investors continued to worsen. Despite shipments of valuable beaver pelts to London, high interest rates actually increased the size of the Plymouth debt. Bradford sent Isaac Allerton to London, and in late 1626 he negotiated a final settlement: the Plymouth colonists would purchase all the shares held by the investors for £1,800, to be paid at the annual rate of £200 pounds. This proposal was debated, accepted and signed by fifty-eight members of the colony, including Samuel Fuller and Edward Fuller's surviving son, young Samuel. To expedite the repayment, eight of the leading members of the colony, including Bradford, John Alden and Myles Standish, entered into an agreement with the rest of the fifty-eight purchasers in which the eight assumed the colony's entire debt in return for all the shares and exclusive trading privileges for a period of time. But this did not end the matter, which dragged on until a final settlement was reached with the last creditor in 1645. See Stratton, *Plymouth Colony*: 69.

458   See *Bradford Journal*, 147-167.

ruddy face which quickly took fire when he lost his temper." A man of great personal courage, he could be quick, decisive and violent. His enemies referred to him as "Captain Shrimp," though probably not to his face.[459]

In March 1623, the Pilgrims faced a moment of great peril. They believed, on apparently reliable evidence, that the Massachusetts Indians were about to attack a settlement at Wessagusett (Weymouth) and, with the aid of other tribes, Plymouth as well. Such an attack could have meant the end of Plymouth. Bradford and the other Pilgrim leaders directed Standish to take an armed force to Wessagusett and nip the conspiracy in the bud. Standish took only eight men. At Wessagusett, Standish met with the most prominent Indian warriors. Pecksuot, a tall Indian, tried to intimidate him while Witawamat, another large Indian, conspicuously sharpened his knife in front of Standish. Edward Winslow, one of the Plymouth leaders, described what happened:[460]

> Pecksuot, being a man of greater stature than the Captain, told him, though he were a great Captain, yet he was but a little man; and said he, though I be no sachem, yet I am a man of great strength and courage. These things the Captain observed, yet bare with patience for the present.

> On the next day...this Pecksuot and Wituwamat both together, with another man, and a youth of some eighteen years of age... and [Standish] having about as many of his own company in a room with them, gave the word to his men, and the door being fast shut, began himself with Pecksuot, and snatching his knife from his neck, though with much struggling, killed him therewith. ...Wituwamat and the other man the rest killed, and took the youth, whom the Captain caused to be hanged...

Standish and his men followed up by attacking the nearby village and killing more Indians. When news of the killings got out, the Indians in the area fled their villages, terrified of Standish and his eight-man army.[461] News of the

---

459 Bradford Smith, *Bradford of Plymouth* (Philadelphia; J. B. Lippincott, 1951), 124.

460 Edward Winslow: *Good Newes from New England* (first published in London, 1624; reprinted by Applewood Books, Bedford, MA), 47-48.

461 While Standish was treated as a hero back in Plymouth, the conflict had unfortunate consequences for the fur trade on which Plymouth depended. The Indians with whom they had been trading had all fled their villages, greatly reducing the availability of furs.

events at Wessagusett reached Robinson, the Pilgrims' pastor in Leiden, who was horrified. He wrote to Bradford:

> Concerning the killing of those poor Indians... You will say they deserved it. I grant it; but upon what provocations and invitements by those heathenish Christians? [The English settlers at Wessagusett]. Besides, you being no magistrates over them were to consider not what they deserved but what you were by necessity constrained to inflict. Necessity of this, especially of killing so many (and many more, it seems, they would, if they could) I see not.

> Upon this occasion let me be bold to exhort you seriously to consider the disposition of your Captain... He is a man humble and meek amongst you, and towards all in ordinary course. But...there is cause to fear that by occasion, especially of provocation, there may be wanting that tenderness of the life of man (made after God's image) which is meet.[462]

Despite Robinson's admonition, Bradford recognized Standish's value as military leader and wise counselor. Both men saw that the Indians could, if they chose, wipe out the Plymouth settlement; both were aware of the Jamestown massacre of 1622, when the Powhattan Indians killed 347 settlers. Standish was a man of boldness and courage, qualities respected by the Indians, and he made sure the Pilgrims were feared. What Robinson, sitting in Leiden, saw as a questionable human quality probably served Plymouth well in the American wilderness.

Outnumbered, never knowing when the Indians might turn to war, hearing rumors that might or might not be reliable about Indian intentions, Bradford relied on Standish to organize the community for rapid response to any attack. A Dutch visitor to "New Plymouth" described an armed community ready for war on a moment's notice:

> New Plymouth lies on the slope of a hill stretching east towards the sea-coast....Upon the hill they have a large square

---

462 *Bradford Journal*, 374-375 (Robinson's letter). See also *Bradford Journal*, 113-119, which contains a brief description of the affair, and Philbrick, *Mayflower*, 146-153, who provides much more detail

house, with a flat roof... upon the top of which they have six cannon, which shoot iron balls of four and five pounds, and command the surrounding country. The lower part they use for their church, where they preach on Sundays and the usual holidays.

They assemble by beat of drum, each with his musket or fire-lock, in front of the captain's door; they have their cloaks on, and place themselves in order, three abreast, and are led by a sergeant without beat of drum. Behind comes the Governor, in a long robe; beside him on the right hand comes the preacher with his cloak on, and on the left hand, the captain with his side-arms and cloak on, and with a small cane in his hand; and so they march in good order, and each sets his arms down near him. Thus they are constantly on their guard night and day.[463]

John Alden: Alden had started out as a young "cooper" or barrel maker looking for adventure. He was not part of the Leiden group, but was one of the "strangers" on the *Mayflower*. Bradford saw potential in him, and he became a leader in the Colony, holding various important positions over a long lifetime. Alden was best known for the story of his courtship and marriage of Priscilla Mullins.[464]

He had been one of twenty-three bachelors on the *Mayflower*. Priscilla Mullins, eighteen, had been one of three single girls. According to the story, in the winter of 1621 after the death of his wife, Myles Standish set his sights on Priscilla and asked his good friend, John Alden, to speak on his behalf to Mr. Mullins.[465] John, tall and handsome, spoke eloquently. Priscilla, listening and

---

463   Sydney James, Jr. ed., *Three Visitors to Early Plymouth* .(Bedford, MA; Applewood Books, 1997), 77
464   Alden was born in 1599, Southampton, Hampshire, England. He was barely twenty-one when he joined the Pilgrims aboard the *Mayflower*. Priscilla was born in 1601 in Dorking, Surrey, to William Mullins and Alice Atwood. After John and Priscilla married, in about 1622, he rose to prominence in the community, serving as one of eight undertakers responsible for paying off the Plymouth debt. Later, he served as assistant to the Plymouth governor from 1633 and as first assistant from 1666 to his death in 1686 at eighty-seven. In 1643 he served on a council of war for the New England colonies, charged with coordinating the military response to warlike actions of the Narragansett Indians. In 1657 to 1658 he participated in the action of the Plymouth Court banishing the Quakers and making it a crime, punishable by whipping or fine, to harbor a Quaker. In a letter of December 1658 to friends in England, James Cudworth, a major figure in the Colony, expressed his disappointment with Alden: "Mr. Alden hath deceived the Expectations of many, and indeed lost the affections of such, as I judge were his Cordial Christian Friends; who is very active in such Ways, as I pray God may not be charged him, to be Oppressions of a High Nature."
465   The Reverend Timothy Alden published the family story in 1814, later embellished by Longfellow in *The Courtship of Myles Standish*.

watching, fixed her eyes on Alden and said "Prithee, John, why do you not speak for yourself?" Alden blushed, bowed, made his excuses and left.[466] Of course he returned, courted and married Priscilla sometime during 1621 or 1622. Theirs was the second marriage in the colony.

It's a nice story and one of the few bright spots in that first horrendous winter when half the settlers died. The story was certainly accepted as true by Priscilla Fuller.[467] But there's no evidence that Standish ever regarded Alden as abusing his trust. The two were lifelong friends and neighbors in Plymouth and later in Duxbury, and Standish, at some personal risk, helped get Alden out of a Boston jail in 1634 where he was being held for the murder of a Massachusetts Bay man.[468]

Dr. Samuel Fuller. Plymouth was a well-established settlement in 1630 having grown from fifty survivors to a robust community of about three hundred. But in 1630, a much larger and better-financed settlement to the north immediately dwarfed Plymouth, as John Winthrop and his well-connected group of Puritans sailed into Boston harbor and established the Massachusetts Bay Colony.[469] Winthrop's Puritans, especially the Cambridge-educated Boston preachers, looked down their noses at Plymouth.

As a goodwill gesture to the newcomers and perhaps to keep an eye on them, Bradford sent Fuller to the Bay to minister to the sick, advise on religious matters, and report back on the situation. Fuller met privately with Governor Winthrop, whom he described as "a godly, wise and humble gentleman, and very discreet, and of a fine and good temper." Fuller noted that "We have some privy enemies in the bay (but blessed be God) more friends….opposers there is not wanting and satan is busy; but if the Lord be on our side who can be against us…."

Bradford had also asked Fuller to go farther North in response to a plea from John Endicott, the Salem leader, for help in dealing with an epidemic. Governor Winthrop had also requested Fuller and his colleagues to advise the Salem leaders

---

466 Alicia Crane Williams ed, *Mayflower Families Through Five Generations (Plymouth, MA; General Society of Mayflower Descendants, 1975—),* Vol. 16, Part 1: 2-3.

467 Conditions in Plymouth during the winter of 1621 were horrendous, with half the colony dying and most of the rest sick. Standish's wife, Rose, died in January; Priscilla Mullins' father and mother died in February. Priscilla was an orphan when she married Alden. Sometime before 1624 Standish married Barbara, who had arrived in 1623 on the *Anne.*

468 *Bradford Journal,* 263-265. Stratton, *Plymouth Colony,* 48. Alden, an assistant to the Plymouth governor, was on a visit to the Plymouth trading post on the Kennebec River (Fort Popham). John Hocking, a resident of the Massachusetts Bay Colony visiting the Kennebec for trading purposes, refused to recognize the Plymouth claim and announced his intention to go up river and establish his own trading post. After remonstrating with him, John Howland, in charge of the Plymouth post, ordered the lines of Hocking's ship to be cut. Hocking shot the Plymouth man who had cut his ship's lines. Hocking, in turn, was shot and killed. On his return trip to Plymouth, Alden stopped at Boston and was promptly arrested on the basis of a one-sided report of the incident. Standish was sent up to Boston to set things straight and get Alden out of jail, which he did.

469 See Bremer, *John Winthrop,* 173-201.

what they could do "to pacify the Lord's wrath." The Plymouth group dutifully laid out a plan of action for the Salem people to pacify the Lord, which included setting aside a day for intense prayer and humility.[470] In addition to his religious counsel, Fuller ministered to the sick in Salem. Apparently, Fuller did a good job representing Plymouth, counseling the Salem settlers on practices in the Plymouth church and allaying their suspicions of Plymouth. John Endicott wrote Bradford:

> I acknowledge myself much bound to you for your kind love and care in sending Mr. Fuller among us, and rejoice much that I am by him satisfied touching your judgments of the outward form of God's worship. It is, as far as I can gather, no other than is warranted by the evidence of truth. And the same which I have professed and maintained ever since the Lord in mercy revealed Himself unto me. Being far from the common report that hath been spread of you touching that particular. [471]

That August, Fuller also visited Charlestown and described the desperate local situation:

> The sad news here is, that many are sick, and many are dead, the Lord in mercy look upon them!...I here but lose time and long to be at home, I can do them no good, for I want drugs and things fitting to work with. [472]

In Charlestown, Fuller encountered the same skepticism about Plymouth that he had found in Salem: "Here are divers honest Christians that are desirous to see us; some out of love, which they bear to us, and the good persuasion they have of us; others to see whether we be so evil, as they have heard... "[473]

Fuller's work among the newcomers in Massachusetts, allaying their suspicions and explaining Plymouth church practices, contributed to the Boston and

---

470 *The Mayflower Descendants*, 7:81.
471 *Bradford Journal*, 223-224.
472 The "drugs and things fitting to work with" were most likely herbal medicines and rudimentary sharp instruments to enable the physician to purge the body of blood and other fluids, consistent with seventeenth-century medical theory that disease was the result of an imbalance in body fluids.
473 *The Mayflower Descendants*, Vol. 7: 81.

Plymouth churches becoming more alike, with the Boston churches eventually adopting the congregational form of governance used in Plymouth.[474]

* * *

Dr. Samuel Fuller died in 1633 at the age of fifty-three. He lacked a formal university education, but left a substantial collection of about thirty books, including "physic books." In his will, Fuller provided for his nephew Samuel, now in his twenties and on his own:

> It. My will is that my Cozen [nephew] Samuell goe freely away
> with his stock of cattle and swine without any further reckon-
> ing wch swine are the halfe of six sowes, six hogges, one boare
> and four shotes. Also one Cow and one heifer. [475]

Fuller also took great pains to provide for the education of his children in the event Bridget, who was in "a weak estate of sickness," died. Bridget Fuller didn't die; a formidable lady, she lived until at least 1667, thriving as a property owner, educator and midwife in the Plymouth community.

William Bradford and Myles Standish long outlived Dr. Fuller. In his last years, still serving as governor, Bradford was a disappointed man. He saw original settlers acquiring extensive lands, moving out of Plymouth and forming new communities along the coast: Duxbury, Scituate, Marshfield and Barnstable. To Bradford this dispersion was driven by greed and the pursuit of material wealth; it ran counter to everything he had worked for: his vision of Plymouth as a self-contained cohesive religious community. His own words convey the sadness he felt:

> And no man now thought he could live except he had cattle
> and a great deal of ground to keep them, all striving to increase
> their stocks. By which means they were scattered all over the

---

474   After 1636 or so, the Massachusetts churches applied the strictest tests for church admission, probing applicants for evidence that they had received saving faith and were thus destined for salvation. The Plymouth and Connecticut churches applied similar tests, but perhaps more charitably. All the Congregational churches were independent, elected there own ministers, and set their own admissions procedures. This form of congregationalism became a distinctive feature of seventeenth century New England. Those Puritans who sought greater uniformity among churches and a governing structure became Presbyterians. See Morgan, *Visible Saints*, 99-112.
475   Robert Charles Anderson, *The Great Migration* (Boston; New England Historic Genealogical Society, 1995), 1: 713-717. A "shote" is a young hog of either sex less than a year old.

Bay quickly and the town in which they lived compactly till now was left very thin and in a short time almost desolate." [476]

William Bradford died in 1657.[477] Like Fuller and Standish, Bradford was self-educated.[478] Standish had died the year before, leaving a library of several dozen books ranging from theology to Homer's *Iliad* and Caesar's *Commentaries*. Bradford had learned Dutch, French, Latin, Greek and Hebrew; written *Of Plimoth Plantation*, one of the masterpieces of American literature;[479] and left a library of a hundred or so books, heavily weighted toward religious topics.

Samuel Fuller (1634-1687). Following the death of his uncle, Dr. Fuller, young Samuel Fuller moved to the new town of Scituate. There he married Jane Lothrop in a ceremony performed by Captain Myles Standish.[480] Jane was the daughter of the Reverend John Lothrop, pastor of the church in Scituate, and his wife Hannah Howes.[481]

In the summer of 1639, dissension in the Scituate church caused the Reverend Lothrop and most of his congregation to move to what is now Barnstable, about thirty-five miles south. The Fullers moved to Barnstable in March 1650, Samuel and his brother Matthew Fuller having bought land on Scorton Neck from Seconke, an Indian.[482]

Matthew Fuller. Matthew Fuller was Samuel's older brother. Matthew arrived in Plymouth with wife and children sometime before October 1640.[483] After he and his brother moved their families to Barnstable, Matthew became prominent in the community as physician, deputy to the Plymouth General Court, chairman of the Council of War, and Captain of Plymouth Colony forces in King Philip's War.[484]

---

476 Bradford, *Journal*, 253.
477 Bradford died at Plymouth, May 9, 1657. Myles Standish died at Duxbury, October 3, 1656. John Alden outlived everybody. He died at Duxbury, 12 September 12, 1687.
478 Myles Standish left a library of several dozen books ranging from theology to Homer's *Iliad* and Caesar's *Commentaries*.
479 Bradford's manuscript was passed down through various Bradfords, but disappeared from a private library in Boston during the Revolution. Late in the nineteenth century, it was discovered in the Bishop of London's library and, after negotiations, returned to Boston in 1897.
480 They married April 18, 1635. W. H. Fuller, *The Edward Fuller Family* (Palmer, MA; C.B.Fiske & Co. 1908), 24.
481 Hannah Howes was born September 29, 1614 at Edgerly, Kent, England. Her father had arrived in Boston in 1634 with his family and thirty church members, moving immediately to Scituate.
482 On March 25, 1650, Fuller conveyed his Scituate property, including "one dwelling house and a barne and Cowhouse" to Peter Collymore, with Jane Fuller giving her consent to the transfer two months later. See *Mayflower Descendants*, Vol. 1:91; Fuller, *Edward Fuller Family*, 28.
483 According to Plymouth records, on October 26, 1640, Matthew Fuller sold to Andrew Ringe of Plymouth, property in Plymouth "lately bought of John Gregory," *Plymouth Colony Records, Deeds*, 1:64.
484 Bruce Campbell MacGunnigle, *Mayflower Families*, Vol.4 (Edward Fuller): 5-6. He was granted 10 acres of land by Plymouth in April 1642.

One history of Barnstable refers to Matthew Fuller as a "hot headed soldier and litigious."[485] When Plymouth imposed a pulpit tax for the support of the church and its ministers, Fuller strongly objected, declaring that, "surely the Devill sat in the stern when the General Court passed this wicked" law."[486] To Matthew Fuller and other "liberals" in the Colony, compulsory support of an established church was the reason they had left England. The Plymouth General Court fined Fuller fifty shillings for his outspoken remarks.

Fuller also took a public stand on the side of the unpopular Quakers, vigorously arguing in favor of religious toleration and condemning the laws passed against the sect. Again, he was fined fifty shillings for speaking up.[487]

In 1676 Matthew Fuller, age seventy, led the Plymouth forces in "King Philip's War,"a war the English almost lost to the Indian alliance forged by Philip, chief of the Wampanoags.

It was a close call. After a year of losses, the English were reduced to a few defensive enclaves on the coast. In 1677 the tide turned, as the English methodically destroyed Indian food supplies and enlisted other Indians to fight Philip's tribes. By the end of the year, the English had cornered Philip, killed him, and hung his head on a pole in Plymouth.[488]

During those two years, war raged over all of New England, from Connecticut to Maine. It was the bloodiest conflict in American history measured by the dead as a percentage of the population. The victors showed no mercy, selling many of the Indian survivors into slavery.[489]

Matthew Fuller died in Barnstable during the summer of 1678, leaving his family one of the largest estates of the time, valued at £ 667. Samuel Fuller died in Barnstable sometime in the fall of 1683. Jane Lothrop Fuller was dead by then, but there is no record of when she died. A granddaughter of Matthew Fuller, Mehitable, married Samuel Fuller's son, John.

In his will, Samuel Fuller left ample real property divided among his two surviving sons. John, the younger, received cattle, a house, a three-year old horse, a "Great Bible," one "fatt cow," and his father's slave, "the Indian, Joel." The two surviving daughters got four pounds each.[490]

---

485   Donald Trayser, *Barnstable: Three Centuries of a Cape Cod Town* (Hyannis, MA; F.B. & F.P. Goss, 1939), 173.
486   Paul Wesley Prindle, *Ancestry of Elizabeth Barrett Gillespie* (Summit, NJ; P.W. Prindle, 1976), 159.
487   Prindle, 159.
488   Eric B. Schultz and Michael J. Tougias, *King Philip's War, the History and Legacy of America's Forgotten Conflict* (Woodstock, VT; Countryman Press 1999), 290.
489   Schultz and Tougias, 5. The death rate as a percentage of the population was 1.5 percent vs. .85 percent of a much larger population during the Civil War.
490   Fuller, *Edward Fuller Family,* 28-29

John Fuller (1656-1726): Connecticut River Valley. In 1694 John Fuller was thirty-eight, and married to his cousin, Mehitable Rowley, granddaughter of Matthew Fuller and great-granddaughter of Edward Fuller (John and Mehitable had grown up together on Scorton Neck). That year, John and Mehitable packed up their family and moved to Haddam on the Connecticut River, about 100 miles south and west, in search of better and cheaper farmland. In Haddam, John and Mehitable were surrounded by Rowleys and Fullers.

In 1694, the Connecticut River Valley already had a long history. Trading posts had been established along the river in the 1620s by the Dutch from Manhattan and the English from Plymouth. Traders streaming into Connecticut soon overran these posts. By the late 1630s both Connecticut and New Haven were colonies, on a par with Massachusetts and Plymouth.[491]

When John and Mehitable Fuller arrived in 1694, there were several hundred people living in Haddam, about twenty miles inland from Saybrook where the river flows into the Atlantic Ocean. That year the small group of people living on the east side of the river, including Fuller's and Rowley's, petitioned for their own church. The petition met determined opposition from the minister of the Haddam church, Rev. Jeremiah Hobart, who felt the settlers on the east side should continue to cross the river for services and support his church on the west side. But the Eastsiders gained the right to establish their own church, doing so in 1702 under Stephen Hosmer, a recent Harvard graduate.[492] The Rowleys and the John Fullers were among the early members of the new church. In 1706 John Fuller was appointed to a committee to assign seats in the new church, a delicate diplomatic assignment.[493]

John Fuller died at seventy on March 23, 1726.[494] In his will, he conveyed land and farming implements to each of his sons and made provision for his surviving wife.[495]

Mehitable received a cow of her choice, eight sheep, four pounds, her bed, and a room of her own. She could make do on the farm with her cow and sheep, and she could count on her sons and daughters to see that she was well cared for.

---

491   English migration to the Connecticut River Valley had led to the Pequot War in 1637. The Pequot Indians, who inhabited much of Connecticut, reacted violently to the inflow of English settlers. Connecticut and New Haven were hit hard by the Pequots and later by King Philip's Indians, but by the time John Fuller arrived in 1694, thanks to the determined and sometimes brutal warfare waged by the New England colonies, the Indians were no longer a serious threat in the southern portion of the Connecticut River Valley
492   Francis Hubert Parker, *Contributions to the History of East Haddam, Connecticut* (Hartford, CT; publisher unknown, 1938), 13-14.
493   Parker, *East Haddam*, 22. East Haddam officially became a separate town in 1734.
494   MacGunnigle, *Mayflower Families*, 4:16.
495   As to Mehitabel's probable date of death, see MacGunnigle, *Mayflower Families*, 4:16; Fuller, *Edward Fuller Family*, 34.

Mehitable's family all lived in East Haddam, and she could expect her daughters to visit, clean, help with the cooking and baking, check on her health, and see that her medical needs were met. She died in 1732.

The daughters didn't get much from John's will. Thankful got "what she has already in brass, pewter, etc"; Elizabeth got "sundry valuables she has already received"; daughter Mehitable, in addition to what she had already received, got "a coverlid, an iron pott which she has not as yet received, and also the bedd I lie upon after mine and my wife's decease, not before." John wanted to make sure nobody took that bed away from his widow. [496]

John and Mehitable were buried in the Old Cove Burying Ground—the original burying ground on the east side of the river—in a grave now unmarked.[497] All of John and Mehitable Fuller's twelve children settled in and around East Haddam.

Thomas Fuller (1679-1772): A Farming Life. Born in Barnstable in 1679, Thomas Fuller was fifteen when the family moved to East Haddam. In about 1714, Thomas married Elizabeth, born in Barnstable about the same year as Thomas.[498] Thomas was a farmer who also rendered long service as a lieutenant in the East Haddam militia.[499]

The Fullers lived to a ripe old age: Thomas died at ninety-four on April 9, 1772; Elizabeth lived through the Revolution and died at ninety-six on November 5, 1784.[500]

Thomas and Elizabeth had seven children—six sons and a daughter—all born and raised in East Haddam. They lived to see a grandson graduate from Yale in 1762.[501] By the time of Elizabeth Fuller's death, with three generations of large families, there were hundreds of Fullers living in and around East Had-

---

496   Fuller: *Edward Fuller Family*, 35; *Connecticut Probate Records*, 1723-1729: 509-510.
In East Haddam, the Fuller and Rowley families continued to intermarry, with five of John and Mehitabel Fuller's children marrying Rowley cousins. Most of the Fuller-Rowley children settled in Connecticut towns: East Haddam, Colchester, Hebron, Kent, and Sharon.
497   Parker, *East Haddam*: 41. Apparently, the earliest burial markers in the graveyard were rocks without inscriptions.
498   There's a record of Elizabeth's formal "dismissal" from the West Church in Barnstable to East Haddam in May 1726, twelve years after their marriage. Perhaps Thomas, as a young bachelor, returned to Barnstable, courted and married Elizabeth there, and around 1726 brought his growing family back to East Haddam to live on the land he inherited that year from his father. Elizabeth was possibly Elizabeth Church, born abt 1689 in Barnstable. (See <www.Ancestry.com> Ebenezer Fuller Family Tree).
499   Parker, *East Haddam*: 30, 47.
500   MacGunnigle, *Mayflower Families* 4: 43; Fuller, *Edward Fuller Family*: 40-42. "Relect" (relict), was a widow.
501   Daniel Fuller, son of Thomas Fuller and Martha Rowley, born April 22, 1739, graduated from Yale in 1762 and served as pastor of the church in Hartan, Nova Scotia. Parker, *East Haddam*, 159d.

dam and Colchester. At one time there were four "Thomas" Fullers, called 1st, 2nd, 3rd and 4th to tell them apart.

Ebenezer and Mary Fuller (1713-1798): French and Indian War. In 1738 Ebenezer Fuller, age twenty-three, son of Thomas and Elizabeth, packed up his belongings and moved to Hebron, a recently settled town (1704) about fifteen miles north of East Haddam, several hours by horse.[502] Like his father and grandfather, Ebenezer was a farmer and he needed land for his own farm.

Ebenezer's grandfather, John Fuller, had divided his farm among seven sons. Ebenezer's father, with one-seventh of the original John Fuller property, had six sons. Ebenezer saw the handwriting on the wall and struck out on his own.

When Ebenezer moved there, Hebron was a young and growing community with plenty of good farming land. From eight families in 1708, the town had grown to almost two hundred families by the early 1740s.[503] The parcel acquired by Ebenezer amounted to several hundred acres near the town center. Ebenezer also owned and operated a mill. A book of Hebron historical sites includes a picture of the "Fuller/Porter Grain Mill," with the caption "In 1740, Ebenezer Fuller ground corn at this mill site."[504]

After moving to Hebron, Ebenezer married his older cousin, Mary Rowley, age thirty, daughter of Moses and Martha Rowley of Colchester and East Haddam.[505] In eleven years of marriage Ebenezer and Mary had six children before Ebenezer died at age 34.[506] Mary, age forty-one, was carrying their sixth child.

Hebron had a one-room school house, built in the early 1700s, and Mary Fuller undoubtedly saw to it that her children attended, but only up to a point, because she also needed them to work and earn money.[507] As an additional source of income Mary transformed her home near Hebron Center into a small tavern to take advantage of the heavy stagecoach travel along the Hartford-New London route. Mary's "inn" was a small one-story home with a couple of rooms for travelers and an adjacent lunch place, where she sold gingerbread and cookies.[508]

With sons of military age, Mary was acutely affected by events beyond Hebron. By 1756, England had been embroiled in a long struggle with France

---

502 Ebenezer was born October 27, 1715 in East Haddam.
503 John Sibun, *Our Town's Heritage, 1708-1958, Hebron, Connecticut* (Hebron, CT; Douglas Library, 1975), 23.
504 *Hebron's Historical Heritage, A Selection of Historic Sites* (Hebron, CT; June 1992), Site 22.
505 MacGunnigle, *Mayflower Families*, 4: 130-131; Fuller, *Edward Fuller Family*, 141-142; *Town of Hebron Vital Records*, 1: 43; 2: 296. They married September 30, 1738. The frequency of Fuller-Rowley intermarriage reflected the insular life people lived, the infrequency of travel beyond farm and community, and that family gatherings were the best opportunity for boys and girls to meet and get to know one another.
506 He died September 30, 1749.
507 Sibun, *Our Town's Heritage*: 98 (picture of the Old Burrows Hill School House).
508 Sibun, *Our Town's Heritage*, 103.

for domination of the continent. That year, the struggle broke out into a full-scale world-wide war. England drew on its New England colonies for manpower. Two of Mary Fuller's boys, Ozias and Ebenezer, fought with the British. Ebenezer served in the campaign of 1758 in Captain Baldwin's Connecticut Company and later in a New York regiment during the 1762 campaign.[509] His brother Ozias enlisted on March 29, 1762, served as a drummer, and died in service at the age of seventeen the following October.[510] The war ended with an English victory in 1763. England sought to recoup the cost of the war by taxing her colonies, a strategy that led directly to the American Revolution.

In 1771, Mary Fuller turned over management of the Fuller Inn to Roger and retired. She lived on in Hebron until her death at age ninety on February 5, 1798.

6. Roger Fuller, Innkeeper (1747-1819). Roger Fuller, born in 1747 to Ebenezer and Mary Fuller, was two years old when his father died. At twenty-four, Roger was put in charge of the Fuller inn. As the local tavern-keeper, Roger Fuller was a man to be reckoned with.

With the outbreak of the Revolution in 1776, Roger was thirty and supporting his mother, wife, and half a dozen children with more on the way.

On Sunday night March 4, 1781, Roger entertained General Washington, and put the tall general up for the night in one of the Fuller Inn's small rooms. Washington was on his way to visit the headquarters of the Duke de Lauzun at Lebanon, where the French troops were quartered. The war would for all practical purposes end the following October 19 with the surrender of Cornwallis at Yorktown in Virginia. But that March, when Fuller entertained General Washington, victory was still far from certain.[511]

Long after the war, Roger transformed Mary's little tavern into a much grander establishment and renamed it "The Hebron Hotel." He continued to manage it until his death in 1819 when his son Erastus took over.[512] During his life as farmer and innkeeper, Roger married four times and outlived three wives.

---

509   According to his enlistment record, Ebenezer was 5'6" and a "taylor" by trade. *Collections of the Connecticut Historical Society*, Vol. X (Hartford; The Connecticut Historical Society, 1905), 92, 349.

510   Fuller, *Edward Fuller Family*, 142-143.

511   John Sibun: *Our Town's Heritage 1708-1958, Hebron, Connecticut* (Hebron 1975): 43, 103; J.R. Cole: *History of Tolland County Connecticut* (New York 1888): 346. According to the entry for Hebron written in 1888: "The hotel is as renowned for its good dinners to-day as it was when Washington stopped over..." Unfortunately, 1888 was not a good year for the Hebron Hotel; it burned to the ground that year. At the time of the fire Samuel Barber Fuller, 85 years old and the town clerk, was living in the hotel surrounded by all the old town records. Fuller survived but the records did not.

512   Fuller completed his rebuilding project in 1790.

Roger Fuller died at seventy-two on September 21, 1819. Of Roger's twelve children, Erastus stayed in Hebron and inherited the Hebron Hotel.

Humphrey Taylor Fuller (1786-1877): The Last Farmer. It was big news on October 24, 1814 when twenty-eight year-old Humphrey Taylor Fuller of Hebron, son of Roger and Violette Fuller, married Emma Johnson, daughter of Jedediah and Eunice (Dyar) Johnson in the Congregational Church of Canterbury, Connecticut.[513] The marriage was widely reported in the Connecticut newspapers, not because of the Fuller family, but because of the prominence of Emma's father.[514]

Emma's father Jedediah Johnson (Priscilla Fuller's great-great-grandfather) was a Revolutionary War veteran and an important figure in the state of Connecticut.

At the age of sixteen, Jedediah had enlisted in the Connecticut Militia and served three months in Captain Benjamin Bacon's Company stationed in Rhode Island near Providence. He served as personal orderly to Colonel Obadiah Johnson, the regimental commander and probably an uncle.[515] The next year, Johnson was drafted for another three-month tour and assigned to guard duty in New London under his father, Captain John Johnson. Drafted again in 1780 for yet another three-month tour in his father's company, he served in Groton. Drafted for a third time, he served one month, hired a substitute and went home.[516]

In 1789, he and other Revolutionary War veterans from Canterbury petitioned the Connecticut Legislature to form a light infantry company, arguing that formation of such a company would encourage military skill and discipline and capitalize on their experience.[517] The Legislature approved the formation of the new company, the men "to be equipped and dressed in uniforms at their own expense." Johnson thrived in the militia; by 1808 he had achieved the rank of

---

513 *Records of the Congregational Church in Canterbury Connecticut* 1711-1844, 171.

514 See *Norwich Courier*, 16 November 16, 1814, 134; *Middlesex Gazette*, November 1, 1814, 96; *Hartford Courant*, November 8, 1814, 191; *Connecticut Mirror*, November 7, 1814, 149; *Windham Herald*, November 3, 1814, 34 (all unattributed items).

515 It appears that Jedediah's father, John Johnson, and Obadiah Johnson were sons of Obadiah and Lydia Johnson. See *Connecticut Vital Records*, Barbour Collection, Windham County, Canterbury Vol. 1:168 (John b. 23 March 1730/31; Obadiah b. 18 February 1735/36.) Their birthdates match the ages on their gravestones in the Canterbury cemetery.

516 He may have served again in 1781, according to his affidavit of 12 April 1834 in support of his pension application, but by then his recollection of events was understandably sketchy. See Revolutionary War Pension Files, Lucy W7943, BLW # 27671-160-55 (National Archives, Washington, DC.)

517 Connecticut Archives, Militia Series 3 1738-1820, Vol. 111: 112b (Connecticut State Library)

brigadier general and commander of the 5ᵗʰ Brigade.[518] A history of Windham County described General Johnson on parade:

> His brief term of command was marked by great military activity. War rumors had re-kindled the flame of martial enthusiasm, for even those who disliked the war delighted in military parade. Mounted on a stately steed, and attended by a negro servant in appropriate uniform, General Johnson added great luster to those popular pageants.[519]

After serving four years as a general, Johnson, feeling a bit old at fifty for military service, submitted his resignation to Governor Roger Griswold on May 18, 1812; the resignation was accepted.[520]

Did Johnson resign because he was too old? Or were there other reasons? Perhaps he needed to spend more time on business—he was the local tavern keeper, among other things. But perhaps there were deeper reasons. The timing of Johnson's resignation is significant, coming just one month before President Madison's formal declaration of war against Britain in June 1812. Did Johnson resign because he was personally opposed to the war? Did he resign because he didn't want the responsibility of leadership in an unpopular war?

In May 1812, antiwar feeling in Connecticut was intense, and the war was denounced as "Mr. Madison's war." The governor refused to obey Madison's call for troops, and the Connecticut Assembly declared the state to be "free, sovereign and independent." The declaration of war in June 1812 produced strong secessionist sentiment throughout New England. Clearly, whoever was a general in the Connecticut militia in 1812 would be responsible for raising and commanding troops under extraordinarily difficult conditions.[521]

Eventually, Connecticut came around and committed its militia to the war, one in which the British appeared all too likely to win until Andrew Jackson's climactic 1815 victory in the Battle of New Orleans. It appears that Jedediah

---

518   Militia Series 3, Vol. X11: 89

519   Ellen D. Larned: *History of Windham County, Connecticut,* Vol. 2: 1760-1880 (Worcester, MA; Heritage Books, 1880), 323.

520   Johnson's letter of resignation began "Having considerably passed that period of life recognized by the laws of this state as suitably proper for military duty..." Militia Series 3, Vol. X11: 99a.

521   Charles and Mary Beard: *A Basic History of the United States,* (New York; Doubleday, 1944), 172-174.

served a two-month tour of duty in 1813 at his Revolutionary War rank of private, under Captain Medad Hotchkiss.[522]

Aside from his military service, Johnson was a prominent citizen of Canterbury. He owned and operated the local tavern on the Canterbury Green.[523] During 1796-1797 he represented Canterbury in the General Assembly at Hartford. In 1800 he was one of the incorporators of the "Norwich & Woodstock Turnpike Company," established to build a public highway from Norwich through Lisbon, Canterbury, Brooklyn, Pomfret, Woodstock, and Thompson to the Massachusetts line, now a scenic back road. Johnson was also a slave-owner: the 1820 census records Johnson as owner of one male slave.[524]

In 1834 Johnson applied for a pension under recent Congressional legislation, which for the first time granted pensions to Revolutionary War veterans.[525] But fifty years after the end of the war, it was tough to find anyone alive who could attest to his service. Johnson had to concede that "in my service at Providence & New London I have no testimony to show the service nor have I any documentary evidence. I have delayed making my application until this time in hopes to find some one who served with me in those services but have been able to find none to furnish evidence, nor one credible person to testify…"[526]

His attorney, Rufus Baker, managed to locate U.S. payroll records that confirmed the dates and places of service of Johnson's superior officers. Apparently that and Johnson's character witnesses were enough. Johnson was awarded a pension of $25 per annum beginning in 1834 (about $625 in current dollars). He died September 18, 1839 at seventy-seven.[527] Engraved on his headstone in the cemetery at Canterbury are the words:

Johnson, Gen. Jedediah
1812 War
Captain Hotchkiss Co.

---

522   His gravestone in Canterbury includes the inscription "1812 War Capt. Hotchkiss Co.," and an 1813 muster roll includes "private" Johnson's name under commander Medad Hotchkiss. *Military Records: Connecticut Officers and Soldiers, 1700s-1800s*; Record of Service of Connecticut Men, Part 11, War of 1812, I-J, p. 74.
523   Leonard Labaree and Catherine Fennelly ed., *The Public Records of the State of Connecticut,* May 1793-October 1796 (Hartford; State of Connecticut, 1953), 226-228.
524   *U.S. Census* 1820, Series M33 Roll 3: 427.The Fullers were also slave-owners. Erastus Fuller, Roger's brother, owned a slave on his Hebron farm, and in Barnstable, Samuel Fuller had apparently owned "the Indian Joel," whom he bequeathed to his son John. Slavery wasn't eliminated in Connecticut until well into the nineteenth century.
525   The law was passed and signed June 7, 1832, a full fifty years after the end of the Revolution.
526   Revolutionary War Pension Files Lucy W7943, (National Archives, Washington, DC), Affidavit of Jedediah Johnson April 12, 1834.
527   Revolutionary War Pension Files, Lucy W7943, Affidavit of Lucy Johnson, widow, October 6, 1853.

The headstone makes two statements that were obviously important to Johnson—or, perhaps, to his widow and second wife, Lucy: he was a general, and he fought in the 1812 War. What is left out is that he fought, not as a general but as a private.

* * *

Humphrey Taylor Fuller and his wife, Emma, raised nine children on the Fuller farm. Humphrey did the farming, supplementing his income by giving dancing lessons in the Hebron homes with ballrooms.[528]

None of the Fuller children stayed around Hebron for long. Henry Fuller married a Brooklyn girl, moved to Brooklyn, and lived there until his death in 1885. Humphrey Roger Fuller married a New York City girl, raised his family in Brooklyn and lived there until his death in 1893. Harriet Fuller married a wealthy merchant from Poughkeepsie, New York, J.H. Hitchcock.[529] When Harriet died in 1867 Hitchcock married her younger sister Mary Fuller, who then moved to Poughkeepsie. Emma Fuller married Newell Brown of Hebron, another wealthy merchant, who moved with his printing business to Kansas. Amelia Fuller, a milliner, married Thomas Kelly, proprietor of a fashionable clothing store, "Millinery, Cloaks & Shawls," in Ballston Spa, New York, a fashionable resort town seven miles south of Saratoga.

Emma Johnson Fuller died at seventy eight on April 27, 1872, while on a visit to her daughter in Ballston Spa. Humphrey Fuller moved to Brooklyn to live with his son and daughter-in-law. A sturdy old farmer to the end, he died at ninety-one on May 18, 1877 of "old age" and "general debility."[530]

---

528   Sibun, *Our Town's Heritage*, 67.
529   U.S. Census 1870, Roll m593_927:34.
530   Humphrey Taylor Fuller death certificate, Brooklyn, NY, No. 4027, May 19, 1877 (New York City Municipal Archives). Humphrey and Emma are buried side by side in the Ballston cemetery.

APPENDIX 2: FAMILY GENEALOGIES

I. GEORG VESTNER LINE

1. GEORG VESTNER (1680- ?): b. abt. 1680, probably Bavaria; d. bef. 1735; m. abt. 1705 Margaretha.[531] Children:

Conrad Vestner, b. Hegenberg, Bavaria 29 Aug. 1713.

2. CONRAD VESTNER (1713-1754): b. Hegenberg, 29 Aug. 1713; d. Altdorf, Bavaria, 14 April 1764; m. Magdalena Mordel, 13 Apr. 1735, Altdorf; she was b. abt. 1710, d. 3 Jan. 1772, Altdorf. Children:

Johann Vestner, b. Oberrieden, Bavaria, 2 Sept. 1735.

3. JOHANN VESTNER (1735-?): b. Oberrieden, 2 Sept. 1735; m. Anna Liebel, abt. 1760, Altdorf; she was b. Feb. 1734. Children:

Johann Vestner, b. Altdorf, abt. 1773.

---

531 · The numbering system for this and the genealogies that follow is that of the New England Historic Genealogy Society. Entries 1-5 are from Vestner ancestry chart compiled by Reinhard Hofer for Eliot Vestner, July 24, 2006 (Eliot N. Vestner Files).

4. JOHANN VESTNER (1773-1840): b. Altdorf, abt. 1773; m. Anna Barbara Friedel, 10 Feb. 1795, Altdorf; she was b. Altdorf, 2 Mar. 1765, to Martin Friedel and Magdalena Volkert, and d. 29 June 1838, Altdorf.[532] Children:

Margaretha Vestner, b. Altdorf, 15 Jan. 1798.

5. MARGARETHA VESTNER (1798-1860): b. Altdorf, 15 Jan. 1798; d. Altdorf, 1 Dec. 1860.[533] Children:

Johann Vestner, b. 16 Dec. 1816; father, Heinrich Roth,
b. Richthausen, Bavaria, 29 July 1792; d. Altdorf, 10 July 1860.

6. JOHANN VESTNER (1816-1872): b. Altdorf, 16 Dec. 1816;[534] d. New York City, 6 Aug. 1872;[535] emigrated to U.S., arriving New York City on the *Hudson,* 29 Oct. 1849;[536] m. Margaretha Barbara Ramming, 28 Oct. 1861, New York City.[537] She was b. Unterdornlach, Bavaria, 26 January 1835, to Adam Ramming and Margaretha Gado.[538] Children:

George John Vestner, b. New York City 2 Aug. 1863.[539]

7. GEORGE JOHN VESTNER (1863-1934): b. New York City, 2 August 1863; d. New York City, 17 Mar. 1934;[540] m. Ruth Noble, 19 Aug. 1891, New

532 Evangelical Central Archives, Regensburg, Parish of Altdorf, Marriage Book 1795, No. 1050, 10 Feb 1795 Johann Vestner and Anna Barbara Friedel.
533 Evangelical Central Archives, Regensburg, Parish of Altdorf, Baptism Book 1798, fi 7-11, No. 9:. 897/No. 6, 16 Jan. 1798 Margaretha Vestner.
534 Evangelical Central Archives Regensburg, Parish of Altdorf, Baptism Book 1816, fi. 7-13, No. 3: .217/No. 174, 16 December 1816, Johann Vestner.
535 Death Certificate, John Vestner, Aug. 6, 1872, New York City, No. 125974 (NYCMA); Keeper's Certificate, Aug. 8, 1872, Cypress Hills Cemetery, showing that John Vestner was buried in Lot No. 230 Section 14 southeast quarter.
536 Ira A. Glazer, ed., *Germans to America, Vol. 7 Oct. 1848-Dec. 1849* (Lanham, MD; The Scarecrow Press, Inc., 2004), entry for "Vestner, J."
537 Marriage Register, New York City, entry Oct. 28, 1861 (New York City Municipal Archives). Marriage Register, St. John's Evangelical Church, 81 Christopher St., New York (showing marriage date of Sept. 28, 1861)
538 Marriage Certificate, Margaretha Vestner and Heinrich Hautan, New York City, Nov. 17, 1876, No. 6570 (New York City Municipal Archives).
539 In the 1900 census, George reported his birth date as August 2, 1863, which is consistent with what he reported in his marriage certificate in 1891. See Federal Census 1900, New York Roll 704. ED 587, VDL 154, Sheet 23, Line 43. But his death certificate lists his birthdate as August 13, 1864. See Certificate of Death, No. 7203, March 18, 1934 (New York City Municipal Archives).
540 Death Certificate, George Vestner.

York City.[541] He was a lawyer, graduate of Columbian Law School, Washington, D.C., and member of the New York Bar. She was b. New York City, 13 July 1866, to John W. Noble and Eliza Woodhall, and d. 16 May 1949.[542] Children:

i Marguerite (Marjorie), b. New York City, 2 July 1895; m.
Victor Bensch, New York City; he was b. Germany 19 Jan.
1887, and d. Hendersonville, NC, 16 May 1965; she d.
Hendersonville, 24 Feb. 1981. They had one child, Ruth, who d. abt. 1975
w/o issue.

ii Noble Ellis (Eliot Noble), b. New York City, 19 Dec. 1897.

8. NOBLE ELLIS (ELIOT NOBLE) VESTNER (1897-1983): b. New York City, 19 December 1897; d. North Conway, NH, 21 March 1983;[543] m. (1) Priscilla Alden Fuller, Brooklyn, NY, 28 May 1931.[544] She was b. Brooklyn, 7 October 1899 to Charles Humphrey Fuller and Mary Everett Webb, and d. Freedom, NH, 15 November 1969. He m. (2) Margaret K. Cunningham, 1975. She was b. 28 May 1913 and d. 9 February 2001. Child with Priscilla:

Eliot Noble Vestner, Jr. b. Bronxville, NY, 4 August 1935.

9.ELIOT NOBLE VESTNER, JR., b. Bronxville, 4 August 1935; m. (1) Elizabeth Thomas Gwin, Boston, MA, 1 Jan. 1966; she graduated Smith College 1959. They were div. 1991. He m. (2) Louisa Richards Cutler, Hamilton, MA, 11 Aug. 1995. He graduated Amherst College, 1957, and Columbia University Law School, 1962. Children with Elizabeth Gwin Vestner:

i Alice-Lee Vestner, b. New York City, 4 Aug. 1967; m. David Lawrence Ackley Jr., Freedom, N.H., 21 Aug. 1999; graduated Hampshire College, 1990 and University of Rochester Medical School, 2000; she is a psychiatrist. He graduated Hampshire College, 1990, PhD English literature,

---

541 Marriage Certificate, George Vestner and Ruth Noble, Aug. 19, 1891, New York City, No. 9804 (New York City Municipal Archives).
542 Birth Certificate, Ruth Noble, New York City, July 13, 1866, No. 2020 (New York City Municipal Archives); Death Certificate, Ruth Noble Vestner, Dist. No. 5922, Register No. 62 (New York State Department of Health, Office of Vital Statistics).
543 Birth Certificate, Noble Ellis Vestner, Dec. 19, 1897, New York City, No. 53219 (New York City Municipal Archives); Death Certificate, Eliot Noble Vestner, March 21,1983, Freedom, Carroll County, NH (NH Dept of Health).
544 Certificate of Marriage, May 28,1931, St. Paul's Church, Brooklyn; Wallace Gardner, Rector

Brown University, 2010, and is a teacher. Child: Lila Gwin Ackley, b. 29 Dec. 2001, Providence, RI.

ii Charles Fuller Vestner, b. New York City, 3 Jan. 1970; m. Mary Grayson Thibaut, New Orleans, LA 27 Jan. 2007. He graduated Dartmouth College, 1992; she graduated Stanford University, 1997 and Dartmouth (MBA, 2002). They are business executives. Child: Violette Rhoades Vestner, b. San Francisco, 18 April 2010

Children of Louisa R.C. Vestner from her previous marriage:

iii Donald Frederick Cutler IV, b. Boston, MA, 10 Oct. 1967; m. Shannon R. Fike, Gloucester, MA, 10 Sept. 2006; he graduated Fort Lewis College, 1991; Univ. of Denver College of Law, 2000 and is a lawyer; she graduated Baker College, 2007 and is a manager.

iv Quincy Adams Shaw Cutler, b. Boston, MA, 13 March 1969; m. Alexandra Berckmans, Ipswich, MA, 8 Sept. 2005; she graduated University of Colorado, 1990, and is a real estate broker; he is an arborist.

2. FULLERS: EDWARD FULLER LINE

1. EDWARD FULLER (1575-1620): b. abt. 1575 to Robert and Francis Fuller of Redenhall, Norfolk, England; m. bef. 1605 in England, but his wife's name has not been established; sailed on the *Mayflower* and was a founding member of Plymouth Colony 1620; he and his wife d. Jan-March 1621, Plymouth.[545] Children:

    i Matthew Fuller, b. Redenhall, Norfolk, England, abt. 1605;

    (2) ii Samuel Fuller, b. Redenhall, Norfolk, England, abt. 1608.

2. SAMUEL FULLER (1608-1683): b. abt. 1608, Redenhall; m. Jane Lothrop, Scituate, MA, Apr. 1635, dau. of the Rev. John Lothrop and Hannah Howse. He d. 31 Oct. 1683, Barnstable, MA.[546] She d. Barnstable, bef. 1683.[547] Children: nine, of whom,

    John Fuller, b. Barnstable, abt. 1655.

3. JOHN FULLER (1655-1726): b. Barnstable abt. 1655; m. Mehitable Rowley abt. 1678 at Barnstable; she was his cousin, dau. of Moses Rowley and Elizabeth Fuller and granddaughter of Matthew Fuller. He d. East Haddam, CT, 23 Mar. 1725/26; she d. East Haddam, abt. 1732[548] Children: eleven, of whom,

---

545   Francis Fuller, "Fullers of Redenhall, England," *New England Historic and Genealogical Register* (1901), 55: 410-414 (extracts from Register of Parish of Redenhall; abstract of will, Norfolk Archdeaconry Court, Norwich); *Bradford Journal*, 446 (reference to deaths of Edward and wife during first winter).
546   Stratton, *Plymouth Colony*, 295.
547   Robert Charles Anderson, *The Great Migration*, 1: 713-717.
548   MacGunnigle, *Mayflower Families*, 4: 16.

Thomas Fuller, b. Barnstable 1679.

4. THOMAS FULLER (1679-1772): b. Barnstable, 1679; m. Elizabeth (Church?), probably in Barnstable, 1714; he was a farmer; d. East Haddam, 9 Apr. 1772; she d. East Haddam, 5 Nov. 1784.[549] Children: seven, of whom,

Ebenezer Fuller, b. East Haddam, 27 Oct. 1715.

5. EBENEZER FULLER (1715-1749): b. East Haddam, 27 Oct. 1715; m. Mary Rowley, Colchester, CT, 30 Sept. 1738; she was dau. of Moses Rowley, Falmouth, MA, and Martha Porter, Windsor, CT. He d. Hebron, CT, 30 Sept. 1749; she d. Hebron 5 Feb. 1798.[550] Children: six, of whom,

Roger Fuller, b. Hebron, 21 July 1747.

6. ROGER FULLER (1747-1819): b. Hebron, 21 July 1747; m. (1) Martha Phelps, Hebron, 21 Dec, 1766, who d. 13 Feb. 1785; m. (2) Violette Taylor, Hebron, 17 Nov. 1785, who d. 14 Jan. 1806; m. (3) Lois Taylor, Hebron, who d. 23 Aug. 1809; m. (4) Susannah Keeney, Hebron, 21 June 1810, who d. 1852.[551] He was a farmer and innkeeper and d. Hebron, 21 Sept. 1819. Children: nine by Martha Phelps and three by Violette Taylor, of whom,

Humphrey Taylor Fuller, b. Hebron, 29 July 1786.

7. HUMPHREY TAYLOR FULLER (1786-1877): b. Hebron, 29 July 1786; m. Emma Dyar Johnson, Canterbury, CT, 24 Oct. 1814, dau.of Gen. Jedediah Johnson and Eunice Dyar; she d. Ballston Spa, NY, 27 April 1872; he d. Brooklyn, NY, 18 May 1877.[552] Children: ten, of whom,

Humphrey Roger Fuller, b. Hebron, 27 Feb. 1827.

8. HUMPHREY ROGER FULLER (1827-1893): b. Hebron, 27 Feb. 1827; m. Isabelle Mercein, New York City, 17 July 1853, dau. of Colonel Thomas Royce

---

549   MacGunnigle, *Mayflower Families*, 43-44; W. H. Fuller, *Edward Fuller Family*, 40.
550   MacGunnigle, *Mayflower Families*, 130-131; W.H. Fuller, *Edward Fuller Family*, 141-142.
551   W.H.Fuller, *Edward Fuller Family*, 143
552   W.H.Fuller, *Edward Fuller Family*, 144-145; "Certificate of Death", Humphrey T. Fuller, Brooklyn, 21 May 1877, No. 4927 (New York City Municipal Archives).

Mercein and Mary Stanbury. He was Cashier, Bank of America. She d. Brooklyn, 6 Apr. 1893; he d. Brooklyn, 8 May 1893.[553] Children: five, of whom,

(9) i Charles Humphrey Fuller, b. Newark, NJ, 14 Jan. 1859.
(10) ii Elise Mercein Fuller, b. Newark, 15 Jun. 1857

9. CHARLES HUMPHREY FULLER (1859-1938): b. Newark, 14 Jan. 1859; m. Mary Everett Webb, Winchester, MA, 5 June 1884, dau.of Francis Everett Webb and Mary Frances Dwight, Winthrop, ME. He graduated Amherst College, 1878, and Columbia Law School, 1880; he was a lawyer, and member, New York State assembly and senate.[554] He d. Bronxville, NY, 5 Dec. 1938; she d. Bronxville, 7 Jan. 1953. Children:

(11) i Dorothy Fuller, b. Brooklyn, 2 July 1889;
(12) ii Everett Webb Fuller, b. Brooklyn, 8 June 1892;
(13) iii Randolph Mercein Fuller, b. Brooklyn, 26 Nov. 1893;
(14) iv Ruth Dwight Fuller, b. Brooklyn, 21 Aug. 1896;
(15) v Priscilla Alden Fuller, b. Brooklyn, 7 Oct. 1899.

10. ELISE MERCEIN FULLER (1857-1941):[555] b. Newark, 15 Jun. 1857; m. William Cox Redfield, Brooklyn, 8 Apr. 1885; she d. Bronxville, NY, 13 Mar. 1941. He was b. Albany, NY, 18 Jun. 1858; president, J.H. Williams Co., director, Equitable Life Insurance Company, congressman, 1910-12; and U.S. secretary of commerce, 1913-1919. LL.D, Amherst College, 1914. He d. Brooklyn, 13 Jun. 1931. Children:

(16) i Elise Mercein Redfield, b. Brooklyn, 22 Apr. 1887;
        ii Marian W. Redfield, b. Brooklyn, 6 Sept. 1888 (d. in infancy);
        iii Isabelle Redfield, b. Brooklyn, 29 Dec. 1890 (d. in infancy);
        iv Rosalie Redfield, b. Brooklyn, 29 Dec. 1890 (d. in infancy);
(17) v Humphrey Fuller Redfield, b. Brooklyn, 1894;

---

553   W.H.Fuller, *Edward Fuller Family*, 146. Marriage Register, entry: "Humphrey Roger Fuller", July 27, 1853 (New York City Municipal Archives). Death Certificate, Isabelle Mercein Fuller, No. 5739, 6 April 1893 (New York City Municipal Archives); *The New York Times*, 21 May, 1893: 1 (Obituaries).
554   Returns of Births, 1859, Vol. L: 555, Newark, Essex County, NJ (NJ .State Archives). Biographical Record, Amherst College, printed 1920; Death Certificate, 6 December, 1938, No. 75484 (New York State Dept of Health); *The New York Times*, 6 December 1938 (Obituaries); *The New York Times*, 8 January 1953, 27 (Obituaries).
555   < www.ancestry.com> under Elise Mercein Fuller (last accessed January 2010).

11. DOROTHY FULLER, b. Brooklyn, 2 July 1889; m. Harmanus Swan, Brooklyn, abt. 1923; d. Bronxville, 4 Oct. 1951; he d. May 1977, Redwood, NJ. No children.[556]

12. EVERETT WEBB FULLER, b. Brooklyn, 8 June 1892; m. Gertrude Gladding, Brooklyn, 15 Sept. 1919, dau. of Walter Gladding and Harriet Priscilla Bowne; he graduated Amherst College, 1915, Phi Beta Kappa; served as a 1st Lt., Chemical Warfare Division, U.S. Army, in World War I. He was a research chemist and assistant to the director, chemical research, Socony Mobil Oil Co, New Jersey. He d. Richmond, VA, 12 Aug. 1965; she d. Richmond, 25 March 1975. Children:

> (18) i Everett Gladding Fuller, b. 6 Dec. 1921;
> (19) ii Priscilla May Fuller, b. 25 Mar. 1924.

13. RANDOLPH MERCEIN FULLER. b. Brooklyn, 26 Nov. 1893; m. Jessie Margaret Catlin, Brooklyn, 16 Feb. 1920, dau. Rufus Catlin and Jessie Mackenzie; he graduated Amherst College 1915; served as 1st Lt. U.S. Army, Mexican Border and World War I. He was managing partner, Patterson, Teale & Dennis, accounting firm, New York City office. He d. Naples, FL, 6 Apr. 1967; she d. Naples, 26 June 1979. Children:

> (20) i Randolph Mackenzie Fuller, b. Brooklyn, 15 Nov. 1924;
> (21) ii Robert Catlin Fuller, b. Brooklyn, Nov. 1930.

14. RUTH DWIGHT FULLER, b. Brooklyn, 21 Aug. 1896; m. Lowell Shumway, Brooklyn, 4 Mar. 1919, son of Prof. Edgar Shumway of Rutgers University and Florence Shumway; he graduated Amherst College, 1914, and served as 1st Lt. U.S. Army, 1917-1919. He was vice president, McCall Corporation, New York City (ret. 1957). He d. Bronxville, 12 Apr. 1979. No Children.

15. PRISCILLA ALDEN FULLER, b. Brooklyn, 7 Oct. 1899; graduated Packer Collegiate Institute, Brooklyn, 1919; m. Eliot Noble Vestner, Brooklyn, 28 May 1931. He was Lt. Col., U.S. Army; served on the Mexican Border, and in

---

556   Charles Humphrey Fuller entry in Amherst College Biographical Record (Dorothy Fuller birth date); U.S. Census 1930 Roll 1659:8B (states Manny thirty when married, which would suggest 1923 as marriage year).

World War 1, World War 11 and Korea. She d. North Conway, NH, 15 Nov. 1969; he d. North Conway, 21 Mar. 1983. Child:

Eliot Noble Vestner, Jr., b. Bronxville, 4 Aug. 1935.

16. ELISE MERCEIN REDFIELD, b. Brooklyn, 22 Apr. 1887; m. Charles Kellogg Drury, Brooklyn, 12 Jan. 1910; She d. probably Bronxville, bet. 1940 and 1950; he d. Bronxville, July 1965. Children: William Redfield Drury, b. 12 Feb. 1912, d. 8 Oct. 1993; Mercein Kellogg Drury, b.10 Jan. 1920; d. Jan. 1984.

17. HUMPHREY FULLER REDFIELD, b. Brooklyn 1895; m. Amy Cowing, 5 Jan. 1918; she graduated Smith College, 1916; he graduated Amherst College, 1916. During the First World War he served as Lt. JG, USN Reserve, and later was president, John Price Jones, Inc., New York City. He d. 8 Sept. 1960, Easton, MD; she d. 8 March, 1962, Chicago, ILL. Children:

> i Amy Lou, b. Bronxville 1921; m. Bronxville, 12, May 1946, Capt. John Davies Gosin. She attended Univ. of Wisconsin, graduated from Hollins College, and served as lieutenant in the Waves. He graduated Univ. of Wisconsin and served in the China-Burma-India Theater during the war. She d. Sept. 1970; He d. 4 Sept. 1999, Du Page, ILL;

> ii. Mary Alan (Molly) b. 27 Oct. 1920; m. Bronxville, June 1943, Lt. Robert D. Brown, Jr., who graduated West Point 1942. She d. Alexandria, VA, 16, July 2006.

(22) iii Jeanne, b. Bronxville, 10 Feb. 1925.

18. EVERETT GLADDING FULLER, b. 6 Dec. 1921, Brooklyn; m. Gladys Heinlein, Riverdale, NY, 10 Aug. 1947, graduate of Hunter College, New York City, 1945. He graduated Amherst College, 1942; PhD, physics, University of Illinois, 1950; served as Capt. U.S. Army Air Force, during the Second World War; physicist, National Bureau of Standards. He d. Gaithersburg, MD, 15 Nov. 1995. Children:

i Wendy Webb Fuller, b. Washington, DC, 3 Feb. 1952; m. Jeffrey Guy Mora, Brookeville, MD, 1991; graduated University of Maryland, 1975; PhD physics UCLA, 1980. She is a physicist with the National Science Foundation;

ii John Everett Fuller, b. Washington, DC, 7 May 1953; m. Kim Marie Curran, Shelburne, VT., 2002, div. 2007. He graduated University of Virginia, B.S. 1975, and he is an architect. Child: Louisa Everette Archer Fuller, b. Plattsburgh, NY, 4 February 2010.

iii Susan Dorothy Fuller, b. Washington, DC, 31 Mar. 1957; m. (1) Robert A. Ohgren 1976-1982; m. (2) John S. Eveler, 1988-1992 m. (3) Vernon C. Tamalavicz, 1993-2006 m. (4) Dr. Robert R. Conley, M.D. 2007. She graduated University of Maryland, B.S. 1978, and is a business executive.

19. PRISCILLA MAY FULLER,[557] b. Springfield, MA, 25 March, 1924; m. L. McCarthy Downs, Jr. Woodbury, NJ, 6 Oct. 1951; she graduated William & Mary, 1946; he attended Hampden-Sydney College and was stockbroker in Richmond, VA and d. Richmond, 27 June 1998. Children:

i Lewis McCarthy Downs, III, b. Richmond, 24 Feb. 1953; m. Marta Jane Schlenz, Williamsburg, 19 Dec. 1976; she graduated William & Mary; he graduated The Citadel, 1976, William & Mary (MBA), 1978 and is a business executive in Richmond. Children: Marta Anne Downs, b. Fort Thomas, KY. 27 Aug. 1980, graduated Virginia Commonwealth University, 2006; Catherine Theresa Downs, b. Fort Thomas, 1 Mar. 1983, graduated Virginia Commonwealth University, 2006.

ii Priscilla Ann Downs, b. Richmond, 9 May 1955; d. Charles City VA, 17 March 1975;

iii William Everett Downs, b. Charles City, 5 June 1959; m. Deborah Hayes Seaman, Charles City, 14 May 1983; he graduated Randolph Macon 1981 and William & Mary (MBA) 1983; she graduated Skidmore College; he is a business executive in Richmond; children: Genevieve Fuller Downs,

---

557 Priscilla Downs is the primary source for much of the information about the family of Everett Webb Fuller, supplemented by Gladys Fuller and Wendy Webb Fuller.

b.Williamsburg, 10 Oct. 1985, graduated University of Virginia, 2008; Julia Melisande Downs, b. Richmond, 4 Mar. 1991, attending Christopher Newport University.

20. RANDOLPH MACKENZIE FULLER, b. Brooklyn, 15 Nov. 1924; m. Marion Moe, Greenwich, CT, 1945; d. Naples, FL, 4 Mar. 1985; attended Amherst College; businessman and antique car collector in Naples; No children.

21. ROBERT CATLIN FULLER, b. Brooklyn, 1930; m. Ann Ball, Rye, NY, 6 April 1956; she d. 17 Feb., 1983, Naples. He graduated from Amherst College, 1952, and is businessman in Naples. Children:

  i Robert Scott Fuller, b. Naples, 25 Oct. 1957;
  ii Clay Randolph Fuller, b. Naples, 30 Nov. 1959.

22. JEANNE REDFIELD BONYNGE, b. Bronxville, 10 Feb. 1925; m. Bronxville, 15 May 1948, Russell Bonynge, Jr., who d. Aug. 1971. She graduated Denison University; he graduated Culver Military Academy and served in the armed forces, Second World War. She worked as lead librarian for the Internal Revenue Service, served as a trustee of UNICEF, and was active in social and political causes. She d. Bend, Ore., 2 July 2005. Children:

  i Terry Bonynge, b. 9 Feb.1952, Indianapolis, IND; m. Cape Cod, MA, 4 Aug. 1977, David Smullin; she d. Bend, OR 6 July 2002. Children: Josh and Emily.

  ii Jeffrey Redfield Bonynge, Grand Rapids, Michigan.

3. FULLERS: WILLIAM BRADFORD LINE

1. GOVERNOR WILLIAM BRADFORD, son of William Bradford and Alice Hanson, b. 19 March 1589/90, Austerfield, Yorkshire, England, d. 9 May 1657, Plymouth; m (1) Dorothy May, 10 Dec. 1613, Amsterdam, Holland who d. Dec. 1620, Cape Cod Harbor, 23 years old; m (2) Alice Carpenter, 14 Aug. 1623, Plymouth who d. 26 March 1670, Plymouth. He was elected governor of Plymouth Colony 1621; re-elected 1621-1633, 1635-1637, 1639-1644, and 1645-1657; author "Of Plymouth Plantation, 1620-1647." [558]Children four, of whom,

William Bradford, b. 17 June 1624, Plymouth.

2. LT. GOVERNOR WILLIAM BRADFORD, b. 17 June 1624, m. (1) Alice Richards, after 23 April 1650, Plymouth; she d. 12 Dec. 1671, Plymouth, 44 years old; m. (2) Sarah Griswold, abt. 1674, Norwich, CT; m. (3) Mary Wood, abt. 1676, Plymouth, who d. 6 Jan. 1714/15, Plymouth. He was elected Deputy Governor of Plymouth Colony 1682-86 and 1689-91. In 1675 he was

---

558   Sources: Ruth Gardiner Hall, *Descendants of Governor William Bradford through the first seven generations* (Ann Arbor, Michigan; Bradford Family Compact,1951); Robert S. Wakefield, *Mayflower Families Through five Generations*, Vol. 22 (Plymouth, MA; General Society of Mayflower Descendants, 2004); Howard Metcalfe, Lineage from Gov. William Bradford to Sybil Chapin (July 14, 2004), at <http://www.lanopalera.net/Genealogy/Bradford.html>; *American Marriages before 1699* [database on-line], Provo, UT, The Generations Network, Inc. 1997 (marriage record, Gov. William Bradford and Alice Southworth, widow);U.S .*and International Marriage Records, 1560-1900* [database on-line], Provo, UT, The Generations Network, Inc. 2004 (marriage record, Maj. William Bradford and Alice Richards; marriage record, Alice Bradford and James Fitch); *Mayflower Births and Deaths*, Vol. 1: 112; Society of Colonial Wars, State of Maryland (service record, James Fitch); *Early Connecticut Marriages* [database on-line], Provo, UT. The Generations Network, Inc. 2006 (marriage record, John Dyar and Abigail Fitch); *Connecticut Town Marriage Records, pre-1870* (Barbour Collection) (marriage record, Elijah Dyar and Elizabeth Williams); Ancestry.com, One World Tree, Elijah Dyer (information on children of Elijah Dyer and Elizabeth Williams); *Windham County, Connecticut, Cemetery Records*, Vol. 1 (death of Elijah Dyer and wife Elizabeth); Ancestry.com, Family Tree, 2008, *Descendants of Deacon. Thomas Dyer of Weymouth, Mass.* (information on Eunice Dyer, spouse and children)

major and commander of the Plymouth forces at the "Great Swamp Fight" in King Philip's War. He d. 20 February 1703/4. Children nine, of whom,

Alice Bradford, b. 1659, Plymouth.

3. ALICE BRADFORD, b. 1659, Plymouth; m. (1) Rev. William Adams, 29 March 1680, Dedham, MA. He was pastor of the Dedham church and d. 17 August 1685, Dedham; m. (2) Maj. James Fitch, 8 May 1687, Norwich, CT, who served as governor's assistant in CT, as captain in King Philip's War, and was an original benefactor of Yale College. He d. 10 Nov. 1727, Canterbury, CT. Children: seven, of whom,

Abigail Fitch, b. 22 Feb. 1687/88, Canterbury.

4. ABIGAIL FITCH, b. 22 Feb. 1687/88, Canterbury, m. Col. John Dyar, son of Deacon Joseph Dyar and Hannah Baxter, 22 Oct. 1713, Canterbury. Col. Dyar served in the French and Indian wars, as judge in Windham County, and was elected a deputy to the Connecticut General Assembly. She d. 19 May 1759, Canterbury; he d. abt. 25 Feb. 1779 at Canterbury. Children: eight, of whom,

Elijah Dyar, b. 10 Sept. 1716,

5. CAPTAIN ELIJAH DYAR, b. 10 Sept. 1716, Canterbury; m. Elizabeth Williams, 16 Nov. 1752, Plainfield, CT. He served as captain, Connecticut Militia and d. 15 Feb. 1795, Canterbury. She d. 1 May 1817, Canterbury. Children: nine, of whom,

Eunice Dyar, b. 2 Dec. 1766, Canterbury.

6. EUNICE DYAR, b. 2 Dec. 1766, Canterbury, m. 4 March 1790, Jedediah Johnson, Canterbury, son of Capt. John Johnson and Phillus Pettet, Canterbury; he served in his father's company at New London during the Revolution, and as general in the Connecticut militia, 1808-1812. She d. 14 June 1808, Canterbury; he remarried 31 July 1811, Lucy Abbe, Canterbury, and d. 18 Sept. 1839, Canterbury. Children: seven, of whom,

Emma Dyar, b. 29 Nov. 1792, Canterbury.

7. EMMA DYAR JOHNSON, b. 29 Nov.1792, Canterbury; m. Humphrey Taylor Fuller, 24 Oct. 1814, Canterbury; she d. 27 April 1872, Ballston Spa, NY. He d. 18 May 1877, Brooklyn, NY. Children: nine, of whom,

Humphrey Roger, b. 27 Feb. 1827, Hebron.

8. HUMPHREY ROGER FULLER, b. 27 Feb. 1827, m. 17 July 1853, Isabelle Mercein, dau. of Col. Thomas Royce Mercein and Mary Stanbury, New York City. She d. 6 Apr. 1893, Brooklyn; he d. 8 May 1893 Flatbush. Children: five, of whom,

Charles Humphrey Fuller, b. 14 Jan. 1859, Newark, NJ.

9. CHARLES HUMPHREY FULLER, b. 14 Jan. 1859, Newark; m. 7 Aug. 1884, Mary Everett Webb, Haverhill, MA, daughter Francis Everett Webb and Mary Frances Dwight; she d. 6 January 1953, Bronxville, NY. Children: five, of whom,

Priscilla Alden Fuller, b. 7 Oct. 1899, Brooklyn.

4. FULLERS: CHRISTOPHER WEBB LINE

1. CHRISTOPHER WEBB, b. England abt. 1599; settled in Braintree, MA abt. 1642.[559] Children: several, born in England, of whom,

> Christopher Webb 2nd, b. England 28 March 1630.

2. CHRISTOPHER WEBB 2nd (1630-1694): b. Crediton Parish, Devonshire, England 28 March 1630; m. Hannah Scott, Braintree, 18 Jan. 1654/55; d. 30 May 1694, Braintree. He was a lawyer, surveyor, representative to the Massachusetts legislature, town clerk and selectman of Braintree. Children: nine, of whom,

> Christopher Webb 3rd, b. Billerica, MA, 23 Mar. 1663.

3. CHRISTOPHER WEBB 3rd (1663-1690): b. Billerica, 23 Mar. 1663; m. Mary Bass, Duxbury, MA, 24 May 1686; d. Braintree 7 Feb. 1689/90 (small pox). Children:

> Christopher Webb 4th: b. Braintree, 19 Aug. 1690.

---

559   Webb genealogy, from Dorothy Webb Huston; Webb family tree by A. S. Ames, Gardiner, ME, 1921. Samuel Bates ed., *Records of the Town of Braintree* 1640-1793 (Randolph, MA; Daniel H. Huxford, 1886), 12, 26-27.

4. CHRISTOPHER WEBB 4th (1690-?): b. Braintree, 19 Aug. 1690; m. Annie White, Boston, 30 Apr. 1713. Children: ten, of whom,

Samuel Webb, b. Boston, 5 Oct. 1716.

5. SAMUEL WEBB (1716-1773): b. Boston, 5 Oct. 1716; d. Woolwich, ME, 27 Apr. 1773; m. Sarah Lincoln, Braintree, 1740. Children:

Christopher Webb 5th b. Braintree, 21 Apr. 1747.

6. CHRISTOPHER WEBB 5th (1747-1840): b. Braintree, 21 Apr. 1747; d. Skowhegan, ME, 18 Sept. 1840; m. Elisa ("Betsy") Smith, Woolwich, ME. Children:

James Webb, b. Skowhegan, 1765.

7. JAMES WEBB (1765-1821): b. Skowhegan, 1765; d. Skowhegan, 1821; m. Rebecca Jewett, Skowhegan, 1790. Children:

Samuel Webb, b. Skowhegan, 30 Dec. 1791.

8. SAMUEL WEBB (1791-1840: b. Skowhegan, 30 Dec. 1791; d. Winthrop, ME, 17 Apr. 1840; m. Olive Lambert, Winthrop, 16 Jan. 1817. He was justice of the peace in Winthrop. Children: seven, of whom,

Francis Everett Webb, b. Winthrop, 13 Mar. 1829.

9. FRANCIS EVERETT WEBB (1829-1869): b. Winthrop, 13 Mar. 1829; d. Winthrop, 20 Nov. 1869; m. Mary Frances Dwight Richmond, Winthrop, 27 May 1858. He graduated Bowdoin College 1857, was attorney and town official in Winthrop, Superintendent of Banks Maine, and represented Winthrop in Maine Legislature. Children:

i Mary Everett Webb, b. Winthrop, 11 Jan. 1862

ii Annie Dwight Webb, b. Winthrop, 22 June 1865; m. (1) John A Page, Bradford, MA, 1886. He d. Haverhill, abt. 1893.

She m. (2) W.W. Holt, 17 May 1897. They had one child,
Kenneth Dwight Holt, b. 7 July 1901. He d. Skowhegan,
ME, June 1983.

10. MARY EVERETT WEBB (1862-1953): b. Winthrop, 11 Jan. 1862; d.
Bronxville, N.Y., 6 Jan. 1953; m. Charles Humphrey Fuller, Winchester, MA,
5 June 1884. Children: five, of whom,

Priscilla Alden Fuller, b. Brooklyn, 7 Oct. 1899.

5. FULLERS: JOHN DWIGHT LINE

1. JOHN DWIGHT (1601-1660): b. Dedham, England, abt. 1601; d. Dedham, MA, 24 January 1660; m. (1) Hannah, in England; (2) Elizabeth Thaxter, Dedham, 20 Jan. 1657.[560] He was a founder and selectman of Dedham.[561] Children: five with Hannah, of whom,

Timothy Dwight, b. Dedham, England 1629.

2. CAPTAIN TIMOTHY DWIGHT (1629-1717)[562]: b. Dedham, England, 1629; d. Dedham, MA, 31 Jan. 1717; m. (1) Sarah Perman, 11 Nov. 1651, who d. 29 May 1652; m. (2) Sarah Powell, 3 May 1653, who d. 27 June 1664; m. (3) Anna Flint, 9 Jan. 1664-5, who d. 29 Jan. 1685-6; m. (4) Mary Edwind, 7 Jan. 1686-7, who d. 30 Aug. 1688; m. (5) Esther Fisher, 31 July 1690,, who d. 30 Jan. 1690-91; m. (6) Bethiah Moss, 1 Feb. 1691-2, who d. 6 Feb. 1717-18. He was selectman, deputy governor of Plymouth and military officer. Children: fourteen (four by Sarah Perman; ten by Anna Flint), of whom,

Henry Dwight, b. Dedham, 19 Jan 1676 (by Anna Flint).

3. CAPTAIN HENRY DWIGHT (1676-1732): b. Dedham, 19 Dec. 1676; m. Lydia Hawley, Northampton, MA, 27 Aug. 1702; d. Hatfield, MA, 26 Mar. 1732. He was judge of the county court and officer in the militia.[563] Children: eight, of whom,

Simeon Dwight, b. Hatfield, 18 Feb. 1719.

---

560 The principal source for information on the Dwight family is Benjamin W. Dwight, *The History of the Descendants of John Dwight of Dedham, Mass* (New York; John F. Trow & Son, 1874) in two volumes.
561 Robert C. Anderson, George Sanborn, Melinde Sanborn, *The Great Migration 1633-1634,* 2:371-377;
562 Benjamin Dwight, *Dwight Family,* 91-96.
563 Benjamin Dwight, *Dwight Family*: 620

4. COLONEL SIMEON DWIGHT (1719-1776): b. Hatfield, 18 Feb. 1719; d. Warren, MA, 21 Feb. 1776; m. Sybil Dwight, Warren, 14 Dec. 1743. He was colonel in the militia and high sheriff of Worcester County.[564] Children: nine, of whom,

Simeon Dwight Jr., b. Warren, 13 Sept. 1755.

5. SIMEON DWIGHT Jr. (1755-1815): b. Warren, 13 Sept. 1755; m. Anna Cutler, Warren, abt. 1783; d. Warren 1 Feb. 1815. He was a "thrifty farmer" and hotelkeeper; a soldier in the Revolution and War of 1812.[565] Children: five, of whom,

Joseph Cutler Dwight, b. Warren, 19 June 1798.

6. JOSEPH CUTLER DWIGHT (1798-1865): b. Warren, 19 June 1798; d. Hallowell, ME 2 Jan. 1865; m. Mary Moore Farrell, Hallowell, 13 Oct. 1826; d. Hallowell, 2 Jan. 1865. He was a merchant and cashier, Northern Bank of Hallowell. His widow m. (2) Dr. Arba Blair, Rome, NY, and d. there, 18 Jan. 1870.[566] Children: three, of whom,

Mary Frances Dwight, b. Hallowell, 29 Mar. 1828.

7. MARY FRANCES DWIGHT (1828-1912): b. Hallowell, 29 Mar. 1828; d. Brooklyn, NY, 19 Apr. 1912; m. (1) Cyrus Clark Richmond, Hallowell, 30 Dec. 1850; he d. San Francisco, 1 June 1852; she m. (2) Francis Everett Webb, Winthrop, ME, 27 May 1858; he d. Winthrop, 20 Nov. 1869; she m. (3) Henry Carter. Haverhill, MA abt. 1887; he d. abt. 1898. Children with Francis Webb,

i Mary Everett Webb, b. Winthrop 11 Jan. 1862.
ii Annie Dwight Webb, b. 22 June 1865.

---

564   Benjamin Dwight, *Dwight Family*, 915
565   Benjamin Dwight, *Dwight Family*, 926; Massachusetts Soldiers and Sailors in the Revolutionary War, compiled by the Secretary of the Commonwealth (Boston. 1896-1908; Wright & Potter Printing), 5:110; War of 1812 Service Records, National Archives, Washington, DC.
566   Benjamin Dwight, *Dwight Family*, 929.

8. MARY EVERETT WEBB (1862-1953), b. Winthrop, 11 Jan. 1862; m. Charles Humphrey Fuller, Winchester, MA, 5 June 1884; d. Bronxville, 6 Jan. 1953. Children, five, of whom,

Priscilla Alden Fuller, b. Brooklyn, 7 Oct. 1899.

6. FULLERS: ALDEN, STANDISH & SOULE LINE

1. MYLES STANDISH: b. England, bef. 1593; military leader of Plymouth; m. (1) by 1618, Rose, who d. Plymouth 29 Jan. 1620/21; m (2) Barbara by 1624; she d. after Oct. 1659; he d. Duxbury 3 Oct. 1656. Children by Barbara: seven, of whom,

    (4) Alexander Standish, b. Plymouth abt. 1626.[567]

2. JOHN ALDEN[568]: b. England, abt. 1598; cooper; m. Priscilla Mullins, Plymouth, abt. 1622; she d. bef. 1687; he d. 12 Sept. 1687 at Duxbury. Children: ten, of whom,

    (4) Sarah Alden, b. Duxbury abt. 1627.

3. GEORGE SOULE, b. England (possibly son of John Soule of Eckington, Worcester) bet 1593-1600; d. Duxbury bef. 22 Jan 1679; m. bef. 1626, probably in Plymouth, Mary Bucket (Becket?); she d. Duxbury, Dec 1676. Soule, who sailed on the *Mayflower* as Edward Winslow's servant, became an office-holder and property-owner in Plymouth and later was a founder of Duxbury. Children: nine, of whom:

    (5) John Soule, b. Plymouth, abt. 1632.[569]

---

567   Anderson, *The Great Migration,* 3: 1741-1747.-
568   Esther Littleford Woolworth, *Mayflower Families Through Five Generations,* 16 (John Alden): 1-12; 363-374. Russell L. Warner: *Myles Standish of the Mayflower and his Descendants for Five Generations,* 2nd edition ed., Robert S. Wakefield, (Plymouth, MA; Gen. Soc. of Mayflower Descendants, 1992), 3.
569   *Mayflower Families Through Five Generations* (Plymouth, MA; Gen Soc. Of Mayflower Descendants, 1992) "George Soule," 1. George Soule was a deputy to the General Court from Duxbury, and apparently served in the Pequot War (1637). Soule and his wife had eight children. Their son Benjamin was killed by natives at Pawtucket, Rhode Island, on 26 March 1676, during King Phillip's War.

4. ALEXANDER STANDISH, b. Plymouth, abt. 1626; m. (1) Sarah ALDEN, Duxbury, by abt. 1660; she d. bef. 1688; he m. (2) Desire Holmes, 1688, who d. Marshfield, MA, 22 Jan. 1731. Standish was constable of Duxbury; he d. 6 July 1702, Duxbury. Children: eight by Sarah, of whom,

      6) Sarah Standish, b. Duxbury, abt. 1666.

5. JOHN SOULE,[570] b. Plymouth, abt. 1632; m. (1) Rebecca Simmons, probably Duxbury abt. 1654; she d. 1675-1678; he m. (2) Esther Sampson, b. 6 March 1640, d. Duxbury 12 Sept. 1735. He d. Duxbury bef. 14 Nov. 1707. Children: nine by Rebecca, of whom,

      Benjamin Soule, b. Duxbury abt. 1665-66.

6. BENJAMIN SOULE,[571] b. Duxbury, abt. 1665-6; m. Sarah STANDISH, Plymouth, abt. 1694; she d. Plympton 4 Mar. 1740.[572] He d. Plympton 1 Dec. 1729. Children: six, whom,

      Benjamin Soule, b. Plymouth, 5 June 1704.

7. BENJAMIN SOULE, b. Plymouth, 5 June 1704; m. Hannah Whitman, Plympton, 31 Mar. 1730; she d. Plympton 3 Oct. 1788; he d. Plympton 19 Apr. 1751. Children: five, of whom,

      Benjamin Soule. b. Plympton, 1 Feb. 1731.[573]

8. BENJAMIN SOULE, b. Plympton, 1 Feb. 1731, m. Mehitabel Bonney, Plympton, 5 May 1757; he d. Plympton, 30 Mar. 1816; she d. Plympton, 4 Sept. 1801. Children: six, of whom,

      Hannah Soule, b. Plympton, April 1761.[574]

---

570   John Soule and Milton Terry, rev. by Robert S. Wakefield and Louise Walsh Throop, *George Soule, Fifth and Sixth Generation Descendants* (Plymouth, MA; Society of Mayflower Descendants, 2006), 2.
571   Soule and Terry, *George Soule*, 12.
572   Plympton was established as a town separate from Plymouth, 4 June 1707.
573   Soule and Terry, *George Soule*, 51-52.
574   <http://trees.ancestry.com/owt/Benjamin Soule>

9. HANNAH SOULE, b. Plympton, Apr. 1761; m (1) Isaac Bonney. After his death she m. (2) Silas Lambert, Winthrop, ME, 20 Oct. 1792. He was b. 15 Oct. 1765, Tisbury, Martha's Vineyard, MA, and d. 26 July 1828, Winthrop. His father, Gideon, was an early settler of Winthrop. She died at Winthrop, 11 Feb. 1828. Children: two, of whom,

Olive Lambert, b. Winthrop, 19 Aug. 1795[575]

10. OLIVE LAMBERT, b. Winthrop, 19 Aug. 1795; m. Samuel Webb, Winthrop, 16 Jan 1817. He d. Winthrop, 17 Apr. 1840; she d. Winthrop, 11 Aug. 1866. Children: seven, of whom,

Francis Everett Webb, b. Winthrop, 13 Mar. 1829[576]

11. FRANCIS EVERETT WEBB, b. Winthrop, 13 Mar. 1829; m. Mary Frances Dwight, widow of Cyrus Richmond, at Winthrop, 27 May 1858; d. Winthrop, 20 Nov. 1869. Children: two, of whom,

Mary Everett Webb, b. Winthrop, 11 Jan. 1862[577]

12. MARY EVERETT WEBB, b. Winthrop, 11 Jan. 1862; m. Charles Humphrey Fuller, Winchester, MA, 5 June 1882. He d. 5 Dec. 1938, Bronxville, NY; she d. Bronxville, 6 Jan. 1953. Children: five, of whom,

Priscilla Alden Fuller, b. 7 Oct. 1899, Brooklyn.

---

575   Everett Schermerhorn Stackpole, David C. Young and Elizabeth Keeene Young, *Stackpole's History of Winthrop, Maine* (Westminster, MD; Heritage Books, 1994), 652; David Thurston, *Brief History of Winthrop from 1764 to October 1853* (Portland, ME; Brown, Thurston, Steam, 1855). <http://trees.ancestry.com/owt/ Silas Lambert>
576   Stackpole, *History of Winthrop*, 652-653.
577   Bowdoin College Biographical Record, Class of 1853, "Francis Webb;" Death Certificate, Mary F.D.Carter, New York City, April 19, 1912, No. 8182 (New York City Municipal Archives).

ACKNOWLEDGEMENTS

My dear wife, Louisa, has put up with ten years of research and writing. But she asked for it; it was her idea of how I should spend my retirement. She also suggested the title, sat and listened as I read chapters aloud, offered helpful criticism, and reviewed chapters with a sharp eye for punctuation. Without her patience and constant encouragement this book would not have been possible.

Thanks also to my son, Charlie. He gave me Ian Frazier's book *Family* in August 1995 to get me started, and has persistently encouraged me ever since. Charlie reviewed various chapters, did research in San Francisco, contributed his recollections about our time in Rye, and most importantly, located my mother's diaries in the old house in Freedom, New Hampshire.

My cousin, Priscilla Fuller Downs of Williamsburg, Virginia, has been a constant source of help and encouragement. She did early research on the family.

Sharon Carmack, an expert in genealogy and family history, has been my principal editor and advisor, reading through two entire drafts and giving me useful criticism and encouragement every step of the way.

John Milton Cooper, an old friend who also happens to be a very distinguished historian and biographer, took the time to read the manuscript, provided a candid critique, and offered numerous excellent suggestions for improving it.

William Shumate read the entire manuscript with a sharp and critical eye for mistakes, grammatical and otherwise. He had a field day doing so, as did Ingrid Powell, Booksurge editor, who did a thorough job. To the extent the book is reasonably free of glaring errors and stupid redundancies, I owe it to them.

Reinhard Hofer, a German genealogist (<u>Hofer-Bavaria@T-online.de</u>) helped me nail down John Vestner's birthplace and records in Altdorf,

Germany. Nancy Ehlers, a genealogist in Sacramento, California, was helpful in transcribing the Richmond letters from 1849-51 in the State Library.

Mina Ellis Otis and Dr. John Gunderson were kind enough to read and critique portions of the manuscript. I am very grateful for their candid and thoughtful criticisms and suggestions. My good friend, Paul Hicks, also read earlier portions of the manuscript, made useful suggestions, and as author of a distinguished biography of Joseph Henry Lumpkin, Georgia's first chief justice, he has been a source of inspiration.

Marilyn Hill, editor of the *Bronxville Journal*, a publication of the Bronxville Historical Conservancy (of which she is also co-chair), agreed to publish my chapter on World War 11 in the *Journal*. As a result, that chapter received a thorough review, with drafts and re-drafts and numerous questions. Bob Riggs, my old friend and co-chair of the Conservancy, arranged for that publication, and I am grateful to him for that.

Penny Vestner, who shared my life for many years, has been very helpful in finding old family photos and documents in the Freedom house, as has my daughter, Alice-Lee.

Heidimarie Burke, owner of Photographic Images in Englewood, Florida, expertly reproduced the 115 photos that I gave her in various shapes and sizes.

I have taken advantage of the good will and skills of a host of librarians. Toni Vanover at the Boca Grande Community Center Reading Room, Ginny Hopcroft and Kathy Peterson of the Bowdoin College Library, and Carol Ganz of the History and Genealogy Section of the Connecticut State Library in Hartford, were all particularly helpful.

In addition to the help I have received with this book, I am also grateful for the help I have received throughout the years from people and institutions too numerous to list, help which I did not always appreciate and acknowledge at the time, but without which I would have driven my car into a ditch long ago. I have been extremely fortunate.

SOURCES

My own files constitute the most important source of information for this book, particularly my father's Army records and mother's letters, diaries, photos and other material.

In addition to family papers, I have used the resources of The National Archives, New England Historic and Genealogical Society, Boston Public Library, Boston Athenaeum, University of New Hampshire Library, Brooklyn Public Library, New York Public Library, New York Historical Society, New York Genealogical and Biographical Society, New York City Municipal Archives, Connecticut State Library, New York State Library at Albany, California Historical Society in San Francisco, Family History Library in Salt Lake City, San Francisco Historical Society, Maine State Archives, and the Library of Congress, which holds the collected papers of William Cox Redfield.

Smaller libraries have also been extremely useful: the Bowdoin College Library, Bronxville Library, local libraries in East Haddam and Hebron, Connecticut, as well as Winthrop and Hallowell, Maine.

In New York, the Municipal Archives on Chambers Street is the main source of vital records (birth, marriage and death) for the five boroughs. For Connecticut, the Barbour Collection, which can be accessed by surname on the Internet, is an invaluable resource for records prior to 1850. In Massachusetts, vital records are available on microfilm at NEHGS, and in Maine at the State Archives in Augusta.

The U.S. census is another critical source of information, and all the census records from 1790 through 1930, with the exception of the 1890 records which were destroyed in 1921 by a fire in the commerce department, are available at the National Archives in Washington and the regional offices as well as on the Internet through Ancestry.com.

As regards ship passenger information, Ancestry.com includes passenger lists, and "J. Vestner???" arriving on the *Hudson* in the fall of 1849 appears there. The huge multi-volume *Germans to America* is also useful for information on German immigrants. "J. Vestner" appeared in one of the 1849 volumes recently published.

City directories are a valuable resource for determining the presence of an individual or family and their address, business and residential. The New York Historical Society has a complete set of New York City directories in book form, 1786-1930, which makes them easily readable. The Boston Public Library has a microfilm collection of city directories for New York, Brooklyn, Newark, and other cities.

Internet companies like Ancestry.com and Genealogy.com have huge databases, usually well-indexed. Google is free and surprisingly useful.

Perhaps the most interesting part of the research is unraveling a mystery. For example, mother listed "Jedediah Johnson, General, War of 1812" on her family chart. He came from Canterbury, Connecticut, and his daughter married Humphrey Taylor Fuller, my great-great-grandfather. I checked the records at the National Archives for the War of 1812 and found nothing. On the Internet, I found a reference to a Private Jedediah Johnson in the Revolutionary War, but that's a long way from a general. Almost as an afterthought at the end of a long day, I was browsing through an index to Revolutionary War pension files at the National Archives when I came across a file on "Lucy, widow of Jedediah Johnson." The file contained extensive material on Johnson's service as a private in the Revolution in Johnson's own handwriting. One document by Lucy's lawyer referred to "General Jedediah Johnson." But where was the evidence that he served as a general?

I called the state library in Hartford to see if they had anything on Jedediah Johnson in their Connecticut militia files. Carol Ganz, a librarian with the History and Genealogy Unit, did some research and sent me a printout of an index to their files on the militia 1738-1820, which included numerous references to Jedediah, including his various promotions and appointment as brigadier general. He had indeed served as a brigadier general in the Connecticut Militia between 1808 and 1812, but resigned in May of 1812 one month before President Madison declared war. Johnson's gravestone in the Canterbury cemetery says "War of 1812, Capt. Hotchkiss Company." Did he re-enter the service after his resignation? And if he was a general why would he be serving under Capt. Hotchkiss? Then I remembered a document from the "Record of Service of

Connecticut Men in the War of 1812" listing a "Jedediah Johnson" as having served as a "private" from September 13, 1813, to November 13, 1813, under the command of Medad Hotchkiss. He appears to have re-enlisted in the U.S. Army at age fifty-one with his old rank of private. So he was indeed a general, and he did serve in the War of 1812; but he didn't serve as a general, he served as a private!

In the case of the Vestners, I was unable to find John Vestner's birthplace. The ship passenger records noted simply that he came from "Germany." Not helpful. His marriage record said he came from "Bavaria;" better, but not good enough. There was no record of him in the naturalization data, and among the Vestners from the Nürnberg area listed in the files at the Family History Library in Salt Lake City, none matched his birthdate. So I hired a German researcher specializing in Bavaria, Reinhard Hofer (<u>Hofer-Bavaria@T-Online.de</u>), who eventually managed to find reference to John Vestner's birth in the parish records of the Lutheran Church in the village of Altdorf. From those records, Hofer was able to trace John's family back to 1680.

BIBLIOGRAPHY

Eliot and Priscilla Vestner

U.S. Army records of Lt. Col. Eliot Vestner, 1919-1956

Memories of District C, Civilian Conservation Corps, 1934

Diary of Priscilla Fuller Vestner, 1911-25, 1932-36, 1948, 1951, 1956-69

Letters, Priscilla Fuller Vestner to Lt. Col. Eliot N. Vestner, September 1953-March 1955 (approximately 350 letters)

American History: Miscellaneous

E. Benjamin Andrews, *The United States in our Own Time: A History from Recon-struction to Expansion* (New York; Charles Scribner's Sons, 1903)

Theodore Baird, *English At Amherst,* ed. William H. Pritchard (Amherst, MA; Amherst College Press, 2005)

Charles A. and Mary R. Beard, *A Basic History of the United States* (Garden City, NY; Doubleday, Doran & Company, 1944)

D.F. Fleming, *The Cold War and its Origins* (two volumes; Garden City, NY; Doubleday, 1961)

David Halberstam, *The Coldest Winter: America and the Korean War* (New York; Hyperion, 2007).

411

William M. Fowler, *Empires at War: the French and Indian War and the Struggle for North America, 1754-1763* (New York; Walker and Company, 2005).

Frank Freidel, *Franklin D. Roosevelt Launching the New Deal* (Boston; Little, Brown and Company, 1973)

William Leuchtenburg, *Franklin D. Roosevelt and the New Deal* (New York; Harper & Row, 1963)

Edward G. Longacre, *Joshua Chamberlain: The Soldier and the Man* (Conshohocken, PA; Combined Publishing, 1999).

David McCullough, *Truman* (New York; Simon & Schuster, 1992).

Thomas O'Conner, *Civil War Boston, Home Front and Battlefield* (Boston; Northeastern University Press, 1997).

Ellen Rothman, *Hands and Hearts, A History of Courtship in America* (Cambridge, MA; Harvard University Press, 1987).

Arthur Schlesinger, Jr. *The Age of Roosevelt* (three volumes) (Boston; Houghton Mifflin, 1957)

William Strauss and Neil Howe, Generations: *The History of America's Future, 1584 to 2069* (New York; William Morrow, 1991).

Laura Thatcher Ulrich, *A Midwife's Tale: The Life of Martha Ballard, Based on Her Diary, 1785-1811*(New York; Vintage Books, 1991)

Gordon S. Wood, *Empire of Liberty, A History of the Early Republic*, 1789-1815 (New York; Oxford University Press, 2009).

Puritans and Pilgrims

Robert Charles Anderson, *The Great Migration,* Vol. 1 (Boston; NEHGS, 1995).

Robert Charles Anderson, George Sanborn, Melinde Sanborn, *The Great Migration* 1633-1634, Vol. 2 (Boston; NEHGS, 2001).

Warren M. Billings, *Jamestown and the Founding of the Nation* (Gettysburg, PA; Thomas Publications, undated).

George Bodge, *Soldiers in King Phillips War* (Boston; The Rockwell and Churchill Press, 1896)

William Bradford, *Of Plymouth Plantation 1620-1647* (ed. Samuel Eliot Morison, New York; Alfred A. Knopf, 2001).

Governor *William Bradford's Letter Book* (Bedford, MA; reprint by Applewood Books, 2001)

Francis J. Bremer, *The Puritan Experiment; New England Society from Bradford to Edwards* (University Press of New England, 1995).

Francis J. Bremer, *John Winthrop, America's Forgotten Founding Father* (New York; Oxford University Press, 2003).

James Deetz and Patricia Scott Deetz, *The Times of Their Lives: Life, Love and Death in Plymouth Colony* (New York; W.H. Freeman & Co., 2000).

Edmund Delaney, *The Connecticut River, New England's Historic Waterway* (Chester, CT; The Globe Pequot Press).

Sir Ferdinando Gorges and his Province of Maine, ed. James Phinney Baxter (Boston; Prince Society, 1890)

Richard Hakluyt, *Voyages and Discoveries, the Principal Navigations, Voyages, Traffiques and Discoveries of the English Nation* (edited and abridged by Jack Beeching, New York; Penguin Books, 1985).

Tony Horwitz, *A Voyage Long and Strange* (New York; Henry Holt and Company, 2008).

Karen Ordahl Kupperman, "The Puzzle of the American Climate in the Early Colonial Period," *American Historical Review*, Vol. 87 (1982): 1262-1289.

Eve LaPlante, *American Jezebel, the Uncommon Life of Anne Hutchinson, the Woman Who Defied the Puritans* (San Francisco; Harper 2004).

Edmund S. Morgan, *Visible Saints, the History of a Puritan Idea* (New York; Cornell University Press, 1963).

Samuel Eliot Morison, "The Pilgrim Fathers: Their Significance in History," *By Land and by Sea: Essays and Addresses* (New York; Alfred A. Knopf, 1953).

Mourt's Relation: The Journal of the Pilgrims at Plymouth in New England 1620, (originally published. 1622; reprinted and edited by George B. Cheever, New York; J. Wiley, 1848); the earliest first-hand account of the Pilgrims' voyage and landing.

Nathaniel Philbrick, *Mayflower* (New York; Viking, 2006).

John Pory, Emmanuel Altham and Isaak De Rasieres, *Three Visitors to Early Plymouth,* ed. Sydney V. James, Jr., (Bedford, MA; Applewood Books, 1963).

Eric B. Schultz and Michael J. Tougias, *King Philip's War, the History and Legacy of America's Forgotten Conflict* (Woodstock, VT; Countryman Press, 1999); includes primary source documents, such as the Benjamin Church Diary.

Bradford Smith, *Bradford of Plymouth* (Philadelphia and New York; J. B. Lippincott, 1951).

Dean R. Snow and Kim M. Lanphear, "European Contact and Indian Depopulation in the Northeast: the Timing of the First Epidemics", *Ethnohistory*, Vol. 35 (winter 1988): 1-32

Eugene Aubrey Stratton, *Plymouth Colony, Its History & People 1620-1691* (Salt Lake City, UT; Ancestry Publishing, 1986).

Alden T. Vaughan, ed., *The Puritan Tradition in America, 1620-1730*, (Hanover NH, 1972).

414

George Willison, *Saints and Strangers* (New York; H. Wolff, 1945)

The Journal of John Winthrop, 1630-1649 (abridged edition), ed. Richard S. Dunn & Laetitia Yeandle (Harvard University Press, 1996).

Edward Winslow, *Good Newes from New England, A True Relation of Things Very Remarkable at the Plantation of Plimoth in New England* (first published 1624; reprint, Bedford, MA; Applewood Books).

Family Histories, Genealogies & Memoirs

Russell Baker, *Growing Up* (New York; Penguin Putnam, Inc, 1982).

Diantha L. Barstow, *The Coleman's of California* (Baltimore, MD; Gateway Press, 2003).

Benjamin W. Dwight, *The History of the Descendants of John Dwight of Dedham, Massachusetts* (New York, 1874).

Ian Frazier, *Family* (New York; Farrar Straus Giroux, 1994).

William Hyslop Fuller, *The Edward Fuller Family* (Palmer, MA; C.B. Fiske & Co., 1908).

Ruth Gardiner Hall, *Descendants of Governor William Bradford Through the First Seven Generations* (Ann Arbor, Michigan; Bradford Family Compact, 1951).

Bruce Campbell MacGunnigle, *Mayflower Families through Five Generations,* Vol. 4: Edward Fuller (Plymouth, MA; General Society of Mayflower Descendants, 1990).

Mina Walleser Ellis Otis, *Our Ellises, a Family Album* (Boston; Quinn Printing Company, 1996).

Stephen Perkins Parson, *An American Family, The Lymans and The Vale: 1631 to 1951* (Ipswich, MA; Publication Resources, 2009).

Paul Wesley Prindle, *Ancestry of Elizabeth Barrett Gillespie* (Summit, NJ; P.W. Prindle, 1976).

Arthur H. and Katherine Radasch, revised by Robert S. Wakefield, *Mayflower Families through Five Generations*, Vol.10: Samuel Fuller (Plymouth, MA; General Society of Mayflower Descendants, 1975—)

John Soule and Milton Terry, revised by Robert S. Wakefield and Louise Walsh Throop, *George Soule, Fifth and Sixth Generation Descendants* (Plymouth, MA; Society of Mayflower Descendants, 2006),

Russell Warner, revised by Robert S. Wakefield, *Mayflower Families through Five Generations*, Vol.14, Myles Standish (Plymouth, MA; General Society of Mayflower Descendants, 1975—)

Robert S. Wakefield and Anne Smith Lanhart, *Mayflower Families through Five Generations,* Vol. 22: William Bradford (Plymouth, MA; General Society of Mayflower Descendants, 2004).

Esther Littleford Woolworth, *Mayflower Families through Five Generations*, Vol. 16, John Alden, ed., by Alicia Crane Williams (Plymouth, MA; General Society of Mayflower Descendants, 1975—).

Jonathan Yardley, *Our Kind of People, the Story of an American Family*, (Weidenfeld & Nicolson, New York, 1989).

Town and State Histories

Barnstable Town Records, transcribed by Robert J. Dunkle from the Gustavus Adolphus Hinckley Collection (NEHGS, 2002).

Samuel Bates, *Records of the Town of Braintree, 1640-1793* (Randolph, MA; Daniel H. Huxford, Printer, 1886).

J.R. Cole, *History of Tolland County Connecticut* (New York; W. W. Preston and Co. 1888).

Robert B. Hanson, *Dedham, Massachusetts 1635-1890* (Dedham, MA, Dedham Historical Society, 1976).

Ellen D. Larned, *History of Windham County, Connecticut* (Bowie, MD; Heritage Books, Inc. facsimile reprint 1998)

Emma Huntington Nason, *Old Hallowell on the Kennebec* (Augusta, ME; Press of Burleigh & Flynt, 1909).

Francis Hubert Parker, *Contributions to the History of East Haddam, Connecticut* (Hartford, CT, 1938).

John Pease and John Niles, *A Gazetteer of the States of Connecticut and Rhode Island* (Hartford, CT, 1819).

John Sibun, *Our Town's Heritage 1708-1958, Hebron, Connecticut* (Hebron, CT; Douglas, Library, 1992).

David Thurston, *Brief History of Winthrop from 1764 to October 1853* (Portland, ME; Brown, Thurston, Steam, 1855).

Donald Trayser, *Barnstable: Three Centuries of a Cape Cod Town* (Hyannis, MA; F.B & F.P. Goss, 1939).

Everett Schermerhorn Stackpole, David C. Young and Elizabeth Keene Young, *Stackpole's History of Winthrop, Maine* (Winchester, MD; Heritage Books, 1994).

German Immigration in Mid-Nineteenth Century

Robert Ernst, *Immigrant Life in New York City 1825-1863* (King's Crown Press, Columbia University, New York, 1949).

Family Tree Maker: Family Archives, Passenger and Immigration Lists: New York, 1820-1850, CD # 273 (1999). The information on this CD was taken from National Archives Microfilm Series M237, rolls 1-95 (Registers of Vessels Arriving at the Port of New York from Foreign Ports, 1789-1919).

Ira A. Glazer, ed., *Germans to America, Lists of Passengers Arriving at U.S. Ports in the 1840s* (Lanham, MD; The Scarecrow Press, 2004).

Edwin C. Guillet, *The Great Migration, The Atlantic Crossing by Sailing Ship Since 1770* (Toronto, London and New York; Thomas Nelson and Sons, 1937).

"Memoirs of the Nohl Family, Trip Diary of Friedrich Nohl, 16 September 1849 to December 20, 1849:" <www.crossmyt.com/hc/gen/nohlmigd.html.>Translated by Eva Krutein and edited by James Nohl Churchyard, included in family genealogy: James Nohl Churchyard *Our Family Museum* (1996) (unpublished).

Stanley Nadel, *Little Germany: Ethnicity, Religion and Class in New York City, 1845-80* (Urbana and Chicago; Univ. of Illinois Press, 1990).

"The Immigration Diary of Michael Friedrich Radke, 1848" in the possession of Judith Radke Craig and family of Huntingburg, Indiana; translated by Mrs. Sabine Jordan and published in 1982: <http://members.aol.com/1hcristen/1848.htm.>.

Carl Wittke, *Refugees of Revolution: The German Forty-Eighters in America* (Westport CT; Greenwood Press, 1952).

New York and Brooklyn History

Dee Andrews, *The Methodists and Revolutionary America*, *1760-1800* (Princeton, NJ; Princeton University Press, 2002).

John A. Barry, *The Barry Case* (New York; Appleton & Co. 1839).

Peter L. Bernstein, *Wedding of the Waters, the Erie Canal and the Making of a Great Nation* (New York; W.W.Norton and Company, 2005)

The Brooklyn Daily Eagle, 1841-1901, available on the Internet at <www.brooklynpubliclibrary.org.>

Walter Barrett, *The Old Merchants of New York City* (New York; Thomas R. Knox & Co. 1885).

Edwin G. Burrows and Mike Wallace, *Gotham: A History of New York City to 1898* (Oxford and New York; Oxford University Press, 1999).

Colonel Emmons Clark, *History of the Seventh Regiment of New York, 1806-1889* (New York; published by the Seventh Regiment, 1890).

Five Points Mission, *The Old Brewery and the New Mission House at Five Points* (New York; Stringer & Townsend, 1854).

Flatbush (published by *The Brooklyn Eagle*, 1946).

Charles H. Fuller, *Address at the Fifteenth Annual Meeting of the Brooklyn League*, April 7, 1913 (Brooklyn, 1913).

Tom Glynn, *Books for a Reformed Republic, the Apprentice's Library of New York City* (Austin, Texas; University of Texas Press, 1995).

Hendrik Hartog, *Man and Wife in America, a History* (Cambridge, MA; Harvard University Press, 2000).

Luther S. Harris, *An Illustrated History of Greenwich Village* (New York; JHV Press, 2003).

Eric Homberger, *The Historical Atlas of New York City* (New York; Henry Holt and Company, 2004).

T. R. Mercein, *Address to Mechanics Society* (New York; W.A. Mercein, 1820).

Hopper Striker Mott, *The New York of Yesterday: A Descriptive Narrative of Old Bloomingdale* (New York; Putnam, 1908).

Gustavus Myers, *The History of Tammany Hall* (Published by the author, 52 William St., New York City, 1901)

The Diary of Philip Hone, 1828-1851, Ed. Allan Nevins (New York; Dodd, Mead and Company, 1927).

New York City Directory 1786-1930, New York Historical Society. The Historical Society has all the Directories in hard copy. Directories on microfilm are available in the microfilm room of the Boston Public Library.

The New York Times, from 1851: Proquest enables one to search the *Times* archives going back to 1851, but is generally available only through libraries.

Henry Reed Stiles, *History of the City of Brooklyn* (Albany, NY; Joel Munsell, printer, 1870).

The Diary of George Templeton Strong, ed. Allan Nevins and Milton Halsey Thomas (New York; The Macmillan Company, 1952), 4 volumes.

Joseph B. Wakeley, *Lost Chapters Recovered from the Early History of American Methodism* (New York; published for the author by Carlton & Porter, 1858).

Edwin Warriner, *Old Sands Street Methodist Episcopal Church of Brooklyn, New York* (New York; Phillips & Hunt, 1885).

John Fanning Watson, *Annals and Occurrences of New York City and State in the Olden Times* (Philadelphia; Henry F. Anners, Chesnut St. 1846; reprinted by Applewood Books, Carlisle, MA).

Edith Wharton, *Old New York* (New York; Scribner, 1924).

William Lee Younger, *Old Brooklyn in Early Photographs,* 1865-1929 (New York; Dover Publications, Inc., 1978).

San Francisco and the Gold Rush

"Across the Isthmus in 1850: the Diary of Daniel A. Horn," ed. James P. Jones and William Warren Rogers, *Hispanic American Historical Review*, Vol. 41 (Nov. 1901).

LeRoy Armstrong and J.O. Denny, *Financial California* (San Francisco; Coast Banker Pub. Co. 1916; reprint, Arno Press, 1980).

T.A. Barry and B.A. Paten, *Men and Memories of San Francisco in the "Spring of 50"* (San Francisco; A.L. Bancroft & Co. 1873).

James P. Delgado, *To California by Sea* (University of Southern California Press 1990): provides useful first-hand information on the trip from New York via the Isthmus to San Francisco around 1850.

U.S .Grant, *Personal Memoirs* (New York; Charles L. Webster & Company, 1885). Grant provides a first hand account of his trip as a young lieutenant through Panama en route to the West Coast in 1850.

J. S. Holliday, *Rush for Riches, Gold Fever and the Making of California* (Berkeley, CA; University of California Press, 1999).

J.S. Holliday, *The World Rushed In, the California Gold Rush Experience* (New York; Simon and Schuster, 1981).

John Haskell Kemble, *The Gold Rush by Panama, 1848-1851* (Berkeley, CA; University of California Press, 1949)

Rand Richards, *Mud, Blood, and Gold, San Francisco in 1849* (San Francisco; Heritage House Publishers, 2009).

C.C. Richmond Letters, SMC 11, Box 13, Folders 3 and 4, California State Library, Sacramento, CA.

Sarah Royce, *A Frontier Lady's Recollections of the Gold Rush*, ed. Ralph Henry Gabriel (New Haven, CT; Yale University Press, 1932).

The Hallowell Gazette, 1814-1870 (Hallowell, ME; Hubbard Free Library).

George R. Stewart, *Committee of Vigilance, Revolution in San Francisco, 1851* (New York; Ballantine Books, 1964).

Mary Floyd Williams, *History of the San Francisco Committee of Vigilance of 1851, A Study of Social Control on the California Frontier in the Days of the Gold Rush* (Berkeley, CA: University of California Press, 1921).

Early Twentieth Century: 1900-1929

Frederick Lewis Allen, *Only Yesterday, an Informal History of the Nineteen Twenties* (New York and London; Harper & Brothers, 1931).

Leslie S. Baker, *The Story of Company B, 106th Machine Gun Battalion, 27th Division, U.S.A.* (New York, 1920).

Ray Stannard Baker, *Woodrow Wilson, Life and Letters* (Garden City, NY; Doubleday, Page & Co. 1927).

Henry Berry, *Make the Kaiser Dance, Living Memories of a Forgotten War* (Garden City, NY; Doubleday, 1978).

William H. Becker, *Dynamics of Business Government Relations, Industry and Exports, 1893-1921* (Chicago; The University of Chicago Press, 1982).

John Milton Cooper, *The Warrior and the Priest, Woodrow Wilson and Theodore Roosevelt* (Cambridge, MA; Harvard University Press, 1983).

Josephus Daniels, *Cabinet Diaries 1913-1921*, ed. by E. David Cronon (Lincoln, Nebraska; University of Nebraska Press, 1963).

Francis P. Duffy and Joyce Kilmer, *Father Duffy's Story: A Tale of Humor and Heroism, of Life and Death with the Fighting Sixty-Ninth* (New York; George H. Doran Company, 1919).

History of Company "E," 107th Infantry, 54th Brigade, 27th Division, U.S.A. 1917-1919 (New York; War Veterans' Association, 1920).

Robert Hennigan, *The New World Power, American Foreign Policy 1898-1917* (Philadelphia; University of Pennsylvania Press, 2002).

Geoffrey Hodgson, *Woodrow Wilson's Right Hand, the Life of Colonel Edward M. House* (New Haven, CT; Yale University Press, 2006).

Michael Kazin, *A Godly Hero, the Life of William Jennings Bryan*, (New York; Random House, 2007).

David M. Kennedy, *Over Here, the First World War and American Society* (New York; Oxford University Press, 1980).

William Gibbs McAdoo, *Crowded Years, the Reminiscences of William G. McAdoo* (Boston; Houghton Mifflin Company, 1931).

Herbert Molloy Mason Jr., *The Great Pursuit: Pershing's Expedition to Destroy Pancho Villa* (New York; Smithmark Publishers, 1970).

John J. Pershing, *My Experiences in the World War* (two volumes, New York, 1931).

William Cox Redfield, *With Congress and Cabinet* (Garden City, NY; Doubleday, Page & Company, 1924).

Henry J. Reilly, *Americans All, the Rainbow at War, Official History of the 42nd Rainbow Division in the World War* (Columbus, OH; F. J. Heer Printing Co., 1936).

Shepley Thomas, *The History of the AEF* (New York; George H. Doran Co. 1920).

A.L Todd, *Justice on Trial, the Case of Louis D. Brandeis* (New York; McGraw-Hill Book Company, 1964).

Papers of Woodrow Wilson, ed. by Arthur S. Link (Princeton, NJ; Princeton University Press, 1978): Sixty-nine volumes.

Financial History

David T. Beito and Linda Royster Beito, "Gold Democrats and the Decline of Classical Liberalism, 1896-1900," *The Independent Review*, vol. 4, no. 4 (Spring 2000), 555-575.

John Brooks, *Once in Golconda, a True Drama of Wall Street 1920-1938* (New York; Harper& Row, 1969).

Robert Bruner and Sean Carr, *The Panic of 1907: Lessons Learned from the Market's Perfect Storm* (Hoboken, NJ; John Wiley and Sons, 2007).

Closed for the Holiday, the Bank Holiday of 1933 (undated publication of the Federal Reserve Bank of Boston, ca. 1993).

Charles W. Calomiris and Larry Schweikart, "The Panic of 1857: Origins, Transmission and Containment," *The Journal of Economic History*, Vol. 51, No. 4 (Dec. 1991).

Henry Dexter, "Reminiscences of the Panic of 1857," *American History Magazine*, Vol. 1, November 1906, No. 6.

John Kenneth Galbraith, *The Great Crash 1929* (Boston; Houghton Mifflin Company, 1954).

John Steele Gordon, *The Great Game, The Emergence of Wall Street as a World Power 1653-2000* (New York; Scribner 1999).

James L. Huston, *The Panic of 1857 and the Coming of the Civil War* (Baton Rouge, LA; Lousiana State University Press, 1987).

Randall S. Kroszner, "Is It Better to Forgive than to Receive? An Empirical Analysis of the Impact of Debt Repudiation" (paper delivered to Graduate School of Business, University of Chicago, 2003).

J.S. McMasters, *Commercial Cases for the Banker, Treasurer and Credit Man*, Vol. 19, (New York; Commercial Book Company, 1906).

Frederic S. Mishkin, "Asymmetric Information and Financial Crises," *Financial Markets and Financial Crises*, ed. by R. Glenn Hubbard (National Bureau of Economic Research, 1991).

Joseph Nocera, *A Piece of the Action, How the Middle Class Joined the Money Class* (New York; Simon and Schuster, 1994).

Peter L. Rousseau, "Jacksonian Monetary Policy, Specie Flows and the Panic of 1837," *The Journal of Economic History*, Vol. 62, No. 2 (June 2002).

Amity Shlaes, *The Forgotten Man, A New History of the Great Depression* (New York; Harper Collins, 2007).

Gene Smiley, *Rethinking the Great Depression* (Chicago; Ivan Dee, 2002).

Robert Sobel, *The Great Bull Market, Wall Street in the 1920s* (New York and London; W.W. Norton & Company, 1968).

Index

Ackley, Dr. David, 380

Ackley, Lila Gwin, 380

Adams, Hon. John Joseph, 32, 36, 37, 38 , 41

Adelphi Academy, 101, 103

Adams, Maude, 57

Albright, Hon. Harry W, 319, 320, 326, 327, 328, 329, 330, 332, 333, 334, 336

Alden, John, 51, 76, 77, 79, 357, 359, 360, 363, 366, 401, 416

Alden family, for more information see 401-403

Alden, Priscilla Mullins, 51, 79, 363, 364, 401

Altdorf, Germany, xi, 18, 19, 20, 24, 25, 377, 378, 405, 409

America, the, 8

Amherst College, 46, 58, 60, 65, 72, 74, 103, 125, 126, 127, 190, 253, 254, 256, 258, 260, 261, 268, 269, 271, 272, 275, 277, 296, 297, 301, 304, 306, 314, 330, 342, 379, 383, 384, 385, 387, 411

Andover, 243, 249, 250, 252, 253, 254, 256, 348

Ann Arbor, Michigan, 297, 298, 389

AT&T, 153, 156, 160, 162, 166, 168, 172, 179, 268, 272

Attica, 327, 328

Austerfield, Yorkshire, England, 76, 351, 354, 389

Baden Baden, Germany, 241

Ballston Spa, New York, 91, 376, 382, 391

Bank of America, 81, 82, 95, 98, 101, 383

Barnstable, Massachusetts, 79, 80, 351, 366, 367, 368, 370, 375, 381, 382, 416, 417

Barry, Eliza Anne Mercein, 82, 93, 94, 95

Barry, John, 82, 93, 94, 95, 418

Battle of Mobile Bay, 117

Bavaria, Germany, xi, 18, 20, 23, 24, 28, 377, 378, 405, 409

Baxter, Channing W, 73, 74, 75, 76

Beecher, Henry Ward, 103, 126, 127

Benedict, George Grenville, 253, 254

Bensch, Marguerite Vestner, 42, 379

Bensch, Victor, 169, 379

Berlin, Germany, x, 21, 27, 209, 211, 223, 224, 232, 233

Berchtesgaden, Germany, 227

"Black Tuesday", 157

Bonynge, Emily, 387

Bonynge, Jeanne Redfield, 385, 387

Bonynge, Jeffrey Redfield, 387

Bonynge, Russell Jr, 387

Bonynge, Terry, 387

Bradford, Alice Richards, 389

Bradford, Alice, see Fitch

Bradford, Dorothy May, 389

Bradford, Alice Southworth, 389

Bradford, Gov. William, xii, xiii, 76, 77, 79, 122, 351-367, 389, 413, 415, 416

Bradford, Lt. Gov. William, 389

Bradford family, for more information see 389-391

Brewster, William, 357

Bronxville, N.Y., 178, 179, 180, 182, 183, 185, 186, 187, 188, 189, 190, 192, 194, 197, 203, 204, 207, 208, 209, 220, 238, 247, 249, 252, 264, 265, 271, 272, 273, 274, 275, 297, 342, 343, 379, 383, 384, 385, 387, 391, 395, 399, 403, 406, 407

Brooklyn Academy of Music, 57

Brooklyn Dodgers, 196, 197, 208

Brooklyn, New York, xi, 4, 12, 15, 26, 30, 31, 44, 49, 50, 53, 55, 57, 58, 59, 66, 68, 70, 71, 73, 74, 75, 76, 81, 84, 100, 101, 102, 120, 122, 123, 125, 126, 127, 128, 129, 130, 131, 132, 133, 134, 135, 136, 137, 138, 145, 146, 150, 151, 157, 164, 170, 173, 174, 190, 196, 211, 213,

216, 227, 277, 305, 334, 335, 376, 379, 382, 383, 384, 385, 387, 391, 394, 398, 399, 403, 407, 408, 418, 419, 420

Bryan, Hon. William Jennings, 40, 128, 129, 130, 131, 423

Cabinetmakers, 23, 25, 26, 29

Canterbury, Connecticut, 79, 80, 372, 373, 374, 375, 382, 390, 391, 408

Carey, Gov. Hugh, 334, 337, 339, 340

Carmel, California, 204, 207

Carter, Judge Henry, 122, 398

Central Congregational Church, 125

Chamberlain, Gen. Joshua, 117, 412

Chappaqua, New York, 312, 322, 325

Chez Mercier, Paris, 244, 245

Christ Church, Bronxville, 180, 199, 253

Church of the Pilgrims, Brooklyn, 103, 126, 127

Civilian Conservation Corps, 169, 170, 171, 172, 173, 174, 175, 180, 181, 295, 349, 411

Civil War, 7, 13, 27, 36, 37, 38, 40, 45, 59, 89, 98, 99, 100, 116, 117, 126, 127, 137, 156, 253, 368, 412, 424

Cleveland, Pres. Grover, 38, 39, 40, 126, 133

Clinton, Gov. Dewitt, 85, 88, 89, 90

Colonial Yacht Club, 42

Columbia University, 1, 32, 73, 74, 92, 103, 131, 298, 299, 300, 301, 302, 316, 330, 379, 383, 417

Columbian University Law School, 32

Coolidge, Pres. Calvin, 71, 72, 150, 164

Covington, Miss Caroline, 201

Craig House, 176, 177

Croker, Richard, 37, 38, 41, 128
Cutler, Alexandra Berckmans, 380
Cutler, Donald Frederick IV, 380
Cutler, Louisa Richards, see Vestner
Cutler, Quincy Adams Shaw, 380
Cutler, Shannon Fike, 380
Cypress Hills Cemetery, 30, 378
Czechoslovakia, 317

Davis, Lee, 136
Davenport, John L, 301
Debevoise, Plimpton, Lyons & Gates, 299, 301, 312, 315, 317, 329, 338
Diamond Cross Ranch, Alberta, 204
Ditzen, Rev. Dr. Lowell, 199
Donovan, Col. William, 13, 193
Dow Jones, 14, 15, 153, 156, 158, 168
Downs, Genevieve Fuller, 386
Downs, Julia Melisande, 387
Downs, L. McCarthy Jr, 295, 386
Downs, L, McCarthy 111, 386
Downs, Marta Anne, 386
Downs, Marta Jane Schlenz, 386
Downs, Priscilla Ann, 386
Downs, Priscilla May Fuller, 188, 295, 322, 386, 405
Downs, Theresa, 386
Downs, William Everett, 386
Duffy, Father Francis, 7, 8, 9, 422
Dutch Reformed Church, 83, 186, 199
Dutton, Dr. David, 282, 285, 322, 323
Dyar, Abigail Fitch, 389, 390
Dyar, Capt. Elijah, 389, 390
Dyar, Elizabeth Williams, 389, 390
Dyar, Emma, see Fuller
Dyar, Eunice, see Johnson
Dyar, Col. John, 79, 389, 390

Dwight, Anna Cutler, 398
Dwight, Mary Frances, see Webb
Dwight, Ella Louisa, see Titcomb
Dwight, Capt. Henry, 397
Dwight, John, 105, 114, 397, 415
Dwight, Joseph Cutler, 108, 398
Dwight, Mary Moore Farrell, 105, 398
Dwight, Col. Simeon, 397, 398
Dwight, Simeon Jr, 398
Dwight, Sybil, 398
Dwight, Timothy, 105, 397
Dwight family, for more information see 397-399

Eagle, Florence, 193
East Haddam, Connecticut, 79, 80, 348, 366, 370, 371, 381, 382, 407, 417
Eisenhower, Pres. Dwight D, 261, 273, 285, 332
Elizabeth 1, 76, 352, 354
Endicott, Gov. John, 364, 365
Erasmus Hall, 46, 55
Erie Canal, 89, 90, 327, 418

Feeman, Col. William, 220, 221, 239
59th Regiment, 4th Division, 11
Financial Crisis, 1817, 89
Financial crisis, 1837, 91, 93, 95
Financial crisis, 1857, 97, 99
Financial crisis, 1873, 101, 102
Financial crisis, 1893, 39, 81
Financial crisis, 1907, 42, 135, 156, 157, 424
Fitch, Abigail, see Dyar
Fitch, Alice Bradford, 389, 390
Fitch, Maj. James, 389, 390
Fitzgerald, F. Scott and Zelda, 177

Flatbush, New York, 45, 46, 47, 49, 54, 56, 57, 59, 81, 123, 128, 130, 131, 133, 153, 160, 163, 173, 178, 179, 180, 182, 282, 294, 342, 391, 419
Ford, Pres. Gerald, 334, 336
Fort Slocum, New York, 247, 254, 261, 265, 274
France, x, 7, 8, 9, 11, 12, 59, 61, 63, 66, 99, 148, 192, 222, 223, 225, 227, 238, 240, 243, 244, 245, 317, 325, 342, 355, 359, 370, 371, 372, 390, 412
Freedom, New Hampshire, ix, xi, xiii, 277-289, 294, 295, 296, 301, 307, 310, 322, 323, 336, 346, 379, 405, 406
French and Indian War, 370, 412
Frost, Robert, 260, 306
Fuller, Bridget, 366
Fuller, Hon. Charles Humphrey, 45, 51, 71, 72, 99, 100, 102, 103, 120, 121, 122, 125, 127-139, 145, 146, 151, 159, 160-164, 179, 181, 182, 325, 379, 383, 384, 391, 395, 399, 403, 419
Fuller, Clay Randolph, 387
Fuller, Daniel, 370
Fuller, Dorothy, see Swan
Fuller, Ebenezer, 370, 371, 382
Fuller, Edward, 76, 79, 351, 352, 353, 354, 360, 367, 370, 371, 372, 381, 415
Fuller, Elise Mercein, see Redfield
Fuller, Elizabeth, 382
Fuller, Emma Johnson, 76, 80, 372, 376, 382, 390
Fuller, Everett Webb, 64, 322, 383, 384

Fuller, Everett Gladding, 384, 385
Fuller, John Everett, 386
Fuller, Francis, 351, 381
Fuller, Gertrude Gladding, 64, 190, 322, 384
Fuller, Gladys Heinlein, 385, 386
Fuller, Humphrey Roger, xi, 80, 81, 96, 99, 101, 102, 108, 181, 376, 382, 383
Fuller, Humphrey Taylor, 76, 101, 102, 372, 373, 375, 376, 382, 391, 408
Fuller Inn/Hebron Hotel, 372
Fuller, Isabelle Mercein, xi, 81, 82, 95, 96, 99, 100, 101, 382, 391
Fuller, Jane Lothrop, 367, 368, 381
Fuller, John, 80, 348, 368, 369, 371, 381
Fuller, Louisa Everette Archer, 386
Fuller, Margaret Catlin, 103, 290, 308, 309, 310, 449
Fuller, Mary Everett Webb, 45, 73, 120, 121, 122, 127, 137, 144, 159, 179, 182, 188, 252, 379, 395, 399, 403
Fuller, Martha Phelps, 382
Fuller, Mary Rowley, 370, 371, 372
Fuller, Matthew, 367, 368, 381
Fuller, Mehitable Rowley, 80, 348, 368, 369, 370, 381
Fuller, Priscilla Alden, see Vestner
Fuller, Priscilla May, see Downs
Fuller, Randolph Mercein, 60, 62, 63, 66, 322, 383, 384
Fuller, Randolph Mackenzie, 384
Fuller, Robert Catlin, 384, 387
Fuller, Robert Scott, 387
Fuller, Roger, 80, 372, 382, 391
Fuller, Ruth Dwight, see Shumway

Fuller, Dr. Samuel, 76, 79, 351, 352, 353, 354, 359, 360, 364, 365, 366, 367, 416

Fuller, Samuel, 79, 80, 360, 366, 367, 368, 381

Fuller, Susan Dorothy, 386

Fuller, Thomas, 348, 370, 382

Fuller, Violette Taylor, 372

Fuller, Wendy Webb, 386

Fuller family, for more information see 381-387

Germany, x, xiii, 7, 12, 17, 18, 22, 25, 27, 28, 30, 31, 59, 144, 190, 202, 209, 211, 121, 224, 227, 228, 231, 232, 240, 244, 258, 294, 302, 325, 379, 406, 409, 418

Gibson, Prof. William Walker, 255, 257, 258

Gierasch, Walter, 249, 250, 253

Gold, 38, 40, 83, 92, 97, 98, 99, 105, 106, 107, 115, 129, 130, 132, 145, 179, 199, 263, 295, 420, 421, 422, 424

Goebel, Prof. Julius, 299

Gramatan Hotel, Bronxville, 186

Green, Prof. Warren and Ethel, 271, 272

Greenwich Village, 90, 304, 306, 310, 419

Gwin, Elizabeth ("Betty"), 311, 316

Gwin, Samuel L, 311

Gwinn, Cong. Ralph, 252

Hagen, Ernest, 525, 26

Hallowell, Maine, 105, 106, 108, 109, 111, 112, 114, 115, 116, 117, 123, 398, 407, 417, 421

Hamilton Institute for Boys, 3

Hannah, 217, 218, 220, 235

Harvard University, 3, 74, 95, 136, 151, 180, 202, 211, 226, 251, 254, 282, 302, 303, 304, 310, 315, 342, 369, 412, 415, 419, 422

Hautan, Henry, 31, 36, 378

Hatfields, Elizabeth and Luke, 168, 277, 278, 282, 289

Hawes, Jack, 249, 251, 252, 256, 348

Hebron, Connecticut, xi, 79, 80, 81, 82, 370, 371, 372, 375, 376, 382, 391, 407, 417

Heidelberg, Germany, 211, 216, 217, 218, 220, 221, 222, 223, 224, 227, 228, 239, 240, 241, 243, 244, 245, 250

Heiser, Henry, 82

Heiser, Rosalie Mercein, 51, 82, 86

Held, Rev. August H. M, 26, 31

Hohly, Rev. Harold, 199

Holmes, Burton, 73

Holmes, Henry E.C, 187, 290

Holt, Annie Dwight Webb, 50, 116, 120, 394

Holt, Kenneth, 120, 394

Holt, William W, 120, 394

Hone, Hon. Philip, 91, 92, 93, 419

Hoover, Pres. Herbert, 156, 16

Huddleston, USNT Jarrett M, 211, 213, 214, 215, 217

Hudson, 17, 20, 378, 408

Huebner, Gen. Clarence, 220, 221, 239, 243, 244

Indians, 77, 79, 105, 356, 358, 361, 362, 363, 368, 369

Irving, Washington, 88, 90
Irving Trust Company, xii, 341

Jaffe, Dr. Ludwig, 318
Jamestown settlement, 78, 79, 356, 362, 413
Japan, 202, 203, 204, 205, 206, 263, 264, 265
Johnson, Emma see Fuller
Johnson, Eunice Dyar, 372, 382, 390
Johnson, Gen. Jedediah, 76, 80, 372, 373, 374, 375, 382, 390, 408, 409
Johnson, Lucy (Abbe), 375

Kennedy, Pres. John F, 285, 306, 317
Kennedy, Sen. Robert F, 310, 313, 314, 316
King, Dr. Martin Luther, 316
King Philip's War, 105, 367, 368, 369, 390, 414
Kipling, Rudyard, 199
Kissel, Kinnicutt & Co., 14
Kleindeutschland, 27, 28, 302, 418
Know-Nothings, 131, 132
Korea, 259, 261, 263, 264, 268, 273, 275, 343, 349, 385

La Pyramide Chez Point, Vienne, France, 245
Lambert, Hannah Soule, 403
Lambert, Olive, see Webb
Lambert, Silas, 403
Lawrence Hospital, Bronxville, 180, 190
Leiden, Holland, 351, 355, 356, 357, 360, 361, 362, 363
Lichtenstein, 241
Lincoln, President Abraham, 131, 306

Lindsay, Mayor John V, 310, 328, 329
Lothrop, Hannah Howse, 367, 381
Lothrop, Rev. John, 367, 381
Lothrop, Jane, see Fuller
Love, Donald, 76, 148, 149, 150, 151
Luneville-Baccarat, France, 8, 9, 10, 11, 243, 293

MacArthur, Gen. Douglas, 7, 205
Macogen Club, 228, 234
Markham, Julia, 193, 198, 199
Massachusetts Bay Colony, 79, 105, 116, 364
Mayflower, xi, 77, 79, 357, 358, 359, 362, 363, 364, 367, 369, 370, 371, 381, 382, 389, 401, 402, 414, 415, 416
Mayflower Compact, 358
McAllen, Texas, 1, 4, 5, 6
McCall Corporation, 177, 188, 189, 196, 272, 342, 384
McKinley, Pres. William, 38, 40, 130, 131, 132, 306
McLaughlin, Hugh, 128, 131, 132
Mercein, Andrew, 82, 83, 84, 348
Mercein, Daniel, 95
Mercein, Elizabeth Royce, 84, 348
Mercein, Eliza Anne, see Barry
Mercein, Imogen, 82, 95
Mercein, Isabelle, see Fuller
Mercein, Mary Stanbury, 82, 85, 95, 383, 391
Mercein, Rosalie, see Heiser
Mercein, Rev. Thomas Fitz Randolph, 82, 95
Mercein, Thomas Royce, 82, 84, 85, 87, 88, 89, 90, 91, 93, 94, 95, 99, 382, 383, 391, 419

Mercein, Thomas R, 95

Mexican border, x, xiii, 1, 4, 5, 6, 7, 60, 148, 221

Midwood Club Literary Circle, 123

Miss Hart's Camp for Girls, 51, 79, 363, 364, 401

Mr. Dooley, 27

Mont. St. Michel, 225

Mugwumps, 126

National City Company, 14, 15, 342

Newark, New Jersey, 96, 100, 383, 408

New York City, xi, 1, 2, 3, 7, 13, 15, 20, 24-32, 35, 36, 37, 41, 66, 73, 80, 81, 82, 83, 85, 86, 88, 89, 90, 92, 95, 97, 100, 101, 108, 128, 129, 132, 135, 150, 165, 173, 298, 301, 317, 318, 328, 329, 330, 337, 338, 346, 376, 378, 379, 380, 382, 383, 384, 385, 391, 403, 407, 408, 417, 418, 419, 420

New York University, 88

Nixon, Pres. Richard M, 285, 286, 319, 320, 327, 328, 332, 334

Noble, Eliza Woodhall, 36

Noble, John W. 13, 36, 37, 41

Noble, Ruth, see Vestner

Noble, William, 35, 36, 37

Nohl, Friedrich, 20, 21, 22, 23, 418

One Beechtree Lane, 185, 186, 198, 239

165th Regiment, 42nd (Rainbow) Division, 7, 9, 10, 11, 12, 13, 423

Orleans, France, 243, 244, 245, 246

Oslo, Norway, 228, 236, 237

OSS (Organization of Strategic Services), 193

Owen, Charles and Mabel, 282

Packer Collegiate Institute, 55, 57, 58, 61, 67-75, 148, 150, 167, 180, 277, 282, 384

Panama, 109, 110, 421

Paris, France, x, 11, 12, 21, 61, 225, 243, 244, 245

Patch, USNT Gen. Alexander M, 238

Pearl Harbor, 185, 192

Pecksuot, 361

Pershing, Gen. John J, 1, 8, 11, 12, 423

Phyfe, Duncan, 25

Pilgrims, 77, 78, 103, 126, 357, 358, 359, 361, 362, 363, 412, 414

Platt, Hon. Thomas C, 129

Plimpton, Hon. Francis T.P, 304, 314, 315

Plymouth, xi, xii, xiii, 31, 76, 77, 103, 126, 127, 151, 351, 353, 357-367, 389, 390, 397, 401, 402, 413, 414, 415, 416

Pokanokets (Wampanoags), 359

Popham settlement, 79, 356, 364

Powell, Rev. Dr. John, 182, 199

Presidio of Monterey, 203

Prohibition, 13, 68, 165

Puritans, xiii, 79, 83, 103, 105, 343, 351, 352, 353, 364, 365, 412, 414

Radke, Michael, 20, 21, 22, 418

Redenhall, Norfolk, England, 76, 351, 354, 381

Redfield, Amy Lou (Gosin), 385

Redfield, Elise Mercein Fuller, 49, 98, 99, 101, 125, 383

Redfield, Elise (Drury), 385

Redfield, Humphrey Fuller, 203, 294, 385

Redfield, Jeanne, see Bonynge

Redfield, Mary Alan (Brown), 385

Redfield, William Cox, 49, 50, 125, 128-132, 137-145, 150, 157, 158, 383, 407, 423

Red Lodge, Montana, 170, 171

Reese, Jack, 162, 179, 183

Reese, Prof. Willis, 299

Republik, 27

Richmond, Cyrus Clark, 106, 107, 108, 111, 112

Riggs, Robert M, 301, 306, 311, 406

Roanoke settlement, 79

Roberts, Helen, 49, 51, 52

Robinson, Rev. John, 354, 355, 357, 358, 361, 362

Rockefeller, Gov. Nelson A, 286, 315, 319, 320, 326, 327, 328, 329, 330, 332, 334, 336, 337

Rogers, Dr. Alfred, xi, 278, 279, 290

Roosevelt, Pres. Franklin Delano, x, 71, 72, 164, 166, 167, 168, 169, 175, 179, 181, 203, 412, 422

Roosevelt, President Theodore, 41, 103, 132, 133, 137

Roth, Heinrich, 18, 378

St. Anton, Austria, 242

St. John's Evangelical Lutheran Church, New York, 26, 378

St. Louis Cardinals, 196, 197, 208, 346

St. Paul's Episcopal Church, Flatbush, xi, 51, 63, 72, 127, 128, 160, 182, 342, 379

San Francisco, California, 106-115, 123, 135, 204, 398, 405, 407, 420, 421, 422

San Francisco Committee of Vigilance, 113, 114

Scott Commission, 326, 330

Separatists, xiii, 76, 77, 353, 354, 355, 356, 357, 358

Seventh Regiment of New York, 1, 3, 4, 7, 85, 87, 98, 419

Shumway, Lowell, 58, 61, 64, 65, 148, 155, 161, 168, 173, 177, 178, 180, 188, 189, 190, 194, 195, 196, 201, 203, 239, 247, 249, 252, 264, 271, 272, 273, 274, 275, 277, 279, 281, 285, 290, 294, 297, 298, 323, 326, 335, 341, 342, 343, 384

Shumway, Ruth Dwight Fuller, 45, 51, 56, 57, 58, 61, 64, 65, 70, 73, 122, 155, 158, 168, 177, 178, 180, 188, 239, 247, 342, 343, 383, 384

Sides, W.M., 253

Sleepy Hollow Cemetery, 182, 253

Smith, Capt. John, 77

Society of Mechanics and Tradesmen, 88

Soule, George, 76, 77, 401, 402, 416

Soule family, for more information see 401-403

Soviet Union/Soviets, 211, 338, 339

Spain, 224, 245, 246, 325, 352, 355, 359

Speedwell, 356, 357

Squanto, 359

Standish, Myles, 76, 77, 79, 359, 360, 361, 362, 363, 364, 366, 367, 401, 416

Standish family, for more information see 401-403

Stockholm, Sweden, 234, 235

Storrs, Dr. Richard S, 103, 126, 127, 129

Strasbourg, France, 221, 222, 223, 24

Swan, Clinton, 62, 66

Swan, Dorothy Fuller, 84, 178, 195, 274, 290, 307, 383, 384, 394

Swan, Harmanus ("Manny"), 342, 384

Switzerland, 82, 225, 227, 238, 241

Tammany Hall, 37, 38, 40, 41, 129, 131, 135, 138, 419

Tariff issue, 38, 39, 40, 126, 138, 139, 140, 141, 142

Tennessee Valley Authority, 174, 175

Tennis Court, Flatbush, 45, 48, 49, 50, 51, 52, 53, 58, 81, 123, 127, 129, 130, 151

The Alps, Bronxville, 179, 194, 208, 274

The Arlington League, 33

The Bossart Hotel, 76, 148, 151, 161

The Crescent Club, 76, 148, 149, 150

The German Society, 24

The Knickerbocker Club, 49, 128

The Shadow, 185

The Tontine Coffee House, 84, 89

The Wall Street Journal, 15, 153, 160, 169, 170

Thomson, Mrs. Alexander, 282, 295, 322

Thomson, Chilton, 280, 284

Tilden, William, 70

Titcomb, Ella Louisa Dwight, 117

Titcomb, Walter, 117

Truman, Pres. Harry, x, 211, 224, 274, 306, 343, 412

Turner, Gen. Howard, 282

Unterdornlach, Bavaria, 26, 27, 378

Urban Development Corporation, 337, 338

Vestner, Alice-Lee, 311, 312, 316, 322, 323, 325, 330, 331, 344, 379, 406

Vestner, Anna Barbara (Friedel), 18, 378

Vestner, Charles Fuller, 325, 331, 344, 380, 405

Vestner, Lt. Col. Eliot Noble,
Boyhood, 1-4
Army:
Mexican border, x, xiii, 1, 4, 6, 60, 148, 231
First World War, 7-13
Civilian Conservation Corps, 170, 171, 172, 173, 174, 175, 181
Second World War, 183, 193, 202, 203
Postwar, 204, 205, 206, 209, 211, 220, 221, 239, 244, 261, 262, 265, 266, 267, 275, 276, 279
Ancestry, 17-44, 379, 384, 385
Courtship and Marriage, 147-160
The Great Depression: 160, 161, 162, 164, 166, 168, 169, 170, 171-183
Andover, 397, 400, 402, 403

Freedom, NH, 277, 278, 279, 280-283, 285, 287, 288, 289, 291, 292, 293, 295, 296
The Sixties: 301, 307, 314, 315, 321, 322, 323
The Seventies, 326, 335, 336, 339
Lowell and Eliot, 341, 342, 344, 345, 346
Reflections, 347, 348, 349
Vestner, Eliot Noble Jr, 180, 187, 194, 197, 198, 199, 215, 237, 249, 251, 252, 253, 259, 269, 270, 271, 272, 278, 282, 296, 297, 298, 299, 300, 307, 310, 311, 314, 315, 316, 317, 327, 334, 335, 337, 338, 340, 341, 377, 379, 385
Vestner, Elizabeth Thomas Gwin, xi, 310, 311, 312, 313, 317, 325, 341, 379, 406
Vestner, George John, xii, 2, 18, 27, 31-43, 128, 129, 130, 151, 152, 161, 172, 173, 378, 379
Vestner, Johann, xi, xii, 17-31, 108, 378, 408
Vestner, Louisa Richards Cutler, ix, 379, 380, 405
Vestner, Margaretha, 18, 30, 378
Vestner, Margaretha Ramming, xi, 26, 27, 28, 29, 31, 378
Vestner, Margurite, see Bensch
Vestner, Margaret K. Cunningham, 345, 346, 379
Vestner, Mary Grayson Thibaut, 380
Vestner, Priscilla Alden Fuller, Girlhood, 45-76

Ancestry: 76, 77, 79, 95, 123, 145, 146, 364, 373, 379, 383, 384, 385, 391, 395, 399, 403
Courtship and Marriage, 147-160
The Great Depression: 160-170, 172, 173, 175, 176, 178-183
Bronxville, Second World War, 187, 190, 193, 194, 195, 197, 198, 199, 201, 202, 203, 204, 207, 208, 209, 261, 264
Postwar Germany: 211, 213, 215, 216, 217, 219, 220, 221, 223, 225, 226, 227, 228, 230-240, 242-246
Andover, 243, 252
Amherst, 72, 74, 260, 268, 269, 270, 271, 272
Bronxville in the 50s, 272, 273, 274, 275
Freedom, NH, 277, 278, 279, 280, 281, 283-296
The Sixties, 301, 307, 309, 310, 311, 312, 314, 315, 316, 317, 321, 322, 323
Lowell and Eliot, 343, 345, 346
Reflections, 347, 348, 349
Vestner, Ruth Noble, 4, 33, 35, 37, 42, 44, 154, 172, 181, 187, 378, 379
Vestner, Violette Rhoades, 380
Vestner family, for more information see 377-380
Vienna, Austria, 27, 228, 229
Villa, Francisco, x, 1, 6, 8, 423

War of 1812, 85, 86, 87, 106, 374, 375, 398, 408, 409

Washburn, Gov. Israel, 116, 117

Washington, General George, 372

Webb, Albert, 47

Webb, Annie Dwight, see Holt

Webb, Annie White, 394

Webb, Christopher, 393

Webb, Christopher 2nd, 393

Webb, Christopher 3rd, 393

Webb, Christopher 4th, 394

Webb, Christopher 5th, 394

Webb, Eliza Smith, 394

Webb, Frank, 47

Webb, Francis Everett, 105, 115, 116, 117, 118, 119, 120, 383, 394, 403

Webb, Hannah Scott, 393

Webb, James, 394

Webb, Mary Bass, 393

Webb, Mary Everett, see Fuller

Webb, Mary Francis Dwight, 105, 116, 120, 123, 394, 404

Webb, Olive Lambert, 116, 394

Webb, Rebecca Jewett, 394

Webb, Samuel, 394

Webb, Samuel Jr, 116, 394

Webb, Sarah Lincoln, 394

Webb family, for more information see 393-395

Whiteman, Paul, 150

Wille, Hon. Frank, 314, 317

Williams, Stephen F, 310

Wilson, Gov. Malcolm, 334

Wilson, President Woodrow, 1, 6, 7, 14, 60, 72, 137, 138, 139, 140, 142, 143, 144, 145, 150, 422, 423

Winslow, Edward, 361, 415

Winthrop, Gov. John, 354, 364, 413, 415

Winthrop, Maine, 45, 46, 47, 105, 106, 107, 108, 111, 114, 115, 116, 117, 119, 120, 123, 383, 394, 395, 398, 399, 403, 407, 416

Witawamut, 361

Yale University, 3, 76, 111, 151, 157, 253, 254, 302, 330, 370, 390

Yugoslavia, 512

Made in the USA
Charleston, SC
26 August 2010